GREAT BATTLES OF THE WORLD
ON LAND, SEA & AIR

GREAT BATTLES
OF THE
WORLD
ON
LAND, SEA & AIR

EDITED BY BRIGADIER PETER YOUNG

Bookthrift Publications
New York

A BISON BOOK

CONTENTS

Peter Young was one of the most decorated soldiers in World War II, and became the youngest brigadier in the British Army at the age of 25. On his retirement from military service he became head of the War Studies Department of RMA Sandhurst. His *History of the Second World War* is a modern classic and he has written and edited over twenty books on the subject of military history.
Chapters 3, 6, 7, 18

John Pimlott was educated at Leicester University, England where he completed a doctorate on the late 18th century British Army. He is a senior lecturer at RMA Sandhurst. He has written a study on *British Light Cavalry 1808-1815* and has made many contributions to the *Journal of Army Historical Research*. He is at present collaborating on the title *Strategy and Tactics of Modern War*.
Chapters 5, 8, 9, 15, 17, 19, 21, 24

Douglas L Welsh was educated at the University of Maryland. He joined US Army Intelligence in 1970 and served in Vietnam as adviser to the XXIV Corps. He is now serving with NATO in the 2nd Military Intelligence Battalion and is pursuing studies in international politics. He contributed to *The Russian War Machine* and is at present working on a study of NATO.
Chapters 13, 22, 23

Judith Steeh was educated at the University of Michigan and then became a journalist. She contributed to the *Olympiad 1936* and co-authored the *Directors' Guide to the USA*. She has also written *The Complete Book of Cats*. She had written numerous articles on historical subjects and is preparing a work on the origins of the Third Reich.
Chapters 2, 4, 11, 14, 16, 20

Patrick Jennings was born in Chicago in 1937. Educated in both the United States and Great Britain, he is a journalist living in London. Among his works is *A Pictorial History of World War II*, a subject in which he has specialized. He is at present working on an illustrated biography of Adolf Hitler.
Chapters 1, 10

Thomas A Siefring was one of the most highly decorated NCOs in the US Air Force. He received a BA from the University of Maryland and a master's degree in international politics from the University of Southern California. He wrote *US Air Force in World War II* and is at present writing a history of the United States Marines.
Chapter 12

INTRODUCTION

Brigadier Peter Young, DSO, MC, MA, FSA.

Will no one tell me what she sings?
Perhaps the plaintive numbers flow
For old, unhappy far-off things,
And Battles long ago.
　　　　WILLIAM WORDSWORTH

The battles in this book cover a relatively brief space in the story of mankind. The earliest is the decisive sea Battle of Tsushima in 1905. The latest, curiously enough, is Vietnam. 'Curiously enough' because one would have been justified in thinking that the operation of the Super-fortress *Enola Gay* at Hiroshima on 6 August 1945 might have proved the last great 'battle' of the World. It seems, however, that atomic warfare was rather too efficient for the military profession and its political employers. And so in the nuclear age we have seen the two atomic victories of Hiroshima and Nagasaki and a multitude of old-fashioned conventional campaigns. Of course, we know that the conduct of war is far too serious a business to be entrusted to the inept hands of soldiers. Lord Zuckerman, in his autobiography, has recently made it perfectly clear that it should be directed by scientists. However war is, in fact, waged at four distinctly different levels, two of them Strategic, and two Tactical. This is not a very difficult concept to master. What it amounts to is that a war is run for political ends and, therefore, at the highest level, it is conducted by the political leaders, who reap what they have sown. (And that very often is the product of years of neglecting their armed forces!) At this level the service chiefs are little more than expert advisers.

The next level is that of the campaign, where the admirals, the generals, and the air marshals operate. At this level the Ministers interfere at their peril, still as we have seen in our own time, they frequently have had the hardihood to do so! Time plays its little jokes. Sometimes a Corsican subaltern is pitted against one from Ireland. A fair match you may say. But what of the days when an Austrian corporal fought to the death with an English lieutenant? But let that pass.

We descend to a lower level: the Tactical level. There are decidedly two tactical levels: Grand Tactics and Minor Tactics. Grand Tactics is the way that the corps commander fights his battle: the way, for example, that Guderian stormed his way across the Meuse at Sedan in 1940, or Dempsey fought XIII Corps up the east coast of Sicily in 1943. This is the level at which Montgomery fought Rommel at El Alamein.

Minor tactics describes what goes on at group, section, platoon, company and battalion level. And you can have some very fine statesmen, some superb generals, a few competent corps commanders and still be damnably beaten for lack of stout-hearted platoon commanders. And this brings us to rather an important point: not everybody really enjoys battle. The Huns, or the Vikings or the Zulus may have done so: but *joie de combattre* is nowadays fairly rare. The late General S L A Marshall, the well-known American military historian and analyst, went so far as to assert that only about a quarter of all 'fighting' soldiers will actually use their weapons against the enemy. He contended that a soldier coming from a Western society is handicapped in combat by his upbringing. 'The teaching and ideals of that civilization are against killing, against taking advantage. The fear of aggression has been expressed to him so strongly and absorbed by him so deeply and pervadingly – practically with his mother's milk – that it is part of the normal man's emotional make-up. This is his greatest handicap when he enters combat.' It may be that Marshall goes rather too far, but whatever the Western soldier may think of slaughtering his enemies, he is not always all that keen to hazard his own person. At the same time, like the officer in A E W Mason's novel *The Four Feathers*, one is only afraid of being afraid. The commander must master his feelings – at least to the point of not being frightened by things that are not particularly dangerous! That point being established it remains for the commander to deploy his forces to the best advantage. And to assist him in this task he has the guidance of the Principles of War. The late Major General J F C Fuller, as a result of a year's study of military history, came to the conclusion that these are:–

Maintenance of the Aim (formerly called the Objective)
The maintenance of Morale (added after World War II)
Offensive Action
Surprise ⎫
Security ⎬ These pairs are
Concentration of ⎫ complementary
Effort ⎬
Economy of Force ⎭
Flexibility (formerly called Mobility)
Co-operation (between Allies, Services and Arms)

These are all very well so long as it is realized that somewhere one has got to include good staff work, a mobilization scheme, which will swiftly put the nation's resources in the field, and an efficient communications set-up. In addition it is of paramount importance that a Military Power should keep abreast of technological advances, weapons development and so forth.

In studying the battles by sea, land and air, described in these pages, the reader will discern, and judge for himself, the skill of the various commanders in 'playing their hand.'

The rules of the art or science of war have been formulated over the years. We have a fairly detailed description in the Old Testament (Judges 7) of the way in which Gideon and his 300 select warriors surprised the hosts of Midian near Beisan one night long ago.

The hosts of Midian who were so disconcerted by the sound of trumpets, and the breaking of earthenware pitchers with lights inside them, were Bedouin tribesmen, ancestors maybe of the Ruwallah, the Beni Sakhr and the Howeitat, who had come in from the Syrian Desert, 'the Sahara,' to raid the Sown – as was their wont right down to the days of Glubb Pasha. It is an interesting case for Gideon showed at least as much skill in personnel selection and minor tactics as the psychologists and the commando leaders of World War II.

Nearly 5000 years have passed since the Sumerians first organized their fighting men in disciplined formations. The elements of the armies of World War I were much the same as those of Alexander the Great, 3000 years ago.

Some years ago the late Major General Hubert Essame, an experienced fighting soldier of two World Wars, pointed out that by his time 'the six military maneuvers were already known that were to form the basis of warfare until after World War II. New weapons evolved, but the basic tactics remained the same.'

[From *The Seven Gambits of War*].

These Gambits are:
1 Envelopment of one flank
2 Envelopment of both flanks
3 Penetration of the center
4 Attack from a defensive position
5 Withdrawing before striking back
6 Surprise thrust at the enemy's rear

The reader may perhaps find it entertaining to seek among the battles here described illustrations of General Essame's theory. El Alamein, for example, is a clear case of Gambit Three.

And then after some 5000 years of respectable warfare Gambit Seven, forecast in the Peninsular War of 1808–1814, was added to the list. This was guerrilla warfare, which first in Indo-China, as a whole, and then in Vietnam paved the way to a victory that was as much political as military.

In the days between World Wars I and II, the publisher of a book like *Great Battles of the World* could scarcely have anticipated a very favorable reception in the United States, or France, or England. Those were the days of the League of Nations, of Disarmament, of a Pacificsm so abject, that the enemies of Democracy were everywhere encouraged in their inordinate demands. Yet it is evident that with the weapons available today, World War III could be more devastating, more terrible in every

way than those we have already seen — since Tsushima. Why then is there such a wide interest today, in civilized countries, in the art of war? It is perhaps due to the fear that ignorance of the nature of war contributes to its outbreak? A widespread knowledge of warfare may serve in its fashion to inoculate Mankind against the disease. It is not impossible.

The soldiers and scholars who study war fall into two main groups. There are those who philosophize about war in general, under the heading of War Studies, the spiritual heirs of the Prussian General Karl von Clausewitz, who, for all his talents, is not easy to understand.

Or there is the more factual approach, which one may describe as Military History. This includes, of course, the memoirs of combatants of every sort, but it also includes the description and analysis of actual operations. From these one may discern the methods of war, and the way that its conduct has been transformed over the years, by new inventions and technological advances.

Long ago the Prince de Soubise managed to lose his army in the famous battle of Rossbach (1757), when he was completely surprised and thoroughly outmaneuvered by Frederick the Great, King of Prussia. In France, they say, everything ends with a song, and this is the song they sang about the unfortunate Prince.

Soubise dit, la lanterne à la main,
J'ai beau chercher où diable est mon armée,
Elle était là pourtant hier matin!
Me l'a t-on prise ou l'aurais-je egarée?

which, being loosely translated, might be:

Quoth Soubise, lantern in hand,
I've searched high and low for my
Army, and

I can't tell
Where the Hell
It is. I can but say
'Twas here at reveille yesterday
Has it been pinched — or just gone
astray?

Soubise was not the last general to lose an army. In these pages we shall find Corap and Huntziger wondering where their armies had got to in May 1940. Theory was no help to them. For those who would perceive the art of war the cool, historical analysis of past operations is a more reliable lantern than all the philosophizings of von Clausewitz and his disciples.

TSUSHIMA 1905

27 May 1905

Tsushima was the decisive battle of the Russo-Japanese War, 1904–1905. It was moreover the greatest naval battle between Trafalgar (1805) and Jutland (1916).

It was the rivalry of the empires of Russia and Japan, in Manchuria and Korea, that led to war. Throughout the nineteenth century the Russians were pushing eastward, with a vigor alarming not only to Japan but to Great Britain and the United States of America. When in 1894–1895 the Japanese had defeated China in a struggle for control of Korea, the Russians, supported by Germany and France, had compelled them to return their gains to China. These included Port Arthur which Russia subsequently obtained on a long lease from the Chinese and developed as a fortress and a naval base. This led Britain and Japan to conclude an alliance (1902), by which it was agreed that should the latter become involved in a war, Britain would come in on her side in the event of any other power intervening. In practice this meant that should Russia, at war with Japan, find an ally in France, Great Britain would fight alongside the Japanese. The Russians' control of Manchuria was bad enough, but their penetration of Korea was 'an arrow pointed at the heart of Japan.' The Japanese, having fought to get rid of the Chinese, now saw the Russians in control, which was a great deal worse, and the Japanese prepared to solve the problem by the invasion and capture of Korea. The Japanese Government, however, in statesmanlike fashion first proposed a peaceful solution, by which the two sides would recognize each other's respective spheres of influence in Manchuria and Korea. The Russians spun out the negotiations. Asked if this policy might not provoke war the Foreign Minister retorted: 'One flag and one sentry; Russian prestige will do the rest.' The idea that Japan would take on a European power was simply incredible. Nevertheless on 10 February 1904 Japan declared war. She had al-

ready struck the first blow, when on the night of 8 February, Vice-Admiral Heihachiro Togo made a surprise attack on the Russian Fleet in Port Arthur. This treacherous operation, comparable in concept with Pearl Harbor, was not altogether successful.

Japan had an efficient modern fleet, and since 1892 she had been spending money on her Navy rather than her Army. In the battle of the Yalu (17 September 1894) the Japanese had outfought the Chinese, and shown that they were well-trained.

In 1896 the Japanese had determined to increase their Navy so that it would be superior to the Pacific squadrons of any other two powers, excepting Great Britain. In practice this meant that she would have a stronger navy than Russia and France together could concentrate against her. Her battleships and armored cruisers were built in British yards, but many of her light cruisers and torpedo craft were built in the Japanese yards at Kure and Yokosuka. None of her battleships were more than ten years old, and all had similar characteristics – range of guns; speed; turning circles and so on. The oldest battleships, *Fuji* and *Yashima* had been launched in 1896. They were each of 12,500 tons, and had a speed of 18 knots. They mounted 4×12-inch and 10×6-inch guns. The *Asahi*, *Hatsuse*, *Mikasa* and *Shikishima*, which were more modern, were of 15,500 tons. Their maximum speed was 18 knots. They mounted 4×12-inch guns and 14×6-inch. The *Mikasa* which had improved protection for her secondary armament was considered one of the world's best battleships of the pre-dreadnought period. Japan had six armored cruisers: *Adzuma*, *Asama*, *Idzumo*, *Iwate*, *Tokigawa* and *Yakumo*. They were 10,000 ton warships with a speed of 20 knots, and 4×8-inch and 14×6-inch guns.

In 1903, when relations with Russia were deteriorating, Japan, with British assistance, bought two new armored cruisers from Argentina. These were the *Kasuga* and the *Nisshin*, 7700 tons with a speed of 20 knots. *Kasuga* had a 10-inch

Above: The Battle of Tsushima, which was almost as easy as the painter depicted it.

gun forward and two 8-inch guns aft. *Nisshin* mounted 4×8-inch guns.

The Japanese had in addition 14 light cruisers, and during the war converted 27 merchantmen to auxiliary cruisers. The Japanese depended to a great extent upon the British for guns, ammunition and coal.

Vice-Admiral Heihachiro Togo, who was to command at Tsushima came of an ancient Samurai family. He had both brains and experience. As a young officer he had been trained in the Royal Navy.

Imperial Russia had three fleets: Baltic, Black Sea and Pacific. In 1898 she had begun a building program and by 1904 she had more battleships than any other powers save Britain and France. Indeed Russian naval expansion was a great factor in deciding the Japanese to strike when they did. They knew that in another year their rival would have six more battleships.

By the Treaty of London (1870) the Black Sea Fleet, which was intended to counterbalance the Turkish Navy, was not permitted to pass through the Dardanelles. It was not, therefore, a factor in the Russo-Japanese struggle. The Pacific Fleet included seven battleships, six cruisers and a number of destroyers.

Togo planned to destroy the Russian fleet at the outset, so that the Japanese Army could occupy Korea, take Port Arthur and advance into Manchuria.

On the night of 8 February Togo attacked Port Arthur, Dairen and Chemulpo. At Port Arthur the Japanese damaged two battleships and a cruiser. At Chemulpo they destroyed a cruiser and a

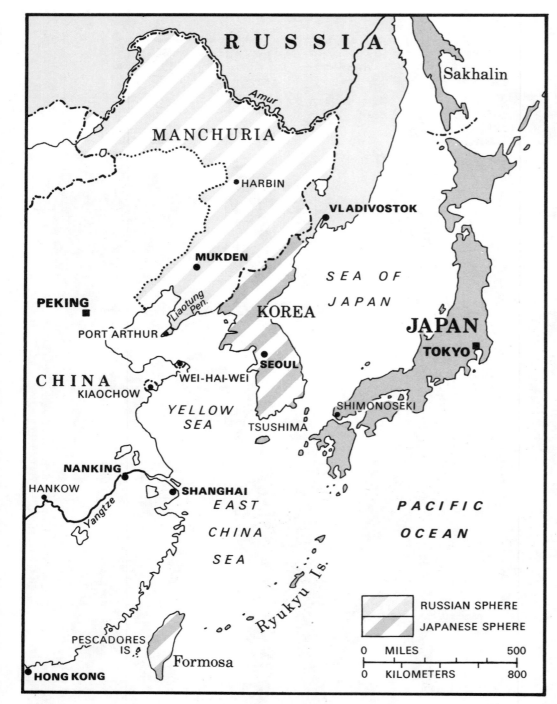

RUSSIA

Sakhalin

Amur

MANCHURIA

• HARBIN

VLADIVOSTOK

MUKDEN

Liaotung Pen.

PEKING

KOREA

SEA OF JAPAN

PORT ARTHUR

JAPAN

TOKYO

CHINA

KIAOCHOW

WEI-HAI-WEI

SEOUL

YELLOW SEA

SHIMONOSEKI

TSUSHIMA

NANKING

HANKOW

Yangtze

SHANGHAI

EAST CHINA SEA

PACIFIC OCEAN

Ryukyu Is.

PESCADORES IS.

Formosa

HONG KONG

| | RUSSIAN SPHERE |
| | JAPANESE SPHERE |

| 0 | MILES | 500 |
| 0 | KILOMETERS | 800 |

Left: The position of Russia and Japan in the Far East prior to the Russo-Japanese War.

and entrusted this so-called Second Pacific Squadron to Admiral Zinovi Petrovitch Rozhestvensky. He was a wealthy and aristocratic officer, aged 56, who had fought as a young man in the Russo-Turkish War of 1877–78. He had been Naval Attaché in London, and had risen to be Naval Chief of Staff. Rozhestvensky, who had served previously in the Far East, had no illusions as to the difficulty of his task, though, according to one of his ministers, 'The Tzar with his habitual optimism expected Rozhestvensky to reverse the war situation.' The admiral was a taciturn, unimaginative man, who was not in the habit of consulting his staff, although his experience in command was as limited as his tactical skill.

The Second Pacific Squadron was organized into five 'divisions.' The first, which was the backbone of the fleet, comprised four new battleships: *Suvorov* (flagship); *Alexander III*; *Borodino* and *Orel*. They were of 15,000 tons, with a speed of 18 knots, and mounted 4×12-inch guns. Their 6-inch guns were in casemates, an improvement on the other battleships of the period. The speed of the squadron was reduced because of the need to carry a great deal of extra fuel and ammunition. It was dangerous for the ships to turn at more than 12 knots with the gun ports open.

The second 'division' was under Admiral von Felkerzam, the second-in-command. His flagship *Oslyabya* was a modern ship like *Suvorov* and the rest. He had two old battleships, *Navarin* and *Sisoi Veliky*, of 10,000 tons, and mounting 4×12-inch guns. An old armored cruiser completed the 'division.' This was the *Nakhimov*, 6000 tons, built in 1882. Of Felkerzam's command only the *Oslyabya* was fit to take its place in a line of battle in 1904.

Admiral Enkvist, flying his flag in the *Oleg*, commanded the third 'division,' which consisted of eight cruisers. The rest of the Squadron consisted of light cruisers and destroyers. There was in addition a multitude of store and repair ships.

The Japanese enjoyed certain advantages over even the best of Rozhestvensky's ships. They were faster. The rate of fire of their big guns was quicker, because they were fired electrically, while the Russians' were still fired by lanyard. The Japanese 12-inch shell weighed 850lb to the Russians' 732.

gunboat, while at Dairen no Russian warships were found. The attempt to destroy the Russian fleet had not worked; nonetheless Togo had seized the initiative and thenceforth the Russians were on the defensive, the greater part of their Pacific squadron being bottled up in Port Arthur, protected by powerful shore batteries. Although Togo made some effort to destroy them the Russians were content to sit idle, making no effort to interfere with the landing of the Japanese Army. With the arrival of Admiral Stephan Makarov, an energetic officer, this changed, but not for long. In April his flagship, the *Petropavlovsk* hit a mine and sank with all hands. Thereafter the Russian fleet, except for a few abor-

tive attempts to get away to Vladivostok, did little or nothing.

The Japanese lost the battleships *Hatsuse* and *Yashima*, mined in May, but their command of the sea remained unchallenged.

Meanwhile the Japanese armies were pushing on. One moved south across the Liaotung Peninsula and laid siege to Port Arthur. Two more pushed the Russians back toward Mukden. The trouble, from the Japanese point of view, was that the further they fell back the easier it was for the Russians to reinforce their Army, as its communications became shorter.

At this juncture the Tsar Nicholas II and his advisers determined to send part of the Baltic Fleet to relieve Port Arthur,

They had a greater muzzle velocity, better penetrating power and a flatter trajectory, which allowed a greater margin of error in range finding. The best of the Russian ships had Krupp armor, and in that area they had the advantage of their enemy. They also had a more advanced armor-piercing shell. The Japanese, who used the conservative British Navy's 'common shell' would have been at a disadvantage here, had it not been for their new explosive, *Shimose*, which was called after its inventor. *Shimose* not only burst the shell case into numerous minute splinters – one unfortunate Russian soldier was wounded in 160 places by a single shell burst! – it caused nausea and headaches, and made it easier for the Japanese to observe the effect of their fire.

Rozhestvensky weighed anchor on 15 October and moved out into the North Sea. The state of training of his Squadron left a great deal to be desired. The new battleships had not even completed their sea trials, while many of the others were too antique to be invited to sail halfway round the world. Most of the ships had engine trouble. A Russian captain wrote afterward: 'Our long voyage was a prolonged and despairing struggle with boilers that burst and engines that broke down. On one occasion, practically every ship's boilers had to be relit in the space of 24 hours.' For ships in such a condition the 18,000 mile voyage, without a single Russian base along the way, was a terrible ordeal. Three of the ships actually had to be sent home, so unfit were they. These were the lucky ones! Coaling had to be arranged by chartering 70 colliers from the Hamburg-Amerika line.

With the Japanese 18,000 miles away one might have been forgiven for supposing that the Russians would have sailed across the North Sea with some equanimity. Not so. It was rumored that Japanese torpedo boats were lying in wait along the route. The admiral had given his ships orders to fire on any unidentified vessel which should come too close.

On 24 October, a day of mist and fog, the battleships of the first 'division' sighted small craft ahead, heard gunfire and opened fire. They could see that the cruisers to westward were also firing. It took Rozhestvensky and Enkvist almost 15 minutes to realize that they were

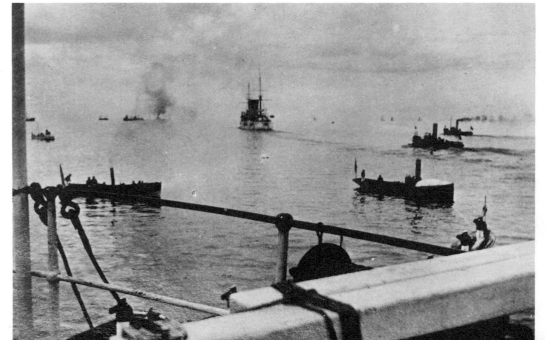

Above: Admiral Rozhestvensky, stopping at Tangiers, with the Russian consul.

Right: The Russian battleship Navarin *in the Baltic, carrying four 12-inch guns.*

engaging each other. The small craft were the Hull fishing fleet. Felkerzam had sailed quietly by, but Enkvist's ships had fired upon the main body of their own fleet. In the panic one trawler was sunk and five others were hit. Five shells struck the cruiser *Aurora*. It was fortunate, perhaps, that Russian gunnery aim was somewhat indifferent.

The British were not pleased by the Dogger Bank Incident. The Press described poor Rozhestvensky as 'the mad dog,' and there were those who talked of war with Russia. Count Reventlow, naval correspondent of the *Berliner Tageblatt*, delivered himself of the opinion that: 'The officers commanding the Russian ships must be all the time in an abnormal state of mind, and it is therefore not altogether unjustifiable to ask . . . whether a squadron led as this squadron is led, ought to be allowed to sail the seas.' Shadowed by British squadrons, on a war footing, the Second Pacific Squadron sailed on toward North Africa. The Russian Government accepted Rozhestvensky's explanation that

Above: Admiral Togo's flagship Mikasa *displaced 15,500 tons (built in England).*

Right: The Hatsuse *launched in England in 1903 but was sunk by a mine in 1905.*

there had not been less than two torpedo boats among the British trawlers. He had not explained why they had loosed off shells rather than torpedoes, or indeed how they had scored hits on a Russian fleet which, as it happened, was 30 miles off course.

On arrival at Tangiers Felkerzam with *Navarin, Sisoi Veliky* and the destroyers made for the Suez Canal. The rest went round the Cape of Good Hope, making for the rendezvous off Madagascar.

Admiral Rozhestvensky endeavored to carry out a little training during the passage, only to discover that many of his officers were incapable of carrying out the simplest maneuvers. The taciturn Rozhestvensky now became even more taciturn than usual. Morale was not high. And when in January the fleet reached Madagascar it was to learn that the Japanese had managed to seize a hill which commanded Port Arthur and its harbor. Before the month was out Rozhestvensky heard the news that Admiral Vitheft, Makharov's successor, had been killed in action (10 August),

and that Port Arthur had fallen (2 January 1905). The First Pacific Squadron was no more. It was no longer a question of joining with the fleet in the Far east in order to relieve the beleaguered fortress. The assumptions upon which the Russian Government had sent forth the Baltic fleet were no longer valid. All that Rozhestvensky could now hope to achieve was, using Vladivostok as his base, to disrupt the enemy's sea communications between Japan and Korea. Even so the problem was not simple for the Vladivostok squadron (Admiral Jensen) had been defeated by Admiral Kamimura (14 August).

To add to his difficulties, upon arrival at Madagascar, Rozhestvensky discovered that Felkerzam's ships required repairs, and could not proceed for another two weeks. Moreover news of disturbances in Russia, the precursors of the Revolution of 1905, had unsettled the crews of the Second Pacific Squadron. Rozhestvensky wanted to sail at once, and to attack the Japanese before they had time to refit after the arduous operations before Port Arthur. The Japanese took this threat very seriously and began to stockpile material in Manchuria.

At this juncture Rozhestvensky was

informed that reinforcements under Rear Admiral Nebogatov were on their way. These were ancient ships, which Rozhestvensky had persuaded the Navy Board *not* to give him in the first place. The *Nicholas II* was an 1882 battleship of 10,000 tons; the *Vladimir Monomakh* an ancient 6000 ton rigged cruiser. Then there were 'the flat-irons,' three coastal defense ships of 4500 tons: *Apraxin*, *Seniavin* and *Ushakov*. Their crews called them the 'sink by themselves class.'

Rozhestvensky waited until 16 March for these unwelcome reinforcements and then set sail. By this time the news of General Kuropatkin's defeat at Mukden, the last great battle of the war, had come through.

Sailing from Madagascar the fleet reached Cam Ranh Bay in French Indo-China, after a nonstop voyage of 4500 miles, without refueling. Here Nebogatov, who had come by way of the Suez Canal, caught up. The Russian fleet, over 40 warships with its attendant store-ships and colliers set sail for the South China Sea (14 May). Togo prudently awaited his opponents in home waters.

There were three possible routes by which the Russians might make for Vladivostok. The first was through the Korean Straits, along the west coast of Japan into the Sea of Japan. The other two were around the east coast, and then through either the Tsugari or Soya Straits to the north of Japan. Rozhestvensky, arguing perhaps that he had little to gain by averting action, chose the former. It seems that the long voyage had left him with a low opinion of his subordinates' talents. He was not in the habit of consulting them, nor did he attempt to make up for their lack of battle experience and seamanlike skill by giving them clear orders, or fighting instructions. It was no 'band of brothers' that now steamed into action, but an ill-co-ordinated, disorganized fleet. To depend entirely upon signals, chancy at the best of times, was unwise in the extreme. Thorough briefing is the key to all tacti-

Above left: The 12-inch turret of the battleship Orel *after its capture at Tsushima.*

Left: Admiral Togo's flagship Mikasa *with his famous signal in Japanese: 'The Empire's fate depends on the result of this battle. Let every man do his utmost duty.' This Japanese Nelson won a victory every bit as great as Trafalgar and lived to tell and retell the story.*

cal success, whether by land or sea. It is not to be hoped that, in the heat of action, officers will improvise the maneuvers, which should be coolly discussed and laid down beforehand. To add to the confusion Admiral Felkerzam, the second-in-command, expired on 23 May. So far from nominating his successor, Rozhestvensky kept the news of his death from the fleet!

Admiral Togo, while mining and patrolling the Tsugari and Soya Straits, was convinced that the Russians would come up the Korean Straits. He concentrated his fleet at Takeshii on the island of Tsushima, which lies in the middle of the Korean Straits. Admiral Kamimura with the heavy cruisers was based at Masampa. Two old cruisers and four armed merchantment formed an outer guard line, supported by Admiral Dewa with four light cruisers. Togo had provided his captains with squared maps of the area, so that they could give him accurate intelligence of Russian moves.

On 25 May Russians had been sighted off the mouth of the Yangtse River, but 26 May passed without further news. That day Rozhestvensky ordered wireless silence, and reduced speed. He meant to pass the Straits in daylight, fearing torpedo attacks during the hours of darkness. At dusk the Russian admiral signaled: 'Prepare for action. Tomorrow at the hoisting of the colors, battle ensigns will be flown.'

In the mist at about 0300 hours on 27 May the *Sinano Maru*, an auxiliary cruiser, ran down a Russian hospital ship, and sighting more ships not long after, at 0500, signaled: 'Enemy fleet in square 203. Is apparently making for the eastern channel.' That meant that the Russians were coming up between Tsushima and the Japanese mainland. At 0634 hours Togo signaled to the Emperor: 'I have just received news that the enemy fleet has been sighted. Our fleet will proceed forthwith to sea to attack the enemy and destroy him.'

First contact was made about 0700 hours with the cruiser *Idzumo* shadowing the Russians through the thinning mist. At 0900 hours Admiral Kataoka's

Top right: A stylized version of the Battle of Tsushima. The rout was no exaggeration.

Above right: The sinking of the Variag *at Port Arthur in 1904. Men from the French cruiser* Pascal *are shown trying to rescue some of the survivors. The collapse of Russian naval power at Port Arthur forced the Tsar to send his Baltic Fleet to Asian waters.*

Below: Admiral Rozhestvensky's long journey to disaster.
Right: Togo's classical crossing of the Russians' T, which destroyed the enemy.

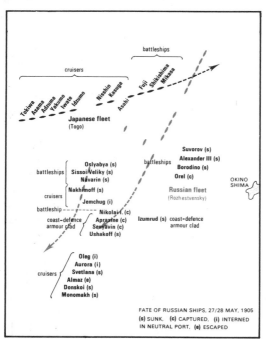

division of four cruisers appeared to port, but moved away again. At 1100 hours the Russians fired a few rounds at four light cruisers, which were sighted in the same direction.

At noon the Russians, steaming at eight knots, were off the southern point of Tsushima, in poor visibility and a heavy rolling sea. Somewhere in the thick mist were the Japanese cruisers but they were no longer visible. At this juncture (about 0145 hours) Rozhestvensky ordered his fleet from line ahead to line abreast, hoping no doubt to cross the Japanese T by a simple turn to port or starboard, whenever Togo should appear. This, the only maneuver Rozhestvensky ordered, was not a success. His ill-trained fleet ended up in two parallel but unequal columns, and this was its formation when, at about 1340 hours the Japanese main battle force, four battleships and eight armored cruisers, were sighted seven miles ahead and to starboard. Since noon Togo had been cruising ten miles north of Okinoshima. He now signaled: 'The Empire's fate depends on the result of this battle. Let every man do his utmost duty.' Not quite a quotation from Nelson, but near enough!

Togo now decided to turn about so that his line would be parallel to the Russians and on the same course. The danger of this maneuver was that his ships must, briefly, mask each other's guns, but thereafter, the side with the faster ships and superior gunnery would have the advantage. The Russian warships were painted black, with canary yellow funnels. The Japanese ships, being painted slate gray, did not show up nearly so well, especially in the dull misty weather prevailing.

The Japanese battleships, *Mikasa*, *Shikishima*, *Fuji* and *Asahi* led the line, supported by the armored cruisers, *Kasuga* and *Nisshin*. Kamimura's squadron followed: the armored cruisers *Idzumo*, *Adzuma*, *Tokigawa*, *Yakumo*, *Asama* and *Iwate*.

When Togo's line reversed its course *Suvorov* and *Oslyabya* opened fire, other vessels in the two somewhat irregular Russian lines joining in as they managed to bring their guns to bear. The Japanese warships concentrated, six of them against *Oslyabya* and four against the *Suvorov*, one of whose officers said afterward: 'Shells seemed to be pouring upon us incessantly. . . .'

Fire broke out in the flagship. *Oslyabya* was hard hit when two 12-inch shells struck her bows simultaneously,

Top: The Russian Fleet's panic when it realized that it was caught in a trap.

Above: Rozhestvensky's flagship, the battleship Suvorov, *brings its 13,516 tons past the Tsar in happier days during a review of the fleet.*

Right: The Illustrated London News dramatically depicted the wounding of Admiral Rozhestvensky during Tsushima.

tearing a great hole at the waterline. Her fore turret was put out of action, and by 1425 hours she was *hors de combat*. The *Alexander III* was also hit, and a serious fire broke out.

Togo's flagship, *Mikasa*, was hit a number of times and *Asama*'s steering gear was wrecked so that she was compelled to quit the line.

At this time the Japanese were veering to starboard and were getting ahead of their slower opponents. It is possible that, had Rozhestvensky turned to port at about 1430 hours, he might have outmaneuvered Togo, and passed across the stern of the rearmost Japanese ships, concentrating his fire upon them. But by this time three of his most formidable ships had been hard hit, so that clever tactics in the teeth of a better trained and more mobile foe were not to be expected. Rozhestvensky now veered to starboard with the result that he threw many of his guns off target. The Russians' formation, never remarkable for its precision, was bunched and confused with the Japanese in a semi-circle ahead, and bringing a terrible cross-fire to bear upon the unfortunate *Oslyabya* and *Suvorov*. Soon the former was stationary

Above: The disaster aboard the sinking Borodino. *Many lives were lost as few survivors were picked up from the sea.*

Right: A Japanese officer scans the disaster from the deck of the Idzumo. *Note the 8-inch gun below the center of this photograph as well as the 25mm machine gun position.*

and the latter was ablaze, her bridge swept by shell splinters. The luckless Rozhestvensky, hit in the head, back and legs, was carried down to the conning tower, hit again, this time in the foot, and evacuated, in an unconscious state, to a destroyer. By 1500 hours the burning *Suvorov*, though her guns were still firing, had fallen out of the line. She was listing to port, and her two funnels had collapsed. With her steering gear jammed, she turned a complete circle.

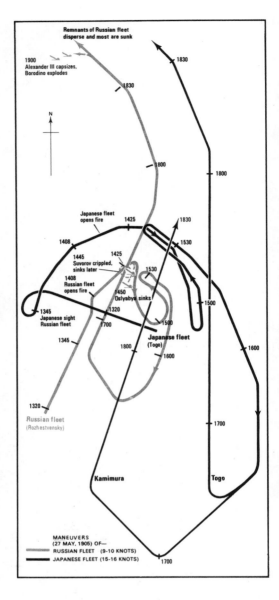

Above: Map of the Battle of Tsushima itself.

Above right: President Theodore Roosevelt.

The *Alexander III* followed. By this time the Russian formation bore little resemblance to a line. Ships steaming past the *Oslyabya* saw her turn over and vanish into the cold depths with Russian sailors clinging to her keel.

A destroyer was sent to tell Admiral Nebogatov that the command had now devolved upon him. Soon afterward the Russians suddenly turned north in an endeavor to pass up the Straits, crossing the wake of the Japanese fleet. Togo was equal to the occasion. The leading Japanese ships, well-drilled, turned together and, protected by their rearmost ships, which continued on the original course and then went round in succession, once more headed off the Russians, who again turned east. At about 1640 hours the Japanese repeated their maneuver steaming southeast again. They were taking some punishment, but

it was nothing to that suffered by the Russians. The Russian line of battle simply disintegrated. In the mist and battle smoke individual vessels strove to break away northward. In the confusion the Japanese lost contact, but at about 1800 hours came upon the *Alexander III*, her fires now under control. She sank, after two attacks, and of her complement of 830 only four survived. At 1900 hours the *Suvorov*, attacked repeatedly by destroyers and torpedo boats, went down with all hands. *Fuji* concluded the main battle with a well-directed salvo. It struck the magazines of the *Borodino* which blew up.

The Russian fleet had lost five battleships and three auxiliaries. Most of the other warships were damaged. Admiral Enkvist with the cruisers *Oleg*, *Aurora* and *Zemchug* made off to the southwest. They were interned at Manila.

Nebogatov managed to collect *Nicholas I*, *Orel*, *Apraxin*, *Seniavin* and *Izumrud*, and by the simple device of steaming without lights, managed to survive the night undetected. The Japanese battle fleet, which had left the destroyers and torpedo boats to finish off the stricken Russian warships, had withdrawn north, and still barred Nebogatov's way

to Vladivostok. *Orel*, his only modern battleship, had been severely damaged, and he decided to surrender. 'I am an old man of sixty,' he said to his crew. 'I shall be shot for this, but what does that matter? You are young and it is you who, one day, will retrieve the honor and glory of the Russian navy. The lives of the 2400 men in these ships are more important than mine.' And so he went to surrender his sword to Admiral Togo. Under all the circumstances it is not impossible that he made the right decision. But who can imagine a Japanese admiral acting similarly?

Of the ships that remained *Ushakov*, *Navarin* and *Sisoi Veliky* were sunk; *Nakhimov* and *Vladimir Monomakh* were scuttled off Tsushima. Rozhestvensky, still unconscious aboard his destroyer, fell into the hands of Admiral Togo. A cruiser and two destroyers actually reached Vladivostok, while a few ships reached neutral ports and were interned.

The Japanese had an armored cruiser and two light cruisers badly damaged; and three torpedo boats sunk. Their battle casualties totaled 700 (110 killed and 590 wounded). This was not much of a price to pay for wiping out the Second Pacific Squadron. The Russians had lost

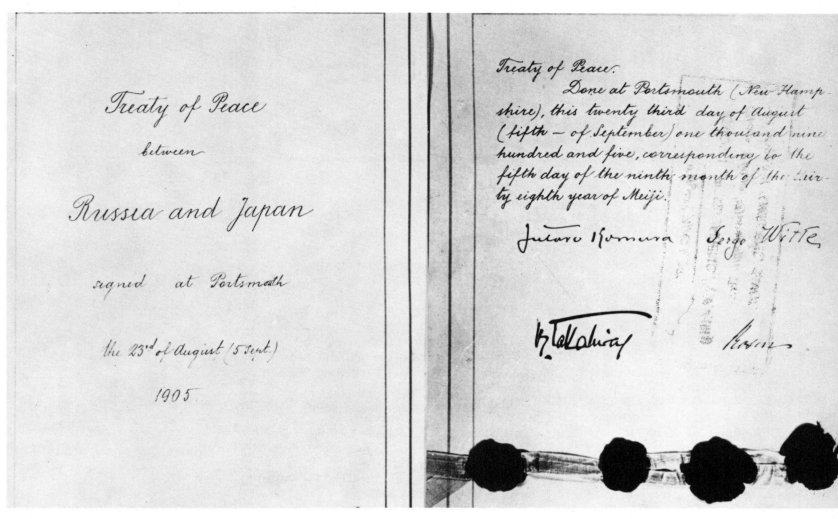

Above: The Treaty of Portsmouth, signed by Baron Komura, Ambassador Takahira, Count Witte and Baron von Rosen.

34 of their 37 warships. Of the crews 4830 were killed, 5917 taken and 1862 interned.

The news of the disaster caused the utmost gloom in Russia. The aristocracy no longer believed in the war. The successive defeats suffered by the Russian armies had not had a moral effect comparable with Tsushima. The catastrophe was so complete that the Tsar and his Government had no alternative but to seek peace.

The Japanese lost no time in asking President Theodore Roosevelt to mediate for peace, and on 8 June he wrote to the belligerents. Thanks to his good offices delegates met at Portsmouth, New Hampshire, and on 5 September signed the Treaty of Portsmouth.

The terms were very favorable to Japan. She received railroad rights in Manchuria, and the ports of Port Arthur and Dairen. Russia recognized her 'paramount political, military and economic interests' in Korea. The southern half of the island of Sakhalin was ceded to Japan. This was of strategic importance for it controlled the approach to the Sea of Japan. The treaty established the islanders of Japan as a continental Asiatic power. The Japanese had defeated a European power. What other Asian power could boast of such an achievement? That Japan had imperialist ambitions could not be denied, but perhaps this could be tolerated if she were to take the lead against Western Imperialism. Japan for her part, her prestige enhanced, began to develop Manchuria.

The Battle of Tsushima completely changed the naval balance of power in the Far East. President Theodore Roosevelt, for all his willingness to act as a mediator, was by no means pleased to see the total destruction of Russian naval power in those waters. He would much rather have seen Japanese and Russian power fairly evenly balanced.

In 1908 the United States and Japan concluded the Root-Takahira Agreement, by which the two governments agreed to respect the 'existing status quo' in the Pacific. The implication was that while the United States would respect Japan's interests in Korea, Japan would not interfere in the Philippines. Still the fact remained that Tsushima had changed Japan from a 'sure' friend to a possible 'enemy' and gradually the Americans began to build up a battle fleet, based on Pearl Harbor in Hawaii. It was not until World War II that the United States was to feel the full consequences of Tsushima.

Tsushima was the first big naval battle of modern times. It confirmed the British and United States naval designers in their view that a new 'all-big-gun' battleship was required. Capital ships had been sunk by big guns: secondary armament had neither the range nor the hitting power to be worthwhile. The lessons of Tsushima were, therefore, the justification for the construction of the new class of battleship of which HMS *Dreadnought*, 17,900 tons, was the first. She was launched in December 1906, had 10×12-inch guns, and could do 21 knots, besides having heavier armor. Roosevelt saw that ships of this class were an absolute necessity if the United States was to maintain its position in the Atlantic and the Pacific. And so in 1905 the United States began to build her dreadnoughts, of which the first was the USS *Delaware*, 20,000 tons The Battle of Tsushima ushered in the dreadnought era in naval warfare.

TANNENBERG 1914

23–29 August 1914

At 0400 hours on 23 August 1914 a retired general, Paul von Beneckendorff und Hindenburg, boarded a train at Hanover. Less than twelve hours earlier he had received a telegram from the German Supreme Headquarters(*Oberste Heeresleitung*, or OHL) instructing him to depart immediately for the Eastern Front where he would take command of the Eighth Army.

As he entered the train, buttoned up in an old blue Prussian uniform that was (to his embarrassment) too tight, he was met by his new second in command: General Erich Ludendorff, hero of Liège. Hindenburg, who came from an old Prussian family, was nearing his 68th birthday. He had been a solid, dependable career soldier prior to his retirement in 1911; his coolness – and the 'von' in his name – were his chief qualifications for the job that lay before him.

Ludendorff – rotund and bull-necked – had won a place on the General Staff through a passionate devotion to duty. He had a harsh, forbidding personality, deliberately modeled on that of his hero, Schlieffen. The two men talked awhile, then went to bed as the train rushed through the night carrying them toward the Battle of Tannenberg – an engagement that was to forge 'H-L' into a partnership that would eventually rule Imperial Germany.

From the commencement of World War I early in August 1914, the French had been begging their Russian ally to begin an immediate offensive. In reply the Russians promised to proceed against Germany on 14 August, despite the fact that it would be impossible for them to mobilize their huge, cumbersome war machine in so short a time. It was a gallant gesture, but an extraordinarily foolhardy one – as such gestures often are. Shortages of equipment posed a major problem. There was a great lack of telephone wire and telegraph apparatus as well as of trained operators; as a result quick communication was impossible and in many cases

one could never be sure that a message had been delivered at all. Motorized transport was at a minimum, which meant that once past their railhead the Army had to depend on horses. The supply system, corrupt and unreliable at the best of times, would not be ready for action until at least 20 August.

In Germany it was becoming more and more difficult to adhere to Schlieffen's master plan, which called for pouring virtually all the Army's resources into the right wing on the Western Front with only token forces on the left and in the East.

On the Eastern Front the Eighth Army, under Lieutenant General von Prittwitz und Gaffron, was charged with defending East and West Prussia. Equal in numbers to but one of the two Russian armies it would soon be facing, its orders were to avoid being overwhelmed or diverted into the fortress of Königsberg at all costs. Prittwitz was instructed to retire behind the Vistula River if either of these dangers threatened.

Prittwitz was an enormous man who had achieved a series of rapid promotions based largely on his talents as a courtier. His Chief of Staff, Count von Waldersee, was a competent soldier; unfortunately he had recently undergone surgery and was not feeling well. This left the Chief of Operations, Major General Grunert and his deputy, Colonel Max Hoffman, as the most energetic members of the Eighth Army staff.

Hoffman, a large, indolent, irreverent man, had nothing if not a high opinion of himself *vis à vis* his superiors. And in many cases his opinion appeared to be justified. He had been the German General Staff's Russian specialist and had previously made a study of the Red Army, working out the probable timing and mechanics of a Russian offensive. An astute student of Russian military thinking and psychology, his ability to predict their movements was excellent, often uncannily correct.

By 14 August the Russian Army was mobilized along the frontier, preparing to move into the long tongue of land that

Above: General Erich Ludendorff, one of the two great architects of the Russian defeat at Tannenberg.

was East Prussia. The 650,000 men were organized into two armies: the First, under General Pavel Rennenkampf and the Second, commanded by General Alexander Samsonov. General Jilinsky, who had been Chief of the Russian General Staff until 1913, was in overall command of the Front.

The plan called for Rennenkampf to enter East Prussia, north of the Masurian Lakes and head for the Insterburg Gap – a stretch of open land about 30 miles wide that lay between the lakes and the fortified area around Königsberg. Here he would keep the Germans busy while Samsonov marched around south of the lakes and came up to hit the German rear.

The Eighth Army, basing their plans on Hoffman's calculations, expected Rennenkampf to appear first. They would, they decided, engage him on 19 or 20 August, around the area of Gumbinnen; this would be early enough to allow them to defeat him before they had to turn and meet Samsonov, but late enough for the First Army to be as far from Russia as possible, thus making it much more vulnerable.

Unfortunately Prittwitz had not counted on General Hermann von François, the hot-headed Commander of the Ger-

man I Corps, who was determined that not a single Slav should defile the sacred soil of Prussia. By 16 August François had moved beyond Gumbinnen, despite orders to halt; by 17 August he had engaged Russian reconnaissance forces at Stilluponen, only five miles from the Russian frontier.

Furious messages from Prittwitz finally forced him to withdraw, but only after he had inflicted severe damage on the Russian 27th Division. He had also managed to hold up the First Army for some hours – which benefited Samsonov far more than Prittwitz.

Rennenkampf's Army renewed its advance for two days. Behind them their incomplete supply lines were already faltering; ahead of them the roads were clogged with fleeing refugees. Then on 19 August the General called a halt for the next day, hoping to lure the Germans forward, away from their prepared positions.

This put Prittwitz squarely on the horns of a dilemma. He was not inclined to lose face by withdrawing François (still ten miles east of Gumbinnen), nor did he have the time to play a waiting game with Rennenkampf. On the other hand, if he allowed François to attack it would be some time before the two and a half corps dutifully waiting behind the River Angerapp could be brought up to join him, and the whole Army would be pulled that much farther away from the XX Corps who were guarding the southern frontier. His problem was solved when word arrived from the XX Corps: Samsonov had crossed the frontier. Von François was ordered to attack on 20 August. Before dawn he was gleefully on his way, wreaking havoc on the Russian right wing.

The early attack, however, alerted the Russians, who were ready and waiting by the time the German XVIII Corps had struggled through the crowds of refugees to the center of the Front. Russian artillery pinned the infantry to the ground; by afternoon the entire German division was in panic-stricken retreat despite the attempts of the Commander, General August von Mackensen, to halt

the rout. General Otto von Below's I Reserve Corps was forced to retreat as well, to cover Mackensen, and the 3rd Reserve Division did not arrive until the battle was over. Thus ended the Battle of Gumbinnen, which set the stage for Tannenberg. It has gone down, quite rightly, as a Russian victory, despite François's action and the successful German retreat.

Prittwitz was unnerved. Soon the First Army would smash through the Insterburg Gap, driving François into Königsberg and the rest of the Eighth Army into Samsonov's arms. He remembered Moltke's last words: 'In case of extreme need abandon the area east of the Vistula.' As he and Waldersee left the house in which their headquarters was located they met Hoffman and Grunert standing outside. From the expressions on their faces the two junior officers knew immediately what was coming. Although they tried to dissuade him, pointing out that there was still time to finish off Rennenkampf while the XX Corps delayed Samsonov, Prittwitz would have none of it. He curtly rejected their advice and telephoned OHL to announce his plans to retire behind the Vistula.

While he was gone Hoffman and Grunert managed to convince Waldersee, with the aid of a map and compass, that retreat was already impossible; only bold action could save the Eighth Army. They decided, therefore, to take advantage of the interior lines by sending François's I Corps by rail to reinforce Scholtz's XX Corps on the right while Mackensen's and von Below's Corps marched south and west by road. Here, then, was the basis of the classic Tannenberg maneuvers.

When Prittwitz returned they managed to get him to agree to the plan, but no one thought to inform OHL of the change. There Moltke, aghast at his subordinate's lack of nerve, had found a 'man of decision' to replace him. On 22 August two telegrams arrived at Eighth Army Headquarters. The first announced that a special train was on its way

Top right: the Tsarist announcement of the declaration of the war against Germany.

Center right: A loyal demonstration in favor of the war by Tsarist supporters in St Petersburg in August 1914.

Right: Russian conscripts join the mobilization, which took several weeks to accomplish.

bringing a new Commander and a new Chief of Staff – Hindenburg and Ludendorff. The second belatedly informed Prittwitz and Waldersee of their dismissal.

Soon orders arrived from Ludendorff. Grunert and Hoffman were to meet him at Marienburg; François's Corps was to be sent by train to reinforce Scholtz; and Mackensen and von Below were to disengage and refit. Whether this was a case where two tacticians arrived independently at the same solution to a problem or whether Ludendorff had seen the orders Hoffman had issued, is not known.

But what of the Russians while all this German reorganization was underway? Rennenkampf stayed where he was, making no attempt to follow up his victory at Gumbinnen. He had lost most of a division to François, and he had no desire to lengthen his already chaotic supply lines while the Germans shortened theirs. Hoffman, who was counting on this inactivity, saw a different reason for it. He had been an observer with the Japanese in their war against Russia and had heard stories of a bitter emnity between Rennenkampf and Samsonov that culminated in a fist fight at Mukden station. Thus, he calculated, Rennenkampf would not be inclined to hurry to his colleague's assistance.

In fact, co-ordinating the two pincers of the Russian attack was an operation beset by so many difficulties that even the Russian General Staff had little hope of success. General Jilinsky, himself under constant pressure from the French, could do nothing but send urgent messages to speed things up – and since Rennenkampf had gone into action first, all those messages were directed to Samsonov.

For Samsonov the constant exhortations to hurry simply added another dimension to the enormous difficulties he was already facing. His men were struggling for every yard along sandy roads and were constantly bogged down with their horse-drawn transport. The Signal Corps was in such a confused state that messages had to be sent over

Above right: The Russian advance into East Prussia, which caught the Germans by surprise. Count von Schlieffen, author of the plan to advance into France and Belgium, expected that Germany would suffer losses initially in the East. General von Moltke, head of the German General Staff on the outbreak of war, was stunned by news of the Russian advances.
Right: Tsarist troops advance to the front.

General Samsonov.

Jilinksy (left) presents decorations to Russian soldiers in the first days of the fighting.

the wireless, in clear. Supply trains had not appeared; ammunition was in short supply for some Corps, food for others. Many men were without boots, marching with their feet bound up in rags. Nonetheless on 19 August Samsonov crossed the German frontier on schedule. On 22 August, in response to yet another message from Jilinsky, he reported that although he was adhering to the timetable his troops were very tired and that there was no food for either men or horses.

That very day the Russian XV Corps under General Martos ran into the German XX Corps. General Scholtz, who had not yet received his reinforcements, retreated, leaving the Russians in possession of two small villages. The next day the Russian VI and XIII Corps, on the right, captured more villages. Scholtz pulled back a little more, at which point Jilinsky ordered an 'energetic offensive' against the 'insignificant forces' facing him.

This would have been precisely the right move – provided Rennenkampf was doing his bit by keeping the rest of the Eighth Army busy in the north. The First Army was moving again, but it was going due west instead of turning south to link up with Samsonov, and was not in contact with the enemy at all. Jilinsky did nothing to alter their line of march, but continued to push the Second Army forward.

Early in the morning on 24 August

A Russian unit moves to the front lines in East Prussia in the sultry summer of 1914.

A German encampment near the Russian frontier.

Front line troops read a Bolshevist newspaper.

Russian infantry in their trench take up a defensive position.

General Martos's XV Corps again fell upon the XX Corps. Greatly outnumbered, Scholtz withdrew to the village of Tannenberg, about ten miles to the rear. The Russians jumped to the conclusion that the Germans were in full retreat, and that night Samsonov issued orders to all his Corps – in clear, of course – giving their orders for the following day's pursuit.

Now Ludendorff had a decision to make. By 25 August François's Corps would be in position to support Scholtz's right. But Mackensen's and von Below's Corps were still halted, about 30 miles from Rennenkampf's Army. Should he pull them southwards for an attack against Samsonov's right wing, or should he leave them where they were, to guard against a possible advance by the First Army? No one knew better than the new Commander that the decision he made would be crucial – and that he would be held responsible for the outcome. Hoffman has described that evening as the 'most difficult' of the whole battle.

Even hearing Samsonov's troop dispositions over the wireless the next morning did not entirely dispel the uncertainty; the Germans could simply not believe that their enemy was being so obliging! Hoffman, however, convinced his superiors that the messages were real. Finally Ludendorff decided to throw the entire Eighth Army against Samsonov. Mackensen and von Below were ordered

south at once, and only a thin cavalry screen was left facing Rennenkampf.

At that point Samsonov belatedly began to realize that he was not chasing an Army in full retreat, but was facing a reorganized and advancing force. However, when he sent a staff officer back to Jilinsky to point out the necessity of veering his army westward, Jilinsky – safely in the rear – replied 'To see the enemy where he is not is cowardice. I will not allow General Samsonov to play the coward. I insist that he continue the offensive.'

Samsonov obediently disposed his exhausted and half-starved troops for the following day's attack. The XV Corps under General Martos and the XII under General Kliouev held the center, along with one division of General Kondratovitch's XXIII Corps. The left flank would be held by the other division of the XXIII Corps and by General Artomonov's I Corps. The VI Corps held the right flank, some 50 miles away. Later Samsonov, not realizing that Mackensen and von Below had reached his front, ordered the VI Corps to march as far as they could to support the center. On the morning of 26 August he changed his mind again and told them to stay and protect the right flank. But by that time the VI Corps was already marching back.

At sunrise on 26 August the Russian XV Corps drove toward the German XX Corps. The XX Corps was composed of

local men fighting for their own homes; Scholtz's line buckled and fell back westward, but did not break. On General Martos's left the division of the XXIII Corps was thrown back, exposing his flank. On his right General Kliouev and the XII Corps had taken Allenstein. They left it, however, to go back and help Martos.

Kliouev assumed that the VI Corps was on its way and would hold Allenstein for him. But as they were marching toward the center, not knowing that their orders had been canceled, one of the divisions heard of enemy soldiers to the north. Assuming these were Germans retreating from Rennenkampf, the divisional commander decided to attack. In fact they were Mackensen's men. The other division was already eight miles ahead. In response to their fellow's desperate pleas for assistance they turned around and marched back again, only to run into von Below's Corps. The Germans were probably as tired as the Russians after two days of forced marches, but at least they had been fed. As day turned to night the battle turned into a rout. By morning the VI Corps was in chaotic retreat. Samsonov's right flank had been turned, and there was still a gap at Allenstein.

Luckily the Germans were too tired to press the Russians and many of them managed to retire safely, but in their panic a few of the Russian soldiers ran straight into Lake Bossau and drowned.

The encirclement of the Russian Army at Tannenberg cost the Tsar many thousands of troops.

This one isolated incident gave birth to the legend that Hindenburg drove the Russian Army to its death in the lakes.

By nightfall Samsonov realized that instead of destroying the enemy he had to save himself from envelopment and destruction. He decided, however, to continue to try and hold the Germans with his Center Corps until Rennenkampf arrived to fall upon them from the rear. He ordered General Artomonov and the I Corps to protect the left flank 'at all costs.'

The 26 August had not been a happy day at German field HQ either. In the morning Ludendorff was suddenly assailed with doubt. Had he made the right decision in committing his whole army against Samsonov? Rennenkampf was still looming on the horizon; if he moved against them, the Germans were finished. Perhaps it would be better to abandon the offensive against the Second Army and return to take care of the First. But at this point Hindenburg, Hoffman, and the rest of the staff rallied round and eventually were able to stiffen his resolve and determination.

Suddenly Ludendorff discovered that François, who had had orders to attack the Russian left wing on the 25th, had refused, and although he had been told to do so on 26 August, had still not begun battle. He had a valid reason for his refusal: his heavy artillery had still not arrived from Gumbinnen and to attack without it would be courting failure. But although both Scholtz and Hoffman supported his position Ludendorff would not tolerate insubordination. Stubbornly he kept repeating his orders to attack. Equally stubborn, Francois managed to procrastinate throughout 26 August.

Then, in the middle of his argument with François, Ludendorff received a telephone call from OHL. Hoffman picked up the extension and the two astonished officers heard Colonel Tappen, OHL's Chief of Operations, propose to send them three Corps and a Cavalry Division as reinforcement. Ludendorff was appalled. He knew, none better, that the success of Schlieffen's plan depended on using every man that could possibly be used to strengthen the

right wing. What could OHL be thinking of?

The answer is easily found. On the Western Front the French Army was in retreat and decisive victory seemed within Germany's grasp. In addition, just as Prittwitz had been too busy to call Supreme Headquarters and tell them he had changed his mind about retiring behind the Vistula, so Ludendorff never bothered to keep his superiors informed of the true situation since his arrival. For three days he had let Moltke brood over the 'disaster' at Gumbinnen and picture hordes of Cossacks ravaging Prussia, all the while besieged by tearful aristocratic ladies who begged him to save their families' lands and fortunes.

Even now, fully realizing the dangers inherent in weakening the line on the Western Front, Ludendorff protested but feebly, telling Tappen that the reinforcements were not 'positively' needed and would in any case arrive too late for the decisive battle. Tappen insisted they could be spared; it is much easier to begin troop movements than to stop them. Ludendorff did not press the point. Though one of the Corps was recalled before it entrained for the Eastern Front, the other two were to be missed at the Battle of the Marne.

The next day, 27 August, saw the decisive moment in the battle as a whole. François's artillery had arrived. Before dawn, at 0400 hours, a furious bombardment lit up the sky and a rain of shells fell upon the men of the Russian I Corps. It is difficult to imbue starving men with the will to fight at any time; under the fierce barrage the Russians broke and fled, leaving half their comrades dead on the battlefield behind them.

But the Second Army was not beaten. The I Corps finally turned, and fought desperately to cover the Army's line of retreat, holding Francois east of Usdau. In the center the formidable XII and XV Corps continued to attack. The German soldiers were as tired as the Russians, and both sides were hampered by the hordes of refugees and livestock that clogged the roads behind the front.

Late that afternoon Jilinsky finally realized that far from retreating to the Vistula, the Germans were actually attacking Samsonov in force. He sent a telegraph message to Rennenkampf belatedly telling him that the Second Army was under heavy attack and that he should support them by moving his left flank as far forward as possible. But he made no mention of any need to hurry.

Meanwhile the two armies – 300,000

men – fought, broke apart, marched, and met to fight again along the 40-mile front. Columns of troops advancing to the front became entangled with prisoners being sent to the rear. The roar of artillery filled the ears of the men, now battling like automatons in the mist and smoke. As night fell men sank where they stood to snatch some rest before the next day's struggle.

At dawn on the morning of 28 August François opened the battle again with another blast from his artillery. But the way ahead of him was empty; the Russian left had fled precipitately across the frontier. So he turned his forces eastward toward Niederburg to cut off Samsonov's retreat. Ludendorff ordered – or rather, begged – him to shift left to relieve some of the pressure on Scholtz's XX Corps. But Francois, as usual, followed his own plan; he continued to drive to the east, leaving battalions as entrenched pickets along the way to prevent the Russians breaking for the south.

Ludendorff and Hindenburg, waiting in Scholtz's headquarters at Frogenau (about two miles from the tiny village of Tannenberg), became increasingly anxious as the Russian center continued to slam into the XX Corps. A series of conflicting orders to Mackensen and von Below left those divisional commanders so confused that they finally sent a staff officer to Headquarters to try and straighten things out. As it turned out, neither of them was where Ludendorff wanted him to be, but by afternoon both were proceeding properly – Mackensen pursuing the remnants of the Russian right wing and von Below moving toward the gap at Allenstein to complete the envelopment of the Russian center.

Ludendorff relaxed and told François he could continue his march eastward. Just then he was told that Rennenkampf's First Army was finally on the move. At the rate he was going, however, he would obviously be too late.

Samsonov realized that the end had come – there would be no glory, no victory, nor even any reprieve. With his Army shattered beneath him he became again a cavalry officer. He ordered his equipment sent back to Russia, cut his communications to the rear and, commandeering horses from some passing Cossacks, set off for the Front with a handful of staff officers.

On the way he met the British liaison officer, Major General Sir Alfred Knox. He told Knox that the situation was 'critical,' that Knox should return 'while

Russian troops on the offensive prior to the Battle of Tannenberg.

A Russian field hospital as the Germans surrounded their positions.

A few hundred of the tens of thousands of Russian soldiers captured in the battle.

Russian troops are marched into German captivity.

Russian prisoners enjoy their rations (above) while others fraternize with Germans (below).

there was still time' so that he could report to his government. As he rode away, Knox recalls, he turned in his saddle and said with a sad smile, 'The enemy has luck one day, we will have luck another.' Throughout the afternoon he rode back and forth behind the lines; that night he ordered a general retreat.

During the next two days, 29 and 30 August, the retreat became an appalling disaster. Hardest hit were the steadfast Center Corps. They had fought hardest and longest, had advanced farthest, and retreated last – and so were the most completely trapped by the German encirclement. They had had almost nothing to eat for four days; some had had no food at all for the last two. They stumbled helplessly through the forests, trying in vain to escape from the ring of François's barricade as the net was drawn tighter and tighter. Thousands were killed or taken prisoner; only one officer of the XV Corps escaped.

General Martos of the XV Corps has described his own capture. On 29 August he and a few of his men were trying to make their way through the forest, with the enemy all around them. One by one they were picked off until by nightfall only four remained. They had had nothing to eat or drink all day; one horse was dead of exhaustion and starvation; they were leading the others. They were trying to guide themselves by the stars, but it was too cloudy. Suddenly a German searchlight blazed out. Martos tried to mount, but his horse was hit and as he fell the German soldiers were upon him. He was taken to a hotel in Osterode where, as he tells it, Ludendorff came and taunted him with defeat. Hindenburg, however, awkwardly tried to comfort him and left with a bow saying, 'I wish you happier days.'

Samsonov, the unfortunate Commander of the Second Army, was not taken alive. Like Martos he was making his way through the forest with a few companions; they were only about seven miles from the frontier, but the Germans had occupied the village ahead of them. They ran out of matches and could not read their compasses. After staggering on for about six miles, hand in hand to avoid losing each other in the dark, they stopped to rest. Samsonov, an asthmatic, was very weak. He moved away from the others into a thicker part of the forest and a few minutes later the sound of a solitary shot rang out. The Russians knew immediately what had happened. They searched for his body until they heard a German patrol approaching, then moved

on toward the frontier and safety. The Germans found Samsonov's body and buried it at Willenburg; in 1916 his widow had it removed to Russia.

The situation need not have been so bleak. If the center Corps had been able to reorganize and make one last concerted effort, they might well have succeeded in breaking out. François's men were spread very thin and, by 30 August, were being menaced from the outside as well. The source of the menace was the Russian I Corps. After its retreat across the frontier the commanding officer, General Artomonov, had been dismissed. His successor, General Sirelius, had collected every man he could, to come up with a unit about the size of a division. He then launched a vigorous offensive that succeeded in breaking through François's lines and retaking Niedeburg. But it was too late and he had no support; on 31 August the I Corps again retreated southward.

Jilinsky, true to form, waited too long and then issued inadequate orders. After he had heard nothing from the Second Army for two whole days, he ordered Rennenkampf's cavalry to break through at Allenstein and find out what was happening. They never made it; the Germans, having virtually destroyed one army, were already reforming to meet the next.

Even the Germans at first had little idea of the magnitude of their victory. Sixty trains were needed to transport more than 92,000 prisoners to the rear; another 30,000 were listed as dead or missing. The XV and XII Corps were wiped out. The XXIII Corps was reduced to about the strength of a brigade and the VI and I Corps to about a division each. Of the Second Army's 600 guns, between 300 and 500 were captured.

Although Ludendorff did not savor the triumph as much as he might have done (the 'strain on [his] nerves' from the menacing presence of Rennenkampf's Army had been too great), the German Commanders soon began to realize that their victory had been a great, perhaps unique achievement. Both Ludendorff and Hoffman claim credit for changing the name of the battle from 'Frogenau' to 'Tannenberg' to offset the memory of an ancient defeat when the Poles and Lithuanians had routed the Teutonic Knights there in 1410.

In the public eye the figurehead commander, Hindenburg, was the victor at Tannenberg. The elderly, dogged figure in its tight, old-fashioned, blue uniform, caught their fancy and was turned into the supreme warlord, the very personification of victory.

Ludendorff was the victor, of course, in the eyes of the General Staff, but Tannenberg was not the carefully planned and deliberately executed 'second Cannae' that appeared later in the mythology. Ludendorff owed much to others. The plan he used had been designed by Hoffman, though Ludendorff does deserve some credit for accepting it and for adding some details. For the courage to carry it out he still had to thank Hoffman, who steadfastly maintained that the First Army would not move. François, who repeatedly defied Ludendorff's orders, was responsible for ensuring the total envelopment of Samsonov's left wing. Jilinsky, the Com-

Above: A Russian soldier mourns some of his slain comrades. Millions were to die in this senseless and futile struggle.

mander of the Russian Northwest Army Group, was an invaluable if unwitting ally, pushing Samsonov forward when he should have held him back, letting Rennenkampf saunter at his own pace when he should have been pushing him forward. In fact, the real responsibility for the German victory at Tannenberg, according to Hoffman, must be attributed to the Russian wireless. Every day the German Signal Corps intercepted Russian messages and decoded or translated them. Once he was convinced of their veracity, Ludendorff came to depend on them; if they did not arrive in his office by 2300 hours he would go out and personally enquire about the delay.

Although Russia won a great victory over the Austrians at Galicia at about this time – in numbers an even greater victory – the disaster at Tannenberg had an irreparable effect. Samsonov was dead, two of his Corps Commanders were captured, and the other three were cashiered for incompetence. The Second Army no longer existed. Rennenkampf retreated eastward and finally deserted his Army entirely. He was discharged, his reputation in ruins, pulling Jilinsky down with him.

The Russian steamroller had fallen apart and all the inefficiency, inadequacy, and incompetence that had gone into its making lay revealed. But despite mounting pro-peace agitation, despite increasing chaos and dwindling supplies, Russia – for whatever reasons – fought on.

THE MARNE 1914

Un joli fleuve la Marne.

MARSHAL JOFFRE

5–9 September 1914

The war which engulfed Europe in 1914 had long been foreseen by the Great Powers. In 1908–1909 there had been negotiations between the Prussian and the Austro-Hungarian General Staffs with a view to deciding upon a common plan for a war with France and Russia. The Germans laid down as its basis that, except for an army of 12 or 13 divisions deployed in East Prussia, Austria-Hungary must carry on the struggle with Russia single-handed, until a decision against France, which was to be sought with all speed, should be obtained. With France defeated there would be a mass transport to the East of important German forces, which would co-operate with those of Austria-Hungary, to obtain a decision against Russia. The Germans hoped that, having beaten the French, their forces would arrive on the Russian front on about the 41st day of mobilization.

In 1914 the Germans officially began to mobilize on 2 August. They expected to have won a decision on the Western Front by the end of that month and to be ready to operate against Russia by 8 September. If their hopes for this breathtaking *blitzkrieg* seem almost ludicrously optimistic it must be remembered that in both their last great wars, against Austria in 1866 and France in 1870, they had been blessed with a quick decision. Moreover preparations had been made with meticulous Teuton thoroughness. From 1890 to 1905 the famous strategist, Field Marshal Graf Alfred Schlieffen, had been Chief of the Prussian General Staff. In 1914 he was in his grave but he had bequeathed to his successor his plan for a new Cannae, a battle of annihilation devised to destroy the French Army – and the British, too, should it intervene.

The Germans were to deploy on either side of the fortresses in the Metz-Thionville area. Their right wing was to be very much stronger than the left; in the proportion of 7–1. This massive right wing was to swing round in a great enveloping flanking movement, which would sweep round south of Paris and drive the French, and any allies they might have, up against their Moselle fortresses, against the Jura and against Switzerland. It was emphasized that the formation of a strong right wing was essential. 'Everything,' said General von Seeckt in a lecture he gave in 1928, 'was risked on the strength and rapidity of the first blow.'

Graf Schlieffen's successor was Generaloberst Helmuth von Moltke, nephew of Germany's greatest soldier, Field Marshal Graf Helmuth von Moltke, the victor of Königgratz and Sedan. It may as well be said at once that even in 1906 the younger Moltke was not the man to drive great German armies on to victory. By 1914 he was 66 and in feeble health. Why then did the Kaiser select him? Perhaps the unpredictable and temperamental Kaiser Wilhelm II, who at least as late as 1908 toyed with the idea of commanding his armies in person, preferred a courtly general who would not stand up to him. It was a disastrous choice. Moltke, who did not really believe that he would ever have the ill fortune to command in war, began to modify the Schlieffen plan. Prudently he dropped the idea of marching through Holland so as not to force her into the ranks of the enemy. A march through Belgium did, however, remain in the plan. This, in the event, was to bring in against him, straightaway, the Belgian Army and the British Expeditionary Force (BEF). Without them Moltke's seven German armies had only to cope with five French armies. The invasion of Belgium, swiftly denounced as a crime, seems with hindsight incredibly stupid. The fact is that the Germans simply did not expect the Belgians to offer armed resistance to a march across their territory. One must remember, too, that in those days the Ardennes were considered to be more of an obstacle to military movement than they were to prove either in 1914, 1940 or 1944. Anything that would slow down the great outflanking movement must hazard the success of the plan, and the safety of the armies on the Russian front. It followed that the invasion of Belgium was not only acceptable but vitally necessary.

In 1909 von Moltke, with fresh formations at his disposal, increased the strength of the German *left* wing from five to eight corps, thus demonstrating, as some critics have said, that he had missed the point of the Schlieffen Plan. It may be that this deployment was intended to be a temporary measure at the beginning of the war, and that after dealing with the French right these troops could be moved by rail to reinforce the wing advancing through Belgium. But this was to leave out of account the possibility of Belgian resistance, for example, that of the fortress of Liège, and of the destruction of railways. To calculate upon the possibility of a second deployment was unrealistic. In war even the simple is very difficult – as Moltke should have known if he had studied his

The French Army during its August mobilization. All artillery was horsedrawn in 1914.

Clausewitz: however, it seems that he was not a very serious student of things military. Cavalry charges or maneuvers, or frontal attacks at war games, were more to the taste of Moltke and his imperial master than a serious study of the Science of War.

Could the Schlieffen Plan have worked with a more resolute man at the helm? It is more than likely. Very soon a partnership was to spring into life, that of Generals von Hindenburg and Ludendorff, which was to achieve great things. Had the Kaiser, and his entourage, shown rather more talent for personnel selection, there were officers available who might have proved more than a match for General Joffre, and Field Marshal Sir John French and King Albert of the Belgians. The story of the 1914 campaign on the Western Front is the story of how von Moltke's modified Schlieffen Plan came unstuck.

This is not, of course, to say that the French did not have a plan of their own. They did – and a fairly unrealistic one, too. The Belgians, who were far from being in a warlike mood, had no real plan beyond the defense of their fortresses. They would ride out the storm as best they could, until their Allies won the war. In the event their army, which was small and inexperienced, did a great deal better than anyone had the right to expect.

The British, as things turned out, merely conformed – more or less – to French strategy, but they might very well have developed a strategy of their own. A maritime, trading nation, with by far the strongest Navy in the world might well have hit upon some strategy other than that of placing their small, but hard-hitting Expeditionary Force, under Joffre's command. It must be remembered that it was the invasion of Belgium,

Top left: Belgian civilians watch as the 2nd Scots Guards march through their village during their approach to the front in the early days of the August 1914 campaign.

Center left: French prisoners under German guard after their capture in Belgium during the long retreat back to the Marne.

Left: French troops and their war dog take up a position near the Aisne. War dogs were used for general reconnaissance and were needed in the first months of the war, particularly by the French, who made excellent targets, wearing their red trousers and other 19th century accoutrements, gratefully abandoned in 1915.

General von Kluck.

not of France, that brought Great Britain into the war. History shows that the English are sensitive about the ports of the Low Countries falling into 'the wrong hands.' From the outset a plan to land and defend Antwerp had its advocates, and, eventually (4 October) a force was sent there. Had the BEF been landed through the Channel ports, from Antwerp to Boulogne, and then developed its operations against the German right the effect upon the Schlieffen Plan must have been tremendous, incalculable: perhaps decisive.

The Allied commander on the Western Front was Joseph-Jacques-Césaire Joffre, a calm, industrious officer of engineers, just old enough to have taken part in the war of 1870. In 1892 he had distinguished himself fighting the veiled Touareg and had taken Timbuktu. He had served in Tongking and Madagascar and, aged 58, had been appointed in 1910 to the *Conseil Supérieure de la Guerre* (War Council). At a time when the French Army was riddled with politics he was considered 'a good republican,' that is to say politically reliable, and on the fall of General Michel, at the recommendation of General Gallieni, under whom he had served in Madagascar, he was appointed Chief of the General Staff and Commander on Chief designate.

Joffre did not have so long to tinker with his predecessors' plans as did von Moltke, and the changes he made between 1911 and 1914 were to prove valuable. It fell to him to make good deficiencies in armament, especially heavy artillery; to offset the Germans' numerical superiority by the introduction of three years military service; to evolve a new plan, and to train com-

Propaganda poster showing Anglo-French solidarity on the Western Front.

manders and their staffs for their part in it.

When Joffre took over in 1911 Plan XVI was in force. It called for a defensive-offensive designed to counter a German invasion towards Metz, Toul and Verdun. It was assumed that Belgian neutrality would be respected.

Plan XVII was not like the Schlieffen Plan. It did not lay down in advance a timetable which was to unroll with Teutonic relentlessness. Plan XVII as General Beaufre has pointed out 'was actually only a plan for concentration with a number of alternatives depending on the assumptions made regarding enemy action. Joffre's main idea was to give himself the possibility of carrying out various maneuvers – the plan amounted to adoption of an "on guard" position

Sixty-pound gun used by the British Expeditionary Force in 1914 from Mons to the Marne.

General von Kluck poses with his staff from the German First Army.

A street in Lille just before the Germans occupied the city in northern France late in August.

before the start of fencing rather than a scenario arranged in advance. Anyone following the preparation and execution of this plan must inevitably be struck by its pragmatic character and the fact that its essence was maneuver. Herein lay its strength and it was this that opened the way to the recovery of the Marne after the initial setbacks.' Plan XVII was no more like the Schlieffen Plan than a bus is like a tram.

Plan XVII was a vast improvement on its predecessor if only because it called for the deployment of far more troops.

	French	German
Battalions	580	600
Squadrons	332	350
Batteries	653	600 [including 100 heavy batteries]

France would now put 1,300,000 men in the field at the outset, whereas Russia with her vast population would not provide more than 800,000 men. Despite the disparity in populations France, taking account of the probability of British and Belgian assistance might even have a degree of superiority over the German invaders.

France like Germany mobilized on 2 August. Great Britain did not declare war until two days later. Both sides now embarked upon the gradual deployment, which by means of countless railway trains was to bring the various armies to their concentration areas. While the patrols probe forward and the first skirmishes take place it is worth pausing for a moment to comment on the merits and defects of the various adversaries.

The French, German and Belgian armies all suffered from a lack of recent battle experience. Few below general rank were old enough to have fought in 1870. In this respect the British with the South African War (1899–1902) behind them had a great advantage. They knew the fire effect of modern weapons; had an excellent rifle and were expert in its handling. In heavy artillery the Germans had a vast superiority. Both the British and the Germans had a practical uniform, devised with some attention to concealment. The French, with their red trousers, showed up rather more than their ancestors had at Waterloo. All the three major armies were imbued with the offensive spirit: very much so. But both the German and the French were inclined to bunch in the attack, and the latter relied too much on the bayonet, as

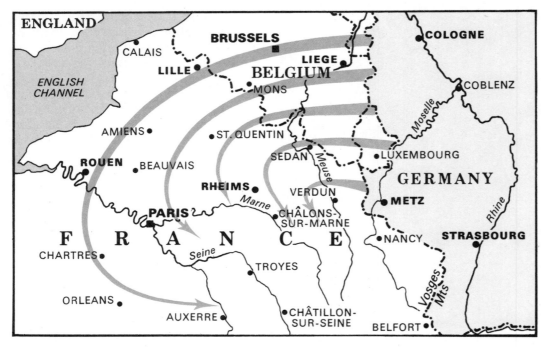

The Schlieffen Plan was a sweep through Belgium and France to the sea to encircle Paris.

opposed to the tactics of 'Fire and Movement.' By modern standards the use of ground and cover was very imperfectly understood, even by the British.

The selection of good generals in peacetime is always a chancy business. It must be said that the Army Commanders of 1914 were an unimpressive lot. It would have been easy enough to find younger and fitter men than Moltke and French, to name but two.

By the standards of the day the armies were reasonably well organized. Moltke might have found it easier to handle the Schlieffen Plan had he organized his forces into three Army Groups, and had the provision of wireless to the German armies been rather more generous. It would not, one would think, have been beyond the wit of man for the Germans to provide some form of motor transport for the reserves of the armies of their right. Some Jäger battalions were moved by truck on at least one occasion. It is also worth observing that when Schlieffen made his plan the possibility of airplanes being used by his opponents for reconnaissance was not a consideration.

One characteristic of the 1914 armies is easily overlooked today. They were horse-drawn. There were a few motorcars for the staff, but the fighting units still relied almost entirely upon horsed transport. This meant that, once beyond railhead, moves of more than 15 to 20 miles a day were not possible.

There was some fighting during the deployment phase, the *Aufmarsch* as the Germans called it. On 5 August von Kluck's First Army attacked the Belgian fortress of Liège, whose capture was essential to the deployment of the two right-hand German armies. Liège was encircled by 12 modern forts, constructed some 25 years earlier under the personal direction of the leading engineer of the day, Lieutenant General Henri-Alexis Brialmont. These forts formed an extensive position and required more than 25,000 men to defend them properly. The forts were from one to four miles apart, and were supposed to be connected by entrenchments, but these did not exist. Consequently the Germans managed to break in and take the city by a night attack, whose success was in doubt until General Ludendorff assumed command of a brigade, which had lost its way, and took the citadel. The Belgian commander, General Gérard-Mathieu Leman put up a spirited defense, but the massive Austrian 42cm Skoda howitzers smashed his forts, the

British cavalry and their artillery on retreat from Mons after their stand on 24–25 August.

British cavalry scouts (Lancers) during the retreat through Flanders back to the Marne.

last of which fell on 16 August. By 14 August the Germans were pouring through the city, but Leman had played his part. Not only was the German timetable getting behind, but the Belgians had had time to do some useful demolition work on their railways.

On 6 August the French wings began to probe forward into Alsace and Belgium, but it cannot be said that they did much to pierce the fog of war. Even so by 16 August it had become clear to Joffre that seven or eight German corps with four cavalry divisions were thrusting westward between Givet and Brussels. There seemed to be six or seven corps, with two or three cavalry divisions, between Bastogne and Thionville, while south of Metz the Germans were keeping quiet. The French had not as yet discovered that their enemy by putting reserve corps in the field at the outset had given themselves a numerical advantage.

It was not only at Liège that the Belgians imposed delay upon the invaders. At Haelen (12 August) Lieutenant General von der Marwitz's II Cavalry Corps was roughly handled by the Cavalry Division under Lieutenant General de Witte.

On 19 August two corps under General von Gallwitz began to invest the Belgian fortress of Namur, and to bombard it with heavy mortars and howitzers. The Belgians had no guns powerful enough to reply and by the evening of 23 August five out of the nine forts were in ruins. The mobile troops of the garrison withdrew southward into France with a loss of 5500 men. The survivors were eventually able to rejoin the main Belgian Army, which had by this time withdrawn into Antwerp.

The XI Hussars at the Marne.

Above: Officers of the 1st Cameronians pause during the retreat from Mons.

Above: French walking wounded on their way to a field hospital in August 1914.
Below: French troops advance toward the Marne front, 4 September 1914.

Wounded men of the British Expeditionary Force at a field hospital near the Marne.

Meanwhile the French were planning a great attack to break the German center. That done Joffre meant to fall with every available man upon the German right wing.

Already, before the general advance had begun the French right, 456,000 strong (First and Second Armies), had been worsted in the Battles of Sarrebourg and Morhange (18–20 August) by the 345,000 men of the German Sixth and Seventh Armies. Despite this on 21 August the Third and Fourth Armies crossed the frontier and launched themselves into the wooded hills and valleys of the Ardennes, advancing from ten to 15 miles. They advanced blind, for in that country cavalry scouts struggled forward with difficulty, and airplanes could observe nothing. The French columns literally collided with those of the German Fourth and Fifth Armies, lost the Battles of Virton and of the Semoy, and after sustaining heavy losses, especially among the officers, fell back to the Meuse.

On this day of disaster (21 August) the BEF was approaching the line of the Mons Canal and the general situation was that:–

The Belgian Army had fallen back into Antwerp.

The BEF was on the eve of making its first contact with the enemy.

The Fifth Army, which was awaiting reinforcements, had not advanced when Ruffey and de Langle did, and was sitting in a salient where it was about to be attacked by two German Armies.

The Third and Fourth Armies had just sustained a serious reverse at the hands of an enemy only slightly superior in numbers.

The First and Second Armies were withdrawing.

It cannot be said that the situation was

Right: A church near the Marne is converted into a field hospital to house French wounded.

Below: French infantry take up a position to repel the long German advance.

a brilliant one from the Allied point of view, but the Germans' advantage, though distinct, was not decisive.

The Germans on the other hand had as yet little cause to be dissatisfied with the progress they had made. By the evening of 17 August their seven Armies had concentrated and were ready to move. Their long front ran from the fortress of Strasbourg up through Sarrebourg, Metz and Thionville, whose fortifications were known as the Moselle Position; on up through the center of Luxembourg, whose neutrality had been violated on 2 August, to Liège and so northwest to the River Gette, where von Kluck faced the Belgians. On the German right, which Schlieffen had intended to be massive, an interesting situation had developed. Three German Armies faced three of the Allies:–

ALLIED ARMIES	Divisions
Belgians	6
BEF	4
French Fifth	10
	20

GERMAN ARMIES	Divisions
First	14 (*)
Second	12
Third	8
	34

* Including IX *Reserve* Corps, which was originally left in Schleswig to oppose a British landing, and then hastened to the front in time to sack Louvain on 25 August.

These 34 German Divisions faced a frontier with no great natural obstacle, and a few obsolete fortresses, where 20 Allied divisions endeavored to bar the most direct route to the French capital. The successful Belgian withdrawal to Antwerp meant that two of Kluck's corps (III *Reserve* and IX *Reserve*) had to be left to invest, or mask, that fortress.

Sir John French landed in France on 14 August and spent the next three days in visits to Monsieur Alexandre Millerand, the French Minister of War at Paris; and his Headquarters (GHQ) at Vitry le François, and Lanrezac at Rethel. The last of the well-intentioned visits was not a success, partly owing to the language difficulty but more to Lanrezac's rudeness, which can perhaps be explained by the strain he was under. And so from the outset there was no good personal accord between the commanders of the BEF and the Fifth French Army.

The BEF crossed the Channel and disembarked, amid scenes of great enthusiasm, during the period 12–17 August. Its task was to move northward and form the extreme left of the French advance, which was about to begin. It assembled in the area Maubeuge-Le Cateau. Except for the Belgians in Antwerp there were few Allied troops between the BEF and the Sea, but General d'Amade, who set up his HQ at Arras on 18 August had three Territorial divisions between the Sambre and the sea, forming a barrier between Maubeuge and Dunkerque in order to protect the railway communications from possible raids by German cavalry.

The British, whose concentration was virtually complete by 20 August, had begun to operate on 19 August when the Flying Corps, which had 63 airplanes at Maubeuge, carried out its first reconnaissances towards Brussels and over Tournai and Courtrai. Next day cavalry patrols pushed forward as far as Binche found no enemy, but aerial reconnaissance spotted an endless German column pouring through Louvain. On this day the main Belgian Army retired into Antwerp and Joffre gave his orders for a general advance. The British were to advance on the axis Soignies-Nivelles. It was thought that Kluck's right would not extend much beyond Mons, and so once Lanrezac was across the Sambre the BEF would be well placed to wheel eastward and envelop the German right. In this it would have the support of General Sordet's cavalry corps which had orders to take position beyond the British left.

On 21 August it became known that the Germans had reached the line Grammont, Enghien, Nivelles, Genappes, Sombreffe, Charleroi, but while Lanrezac's Army was in contact with von Bülow, the BEF had not yet crossed swords with von Kluck. It was still intended that the BEF should take the offensive. Soon after dawn on 22 August a patrol of the 4th Dragoon Guards fired the BEF's first shot of the war, when it drove off a German cavalry piquet near Obourg.

On the next day the BEF, in position nine miles north of Lanrezac's left flank, was assailed by three corps of von Kluck's army. Well entrenched and completely hidden in the mining area around Mons the British rifles took a heavy toll of the German infantry, who attacked with great dash. Frontal attacks against such a position were murder. Captain Bloem, the only surviving company commander left in his battalion (12th Brandenburg Grenadiers, III Corps) tells us that his unit lost 25 officers and 500 men. The 75th Bremen Regiment (IX Corps) lost five officers and 376 men in a single attack.

Lanrezac had not done so well against von Bülow. His men did not like digging, and their red trousers betrayed their positions. Their rifles were obsolescent and their musketry was indifferent. Did they not depend on the bayonet? At 2300 hours Lieutenant Spears, his liaison officer, told Sir John French that the temperamental Lanrezac had retreated! The BEF, left with its right in the air had no alternative but to fall back. And so on the morning of 24 August Captain Bloem found to his astonishment that his battalion was still to advance.

Sir John French, no less volatile than his French neighbor, now began to contemplate departure. 'I think,' he wrote to Lord Kitchener, the Secretary of State for War, 'immediate attention should be directed to the defense of Le Havre.' By 24 August even the phlegmatic Joffre saw that the French, condemned to the defensive, must hold out, making use of fortified lines and wearing down the Germans until the favorable moment for a counterattack should present itself.

Joffre had the self-confidence to attribute the failures up to this point, not to himself but to 'grave shortcomings on the part of commanders.' Nor did he hesitate to sack any whom he found wanting. At least one divisional commander saved him the trouble by committing suicide. Although himself an engineer officer, Joffre now (24 August) issued a training instruction on elementary tactics. Infantry and artillery were to collaborate in the capture of *points d'appui* (strong points). 'Every time that the infantry has been launched to the attack from too great a distance before the artillery has made itself felt, the infantry has fallen under the fire of machine guns and suffered losses which might have been avoided. When a *point d'appui* has been captured it must be organized immediately, the troops must entrench, and artillery must be brought up.' This was pretty elementary, but it was practical and a great deal better than the original French tactical doctrine – infantry attack head down, regardless of fire and of artillery support. Unfortunately, by the time these wise words reached the battalions, many of the

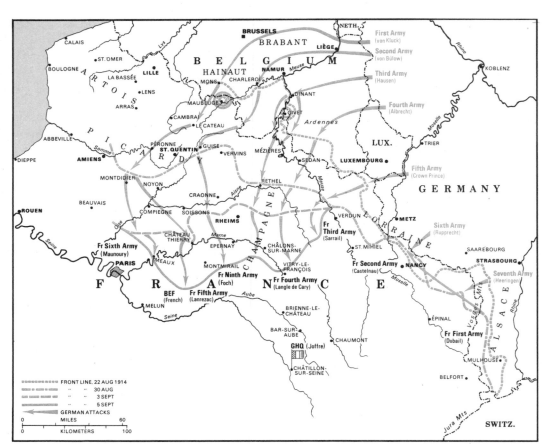

The German advance into France wheeled down toward Paris contrary to the Schlieffen Plan.

Parisiennes hail the advance of the cuirassiers *as they move up to the Marne.*

German troops take cover in shell holes as they shell French positions.

officers who should have seen them put into effect, were already dead. But black though things were the resolute Joffre never despaired of resuming the offensive at some future time, and meanwhile, realizing that his left was in danger of being swept away by the German onrush, ordered (25 August) the formation of a new Sixth Army, made up of divisions drawn from the now static front in Lorraine. This army under General Maunoury was to take up its position on the left of the BEF.

While the French commander was influencing the battle in this decisive fashion, his opponent was giving him timely relief. Von Moltke worried – not without reason – at the mess von Prittwitz was making in East Prussia, had decided to reinforce him with two corps. These could in fact have been spared from Lorraine, though they would still not have reached the Eastern Front in time for the Battle of Tannenberg. Von Moltke, however, chose to withdraw them from the right wing, where an overwhelming superiority was vital to the success of the German plan. It was an astonishing decision, and it was made worse by von Kluck's having to drop a corps to invest the fortress of Maubeuge. The truth seems to be that by 24 August the Germans thought that they had nothing but beaten troops in front of them. If this was von Kluck's opinion he was rudely disillusioned on 26 August, when the tired II Corps (General Sir Horace Smith-Dorrien) turned to fight at Le Cateau.

Von Kluck only managed to get two infantry and three cavalry divisions into action, but they had tremendous artillery support. On his right Sordet's cavalry and a French territorial division engaged two German corps. Eventually a corps, which had marched and countermarched for 11 miles during the day, came in on von Kluck's left, and Smith-Dorrien extricated his force, with a loss of about 8000 men and 38 guns. The Germans painfully impressed by British musketry solemnly concluded that the BEF had 28 machine guns to a battalion, whereas the correct figure was *two*. The BEF, said von Kluck after the war, 'was an incomparable army.' Be that as it may, it certainly did not have an incomparable commander.

While battle was raging at Le Cateau Joffre was in conference with Lanrezac and French at St Quentin. He was astonished by the latter's complaints. The sudden withdrawal of the Fifth Army had left his right flank in the air. His men

British infantry in an advance position near the Aisne after the Marne counter offensive.

were too tired to go over to the offensive. The querulous Irishman left the stolid Frenchman wondering whether the BEF had lost its cohesion. No such thing had happened. It was simply that French had lost touch with his army.

But if French took too gloomy a view of the situation the Germans were feeling, as von Moltke put it, the 'universal sense of victory.' Their outlook was no more realistic. Things were by no means as bright as they appeared. The First Army had suffered heavily at Haelen, Mons and Le Cateau. On the Meuse de Langle was holding up the Fourth Army (26–28 August); the Sixth and Seventh had been repulsed from Toul, Nancy and Epinal by de Castelnau and Dubail (26–28 August). Worse still on 29 August the Second Army blundered into Lanrezac's columns and was severely checked at Guise and St Quentin. Joffre was present at Fifth Army HQ during three vital hours of the battle, and gave a reluctant Lanrezac a direct order to counterattack. In this, the I Corps under General Franchet d'Espèrey, though their tactics do not seem to have been particularly clever, won an astonishing success. Bayonets fixed, the battalions went into action, bands playing and colors flying. This superb parade at least had the benefit of covering fire from a mass of the quick-firing 75mm field

The French Sixth Army at the Marne.

French infantry with their Lebel rifles.

guns, easily the best weapon in the French armory. The Germans gave way. Probably the whole thing was simply too unexpected. When that night the Fifth Army withdrew it did so unmolested.

Still, the sheer impetus of the German onslaught carried the armies of their right wing onwards towards Paris, though with five corps missing from their Order of Battle, gaps were beginning to appear in their array. The BEF disappeared south of Compiègne and von Kluck turned his attentions to Lanrezac. Crossing the Oise (1 September) he reached Crépy-en-Valois and Villers-Cotterests. He had brought the First German Army within 30 miles of Paris, where that very day an interesting interview was taking place. Two British field marshals, both in uniform, met in the British Embassy, and a masterful Kitchener told a resentful French that the BEF would stay in the line and would conform to the movements of its French Allies. Of the many services which Lord Kitchener rendered his country this was perhaps the greatest.

Still the German war machine came rumbling and rattling forward. Von Moltke, running things by remote control from Luxembourg, was now taken by the idea of driving the French southeast and cutting them off from Paris. To this end he ordered von Kluck to remain in rear of the Second Army, so as to cover this movement from the direction of Paris. This did not appeal to von Kluck, who was nothing if not independent minded, and who anticipated no danger from the French capital. On 2 September he gave orders for the passage of the Marne next day, with a single weak corps detailed as flank guard.

On the evening of 2 September the French Government departed for Bordeaux, leaving Paris in the firm hands of the veteran General Joseph-Simon Gallieni, who, on the next day, issued a Proclamation which expressed his determination to defend the place to the end, in the most unequivocal fashion.

At noon on the same day an aviator reported that the German columns had changed direction. Gallieni saw at once that the Germans were no longer advancing on Paris, but were moving in a southeasterly direction. Maunoury's staff refused at first to believe it, but in the evening it was confirmed.

'We must strike!' said Gallieni, and issued a warning order. He sent an officer to ask Joffre's permission to attack.

GHQ was now at Bar-sur-Aube, where early on 4 September the in-

The French held firm and then advanced, splitting the First and Second German Armies.

telligence staff was tracing von Kluck's movements on a wall map. 'But we have them,' they cried. 'We must stop the retreat and seize our heaven-sent chance at once.' The great man appeared in person and was shown the map. 'A remarkable situation,' Joffre commented. 'The Paris army and the British are in a good position to deliver a flank attack on the Germans as they are marching on the Marne.' But would Sir John French co-operate?

There was no longer any difficulty where the Fifth Army was concerned, for Lanrezac had been replaced by a real fire-eater, General Louis-Felix-Marie-François d'Espèrey. D'Espèrey, so far from needing any prodding, had drawn up his own proposals for an attack on 6 September. In this Major General Henry Wilson, French's Deputy Chief of Staff, an ardent francophile, had acted in concert with him. Gallieni shrewdly pointed out that by 7 September the Germans would have got wind of their danger from the direction of Paris.

While the Allies were screwing up their courage for a great counterattack, von Moltke's morale was alternated be-

tween elation and depression. Where were the masses of prisoners, the batteries of captured guns, which should be the trophies of a victorious advance such as his armies had made? On the evening of 4 September he sent out a wireless message: 'The First and Second Armies will remain facing Paris, the First Army between Oise and Marne, the Second Army between Marne and Seine.' Kluck, who received this on the next day, when he was already across the Marne, interpreted it in his own fashion. He continued to advance towards the Seine, but left one corps behind the Marne. That afternoon (5 September) Joffre visited French at GHQ (Melun). 'I put,' he was to write afterward, 'my whole soul into convincing French that the decisive hour had come and that an English abstention would be severely judged by history. Finally, striking the table with my fist, I cried: "*Monsieur le Maréchal!* The honor of England is at stake!" French blushed, and murmured with emotion, "I will do all that is possible," and for me that was the equivalent of an oath.'

The Battle of the Marne had begun.

The cost of the French victory, although this painting is from 1915 as blue uniforms indicate. *Below: German Jaeger troops.*

Thus, at a moment when von Moltke was losing his control, not only of the German machine, but of himself, the Allies unwilling to accept the decision of their first setbacks, found in themselves hidden reserves of nerve and sinew. The battle was in fact a series of separate battles and combats more or less connected by the general concept of an Allied counterattack. It was fought by 57 tired and depleted Allied divisions, against 53 Germans who had been marched off their feet, and had also suffered some pretty heavy casualties. It was a battle in which the presence of the five German corps, which for various reasons were no longer in the line, would have made all the difference.

The battle began when on the afternoon of 5 September the new French Sixth Army, moving up to the River Ourcq, its Start Line, ran into von Kluck's flank guard (IV Reserve Corps) in the hills above Meaux. That evening Oberstleutnant Hentsch, Chief of Intelligence Branch, arrived at von Kluck's HQ. He had been sent by von Moltke upon a mission whose object was to explain the situation and to persuade von

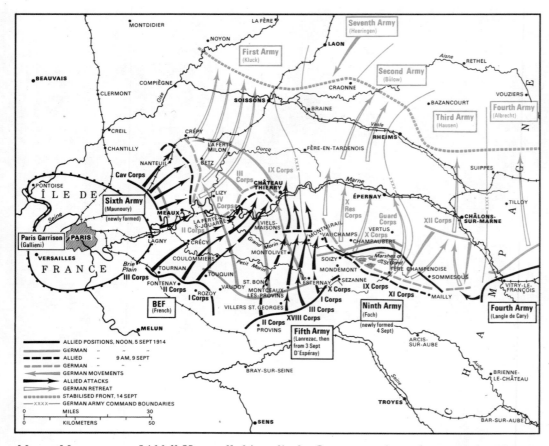

Marne Maneuver, as Liddell Hart called it, split the German armies and stopped the advance.

Kluck to be, if possible, a little less independent. The general grudgingly agreed to fall back – he had not as yet heard the news from the Ourcq – and made a leisurely withdrawal which left most of the First Army south of the Marne.

On 6 September the First and Second French armies successfully held Prince Rupprecht of Bavaria and the two armies forming the German left. In the center, too, the Third Army, now under General Maurice Sarrail and the Fourth Army proved a match for the German Fourth and Fifth Armies. But a small new French Army, the Ninth, under General Ferdinand Foch, was hard-pressed by von Hausen's Third Army. On the Allied left the three Allied Armies might have made more progress, but the long retreat had left them surprised at their own temerity in moving forward at all!

On the following day General von Gronau (IV Reserve Corps), reinforced by two corps from farther south, held Maunoury without much difficulty. The pugnacious and enterprising von Kluck now determined to attack the French Sixth Army from the north, and, driving it back into Paris, to enter the capital on its heels. With this object he swung his two remaining corps from south of the Marne to his right flank, thus opening a 20 mile gap between him and von Bülow.

This breach he intended to mask with two cavalry corps and nine infantry battalions, eight of which were *Jäger* or riflemen.

Into this gap the BEF thrust itself while the Fifth and Sixth French Armies engaged the troops on either flank. From 6–9 September the Allied left wing struggled forward, gaining considerable tactical advantages, which the troops were usually too exhausted to exploit and turn into decisive successes. That there was a considerable amount of panic on the German side is attested by Lieutenant Colonel Hentsch who saw trains and wounded going back 'in wild haste' for fear of being cut off by the English cavalry.

That the Allied advance was entirely unexpected by the Germans is evident. General von Kuhl, Chief of Staff to von Kluck writes: 'Neither OHL (Supreme Command) nor the First Army staff had the remotest idea that an immediate offensive of the whole French army was imminent. The continuation of the French retreat was accepted as certain ... not a sign, not a word from prisoners, not a newspaper paragraph gave warning.'

Incredible though it may seem von Moltke issued no orders of any kind on either 6 or 7 September! But on 6 September a copy of Joffre's Order of the

Day, issued at 0900 hours that morning, fell into the hands of Fourth Army near Vitry-le-François and that evening was telephoned to OHL where it had a depressing effect, confirming von Moltke in his opinion that it had been a terrible mistake to believe that the French were beaten: 'the foe had obviously retired according to plan and during the retreat had regrouped his forces. . . . His plan of battle seemed clear. While his front brought the German pursuit to a stop between Marne and Seine, carefully concealed offensives from Paris and Verdun against the momentarily unprotected German flanks would bring about the decision.' Thus did imagination flatter Joffre's planning with elements of forethought and precision which it did not in truth possess.

The generals now began to take counsel of their fears. 'Would the German troops, worn out by the superhuman efforts of the past week, their ranks reduced about 50 percent by march and battle casualties, stand the shock.'

The four day battle of the Marne was a strategic victory, not a tactical one. The crisis of the battle came on 8 September when OHL, confused by the breakdown of its signal communications, lost grip on the battle. Colonel Bauer has described how Moltke sat apathetic, a broken man, while General Stein, his deputy, said 'we must not lose our heads,' but did nothing. Eventually they decided to send Colonel Hentsch to the front to find out what was going on. He had only verbal instructions from von Moltke. Hentsch traveled 400 miles by car visiting the Fourth and Fifth Armies which were holding their own; the Third which, though divided, was not in trouble. He spent the night at Second Army HQ, where despondency prevailed and the transport was facing northward. Bülow and Hentsch agreed that should the Allies cross the Marne in considerable strength and get in the rear of the First Army, the Second Army should retreat northward.

On 9 September Hentsch pushed on to von Kluck's Headquarters, but owing to congestion and panic on the roads he did not arrive until 1130 hours. Von Kluck was out. By this time the British columns were across the Marne, the Second Army had begun its retirement, and the First Army had already issued preliminary orders for a retirement. It only remained for Hentsch to indicate to von Kuhl, the Chief of Staff, the direction it should take. By noon the battle was virtually over. The Miracle of the Marne had

French troops pause in their counteroffensive, overlooked by a watchful cuirassier.

The Germans shell a village on the Marne as their advance petered out.

Toujours l'attaque! *as the French advance past the Aisne in the November race to the sea.*

happened.

By the evening of 9 September it became apparent to the Allies that the German First and Second Armies were quitting the field. This was the end of the Kaiser's hopes that Germany would win the war by rapidly knocking out her enemies before they were properly prepared.

The French did not really exploit their success. On the eastern wing the position had remained virtually unchanged. In the center von Hausen contented himself with helping his neighbors instead of thrusting between the French Fourth and Ninth Armies, where there was a gap. Von Kluck, obedient for once, secured the German right flank against Maunoury, but in doing so exposed his flank and rear to the BEF. D'Espèrey, instead of supporting the BEF in what was after all the main offensive, turned aside to help Foch, who, instead of holding on to the marshes of St Gond, had gone over to the attack and been repulsed.

The BEF having crossed the Grand Morin and the Petit Morin and then the Marne itself, between Château-Thierry and La Ferté-sous-Jouarre, found itself isolated. For lack of D'Espèrey's support they were compelled to abandon the pursuit. By that time the British were six or seven miles north of the Marne, while not a single French unit was across the river.

What had gone wrong with the German war machine? It had outrun its supplies and its reinforcements; its signal system had failed, its tactics had proved costly. But these failings might not have proved fatal had there been a man at the helm, who, when the crisis came, would not allow himself to get rattled. What a contrast there is between Joffre, with his calmness and strength of character, and his opponent! Gallieni, too, had proved himself a tower of strength, but the fact is that the French General Staff as a whole controlled the battle a great deal better than the German did. As General Beaufre said in a perceptive passage: 'The main characteristic of this great battle ... was that it was nothing less than a gigantic war game, in which the generals of the period, who had no experience of major war, played according to known rules, considering themselves beaten when the situation seemed to them abnormal.'

The loss of the Battle of the Marne was fatal to the Germans. General Erich von Falkenhayn, who now succeeded Moltke, said on taking over that the war was *eigentlich verloren* – 'practically lost.' The advantages gained by getting in the first blow, thanks to speed of mobilization and a rapid advance through neutral Belgium and Luxembourg, could never recur. The best the Germans could hope for was a compromise peace. If the Allies were not disposed for any such thing, it was largely thanks to the policy of 'Frightfulness' which had led to the sack of Dinant, Louvain and other places.

The war had still more than four years to run, but after 9 September 1914 there was little likelihood that the Kaiser would be the victor. He had chosen the wrong general.

Chart A

1914

Soldiers available on mobilization

Germany	8,500,000	
Russia		4,423,000
France		3,500,000
Austria-Hungary	3,000,000	
Great Britain		711,000
	11,500,000	8,634,000

Chart B

French and Allies		German	
Belgians King Albert	117,000	First von Kluck	320,000
BEF Sir John French	111,000	Second von Bülow	260,000
Fifth Lanrezac	254,000	Third von Hausen	180,000
Fourth de Langle de Cary	193,000	Fourth Duke Albrecht of Württemberg	180,000
Third Ruffey	168,000	Fifth Crown Prince of Germany	200,000
Second de Castelnau	200,000	Sixth Crown Prince Rupprecht of Bavaria	220,000
First Dubail	256,000	Seventh von Heeringen	125,000
	1,299,000		1,485,000

Above left: A French cannon is elevated to act as a primitive anti-aircraft gun to strike reconnaissance aircraft at the Marne.

Left: Gunners wearing crash helmets take up positions next to a railway track which probably brought them forward.

Above: French cuirassiers pass a group of British sappers behind the lines.

Below: This time it was the French turn to take prisoners. These soldiers of the German Second Army were seized at the Marne and marched back toward Paris into captivity.

JUTLAND 1916

31 May 1916

In May 1916 the British and German fleets took to sea, each hoping to find and destroy the other. The supremacy of the seas was in the balance, and with it the outcome of World War I. They met off the Danish coast in a momentous battle the likes of which had not been seen before, nor would be since – the Battle of Jutland.

For more than a hundred years (ever since Nelson had smashed the combined fleets of France and Spain at Trafalgar in 1805) Great Britain had ruled the seas without serious challenge.

In the end the great victory at Trafalgar proved almost a disaster for the Royal Navy. The absence of so much as a potential enemy led to complacency. As the decades peacefully succeeded each other, generations of naval officers entered the Service, grew old, and retired without ever hearing a shot fired in battle. The spotless, gleaming, decks and guns became the touchstones of efficiency and quality. 'Parade-ground' maneuvers replaced battle exercises. Gunnery practice consisted of firing at stationary targets from short range. Despite technological advances, tactics remained almost the same as in the days of the old sailing ships of the line. In other words, the attitude of the Royal Navy had changed from that of a tough, fighting service to that of a well-fed police force in a world virtually without crime.

But on the other side of the North Sea a new naval power was rising. In 1888 Kaiser Wilhelm II had taken control of Germany's destiny. He had a passion for ships and the sea, and saw a strong fleet as the means of securing a piece of the colonial pie for his country. With his support, unlimited money was lavished on building a High Seas Fleet that would be second to none, and German shipyards became hives of feverish activity.

At the same time, a revolution in naval weaponry was taking place. The self-propelled torpedo had evolved into an effective, dangerous weapon with a range as great as that of most naval guns. The long-range naval gun, whose power would mitigate the effects of the torpedo to a large extent, was under development. Primitive aircraft carriers were already in the planning stages, and although the submarine still had not reached acceptable standards of seaworthiness and endurance, its potential in naval warfare was evident.

Secure in their formidable tradition of sea supremacy, most British naval officers were content to ignore both the possible effect of the new weapons and the rising German menace. Fortunately a small group of younger officers saw only too clearly both the hidden decay within the Royal Navy and the hidden danger from ambitious Germany. Their chance came when one of their number, 'Jacky' Fisher, was appointed First Sea Lord in October 1904.

Fisher was a well-known, controversial figure in the Navy, a firebrand and an innovator who was once described as a 'mixture of Machiavelli and a child.' Eccentric in his personal life, he signed his letters 'yours till hell freezes' and on occasion entered society parties dancing the hornpipe. Of himself he said, 'I entered the Navy penniless, friendless, and forlorn. I have had to fight like hell, and fighting like hell has made me what I am.'

Professionally his goal was to get the Royal Navy refitted, reorganized, and redeployed in time to meet the German menace. One of his first major decisions was to concentrate three-quarters of his battleship strength in home waters.

A technical rather than a 'salt water' sailor, Fisher embarked on a campaign to pull the Navy into the new technological age. In 1902 submarines had been considered 'underhand, unfair and damned unEnglish.' Under Fisher, their development was supported to the hilt.

Working with the complete support of King Edward VII, he set out to introduce a radically different type of battleship. It was no easy task; critics questioned the wisdom of producing a ship that would immediately make Britain's large existing fleet obsolete and give

Above: HMS Warspite, *the only survivor of Jutland to fight again in World War II at Britain's victory at Matapan.*

Above: The opposing German High Seas Fleet and the British Grand Fleet.

Germany an even start in the armaments race. Fisher recognized the danger, but also knew that if Britain did not develop the new ship some other nation (probably Germany) would. Plans were developed and the first ship built with great speed and secrecy. In 1906 the HMS *Dreadnought* was launched; before any other nation had even begun to design

British battleships Royal Oak *and* Hercules *at Jutland with their guns trained to starboard.*

British cruiser Southampton *exhibits some of the damage inflicted in the battle.*

'dreadnoughts' of their own, the Royal Navy had all the knowledge needed to build improved versions of the type that was to form the line of Battle at Jutland eight years later.

The HMS *Dreadnought* had two revolutionary features: its main armament of new long-range guns and its turbine engines. With the advent of the torpedo, it was imperative that ships be able to fire accurately over long ranges. So, the biggest naval gun in existence, the 12-inch was selected, and ten were housed on the *Dreadnought*. Other ships had carried big guns before, but the *Dreadnought* was the first to carry only one size for her main armament. The master touch, however, was in the engine room where turbine engines capable of pushing the *Dreadnought* through the water at a hitherto unprecedented 21 knots hummed steadily. Not only could the turbines produce more speed, but they could operate at top speed longer and with fewer repairs than the monstrous reciprocating engines of the past.

Later, the efficiency of the dreadnoughts' engines as well as the size and range of guns and the weight of the broadside they fired, were to be increased. The five ships that formed the *Queen Elizabeth* Class, completed not long before war broke out, were capable of making 24 knots and mounted eight 15-inch guns.

Fisher also pioneered development of the battle cruiser. It was to be a ship fast and powerful enough to hunt down armed merchant cruisers, to keep an enemy under observation in the face of hostile fire, and to reinforce battleships if necessary during a general engagement. The first British battle cruiser, *Invincible*, was launched in 1908. She carried eight 12-inch guns and sixteen 4-inch guns, and had a top speed of 26.6 knots. Protective armor was deliberately reduced to a minimum in order to gain speed. This lack of armor has been criticized, but in fact when British ships failed it was usually because they had not been able to hit first or hit hard enough due to their badly designed armor-piercing shells.

As war became, to many, inevitable, the Royal Navy abandoned its superficial polish to get into fighting trim. With the advent of director firing and the establishment of new gunnery drills, Admiral Percy Scott and Rear Admiral John Jellicoe improved the shooting of the fleet by more than a third. Both officers and men perfected the new technical skills demanded by the more sophisticated vessels. The quality of material

British battlecruisers Indomitable *and* Inflexible *at high speed, probably 34 knots.*

continued to improve: torpedoes and mines were becoming more efficient and reliable; destroyers were superseding the old torpedo boats; and even submarines were slowly approaching seaworthiness.

When it came to tactics, however, the Old Guard won a decided victory in the struggle of line-vs-maneuver. The single-line-of-battle principle had been first used in the seventeenth century and persisted into the twentieth. At sea the battle-squadrons usually performed in parallel columns, screened by cruisers and destroyers against torpedo and submarine attack. When the enemy fleet was sighted, the battleships were expected to form a single line, several miles long. This maneuver was known as 'deployment' and the aim of the Commander in Chief was to deploy his entire column so that it would move across the head of the enemy's column ('crossing the T'). The purpose of the maneuver was to ensure that the big guns of the British battleships could rake the leading enemy ships while the enemy could only open fire with his forward guns. Despite its serious disadvantages and the fact that increased speed and maneuverability made more flexible tactics possible, even Fisher and Jellicoe still favored the line system, to the disappointment of younger officers like Vice-Admirals Sir F Doveton Sturdee and Sir David Beatty.

Meanwhile the German Navy was developing along similar lines, but with important differences. Their ships, which were skillfully designed and carefully built, were as good as their British counterparts – but there were fewer of them. This meant that when war came

Above: British battleship Barham *and the Grand Fleet at Scapa Flow.*

Below: The Grand Fleet patrolling the North Sea watching for the High Seas Fleet.

they would have to use defensive strategies and tactics so that they would have to deal only with selected parts of the British fleet at any one time.

Since their ships were designed for service, primarily if not solely, in the North Sea, German shipbuilders could use space and tonnage that normally would be allotted to fuel storage for defensive features such as heavier armor and more speed. Ships did not have to be as comfortable for shorter voyages, which allowed them to be divided more thoroughly into watertight compartments. German ships invariably carried smaller guns – another sacrifice of offensive to defensive features.

By July 1914 on the eve of the outbreak of war, Britain had 29 dreadnoughts with 18 more under construction. Germany had 20 and was building seven others.

At the end of July the British First Fleet, renamed the Grand Fleet, sailed north from Portland to the lonely waters of Scapa Flow in the Orkneys. The great, isolated sea loch was well situated to control the northern exit from the North Sea; it was also the only enclosed stretch of water on Britain's east coast that was large enough to hold the enormous number of battleships, cruisers, destroyers, depot ships, and colliers that made up the Grand Fleet. Its location had one disadvantage: it was so far north that the fleet could not adequately defend the east coast of England from seaborne raids. The danger from minor raids, however, was felt to be less important a consideration as the invisible, unrelenting pressure Britain was able to exert on Germany's naval arteries throughout the entire war.

As soon as war was declared, Admiral Sir John Jellicoe was appointed Commander in Chief of the Grand Fleet, flying his flag on *Iron Duke*. A small man, he had been picked out by Fisher several years earlier for his intellect and organizing ability. He was a superb tactician with a meticulous mathematical mind. Although this was generally an advantage when dealing with the minutiae of maneuvering a huge fleet, it had one unfortunate side effect. Jellicoe was always unwilling to delegate full freedom of action to his subordinates during a battle, for fear they might change the orderly course of events into a chaotic free-for-all.

His second in command, Vice-Admiral Sir David Beatty, had quite a different temperament; he was a high-spirited, dashing, unintellectual young

Above: Graf von Spee, whose actions tied up units of the Royal Navy in the South Atlantic until the Falklands victory. The British Grand Fleet was then free for action in the North Sea.

Above: Admiral John Jellicoe.

52

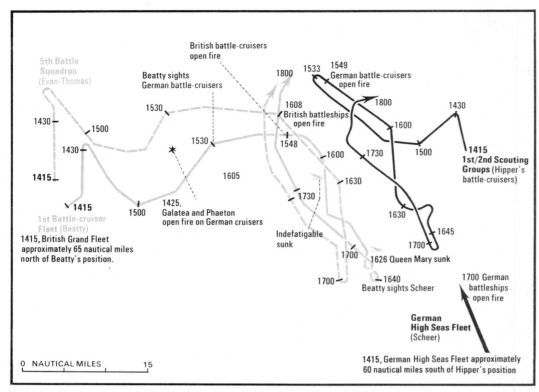

Figure labels:
5th Battle Squadron (Evan-Thomas)

British battle-cruisers open fire

Beatty sights German battle-cruisers

1533 1549 German battle-cruisers open fire
1800   1800
1530   1600   1430
1430   1500
1430   1608 British battleships open fire
1415   1530   1548
1415   1425, Galatea and Phaeton open fire on German cruisers
1500   1605   1600 1730 1500   1415 1st/2nd Scouting Groups (Hipper's battle-cruisers)
1st Battle-cruiser Fleet (Beatty)
1415, British Grand Fleet approximately 65 nautical miles north of Beatty's position.

1730
1630
Indefatigable sunk   1630
1700   1645
1700   1700
1640 Beatty sights Scheer   1700 German battleships open fire
1626 Queen Mary sunk

German High Seas Fleet (Scheer)

0 NAUTICAL MILES 15

1415, German High Seas Fleet approximately 60 nautical miles south of Hipper's position

The battlecruiser action, which opened the hostilities in the late afternoon of 31 May.

Irishman married to an American heiress, the daughter of Chicago millionaire Marshall Field. In 1910 at the age of 38 he had become the youngest Admiral since Nelson. The First Lord of the Admiralty, Winston Churchill, placed him in command of the Battle Cruiser Fleet, which was moved south to Rosyth on the Firth of Forth to stiffen public morale after a series of German raids on the east coast.

Across the North Sea, the German High Seas Fleet was based at Wilhelmshaven, in the Schillighörn at the mouth of the Jade River. After several changes Vice-Admiral Reinhard Scheer was placed in command in 1916, with Vice-Admiral Franz von Hipper leading the battle cruiser force, or First Scouting Group.

Since August 1914 naval strategy on both sides had been concerned with avoiding a decisive conflict. The British realized that maintaining sea supremacy was more important than defeating the German fleet, since Britain's very existence depended on control of the oceans. Thus, despite the fact that the U-Boat blockade was contributing heavily to the collapse of Russia and the near-starvation of Britain, Jellicoe had to avoid conflict that would cost him too dearly.

German strategy called for avoiding a confrontation until the British fleet had been weakened by torpedo attacks and mines to the point that the High Seas Fleet had at least a fair chance of defeating it. The Admiralty was well aware of this and its fear of underwater weapons made it even more cautious.

At the time when Scheer, who had long advocated a more aggressive policy, was placed in command of the High Seas Fleet however, the pressure of the British blockade had induced a more offensive inclination. When Scheer heard a rumor that the British fleet was to be divided as a result of German raids on the east coast, he was even more encouraged. By mid-May 1916 he had his plans ready.

Scheer first planned to stage a cruiser raid on Sunderland, hoping to lure part of the British fleet out onto the high seas where the submarines and the rest of the German fleet would be waiting to pounce. Bad weather, however, prevented zeppelin reconnaissance, and Scheer would not move without it for fear of accidently meeting the rest of the Grand Fleet on one of its periodic sweeps southward to clear the shipping lanes. On 30 May, therefore, he fell back on an alternative plan. Instead of bombarding Sunderland, the Scouting Force – which was composed of battle and light cruisers under the command of Admiral Hipper – was to proceed northward from Wilhelmshaven as if it were going to attack British shipping off the Danish and Norwegian coasts. Scheer hoped that when Hipper's presence was reported to Scapa Flow, a part of the Grand Fleet would be

sent out to attack him. At which point Scheer and the rest of the High Seas Fleet would sail north and destroy them. At 1540 hours on 30 May the wireless signal '31 Gg 2490' went out to the fleet assembled at Schillighörn. It meant 'carry out Top Secret Order 2490 on 31 May' and was to send 100 ships carrying 45,000 officers and men out to meet, all unknowing, the more than 140 ships and 60,000 men of the Grand Fleet.

Scheer was being a bit naive when he assumed that the British would only have whatever knowledge of his movements he cared to reveal to them. In fact, the Admiralty had a very efficient intelligence service based on radio interceptions. The abnormal bustle at Wilhelmshaven had been duly noted. The wireless message, though incomprehensible to the British, was clearly an operational order – and from its wide distribution and method of transmission, it was obviously an important one. Jellicoe had been vainly trying for some time to bring the High Seas Fleet to battle. The German message arrived at the Admiralty at 1700 hours, and almost at once the Grand Fleet was prepared to put to sea.

At Scapa, Rosyth, and Invergordon, signals were run up the yard arms of *Iron Duke*, *Lion*, and *King George V*. Funnels belched black smoke as sailors recalled from liberty scurried back on board; anchor chains rattled and on ship after ship the signal was raised: 'ready to proceed.' By 2230 hours that evening, all were at sea except the seaplane carrier *Campania*, which had not received the sailing signal. She wound up so far behind the others that she was ordered back to port, thus depriving Jellicoe of vital air reconnaissance support the next day.

At 0100 hours on 31 May, Hipper's

Admiral Hipper, leader of the battlecruisers.

The battlecruiser Indefatigable *steams into the struggle.*

Right: Admiral Sir David Beatty, whose actions at Jutland have been widely criticized for decades since the battle.

Scouting Group began to make their way north, while on the flagship of the High Seas Fleet, *Friedrich der Grosse*, Scheer's staff reviewed their plans – not knowing that at that very moment the entire Grand Fleet was already on its way to a rendezvous that would result in one of the greatest naval battles of all time.

The 31 May was a calm day. According to plan Beatty and his battle cruisers, along with four of the splendid new *Queen Elizabeth* Class battleships with their 15-inch guns, were sailing eastward. At 1400 hours he was to turn northward to meet Jellicoe. The Commander in Chief, who had also been moving eastward from Scapa Flow, planned to turn southsoutheast if he had not sighted the enemy by 1400 hours. Following their rendezvous the two fleets would sweep on south toward Heligoland Bight.

Beatty was just turning north at the assigned hour when the *Galatea*, one of his screen of light cruisers, spotted a small steamer to the eastsoutheast. Commodore Alexander Sinclair, commanding the First Light Cruiser Squadron, decided to investigate; *Galatea*, along with the other ships in the Squadron – the *Phaeton*, *Inconstant*, and *Cordelia*, continued to hold its easterly course.

And now fate was to take over for the first – but not the last – time during the engagement. Hipper's Scouting Groups were far to the east of Beatty's force, sailing on a northwesterly course toward Jellicoe, when the left wing cruiser of the scouting line, the *Elbing*, also saw the steamer and, with two torpedo boats, set off to examine her. As the British and German ships steered toward the innocent Danish steamer, the *NJ Fjord*, they saw the mast heads and funnels of

Bottom: The first engagement between the battle fleets in the night action of 31 May.

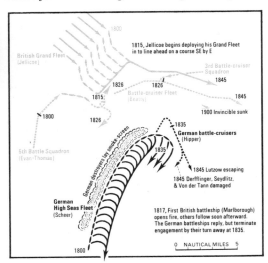

the enemy appear on the horizon. At 1420 hours *Galatea* signaled 'Enemy in sight. Two cruisers probably hostile bearing southeast, course unknown.' At 1428 hours she opened fire. The Battle of Jutland had begun.

This premature contact between the light cruisers was a bit of luck for the Germans, for it sprung Jellicoe's carefully planned trap too soon, while he was still 65 miles to the north and Scheer some 50 miles away in the opposite direction. Soon after *Galatea*'s first signal was read on board the *Iron Duke* a second signal arrived: 'Have sighted large amount of smoke as though from a fleet bearing ENE.' By 1443 hours the Grand Fleet was heading for the conflict with all speed. Admiral Scheer, in the *Freidrich der Grosse*, got a later start, but soon he too was racing toward the battle – each commander still unaware of the other's presence.

The sound of guns – as *Galatea* and *Phaeton* engaged *Elbing* and the two German torpedo boats – arrived on the *Lion* along with *Galatea*'s second signal, and at 1432 hours Beatty immediately turned southeast again to cut off the German retreat. In the haste and confusion, however, his signal to turn – which was made by flags – could not be read by Evan-Thomas' squadron of battleships five miles astern. The signal had to be sent again with searchlights and, as a result, Evan-Thomas did not turn until 1440 hours, which left him some ten miles behind the cruisers.

Beatty has come in for much criticism since the event for his haste in not waiting for Evan-Thomas to catch up to him. However, it must be remembered that as far as he knew he was only going to meet another force of cruisers that was in any case smaller than his own – and he had every reason to think that unless he hurried they would give him the slip, as they had done in the past.

Beatty also ordered the seaplane carrier *Engadine* to send an aircraft up for reconnaissance. Delay in launching the seaplane, combined with poor scouting and finally a hit that badly damaged the plane, meant that on that first day the air arm made no contribution to the battle.

Meanwhile, the *Elbing* had mistakenly identified the light cruisers as battle cruisers, and a later report was misinterpreted aboard Hipper's flagship, *Lützow*, as saying he had sighted 24 to 26 battleships. This was enough to send Hipper racing to the northwest at his top speed of 25 knots.

At about 1530 hours Beatty and Hip-

Attempting to cross the T the British battle fleet lets forth an initial salvo on 31 May.

per were in sight of one another. Hipper promptly turned his ships around 180 degrees onto a southeasterly course and prepared to engage; here was the perfect opportunity to spring Scheer's trap by catching Beatty between two forces as the High Seas Fleet came up. Beatty turned on a parallel course, and at 1545 hours both sides opened fire.

With the westerly sun at their backs the British ships were clearly silhouetted against the horizon. Their range finders miscalculated badly, and the first shells from the *Lion* landed at least a mile behind the German line. With their excellent Zeiss optical range finders, the Germans had no such problems; all around the British ships the sea was pitted with shell splashes, and within three minutes *Lion* and *Princess Royal* had each been hit twice, while the *Tiger* had been hit four times.

The *Queen Mary*, champion gunnery ship of the fleet, finally managed to land two shells on the *Seydlitz* at 1555 hours and another on *Derfflinger* at 1558 hours.

Just after 1600 hours disaster struck the British. A heavy shell from the *Lützow* struck the midship turret of the *Lion* and burst into the gun house, killing or wounding every man on the gun crew. With both legs shattered, Major F J W Harvey of the Royal marines managed, with his dying breath, to call out an order to flood the magazines, thus saving the ship from being blown up. The *Lion* was hit six more times, and the *Princess Royal* had her after-turret knocked out of action.

But there was worse to come. At the rear of the line the *Von Der Tann* landed three heavy shells on the *Indefatigable*. As the British ship staggered out of the line, enveloped in smoke and flame, another salvo struck. She capsized and sank, taking with her all but two of the 1017 men aboard.

Just at the critical moment, at 1605 hours, Evan-Thomas and his battleships came through the first smoke barrier and caught sight of the enemy for the first time. Almost immediately the rear of the

Prince Henry of Prussia (with field glasses) and Admiral von Scheer attempt to view the action.

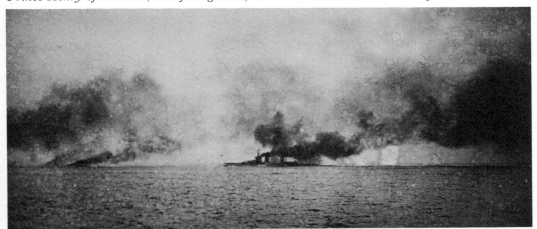

British battlecruiser Lion *is hit on the 'Q' turret as destroyers prepare for a new attack.*

German line was smothered by salvos from the big 15-inch guns, and the *Von Der Tann* and *Moltke* were repeatedly hit. The poor-quality British shells, however, could not inflict much vital damage on the heavier German armor.

At 1626 hours the *Queen Mary* was hit by a salvo. As a pillar of smoke rose 800 feet into the air she exploded, and debris showered on the decks of neighboring ships as she disappeared with her crew of 1266.

In spite of his successes Hipper was still in a serious position, for he had to hold out against Beatty's four remaining cruisers and Evan-Thomas' four battleships until Scheer could come to his assistance.

At 1620 hours the destroyer flotillas had entered the fray, the Germans on their own initiative and the British on Beatty's orders. The two groups of slim little ships raced toward each other down the corridor between the battlelines, through a turmoil of water spouts, as the battle cruisers opened up with their secondary armaments. Guns barked and torpedoes flew in all directions. Two German ships were sunk and the rest retired. The British destroyers were still battling at 1643 hours when a signal was run up the yardarm of the *Lion*: 'Destroyers recalled.' Not knowing the reason for the order, the destroyers reluctantly turned away as they saw *Lion* suddenly reverse her course and start heading northward.

While they had been fighting, the Second Light Cruiser Squadron, commanded by Commodore Goodenough in the *Southampton*, had managed to get in scouting position about two miles southeast of Beatty. At 1633 hours the topmasts of the High Seas Fleet hove into sight. Goodenough immediately sent a priority wireless signal to Jellicoe. Beatty, for his part, held his course until he was sure Scheer had seen him before turning to draw the High Seas Fleet toward Jellicoe's approaching fleet.

Evan-Thomas again missed the signal to turn, and continued steaming south until he passed Beatty's cruisers moving north. His ships were the ones, therefore, to come under fire from the leading ships of Scheer's force, and became not only the bait but a screen for Beatty. Beatty's turn was helped, in part, by two destroyers – *Nomad* and *Nestor* – who had been disabled and were still floating helplessly between the battle lines. Refusing all offers of assistance from their sister ships, the two crews destroyed their records and secret papers and impudently fired off their last torpedoes before the ships were torn apart by a score of hits. German destroyers courteously stopped to pick up the survivors.

By 1730 hours the British ships were beyond the range of either Scheer's or Hipper's ships, and the big guns of the Fifth Battle Squadron were still able to inflict heavy damage on the German battle cruisers who appeared intermittently through the mist to the east. Of Hipper's five ships, only the *Moltke* remained relatively undamaged.

Meanwhile, Jellicoe had been starved

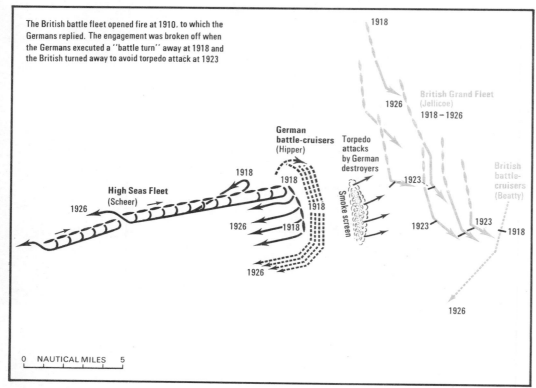

The British battle fleet opened fire at 1910, to which the Germans replied. The engagement was broken off when the Germans executed a "battle turn" away at 1918 and the British turned away to avoid torpedo attack at 1923

High Seas Fleet (Scheer)

German battle-cruisers (Hipper)

Torpedo attacks by German destroyers

Smoke screen

British Grand Fleet (Jellicoe) 1918–1926

British battle-cruisers (Beatty)

0 NAUTICAL MILES 5

The second engagement of the battle fleets, which forced a German withdrawal.

The battlecruiser Seydlitz *after having suffered heavy damage in the battle.*

The sinking of Queen Mary *during the day action.*

all day of the information he so desperately needed. Since the start of the retirement he had received four messages from Goodenough, only one from Beatty – whose wireless had been shot away, so that he had to transmit signals by semaphore to the *Princess Royal* – and none at all from Evan-Thomas.

But the failure of his junior commanders to keep him informed was not as important as the combined effort of errors in the plotting of positions of both sections of the fleet.

Jellicoe was advancing in six parallel columns, in a formation about four miles wide. Light cruisers and destroyers formed an anti-submarine screen. Some eight miles ahead was a scouting screen of heavy cruisers: the First Cruiser Squadron commanded by Rear Admiral Heath in the *Minotaur*. Twenty miles further ahead was the Third Battlecruiser Squadron under Rear Admiral the Honourable Horace Hood: his flagship, the *Invincible*, along with *Indomitable* and *Inflexible*.

Hood was sent ahead to support Beatty, but due to incorrect positioning, ended up not only east of Beatty, but east of Hipper as well. Hipper, who was steaming parallel to – but out of sight of – Beatty, suddenly caught sight of him to the west at 1740 hours and swerved eastward. At 1834 hours he heard Hood's guns firing on his light cruisers and turned away to the southeast. Catching sight of Hood's destroyers, he turned again, this time to the southwest.

At 1815 hours Jellicoe finally received a message from Beatty giving the Germans' course if not their position, and the Grand Fleet was ordered to deploy on the port column on a course southeast by east. It was the high point of his career, the moment he had spent years preparing for. If his calculations were correct, he would have time to 'cross the T' and bring the full power of his battleships to bear on the head of the German line.

Scheer, racing northward at top speed, suddenly found himself confronted with a line of gray battleships stretching as far as the eye could see. It was an appalling moment. But such a situation had been foreseen and a special simultaneous turn-about maneuver had been formulated and practised. At 1830 hours he sent the necessary signal, hoping that the maneuver that worked so well in practice could be carried out under battle conditions. All together, every ship in the line made a 180 degree somersault, while German torpedo boats steamed across their rear to add a black smoke screen to cover the retirement. In the dim light and smoke-filled air Jellicoe was left wondering what had happened.

The firing died down and by 1845 hours unnatural silence spread over the battle area. Their ears still ringing from the shattering blasts of the heavy guns, both sides took account of their situation.

Scheer was in a perilous position. He had turned westward, away from his own harbor, and had to assume that behind the smoke Jellicoe was turning in pursuit, cutting off his line of retreat. Hipper's flagship, the *Lützow*, was limping away to the southwest, almost sinking, while Hipper tried to find a way to transfer his flag to another ship in the squadron. The light cruiser *Wiesbaden*, damaged during Hipper's withdrawal, had been pounded unmercifully by every British ship that came within range and was a tangled, smoking wreck drifting between the lines. The very fact that she was still afloat was a tribute to the excellence of German ship design – and the fact that she still had a role to play in the battle was a tribute to the bravery and devotion of the men of the German Navy. For as she floated toward the British line, a few remaining crewmen managed somehow to prepare a torpedo tube, train it, and fire in one last act of defiance. The torpedo struck Admiral Barney's flagship, *Marlborough*, and inflicted damage heavy enough to drive her out of the battle, while *Wiesbaden* drifted off to an unseen end.

The Germans had inflicted some heavy blows on the British that afternoon, however. The *Derfflinger* had sunk the *Invincible*; the *Defence* had been blown up; the *Warspite* was forced out of action; and the *Warrior* was so badly damaged that she had to be abandoned the next day.

Aboard the *Iron Duke*, however, Jellicoe had decided against direct pursuit and was holding his fleet to their southeasterly course, gradually shifting, by divisions, to head due south. Jellicoe has sustained much criticism for this move, but considering that there were only two hours of daylight left, and no such thing as radar, his decision is understandable. He was still suffering from lack of information about the Germans' movements; of all the light cruiser squadrons detailed for reconnaissance, only Goodenough's did the job required.

As soon as the firing died away at 1845 hours, he led the Second Light Cruiser

Indomitable and Inflexible *seen through the late afternoon haze at* Jutland.

Rear Admiral Horace Hood, who was lost with Invincible *at* Jutland.

Above: A stylized view of the approach of the battlecruisers during the start of the day action.

View of the German High Seas Fleet at the moment when the first British fire struck it.

Below: A British ship is struck cruising.

A German battlecruiser fires a salvo in response to the British onslaught.

Squadron south to find the vanished Germans. In a few minutes he had caught up to the rear ships; despite heavy fire he held his position and at 1904 hours was able to report to Jellicoe that Scheer had turned around and was once more heading east.

Scheer was to claim in subsequent despatches that his aim had been to strike a second blow at the enemy in order to retain the initiative and maintain German prestige. In fact, he probably miscalculated, thought that the Grand Fleet was further south than it really was, and counted on crossing its tail and heading for home. In fact, when he came out of the mist at 1910 hours he found himself staring into the steel jaws of the center of the British Line. He was so anxious to get away that he not only executed another somersault maneuver under a smoke screen, but launched his cruisers on their now-famous 'death ride.'

It was the Germans' turn to face an indistinct target while they themselves were silhouetted against the western sky. Within a few minutes they were coming under concentrated fire from virtually the entire British line. At 1913 hours, Scheer issued his sacrificial order to the four remaining battle cruisers: 'Battle-cruisers charge the enemy without regard for consequences. Ram.'

Without flinching, the *Derfflinger*, fol-

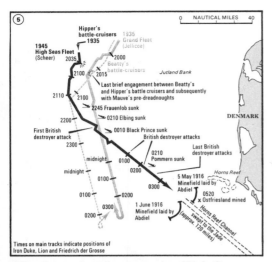

Hipper's battle-cruisers 1935
1935
1945 High Seas Fleet (Scheer) 2035
Grand Fleet (Jellicoe)
2000
2100
2015
Beatty's battle-cruisers
Jutland Bank
Last brief engagement between Beatty's and Hipper's battle cruisers and subsequently with Mauve's pre-dreadnoughts
2110 2100
DENMARK
2200 2245 Frauenlob sunk
0210 Elbing sunk
First British destroyer attack
0010 Black Prince sunk
British destroyer attacks
2300
0210 Pommern sunk
Last British destroyer attacks
midnight 0100
0200
Horns Reef
midnight
0100 0200
5 May 1916 Minefield laid by Abdiel
0300
0100 0200
1 June 1916 Minefield laid by Abdiel
0520 x Ostfriesland mined
Horns Reef Channel swept to the Jade (approx. 120 miles)
0300
0200

Times on main tracks indicate positions of Iron Duke, Lion and Friedrich der Grosse

The chase after the retreating High Seas Fleet after the night action of 1 June.

lowed by *Moltke, Seydlitz,* and *Von Der Tann,* already badly damaged, set off into a hell of exploding shells as, at 1916 hours Scheer sent his second signal to the High Seas Fleet: 'Battle turn-away to starboard.' They were saved from certain destruction by the destroyer attack that was helping cover Scheer's retreat. As they too rushed toward the British line, Jellicoe, in the standard counter to such an attack, moved away in the opposite direction.

Jellicoe's last chance of closing with the Germans slipped away during the next half hour. At about 1950 hours Beatty, who had not been forced to turn during the torpedo attack and had therefore maintained sporadic contact with the Germans, sent a wireless message suggesting that if the van of battleships were to follow the cruisers, the German fleet could be cut off. In fact, Jellicoe had already turned the Grand Fleet so that the two forces were again converging on each other, the British moving westward and the Germans south. Beatty himself caught up with the forward German ships at about 2023 hours; when they came under fire they promptly swung westward again. Beatty had checked their move south and ironically had thus helped them slip through the British rearguard later.

The light was fading fast and by about 2100 hours the sea was pitch black. Faced with the prospect of a night battle, Jellicoe properly rejected it in favor of spreading a screen between the Germans and their home base to prevent them returning during the night. At 2117 hours therefore, the fleet took up night cruising stations, moving on a course due south at 17 knots. The battleships were closed up in three parallel columns. Five miles astern were the destroyers; this

disposition protected the rear of the battle fleet from torpedo attacks and also helped alleviate the dangers of mistaken identity in the darkness. Ahead of the fleet, and on the western flank, were Beatty and the cruisers – the eyes and ears of the fleet.

Scheer, meanwhile, had taken a good hard look at his situation. For the time being his desperate disengagements had been successful and he was in the clear. Serious damage had been confined to only three of the battleships – *Markgraf, Grosser Kurfurst,* and *König.* It was enough, however, to indicate that he must avoid a renewal of the fighting next day. His plan was simple and direct; he would take the shortest route home via the Horn Reefs, breaking through the British line regardless of losses.

From 2220 hours until 2330 hours that night the British tail was in frequent contact with the enemy, playing a mad game of blind man's bluff as the Germans elbowed their way through. A torpedo from a badly battered *Southampton* sank the light cruiser *Frauenlob.* A German light cruiser, *Elbing,* was rammed by the German battleship *Posen* and left to sink. *Spitfire,* a destroyer, managed not only to ram the German battleship *Nassau,* but got away with a long strip of the big ship's plating as a prize.

For some hours afterwards the British hornets harassed the Germans – and through all that time, Jellicoe knew nothing of what was happening. He had received a message from the Admiralty

giving him Scheer's disposition, course, and speed, but he had received so many outdated or useless Admiralty messages during the day that he doubted its importance. Lack of sufficient information from his subordinates must again be named as the cause; several dreadnoughts at the rear of the battle fleet heard the sounds of fighting during the night, but assumed the destroyers were simply beating off a torpedo attack and did not inform the Commander in Chief. One officer, Captain Stirling of the 12th Destroyer Flotilla, did send a wireless message at 0152 hours before his ships torpedoed and sank the battleship *Pommern* (thereby achieving more than the whole Grand Fleet had done). It was never received.

Shortly after 0230 hours the sun rose on a horizon that was blank and empty to the anxious eyes of the British Fleet. Jellicoe turned northward, still hoping against all odds, but at 0355 hours a message arrived from the Admiralty giving him the Germans' new position. There was nothing to do but sweep the battle area for disabled German ships and head for home. There were no ships to be found; the crews of the *Lützow, Elbing,* and *Rostock* had abandoned and sunk their vessels at daybreak. A subdued group gathered on board the *Iron Duke* to begin the first draft of the battle report, as details of losses and casualties began to filter in. It was not until 1000 hours that Jellicoe finally learned of the loss of the *Indefatigable* and *Queen Mary* – one final example of the incredible

A German salvo falls short of a British cruiser of the Birmingham *class.*

breakdown in communication between the Commander in Chief and his officers.

Things were very different aboard the *Friedrich Der Grosse* as light dawned to show that same sea empty of the enemy. Scheer's policy of dogged determination to bludgeon his way through at any cost had succeeded beyond his wildest hopes. At 0324 hours he thankfully ordered his fleet back to harbor.

Even the combined losses of this one great naval battle of World War I are paltry compared to the millions who fell on land. The Grand Fleet lost three battle cruisers, three light cruisers, and eight destroyers, with two badly damaged battleships; the Germans were missing one battleship, one battle cruiser, four light cruisers, and five destroyers. The Royal Navy recorded 6097 men killed and 177 taken prisoner to the Germans' total of 2545 killed.

Who won the Battle of Jutland? Both sides have claimed the victory; the British on the grounds that the High Seas Fleet fled the field and never again risked an encounter with the British Fleet; the Germans because against heavy odds, they inflicted more damage than they received. But against British claims must be noted the fact that their failure to bring the High Seas Fleet to action and destroy it meant that the German Navy remained a threat throughout the war. For the Germans, the fact they were driven from their own waters after the briefest encounter with the Grand Fleet must affect their claim to victory.

In other words, no one won, and it probably would have been better had the battle never been fought at all. This was especially true in Britain where the loss of prestige suffered by the Navy could not offset the fact that naval superiority had been maintained. The controversy that raged long after the battle had ended cast a shadow on Jellicoe's reputation that was never quite removed while Beatty, whose fleet had suffered the most losses, rose in favor with the public and the Admiralty alike.

Jutland merits its place in history as one of the greatest naval battles by virtue of its scope alone, and the sheer magnitude of the forces that faced each other. And in fact, it may well be that their size prevented the battle being fought to a decisive conclusion at all – that with such primitive communications and technology, and without radar, it was impossible to deploy such huge fleets effectively against each other.

Neither country has any reason to be ashamed of its navy, however, and both have heroes they can be proud of: the crew of the *Wiesbaden* who fought on after their ship had been reduced to a flaming wreck; the *Nestor*, firing her last torpedo at the approaching German battleships as she sank under a hail of shells; Hartog, on *Derfflinger*, leading the German cruisers on their gallant 'death-ride,' and Major Harvey, who saved *Lion* from destruction with his dying breath.

If the short-term effects of Jutland were negligible, its long-term impact was important not only to the rest of World War I, but to the whole body of naval techniques and technologies – and as a tribute to the bravery and dedication of the men of both navies it stands alone.

The German battlecruiser Derfflinger *shows heavy damage by shell fire after the chase upon her return to port on 2 June.*

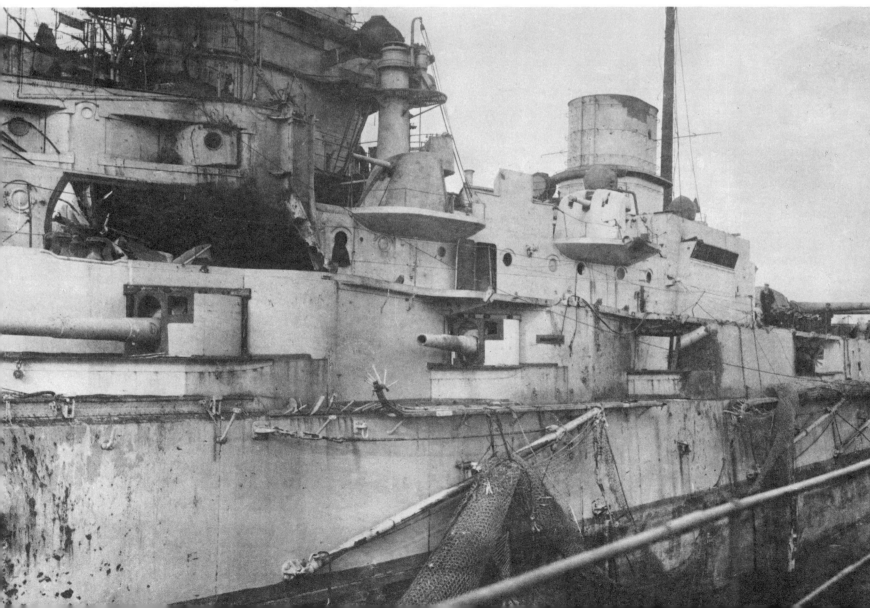

THE BATTLE OF BRITAIN 1917-1918

The history of air power has been short and violent. The initial flight in a heavier-than-air machine took place less than 75 years ago, when on 17 December 1903 the Americans Orville and Wilbur Wright successfully took to the air in their aptly named *Flyer*, and since that time the aircraft has contributed more to the horror of modern war than almost any other technological invention. Without the aircraft there would have been no civilian bombing on a large-scale and no atomic attacks in 1945. War would probably have remained as a process – albeit an increasingly violent one – between rival armed forces, and civilian populations outside the battle area would have been spared the effects of aerial bombardment: effects which stand out as the more obvious manifestations of total war. Even when the picture is balanced by the many peaceful contributions of the aircraft to society, it still remains as one of the most potent and devastating weapons invented by man.

Although the idea of strategic bombing – the destruction of the enemy's industrial base and the demoralization of his people through aerial bombardment – is invariably associated with World War II, it was also a feature of the 1914–18 conflict, particularly so far as Britain was concerned. During this war the Germans launched a total of 103 bombing raids upon the British Isles, using Zeppelin airships for 51 of them and both Gotha and Giant aircraft for the rest. Altogether some 1400 people were killed and 3400 injured, with material damage amounting to more than £3,000,000, and although this may seem minor compared to the results of World War II raids, the effects were dramatic and far-reaching. Without the German attacks, especially those delivered by aircraft in 1917 and 1918, there would have been little evidence upon which to base the theories of strategic air power which emerged between the two world wars, no Royal Air Force and, perhaps most important of all for the future, no air defense of Britain. The air battle of 1917–18, fought between the incoming

German bombers and an increasingly sophisticated British defensive system of anti-aircraft guns, interceptor fighters, searchlights, observer stations and barrage balloons, may not have seemed as important at the time as events on the Western Front, but in retrospect it is apparent that without it the second Battle of Britain in 1940 might well have had an entirely different outcome.

Proposals for air attacks upon southeast England were put to the German High Command as early as October 1914, when Major Wilhelm Siegert suggested raids from Calais upon the embarkation ports then being used by the British Expeditionary Force. Approval was granted and a squadron of single-engined *Taube* aircraft made ready. But Calais was never captured and Siegert was forced to remain at an improvised airfield near Ghistelles in Belgium, out of range of the English coast. As the trench deadlock set in, his squadron was used more and more for tactical support of the armies in the field, until in April 1915 it was withdrawn to Metz and disbanded.

Siegert's idea was not forgotten, however, for in the early months of war a full-scale strategic debate took place within

Germany over the concept of air attacks. Moderates in political circles held the upper hand for some time, exploiting the Kaiser's reluctance to bomb his English cousins, but gradually Admiral Hugo von Pohl of the Imperial Naval Staff, tilted the balance. Solving the problem of range by suggesting the use of Zeppelin airships, he persuaded the Kaiser to permit limited air attacks upon coastal targets in England, on the understanding that only military installations would be hit. The Zeppelins began their campaign in January 1915, but lacked the bomb-aiming equipment to achieve the required degree of accuracy. After a series of apparently aimless raids, the targets were extended to include the huge dock-yard area of London, in the hope that something of value would be destroyed,

Below: A BE 2a, number 347 of 2 Squadron on 13 August 1914, preparing to take off from Dover for Amiens. This machine of the Royal Flying Corps was the first to arrive in France.

but in fact it meant vast tracts of the city came under aerial bombardment. Presented with a virtual *fait accompli* as residential districts of eastern London were hit in late May 1915, the Kaiser had little choice but to relent entirely and permit unrestricted assaults upon any part of England.

By this time both the Army and Navy were sending their airships against Britain, the Zeppelins being able to range far and wide over much of East Anglia and the Midlands as well as the southeast. However, little of strategic value was achieved. Flying by night to avoid detection, the airships were so unwieldy and slow that they could obtain neither accuracy nor concentration of force. When they dropped their bombs it was not unknown for British civilians to

Above: Germany's first dirigible used in World War I, Zeppelin 1.

One of the first dirigibles carried aboard a ship intended for release over Britain.

show signs of panic, but as the war continued into 1916 the Germans began to doubt the value of sending expensive airships into action. In addition, although the British government tended to regard the raids as little more than irritants, they were forced by public pressure to provide at least the basics of an air defense system, and this slowly began to take effect. In early September 1916 the first Zeppelin was shot down by an interceptor fighter (the pilot, Lieutenant Leefe Robinson of the Royal Flying Corps, was immediately awarded a Victoria Cross). Three months later, on 28 November, two airships were destroyed off the East Coast by anti-aircraft fire. The latter catastrophe, coupled with bad winter weather, finally persuaded the Germans to review their strategy and, for a time at least, the airship threat to Britain receded.

By a strange coincidence the future direction of German air strategy became apparent on the same day, 28 November, for as the second Zeppelin crashed into the sea off Norfolk, a single-engined *LVG (Luft-Verkehrs-Gesellschaft)* biplane of the Imperial Navy, using the extra range which its normal reconnaissance role allowed, approached London from the Thames Estuary. Catching the city and its Zeppelin-orientated defenses completely unawares, the aircraft dropped six 20lb bombs onto the West End at approximately noon. Ten people

were slightly injured. At the time the attack was barely reported, but in the light of subsequent events it was recognized for its true importance. Siegert's original proposal for daylight raids, using heavier-than-air machines with their speed and flexibility, was about to be put into effect on a sustained level.

Known by the code name *Turkenkreuz* (Turk's Cross), the campaign had its roots in 1915, when a number of German aircraft manufacturers had been asked to submit designs for machines capable of carrying bombs to London from bases in occupied Belgium. The *Grosskampfflug,* or G-type bombers were the result, and the early versions of these – the G I and G II were available by the middle of 1916. The military situation on the Western Front at that time precluded their use against London, however, as every German aircraft was required for tactical support, and it was not until General Ernst von Hoeppner was appointed to command a re-organized air arm in late 1916 that the idea of raids against England was again raised. Hoeppner proposed the formation of a squadron of 30 Gotha G IVs – twin-engined bi-planes which were capable of carrying up to 1000lb of bombs to England at over 80mph – which would raid London by day from the Belgian bases, commencing in the spring of 1917. This was accepted and command of the squadron, officially

named *Kagohl 3* but generally known as the England Squadron, given to Ernst Brandenburg. He set about training his crews immediately in the difficult and novel art of formation flying over water on navigational 'dead-reckoning,' and despite a delay in the delivery of his bombers to the bases around Ghistelles, he was able to report his squadron ready for action by mid-May 1917.

The first raid was launched on 25 May, the target being specified as London, but a series of problems emerged to alter the plan. To begin with, although 23 Gothas took off from Ghistelles, they were forced to refuel near the Belgian coast and lost two of their number in the tricky process of landing at a strange airfield. The remainder crossed the Channel without incident, but as they approached the target over Essex, towering cumulus cloud above a ground haze protected the English capital. Brandenburg had no choice but to change course, looking for targets of opportunity. The one he chose was Shorncliffe Camp, near Folkestone in Kent, then full of Canadian soldiers awaiting embarkation for the Western Front. Unfortunately accuracy was still a problem, despite the switch to daylight bombing, and although a few bombs hit the camp, the vast majority – totaling nearly five tons – fell on Folkestone itself, killing 95 people and injuring a further 260. The British managed to put 74 fighters into the air in pursuit, while the artillery defenses of Dover put up an impressive barrage, but Brandenburg and his bombers managed to get home, where two of the Gothas crashed on landing. Eleven days later, on 5 June, the pattern was repeated. Twenty-two Gothas were forced away from London by adverse weather, raiding Sheerness and the Isle of Sheppy as secondary targets. Forty-five people died and one of the bombers was destroyed by anti-aircraft fire, but interceptor fighters had little discernible effect.

Presented with the results of these two raids, it might be expected that both sides should have reviewed their respective positions. On the one hand Brandenburg had experienced a number of problems, chief among which were his aircraft losses due to accident and his lack of long-range weather information. If he was ever to hit London, these needed to be solved. On the other, British defensive measures had been poor, lacking co-ordination and effect. Fighter pilots had received no warning of incoming bombers and, as 'the distances in time from the coast to important places like London is less than the time required by most of the machines we have got to ascend to the necessary height' (12,000 feet), little success could be expected. Similarly, although anti-aircraft guns were sited round the major ports of southeast England, the gunners had shown an inability to assess the altitude of the bombers and most of their shot had fallen short. Their destruction of a Gotha on 5 June had been more by good luck than good management.

In the event it was Brandenburg who retained the initiative by employing trained meteorologists and fitting extra fuel tanks to the Gothas to cut out the need for intermediary refueling stops, and he showed this exactly a week after the Sheerness raid, before the British had even begun to react. On 13 June 20 Gothas took off in good weather, and although six were forced to turn back or to bomb secondary targets because of engine trouble, 14 bombers made it all the way to London. Concentrating upon the main-line railroad stations as legitimate military targets, the first major daylight raid on the capital began at 1135 hours when eight people were killed in East Ham. Five minutes later, Liverpool Street Station came under sustained bombardment as 72 bombs fell within a one mile radius, three of them actually hitting the terminus itself. Brandenburg then split his formation, with one part

LIGHTS OF LONDON

The lights along the Thames Embankment when one of the dirigible raids was expected.

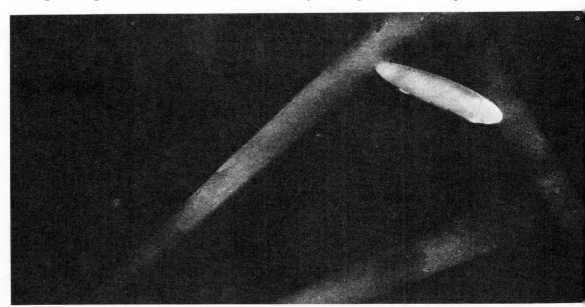

A Zeppelin on an air raid during the night of 13 October 1915 appears over London.

flying north to hit other railroad targets and the other south towards the dockyards. It was a random bomb from the latter group which caused the most damage, ripping through an infants' school at Poplar, killing 18 and injuring 30, the majority of whom were small children under the age of five. Once again the British defenses were ineffective, with interceptor fighters and guns alike failing to make contact. The Gothas returned to Belgium virtually unopposed, landing at 1500 hours having suffered neither losses nor any further incident.

The public reaction to the raid in Britain was dramatic. Many workers, fearful that the bombers would return, stayed away from factories in the East End and the production of war materials fell significantly. In Poplar there was uproar as a mob ran riot, demanding retribution and smashing shops displaying German names. At a more official level, the Government came under intense political pressure to improve defensive measures, and was forced to withdraw two fighter units from the Western Front. Numbers 56 and 66

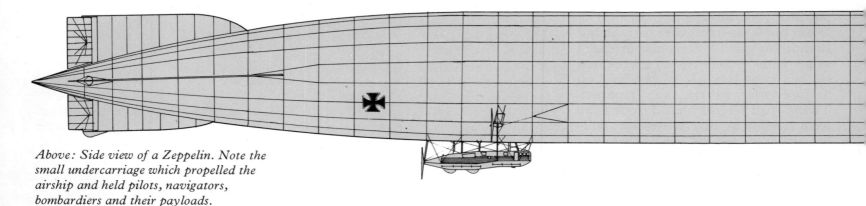

Above: Side view of a Zeppelin. Note the small undercarriage which propelled the airship and held pilots, navigators, bombardiers and their payloads.

Squadrons, equipped with SE 5s and Sopwith Pups respectively, were transferred from Flanders to home defense bases, although in deference to Major General Sir Hugh Trenchard, commanding the Royal Flying Corps at the front line, their return was promised within two weeks. In the event, neither squadron so much as saw a Gotha, for during their short period of transfer only one minor raid on Felixstowe and Harwich took place.

The reason for this lack of German action was an unfortunate flying accident, far behind the front line, in which Brandenburg was badly injured. He was replaced in the England Squadron by Captain Rudolf Kleine, a man who never commanded the same respect or admi-

ration from the Gotha crews. Nevertheless, he was determined to continue the bombardment of London and led 22 bombers on a second raid on 7 July – ironically, less than 48 hours after 56 and 66 Squadrons had returned to army support. Expecting strong opposition now that the element of surprise was lost, Kleine approached the target by a roundabout route, delivering his attack from the northwest. He need not have worried. As his bombs dropped onto the residential districts of eastern and northern London, killing 57 people and injuring 193, a total of 95 interceptor fighters took to the air. A small number actually found the Gothas but, still lacking co-ordination, could only put in single, head-on attacks; a tactic which

resulted in the destruction of two of their number. One Gotha was eventually destroyed, but the expenditure of effort and lives was out of all proportion to the gains. In addition, as many commentators were quick to point out, it was far more important to protect civilians by preventing the bombers reaching London, than it was to destroy them as they returned triumphantly to their bases. As it happened, Kleine was more worried about landing accidents than defending fighters, for four of his bombers crashed on their return to Belgium: the loss rate was approaching a prohibitive 25 per cent per raid.

The British, of course, did not know about this interesting statistic and could only announce the destruction of one of

A Sopwith F1 Camel of 46 Squadron of the RFC is loaded with 25lb Cooper bombs for a British counterattack.

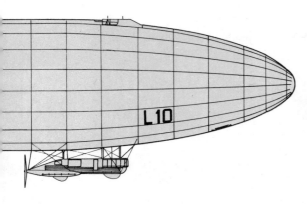

the raiders: a fact which did nothing to allay the fears expressed by the public on 7 July. Almost as soon as the bombers had gone, mobs once again took to the streets and smashed German property, even barricading large areas of the East End to prevent official interference. That night a huge crowd, estimated to number some 5000 people, continued the process, running riot through Hackney, Tottenham and Highgate. Presented with such a violent reaction and under renewed political pressure, Lloyd George's government was forced to act quickly. To their credit they did, transferring No 46 Squadron, equipped with Sopwith Pups, from France to Romford in Kent on a permanent basis and keeping newly-manufactured fighters, earmarked as reinforcements for the Western Front, back in Britain.

This was only a short-term solution, for the problem of air defense in 1917 was far too complex to be rectified by the provision of a few fighters. The lack of co-ordination which had been seen during every Gotha raid was a sad reflection upon the dual control of air services in Britain, for ever since the formation of the Royal Flying Corps in 1912 the Army and Navy had been at loggerheads over its command, demanding that their own particular air needs should take precedence. The Navy had in fact gone its own way, leaving the RFC to the military and raising a separate Royal Naval Air Service, but although this unit was both professional and effective during the early months of World War I, by 1917 it was acting in dangerous competition with its Army counterpart. A dissipation of effort, research, aircraft development and money was the inevitable outcome, leading many influential politicians and servicemen to demand a unified air service capable of defending Britain and answering the needs of the Army and Navy together. It was in the light of such demands, coupled with the need to defeat the Gotha threat in the

long-term, that prompted Lloyd George to announce the creation on 11 July of a special 'Committee on Air Organization and Home Defense against Air Raids,' to be chaired by the South African, General Jan Smuts. The findings of this Committee were to lay the foundations of British air policy for the next 30 years.

Smuts worked with considerable speed, as the pressure of events demanded, and his first report was submitted to the Cabinet in early August. It dealt entirely with the organization of an effective air defense system around London and was put into practice without delay. Recognizing the weakness of dispersed command, Smuts recommended a single defense command authority in charge of all defenses in southeast England. Known as the London Air Defense Area (LADA), this was designed to co-ordinate all guns, observer stations, interceptor fighters and early warning systems then in existence. Anti-aircraft guns were re-deployed to cover the approaches to London from the north, south, and east, with fighters, flying at likely bomber altitudes in preset patrol areas, behind the gun lines to catch any Gothas which penetrated that far. Three regular home defense fighter squadrons were assigned to this task and based in the immediate vicinity of London – No

44 at Hainault Farm to the north, No 61 at Rochford to the east, and No 112 at Throwley to the south – while six other squadrons, deployed the previous year against the Zeppelins, backed them up. Within London itself there was a further ring of guns, known as the Inner Defenses, and the whole arrangement was placed under one commander, Brigadier General Ashmore, an artillery officer with air experience. Virtually overnight the city of London was altered from a defenseless location to a fortified strong point, ready to counter the continuation of daylight raids.

Smuts realized, however, that these measures would probably be inadequate against prolonged assault, and in his second report, submitted on 17 August, he took his findings to their logical conclusion, arguing the need for a complete re-organization of Britain's air forces. Unlike many of his contemporaries, he recognized the possibility of using aircraft for strategic purposes and concluded that the destruction of Britain's industrial base, either through the bombing of factories or the demoralization of working people, was the main aim behind the Gotha attacks. Defense against such attacks, he surmised, could be either passive, in the form of LADA, or active, in the form of a strategic

The damage caused by an early Zeppelin raid on Kings Lynn in East Anglia in 1915.

counteroffensive designed to persuade the Germans to stop their campaign and, ideally, to destroy the German industrial base itself. But in the prevailing atmosphere of naval – military rivalry, there was no portion of the British air services capable of putting such an offensive into operation, and Smuts was driven inevitably to conclude that it was time to establish a separate Air Ministry, with control over all portions together – that is, a separate and independent air force, free from the strictures of service rivalry. Needless to say, he encountered almost universal opposition, and the plan was shelved. It was to be resurrected by the end of the year as the only remaining answer to a new German bombing campaign.

During the period of Smuts' deliberations, only two further daylight raids had taken place – on 12 and 22 August – neither of which had penetrated beyond the coast. Kleine was presented with a noticeable drop in crew morale as losses, mostly from flying accidents, continued to mount and British defenses scored their first successes. He decided upon a change of tactics, arguing that the element of surprise might be regained if the Gothas attacked by night, and this was quickly put into effect. By 3 September four crews were sufficiently proficient to mount a raid on coastal targets in North Kent. Under full moon conditions they dropped their bombs on an unsuspecting population, causing unprecedented casualties when one 110lb bomb hit a drill hall full of naval ratings in Chatham, killing 131 and injuring 90. The defenses were taken completely by surprise, finding it impossible to track the incoming raiders or to co-ordinate any form of organized opposition to them. Anti-aircraft guns fired sporadically and without effect, while interceptor fighters were grounded by a total lack of provision for night flying. Kleine's argument had been correct: the elaborate defenses recommended by Smuts had been largely by-passed through a simple change in tactics. The initiative had returned to the Gothas, and they proceeded to make full use of it.

The four month period between September and December 1917 saw the most sustained German bombing offensive of World War I, involving not only new tactics but also new weapons. Amongst the latter were the *Reisin* or *R*-type bombers, developed initially in 1915 for attacks upon Russia. Two squadrons – Nos 500 and 501 – had used these aircraft – popularly and aptly known as Giants –

Searchlights comb London skies over Battersea Bridge during a night raid of Zeppelins.

Wreckage from a Zeppelin raid over East Anglia, which caused a great panic.

The remains of St Peter's House in Yarmouth on the North Sea coast after a raid in 1915.

to good effect in the East throughout 1916, sometimes hitting targets up to 300 miles behind the enemy lines. In the summer of 1917 Squadron 501, under the command of Captain Richard von Bentivegni, had been withdrawn to Germany and re-equipped, chiefly with the new Staaken RV1, a four-engined machine which sported a wing span in excess of 130ft and a capability of carrying bomb loads five times greater than the Gotha G IV. In September the squadron flew to Belgium to join Kleine's offensive upon London.

By the time that Bentivegni and his crews arrived, Kleine had in fact stepped up his bombing efforts and was in the process of a campaign which was to have a dramatic effect. Known in retrospect as 'the raids of the Harvest Moon,' the campaign had begun on 24 September and was to continue until bad weather intervened on 2 October. During that eventful week the people of London grew used to the idea of nightly attacks and reacted accordingly. Shops and business premises closed early, industrial production diminished dramatically, particularly in the essential area of munitions, and civilians tried to ecape the raids by flocking into the Underground or leaving the city altogether. Casualties were in fact remarkably light – 69 killed and 260 injured during the entire period – but the psychological impact was enormous. It was not lessened by the fact that not one enemy aircraft was destroyed by the LADA

Damage from one bomb during a raid on London in August 1917.

A crowd gathers after a 300kg bomb fell on Warrington Crescent, St John's Wood, London during an air strike on 7–8 March 1918.

guns or fighters, even though on one occasion a staggering total of 14,000 rounds of anti-aircraft ammunition was fired in a single night. The only results were a great deal of damage to London property from falling shrapnel and a chronic shortage of munitions.

If Kleine – joined by Bentivegni and the Giants on 28 September – had been able to sustain his offensive at this level, it is quite possible that considerable long-term damage could have been inflicted upon the British war effort. But poor weather was not the only problem. During the Harvest Moon raids 92 individual Gotha sorties had been flown, with disappointing results, for only 55 of these had got as far as the English coast, with a mere 20 making it all the way to London. Engine failures, inexperienced pilots and poor navigation had combined with the inevitable accidents to blunt the full potential of the assault and to destroy a total of 13 aircraft – a third of Kleine's strength. In addition, the Giants had not fulfilled their promise, flying five sorties of which only one had managed to reach the English capital. A pause for rest and re-equipment was clearly essential, but the pressure was maintained by a temporary return to the use of Zeppelins.

They attacked London and the Midlands in mid-October, suffering heavy casualties in landing accidents upon their return but adding considerably to the confusion of British defenses.

The Gothas returned to the assault on 31 October, when 22 of them took off to try another new tactic – the fire raid. Carrying over six tons of bombs between them, half of which were incendiaries, they attempted to swamp the fire-fighting capacity of London and cause a conflagration which would disrupt the city completely. In theory it was a sound idea, but in practice many of the new bombs failed to ignite and the fires that were started could quite easily be contained. Bad weather then set in, and it was not until 6 December that Kleine could try again, this time with Giant support. Almost 20,000lbs of bombs were scattered over London and Kent on that night and a number of serious fires were started. The pattern was repeated on 18 December, when almost a quarter of a million pounds' worth of damage was inflicted, but that raid turned out to be something of a watershed. Kleine had been killed on 12 December flying an army support mission over the Western Front, so the England Squadron was

temporarily leaderless and somewhat demoralized, but more importantly, the British defenses had recovered their composure. On 6 December alone, six Gothas had failed to land safely, three of them falling to anti-aircraft fire.

Credit for this recovery must be given to Ashmore, who reacted remarkably quickly to the night-time raids. Almost immediately he organized an ingenious system of barrage firing for the LADA guns, whereby the skies above London were divided into a number of specified areas. As soon as bombers were reported in one of these areas a pre-set barrage was fired, the idea being to create a 'curtain' of steel through which the Gothas would be forced to pass. By late November 1917 the whole of LADA was covered by these curtains, and in order to ensure that the bombers flew at predictable altitudes, balloons were floated above the city, joined together by steel cables which forced the German pilots into the barrage traps. In addition, extra anti-aircraft guns were redeployed from cities in the Midlands, where they had been idle since the reduction of the Zeppelin threat in 1916, and were concentrated around London, while fighter pilots hurriedly gained experience in night flying.

Success did not come from these measures immediately, as the events of the Harvest Moon period showed, but they were a good foundation upon which to base more long-term innovations.

Ashmore began to plan for the future during the relative lull in November 1917 and a whole series of new measures were thought out and introduced before the end of the war 12 months later. So far as air defenses were concerned, one of the first priorities was to replace existing interceptor fighters, developed originally for daylight flying only, with machines which could be used at night. The answer was found in the Bristol Fighter, a two-seater aircraft equipped with a forward-firing Vickers gun and one or two Lewis guns in the rear cockpit, which, beyond its ability to fly at night, had advantages of both speed and altitude over the Gothas and Giants. No 141 Squadron, based at Biggin Hill to the south of London, was the first to receive these machines in early 1918, and as the year progressed the Sopwith Camel and SE5 day-fighters were gradually phased out. The process was never completed, but by the summer of 1918 nearly 200 Bristol Fighters were available for home defense. Furthermore, by that time the problem of aircraft control had been recognized, for it was no use having the interceptors if they could not be guided onto the incoming bombers. At first, the pilots were controlled by flashing searchlights and even, during the hours of daylight, by special white arrows on the ground which were rotated to point the fighters in the general direction of the raiders, but by the end of the war successful experiments were being made with ground-to-air radio telephones.

The efficacy of these measures would have been limited, however, if similar improvements had not been made to the ground defenses and observer stations, for without them co-ordination and control would have been impossible. Good communications were the key, and the original, rather haphazard, process of depending upon the civilian telephone network was gradually replaced by a special series of 'tied' lines between defense headquarters in London and the gun batteries and searchlight companies. At the same time the observer corps, hitherto composed of elderly or unfit soldiers, was placed in the hands of the civil police forces, who began to train in the difficult art of aircraft recognition. Finally, to prevent the interceptors from being shot down by their own anti-aircraft guns, rigid areas of priority were

German Gotha bombers dropped a 50kg bomb on Odhams printing works during the night of 28–29 January 1918. This raid wiped out half the building and caused the death of 38 people.

The rotary-engined Sopwith 7F.1 Snipe. By 1918 Britain's defenses were far better prepared for air strikes than they were in 1914.

established, based upon a 'Green Line' drawn around London. Outside this line the guns had priority, unless the fighters were in a particularly favorable position to attack, but inside it they were ordered to 'give preference to our machines' as soon as they arrived on the scene. This was not particularly easy to put into effect, but it had the added advantage of preventing the massive expenditure of anti-aircraft ammunition which had characterized some of the early night-time raids. By November 1918 Ashmore's command had become a tightly-controlled and relatively sophisticated defensive system.

But it took time for the full effect of these innovations to be felt, and after the shock of the night-time attacks in late 1917 the British public was in no mood to sit back passively and await events. They demanded immediate retaliation against German cities, relaying their message to Lloyd George and the Cabinet through the medium of the Press. At first the politicians attempted to satisfy these demands by ordering a series of sporadic raids upon the German homeland, using aircraft withdrawn from army support on the Western Front, but in early November 1917 they were roused from their complacency by the first detailed reports about the Giant bombers. According to Intelligence sources, the Germans were building 4000 of these in preparation for a knock-

A Gotha G Vd heavy bomber powered by two 260hp Mercedes engines.

out blow against England, and although this later turned out to be a gross over-estimation (the largest Giant raid of the war was carried out by only six aircraft), it created instant alarm. Calls for a counteroffensive, based upon a force of at least 2000 British bombers, began to

be heard, and this immediately resurrected all the arguments which had led Smuts to advocate an independent air service. This time, however, the government was convinced and hurriedly introduced an Air Force (Constitution) Bill which, in the prevailing atmosphere of fear, became law on 29 November. Thirty-four days later, on 2 January 1918, the Air Ministry was formed, and three months after that, on 1 April, an independent Royal Air Force came into existence, charged primarily with mounting a strategic counteroffensive against the enemy nation.

A combination of factors, ranging from political problems at the Air Ministry to a lack of suitable aircraft, prevented the formation of a viable British bombing force until June 1918, and by that time the German raids upon England had died out. The Gothas and Giants together had tried to maintain the pressure of their attacks in early 1918 but, despite some successes – notably on 28 January when they inflicted fairly heavy casualties upon London – they could never quite regain the initiative they had enjoyed the previous September. Indeed, in early February 1918 when Brandenburg resumed command of the England Squadron, he was so shocked by its low state of morale that he gained permission to withdraw the Gothas entirely until the end of March. During that period the Giants bore the full responsibility for continuing the offensive, flying a series of raids which were remarkable for their lack of effect upon British morale, even though they entailed the introduction on 16 February of the one ton bomb. The populations of London and the southeast were gradually learning to live with the bombing, so much so that even when the Gothas returned to the attack in May, after nearly two months of army support, the results achieved were nowhere near as dramatic as those of 1917. In addition, of course, Ashmore's defensive system grew stronger every day, and it was perhaps no coincidence that the last German attack, on 19 May, was also their most costly. No less than 28 Gothas crossed the English coast, straggling over Kent and Essex for nearly two hours as they fought toward London against an amazing barrage of 30,000 shells and numerous patrolling fighters. Six of the bombers fell to the LADA defenses that night: a figure which represented a 20 percent loss rate – something which neither Brandenburg nor the German High Command could sustain. Thereafter the Gothas and Giants were used more and more as tactical support aircraft on the Western Front, until in October 1918 they were forced to withdraw from the Belgian bases in the face of the Allied land advance. Hostile aircraft did not fly over England for 21 years.

The first Battle of Britain therefore ended in something of an anticlimax, with neither side really winning in the conventional sense. So far as the Germans were concerned, they had succeeded in forcing a redeployment of British aircraft away from the Western Front, but had failed to destroy either the industrial capacity of Britain or the morale of her people. In other words, what had begun as a strategic offensive had declined into one of tactical importance only: a consideration reinforced by the apparent lack of interest shown by the German High Command once the land war began to move out of the trench deadlock. On the British side the results were a little more concrete, comprising a viable defensive system and an independent air force which were to stand the country in good stead for the future, but neither had contributed decisively to the ending of the German raids. It was almost as if each side had shown its potential, but had been prevented from testing it to the full by a sudden cessation of hostilities on the military front.

But this is to ignore the long-term results of the battle, for between the two world wars a number of air strategists, using the inconclusive evidence of 1917–18 as a base, worked out what appeared to be a viable theory of aerial bombardment. Looking at the most successful German raids, particularly those of June and July 1917, people like the Italian Giulio Douhet and the American Billy Mitchell surmised that in the future, with full political backing and new technological aids, the bomber would always get through to destroy the enemy nation. The theory was believed, and the true legacy of the first Battle of Britain is to be found in the massive devastation of Europe and Japan during World War II. The Gothas and Giants were the trail blazers of total war.

Below: A squadron of Fokker D-VII biplanes in 1918. Aerial raids created public fear of what more modern aircraft could accomplish in any subsequent war.

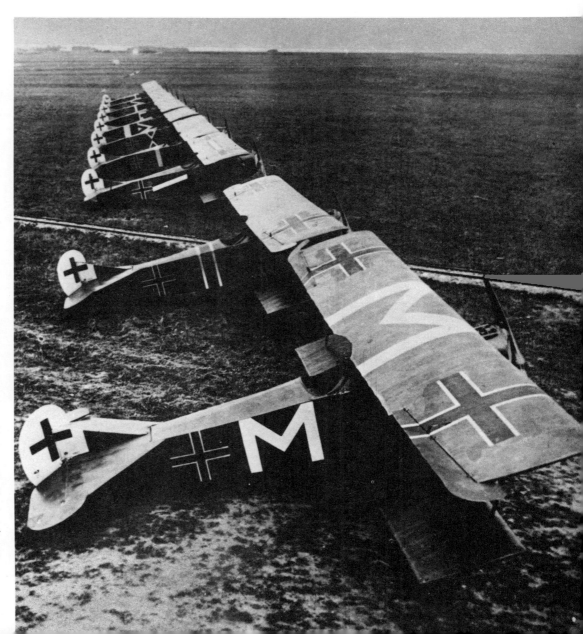

THE BLACK DAY 1918

8 August 1918

'Mon général, voilà l'aurore d'un jour de gloire.'

LIEUTENANT COLONEL JACOMET
to General Deville, 42nd (French) Division. Dawn, 8 August 1918.

France had survived the great onslaught of 1914, when the Germans had tried to knock her out of the war before turning against Russia. As things turned out it was the Tsarist Empire, not the French Republic, that fell. Despite terrible casualties at Verdun and on the Somme, France was holding out. But in the winter of 1917–18 the Germans were able to build up their armies on the Western Front with no less than 44 divisions from the Eastern Front.

Thus reinforced the Germans carried out five great offensives, all of which gained ground, but all of which were eventually held, so that in effect the attackers merely succeeded in creating vulnerable salients along their front. Meanwhile the Allies, too, too had been reinforced. By mid-July 25 strong, fresh American divisions were available. By 1 July there were 1,700,000 Americans under training in France with a few divisions actually under fire.

The Germans began their last offensive of the war, the Second Battle of the Marne, on 15 July. It met with but mixed success and by midday on 17 July had failed. Next day the French counterattacked the Soissons salient, driving back the German Seventh and Ninth Armies for more than four miles; Mangin's Army alone taking over 15,000 prisoners and 400 guns. In the days that followed a steady pressure was kept up. The tactics were well-described in an order by Lieutenant General Godley, Commander of the Anzac Corps, which was operating under French command: 'The enemy should be engaged and worn down by a continuous series of advances undertaken with sufficient deliberation and artillery preparation to secure eco-nomy of men, whilst giving him no rest.' By 5 August the Germans were back behind the Vesle and the Aisne, well entrenched, but with their Soissons salient obliterated. They had lost 793 guns, 3723 machine guns, and perhaps 168,000 men, including 29,367 prisoners. Lacking adequate reinforcements, the Germans were compelled to break up ten divisions. This successful offensive had cost the French 95,165 casualties and the British 16,552. It also won General Foch, who had been in supreme command of the Allies since 26 March 1918, his marshal's baton.

Allied Intelligence now calculated that the Germans had lost a million men on the Western Front since their first great offensive began on 21 March, and this was, if anything, an understatement.

This then was the situation on the eve of the great Allied offensive which Foch had been waiting to launch ever since he had been given command.

When, in May, German pressure on the British in Picardy and Flanders had eased, Sir Douglas Haig had ordered General Rawlinson (Fourth Army) to begin planning an attack from the Amiens front. This was to be carried out in co-operation with General Debeney, whose First French Army, was on Rawlinson's right.

On 12 July Foch had asked for an offensive on the La Bassée front so as to liberate the Béthune mining area. Haig rightly objected to an advance across 'the water-logged basin of the upper Schelde.' He went on: 'the operation which to my mind is of the greatest importance, and which I suggest to you should be carried out as early as possible, is to advance the Allied front east and southeast of Amiens, so as to disengage that town and the railway. Foch, eager to attack, was not the man to make difficulties as to where a particular battle should take place. For he had worked out in his mind that, given the slow rate at which 1918 armies could advance, his final victory must depend on a series of *limited* offensives designed to exploit to the full the *initial* superiority of the firepower of the offensive. This was not precisely the Ludendorff recipe as demonstrated in his five offensives earlier in the year. For Ludendorff's solution was one evolved on the Eastern Front and in Italy at Caporetto. Its elements were complete surprise; brief and violent artillery preparation designed, if not to destroy, at least to neutralize; infantry exploitation by rapid infiltration to the greatest possible depth. But on the Western Front, Foch, who for all his *panache* was a *thinking* general, had found that the defender could switch his reserves to the broken front by rail and by road far more quickly than the infiltrating German infantry could plod forward on their flat feet. Since he was like Joffre before him essentially a pragmatic commander, he decided that his great offensive, which was to rid French and Belgian soil of the invader, must be the sum of a score of limited offensives, rather than the result of some great Cannae or Blenheim or Gaugamela. The conditions prevailing on the Western Front in 1918 simply did not allow for a knockout in one round. The relatively short range of field-artillery on which so much depended and the slow pace of horse transport ruled out the possibility of a fast advance.

And so Foch now wrote to Haig that the offensive he had conceived 'seems to me the most profitable to execute at the moment,' adding, 'General Debeney on his part, has been studying an offensive with the same objective.'

On 24 July Foch held a conference with Haig and General John Pershing, the American commander, and outlined

Marshal Ferdinand Foch, Allied C in C.

Field Marshal Sir Douglas Haig, British C in C.

General Rawlinson, Fourth Army.

Marshal Foch.

Hindenburg, Kaiser Wilhelm and Ludendorff study German defense plans at the Spa HQ.

his plans, in which the main factor was the freeing of three strategic railways:—

1 The Paris–Verdun line, which passed ten miles south of Château-Thierry, and was probably going to be cleared by the Second Battle of the Marne, which was then in progress.

2 The Paris–Amiens line – as proposed by Haig.

3 The Verdun–Avricourt line – as proposed by Pershing. This would be achieved by a reduction of the St Mihiel salient.

Foch envisaged that these operations would be followed up by others designed to recapture the mining areas of the north and to drive the Germans back from the neighborhood of Calais and Dunkirk. Two days later Foch confirmed the decisions taken at this conference by written orders defining the object as to 'disengage Amiens and the

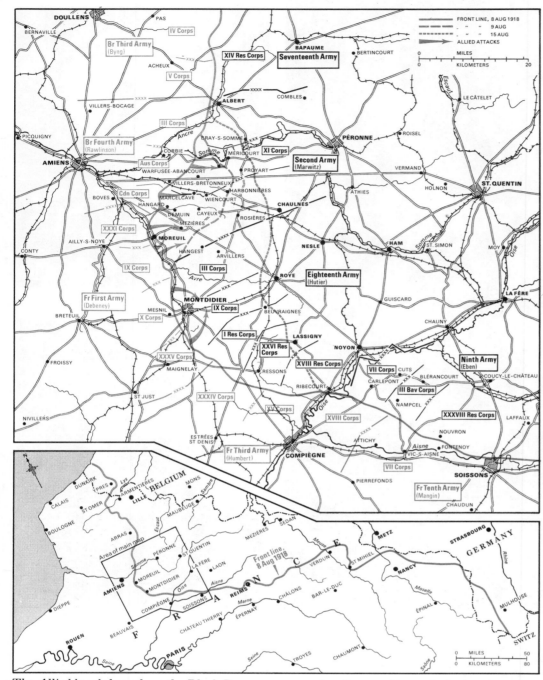

The Allied breakthrough on the Black Day meant an end to German hopes of winning the war.

German shock troops on one of their last frontal assaults.

Paris–Amiens railway, also to defeat and drive back the enemy established between the Somme and the Avre.' On 28 July he placed Debeney under Haig's command for the forthcoming advance, which he wanted to take place on the 8, not 10, August. This meant that the Fourth Army had to get a move on and overhaul its concentration timetables.

Fortunately the Germans were not expecting an offensive in the Amiens Sector. On 2 August OHL had sent out an appreciation which stated the opinion that: 'Since the Entente has engaged large forces between the Vesle and the Marne, full-dress attacks by the enemy within a short time at another place are as little to be expected as a counterattack by us is to be reckoned by him.' This was a very nice piece of wishful thinking on the part of the strategists of the German General Staff (OHL), who were, it seems, not precisely infallible.

Secrecy was the keynote of Haig's plan. In outline it called for three corps, their flanks well guarded, to break through the German line and advance eastward for about five to seven miles. Haig later ordered Rawlinson to push on another seven miles towards Roye. Rawlinson laid the greatest stress upon Secrecy, and a small notice headed *keep your mouth shut* was posted into every soldier's pay-book. By day normal work was carried on. By night all the necessary preliminary moves were made. The *pavé* roads were carefully sanded so as to cut down noise. Ammunition dumps were camouflaged, and aircraft flew over the concentration area looking for clues that might give away the preparations that were in progress. German air reconnaissance was discouraged by a strong ack-ack barrage. Amiens itself, which had been evacuated in March, was practically kept free of civilians.

The Allied Order of Battle was formidable. The French First Army had ten divisions in the line, with four more and II Cavalry Corps (three divisions) in reserve. The Fourth Army had nine divisions in the line and the Cavalry Corps (three divisions) in reserve.

There was a tremendous concentration of heavy guns and howitzers. The French had 826 (one per 42 yards), the British: 684 (one per 59 yards). The French had 72 light tanks; the British had 72 whippets, 120 supply machines and 342 fighting tanks. The French had 1104 aircraft in support, the British had 626. To these the Germans could immediately oppose only some 365. From 1–7 August the weather was not favorable for flying.

Against this array the Germans had the two armies of von Hutier (Eighteenth) and von der Marwitz (Second), 14 divisions in all. The overall commander was Prince Rupprecht of Bavaria.

The battle ground was the Santerre plateau, flat in the French area, but more undulating on the British front. Small woods and villages were few and far between.

Nothing aroused the suspicions of the Germans. Prince Rupprecht had decided that the British had long been preparing 'a full-dress' attack on the Ypres front. The noise of ammunition and materials being dumped near the front line had been heard, but when some German troops reported the sound of approaching tanks, where, incidentally, none could have been, the High Command dismissed the report as 'phantoms of the imagination, or nervousness.' A German officer wrote, 'not even a request to keep a sharp look-out was made. The Army staff were astonishingly indifferent.'

In these anxious days the Germans carried out some minor withdrawals at various points along the front. On the night before the battle the Germans took it into their heads to fire off a concentration of gas, which caused over 500 casualties in the back area of III Corps. In the early morning of 29 July the 5th Australian Division had carried out a piece of 'peaceful penetration,' in other words a fairly big raid, and had taken 138 prisoners. By way of riposte at dawn on 6 August the 27th (Württemberg) Division, a very good formation raided the III Corps, and catching the left of the 58th and the right of the 18th Division in the process of relief, gained some ground. This dislocated the III Corps' plan to some extent.

8 AUGUST

The night, though dark, was fine: there was no moon. Toward dawn mist began to form in the valleys of the Avre and the Luce, gradually spreading across the plateau. It was not until after 0900 hours that the RAF could intervene in the battle. The French *Division Aérienne* played no part on that day.

Zero hour was 0420 hours and a few minutes earlier the 435 British tanks began to move up from their assembly areas. When the barrage went down they went into the mist along with the infantry.

The Canadian and Australian Corps

German 6-inch howitzers in action along the Western Front after the Allied breakthrough.

German troops advance through barbed wire near the Aisne.

German infantry clamber over a captured trench near Montdidier on their final offensive.

Heavy artillery fire drove the Germans back toward the French frontier after four years of stalemate on the Western Front.

Field Marshal Sir Douglas Haig and a French general gloat over their victory.

carried all before them, both gaining their third objectives. The III Corps, its preparations put out by the Württemberger's raid, only gained its first objective. The British had less than 9000 casualties, but suffered heavily in armor and aircraft. Only 145 tanks were still in action.

On the immediate right of the Canadians the French 42nd Division, a crack formation, attacking behind a creeping barrage, broke into the German line wreaking havoc and carrying all but its final objective.

The Germans formed a new line and brought up five reserve divisions to support the remains of the ten which had been manning their front line. They flew up squadrons from neighboring sectors, Captain Hermann Goering's among them. But they had lost some 27,500 men, including 15,000 prisoners, and over 400 guns, and as the German official monograph put it: 'As the sun set on the battlefield on 8 August the greatest defeat which the German army had suffered since the beginning of the war was an accomplished fact.'

On the Allied side there were the usual difficulties. The two Dominion Corps were practically beyond the range of the fire support of the heavy artillery. Communications by runner, galloper and cyclist were as difficult as they were unreliable. It is easy to forget, too, that the troops were exhausted, both mentally and physically by the dangers they had survived and the effort they had made. A letter written next day by a French officer, Sous Lieutenant Bourdot

(5 company, 16 battalion of Chasseurs: 42nd Division), brings this out:

'Night came, and everyone, maddened by fatigue and thirst, stayed where he was, stunned, under the splendid night sky, stretched out in his slit trench, too tired to sleep, or even to dare to turn over. One's whole battered body ached, and still one's heart thumped fast . . . fast. . . . Half an hour later everyone had finished digging his hole, sentries signaled that the enemy was creeping around us. Stand to! The MGs mounted in the front line were on the alert .... Nothing. We drank and drank ... I swallowed two litres of coffee and a half litre of gnôle during the day. Then one slept, but at three in the morning the glacial cold woke everyone up.'

9 AUGUST

The day broke fine and clear, but Allied progress was disappointing. There could, in the nature of things, be no setpiece attack as on the previous day, and divisions and brigades went forward at different times. Some at 1100 hours; some as late as 1300 hours. Some with artillery support; some without. Some with tanks; and some without. The Germans, however, were not able to stage any real counterattack. Cavalry and whippets were pushed forward but soon ran into the German rearguards and were held up.

Debeney and his men were in unadventurous mood and despite Foch's telephonic exhortations made but little progress.

The British III Corps, north of the Somme, put a regiment of the American 33rd Division into the attack at 1730 hours. It made good progress and took 2960 prisoners.

10 AUGUST

This was another disappointing day of disjointed attacks, made in the belief that it was only a question of pursuit. But the German resistance was stiffened by the arrival of seven divisions. Another seven were on their way. Ahead of the British lay the area devastated by the Germans, when in 1917 they had retreated to the Hindenburg Line, and part of the old Somme battlefield, an area of trenches, craters, and uncut barbed wire. The biggest thrust was made by the Canadian Corps which advanced two miles.

The French did better on this day. Their Third Army (General Georges Humbert) advanced, and the Germans abandoned Montdidier. Foch concluded that the enemy was becoming demoralized.

At 1100 hours Foch visited Haig at his advanced headquarters, which was in a railway train in a siding, to discuss future operations. Foch wanted to continue with the frontal attack so as to secure bridgeheads across the Somme. Haig thought this could only work if the Germans were absolutely demoralized. He preferred to bring the British Third and First Armies into the battle, with an advance southeastward calculated to outflank the enemy facing Rawlinson and Debeney. Foch agreed to this, but

Above: German troops await the next Allied onslaught during their long retreat.

Below: German troops in flight.

insisted that these last continue their eastward advance from Amiens. Haig ordered Byng to carry out raids to test the German position, and push forward advanced guards if the time seemed ripe.

British 13-pdr anti-aircraft guns keep watch as German prisoners are taken.

11 AUGUST

Little progress was made. The Army commanders knew that their troops were very fatigued. The Germans now had 12 fresh divisions, besides the debris of the seven defeated on 8 August to oppose ten tired Canadian and Australian divisions. The cavalry divisions were withdrawn for it was obvious that there was going to be no opportunity for them to go through. Haig visited the Fourth Army, seeing Rawlinson and the corps commanders, as well as a number of the divisional generals. He decided to halt the advance until the heavy artillery could be brought up. This was the end of the Battle of Amiens, or as the French call it, Montdidier. Foch, eager to keep up the momentum of the advance, visited Haig in his train at 2200 hours, and urged that the offensive should be continued, and that the British Third Army should attack as soon as possible, but next day he relented somewhat. He would be content with local actions designed to exploit the success, and particularly the capture of Roye, which was important as a road-center.

The four day battle had cost the British 22,000 casualties, 9000 of them in the Canadian Corps. The French lost 24,232 between 6 and 15 August, so that the Allied total was in the region of 40,000. German losses, it is calculated, numbered about 75,000, including 29,873 prisoners, 11,373 of whom were taken by the French.

The brunt of the fighting was borne by the Dominion troops, Canadian and Australian. It would be a mistake, however, to think that the war-weary French contented themselves with the role of onlookers. The 42nd Division, whose performance was particularly important to their Canadian neighbors, fought with skill and *élan*. When their general, Deville, reviewed them on the battlefield on 12 August, their trophies included 33 guns and 13 howitzers. They had taken 2200 prisoners from three different divisions (14th Bavarian; 192 and 225), all of which were so badly knocked about that they had to be withdrawn from the line.

The Battle of Amiens was the beginning of the end. After a lull operations were resumed on 21 August and in the next 50 days the British advanced, taking Albert and Bapaume, breaking the Drocourt Position and the Hindenburg Line, in a campaign which cost about 189,976 casualties. In that time they took 111,606 German prisoners. In the 29

German trench mortar in action as some of the men take cover in shell holes.

An Australian 18-pdr goes into action on the Somme during the Allied August offensive.

A New Zealand division prepare to fire a captured 4.2 battery near Villers on 8 August.

days, 21 August–18 September, the British advanced 25 miles on a 40 mile front. Compare this with the Somme where, during four and a half months, an advance of 8 miles on a 12 mile front had cost 420,000 casualties. The improvement was due to surprise; to better tactics; and more artillery with better ammunition. Co-operation with aircraft and tanks had improved. No longer did the troops cross the Start Line in broad daylight. Small groups now worked forward in depth, using ground and the tactics of Fire and Movement. No longer did wave after wave of men plod forward in extended order, offering the German machine-gunners the very target that the Beaten Zone of their weapons demanded.

At the same time it must be said that the German soldier was not the man he had once been. No longer did it take a superiority of three to one to turn him out of a position. Verdun, the Somme and the failure of Ludendorff's five great offensives had knocked the stuffing out of the steadfast German soldiers. There were still officers and men who would hold an untenable position to the death, but there were droves of others, who were only too willing to put up their hands and declare that they came from Lorraine. . . .

It may be also mentioned that the British push eastward had the effect of shortening the Allied Front so that the French Sixth Army could be withdrawn (7 September) and built up again in Flanders. The French Third Army was taken into reserve (14 September). These were solid achievements, paving the way for the final advance on the Western Front (26 September–11 November).

Truly 8 August 1918 was a turning point. Well might Ludendorff call it 'the Black Day of the German Army.' It was exactly that, and moreover it had destroyed his belief in a German victory.

London Irish Rifles on a dawn patrol on 9 August, as the Allies followed in swift pursuit.

	Allies		Germans		
Haig	Belgian Army	King Albert			
	Second	Plumer	Fourth	von Arnim	**Crown**
	Fifth	Birdwood	Sixth	von Quast	**Prince**
	First	Horne	Seventh	von Below	**Rupprecht**
	Third	Byng	Second	von der	**of**
	Fourth	Rawlinson		Marwitz	**Bavaria**
Fayolle	First	Debeney			
	Third	Humbert	Eighteenth	von Hutier	
	Tenth	Mangin	Ninth	von Eben	
					Crown
Maistre	Sixth	Degoutte	Seventh	von Boehm	**Prince**
	Ninth	de Mitry			**Wilhelm**
	Fifth	Berthelot	First	von Mudra	
	Fourth	Gouraud	Third	von Einem	

Below: German dead on the road to Chipilly on the Black Day.

A lone British soldier in Cambrai the day after the Germans were driven out: 9 October.

THE MEUSE 1940

Below: Wehrmacht troops watch the burning of a town in northern France taken during their sweep through in early June 1940.

For every battle of the warrior is with confused noise, and garments rolled in blood; but this shall be with burning and fuel of fire.
ISAIAH, IX, 5.

The 1940 campaign in France and the Low Countries lasted a little over six weeks: it was a real *Blitzkrieg*. The campaign fell into two phases. The first, which lasted from 10 May to 4 June ended with the evacuation of 338,226 British and French troops from Dunkirk. The second ended when on 22 June the French accepted Hitler's armistice conditions. But in fact the campaign was lost right at the outset. Between 13 and 15 May the Germans made a breach 50 miles wide in the French front and this, for a variety of reasons, the French were never able to repair.

The Battle of the Meuse consisted of three separate actions. In each a German Panzer Corps attacked a sector of the French line: XV Panzer Corps (Hoth) from Fourth Army attacked XI Corps (Martin) of Ninth Army (Corap) at Dinant; XLI Panzer Corps (Reinhardt), belonging to von Kleist's Group (of Twelfth Army), attacked at Monthermé and Nouzzanville; XIX Panzer Corps (Guderian) also from von Kleist's Group, attacked X Corps (Grandsard) of Second Army (Huntziger) at Sedan; XIV Corps (von Wietersheim) of mechanized infantry, also belonging to von Kleist's Group, followed up Guderian. At Dinant and Sedan the Germans met with spectacular success. Between Monthermé and Mézières part of 102nd (Garrison) Division of Ninth Army held up Reinhardt for two days, while everything on either flank was collapsing. When the battle was over there was a gap, 50 miles wide, in the French front and the 10th German Panzer divisions were poised to exploit it. That, briefly, is the story of the Battle of the Meuse, but in order to understand how it all happened we must not only go into rather more detail: we must constantly remind ourselves that a 1940 Army, with fresh ideas, and well-organized air support, was attacking a 1918 Army with 1918 theories.

When, in 1914, the French marched out to meet the German Armies of Kaiser Wilhelm II, their commanders were wedded to the ideas of Colonel de Grandmaison, and he was influenced by the inept way in which the French had endeavored to ward off the Prussian onslaught of 1870. Metz and Sedan had taught him that a passive defense was useless. He had sold his contemporaries the idea of the *attaque à l'outrance*: the all-out attack, and this, in August and September 1914, had sprinkled the battlefields of the Ardennes, Alsace, the Sambre and the Marne with the blood of 385,000 of his countrymen, 110,000 of whom were dead. Before the war was over the French had lost 1,500,000 killed. Small wonder if from 1924 onward a pacifist lethargy overwhelmed the nation. France, a nation of 42,000,000 was not eager to find herself once more at war with 78,000,000 Germans. The elections of 1932 and 1936 confirmed that this feeling was widespread. Nevertheless successive French governments voted vast sums of money for their army, and their fortifications – the celebrated *Ligne Maginot*, covering part of their frontier with Germany. They were not so willing to spend money on their Air Force, which from 1930 onward, was seriously neglected, even when the exploits of Hitler's 'Condor Legion' in Spain had shown that a modern war machine can not afford to be weak in the air.

The British for their part suffered from the same wave of pacifism. In addition their politicians neglected the armed forces, starving them of funds, so that in 1939 they went to war in an astonishing state of unpreparedness. The Navy, with unrivalled personnel, had for its warships a magnificent collection of old iron. The Royal Air Force simply had insufficient planes for all the tasks it was to take on, especially as it was to be invited to make up for the deficiencies of its Allies.

On 10 May 1940 the Army, which in World War I had risen to 60 divisions, could field but ten (four of them incomplete) with a single brigade of tanks. The Germans by this time had ten Panzer Divisions, and the wit to concentrate them for battle.

There were then three main reasons for the defeat of the Allies and the fall of France. The first was that the politicians, both in France and in Great Britain, though Hitler's ambitions were all too obvious, had neglected to prepare their armed services for modern war. The second was that the majority of the generals were living in the past – in 1918 to be precise, when the horse-drawn armies of Western Europe could manage 15–20 miles a day if they were lucky. The third reason was that a handful – no more – of German generals had grasped the idea of what we have come to call the *Blitzkrieg*: lightning war. Pace, horror, mere effrontery, rumor, confusion; these were going to put the slow-moving Allied war machine off the road.

Military operations are governed by various factors, which are more or less constant. Lieutenant Colonel Burne in *The Art of War on Land* suggested that these are:

I   The quality and capability of the *commander*
II   The quality and capability of the *troops*
III   *Morale*
IV   *Resources*

It is well worth looking at the 1940 Armies with these strands in mind.

I *The Commanders*

In general, most of the German commanders had the advantage that they had taken part in the Polish Campaign of 1939, and they were, therefore, confident that the new technique of the *Blitzkrieg* really worked. Still, with the exception of Hitler himself, von Manstein, Guderian and Rommel, it is not all that easy to name German commanders, who were whole-hearted exponents of the new style of warfare.

Another point, and an important one to a professional corps of officers, is that the advent of Hitler and the expansion of the German Army had spelled promotion for hundreds of officers, both senior and junior. Men who had soldiered on after 1918 with the 100,000 strong Army allowed by the Treaty of Versailles, felt that their years of self-sacrifice had not been in vain. Even so some of the senior officers were pretty ancient: von Rundstedt, for example,

General Gamelin, C in C of Allied forces on the Western Front, who has just given General Lord Gort, British commander, the Legion of Honor during a visit by Winston Churchill to France in January 1940 in his capacity as First Lord of the Admiralty.

German commanders. For the conditions of 1918 were not to be repeated on the battlefields of 1940. In Poland the Germans had had a dress rehearsal of the new methods which were to distinguish World War II from the First. The French and the British were now for the first time to see a whole series of new techniques. Air forces would assist ground troops in attack, and would transport men and supplies; airborne troops would fly ahead to seize positions of tactical importance; massed tanks would exploit breaches in the line; mechanical transport by specially designed vehicles, such as the British Universal Carrier, would be employed; the swift-moving battle would be controlled by wireless. All this could be bewildering to men who had never seen an army move more than 15 or 20 miles in a day.

II *The quality and capability of the troops* and
III *Morale*

There seems to be no point in attempting to treat the IInd and IIIrd strands separately.

The morale of the German troops at this stage in the war was, on the whole, excellent. Their army had already shown its paces in Poland and Norway. The men had confidence in the Führer and in their commanders. They were adequately trained and it is no exaggeration to say that they were a self-confident lot.

None of this applies to the French, though it must be said that even when things are at their worst, there are always some good units in the French Army. The terrible casualties at Verdun and elsewhere in World War I had led the French High Command to adopt a defensive policy. It was as if they were planning and training for a defensive phase of the earlier war. *We will win, because we are the stronger* was the rather uninspiring slogan to be read on many a poster. It was hardly a clarion call, but it was typical of the mentality that had led the French to invest in the Maginot Line. There was little confidence in politicians or generals, and it was widely suspected that the Air Force was inadequate.

The morale of the British Expeditionary Force was to prove quite equal to the trials that lay ahead. It cannot be said that there was any great enthusiasm for the war, but there could be no doubt as to the justice of the cause. The BEF, containing as it did large numbers of reservists, territorials and young conscripts, was not a particularly well-

was 65, and had been recalled from retirement.

The French, too, employed generals, who were well advanced in years – rather as if it was necessary to keep the military hierarchy in line with senior civil servants! Weygand was 73; Gamelin was 68. At their age, quite apart from being physically past their best, they were unlikely to have any experience or understanding of the new mobile, armored warfare. In addition, both were staff officers rather than fighting generals.

The British commander, Lord Gort, was much younger (53), without a truly heroic fighting record, but plenty of staff experience. Some of his subordinates, notably Brooke (II Corps) and Montgomery (4th Division) esteemed themselves to be better officers than he, and

though they may have been right, Gort was probably the best possible Commander the British Army could have provided for the BEF in 1939/1940. Being a Viscount, a Guardsman, and a VC, he was liable to do what he thought right regardless of the consequences to his own career.

For the rest, commanders in all three armies, German, French and British were on the old side. In the British Army most battalion commanders were in their late 40s, and the majority of the company commanders had seen service in the 1914–18 war, and were also rather elderly, though their experience of active service was invaluable. But experience can be a double-edged weapon. It certainly was with the French general staff, and possibly with some of the older trained army, and it spent far too much time digging defensive positions, when it might have been shooting, or marching or doing tactical training.

For some reason it never seems to have occurred to the British soldier that he might be beaten, and that, however illogical, was a pearl of great price.

IV Resources

The Germans had a great advantage in the Air, simply because they had more planes. In addition they had dive-bombers and airborne troops, which their opponents had not. They had much better wireless communications than the Allies.

Both the French and the Germans used horsed cavalry, and had masses of horsed transport. The BEF did not have a single horse – that, considering the rearguard action by the cavalry school, you may say was the real 'Miracle of Dunkirk.' Besides being more mobile than the other armies the BEF had a good and numerous artillery.

The British, though they had invented tanks, had very few in France, and no transporters. The Allies had more tanks than the Germans, and their best tanks were superior to those of their assailants. The apparent superiority of the German armor was due to their concentrating their ten Panzer divisions, and supporting them with their Stuka dive-bombers. In addition the Germans were much better organized. The Panzer Corps included a motorized infantry division: the Panzer Division was a balanced force of all arms, even though not all the divisions were complete.

The Germans had: Pzkw IV 278
Pzkw III 349
———
627

These could take on the best Allied tanks on terms of equality. They had another 2063 tanks which were either obsolescent Pzkw I and II or Czech tanks. There were some 800 tanks in reserve in Germany.

The French could put about 3000 tanks into the field. Of these perhaps a sixth belonged to units which were in training or were still forming. They had a reserve of older machines.

The British had 310 tanks in France and another 330 in southern England awaiting transport to France.

The French heavy tank, Char B-1, was pretty formidable, but the Somua S-35 (medium) and Hotchkiss H-39 (light) were considered by Major General G le Q Martel, the British expert, to be

Above: General Gamelin was ready for 1914 in 1940.

Below: German infantry press forward with rifles and grenades.

under-engined and slow. The British Infantry Tank Mark II (Matilda) was also very slow (15mph), but it was thickly armored so that German anti-tank shells simply bounced off it.

For one reason or another most of the tanks used on either side in 1940 were already obsolescent, formidable though they seemed to the unfortunate infantrymen who met them in that campaign. The real advantage that the Germans enjoyed was that several of their generals were genuinely 'tank minded,' and that their formations were much better organized. This quite offset the disparity in numbers.

Lastly, the Germans had their 'fifth column.' Neither the French or the British had thought up anything so deceitful! There came a time when no Belgian peasant could hang out her washing, without some idiot thinking she was signaling to the Stukas! Everywhere nuns seemed to be loading their schmeissers. . . .

On 10 May 1940 the Germans struck. Their plan was a mixture of Hitler's intuition and General von Manstein's tactical skill. It called for a breakthrough on the Meuse, followed by a great scything armored stroke, which would reach the Channel at Abbeville and cut off the Allies' Northern Group of Armies from the rest of the French Army. Fortunately for the Germans their original plan which, in Manstein's opinion, could only lead to sterile and bloody trench warfare from the estuary of the Somme to the Maginot Line, had been prejudiced on 10 January. A plane, piloted by Major Hoenmans, had crashed in Belgium, and its passenger, Major Reinberger, was not able to destroy the Operations Orders, which he had with him. Despite considerable opposition from his more conservative generals Hitler gave von Manstein's plan full approval.

The French also had a plan, the Dyle Plan, devised by General Gamelin, it called for a swift advance with the object of relieving the Dutch and the Belgian Armies. It has been much condemned as playing into the hands of the Germans. Still the French and British could hardly abandon Holland and Belgium without the least attempt to relieve them. The difficulty was that the Belgians, fearful of compromising their neutrality, had allowed the minimum of reconnaissance and joint planning.

It may be that the original Allied plan, which only called for an advance to the Escaut (Scheldt), though less ambitious, was sounder in that it called for a shorter advance, but it meant the abandonment of more Belgian territory, while demanding a longer Allied line. The real weakness of Gamelin's plan was in his strategic layout, which provided no real reserve or *masse de manœuvre*. This rôle had originally been allotted to General Giraud's Seventh Army, but it had later been decided that Giraud should advance to Breda in order to support the Dutch. Since the initiative lay with the Germans it should have been obvious that the Allies, French and British, required a strong reserve army. In 1940 the French High Command was not remarkable for perceiving the obvious.

But General Joseph Georges, Commander of the North East Front saw the problem. On 5 December 1939 he wrote: 'It is obvious that our defensive ma-

Anti-British posters helped to sap public morale and promote defeatism in France, making the Nazi victory all the easier.

neuver in Belgium and Holland should be conducted with an eye to preventing ourselves from committing the bulk of our resources in this theater to meet a German move which might be only a diversion. For example, should an attack in force be launched against the center, on our front between the Meuse and the Moselle, we could well find ourselves deprived of the resources for a counterattack.' He was to prove a true prophet, though in fact he wrote these wise words *before* the Manstein Plan had been hatched.

Gamelin received a number of warnings that the Germans were interested in the Longwy-Givet front, and the roads between Sedan and Abbeville. These came not only from King Leopold and the Belgian general, van Overstraeten, but from Colonel Paillole, the head of the German section of his own counterespionage section. The French Military Attaché in Switzerland even got the date right when, on 30 April, he cabled to Vincennes. 'The German Army will attack along the whole front, including the Maginot Line, between 8–10 May; the

Above: A turret of the Maginot Line riddled with German shell holes; it was easily taken.
Below: Rafts such as these were used by the Wehrmacht to cross the Meuse.

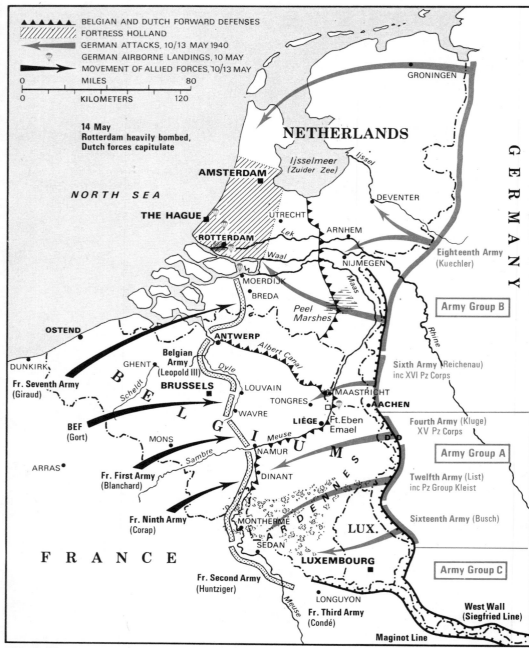

The attack through the Low Countries drew Allied forces northward into the German trap.

A British anti-tank post in Louvain.

region of Sedan, Belgium, Holland and northern France will be occupied in a week, and France within a month.' To react to these warnings by, say, redeploying Seventh Army in the Reims area, would have meant scrapping the Breda maneuver, but this Gamelin was not prepared to do and so when, at dawn on 10 May, the German airborne assault began, Gamelin's forces were thoroughly off balance.

10 May

Holland and Belgium – Supported by Kesselring's *Luftflotte* II, two German divisions went into the attack. General Student's 7th Airborne Division was charged with the capture of key points on the Dutch front, bridges over the Albert Canal and the modern fort, Eben Emael.

General Graf von Sponeck, in full dress as he trusted that Queen Wilhelmina would receive him in audience, commanded 22nd Division, whose mission was to seize The Hague as soon as possible and to compel the Dutch Royal Family to submit, if not to co-operate. The parachutists surprised the airfields at Valkenburg, Ypenburg and Ockenburg, but the Dutch I Corps, alerted in time, ejected the 22nd Division, took 1000 prisoners and wounded von Sponeck. That evening the captured Germans were shipped to England from Ijmuiden.

Though not all fell in the right places the men of Student's Division did much better, seizing Waalhaven airport and gaining a foothold in Rotterdam. With close support from Kesselring they held

out against Dutch counterattacks. The Moerdijk bridges over the estuary of the Maas fell into German hands, clearing the way for the German Eighteenth Army (von Küchler) to drive into *Vesting Holland*.

At dawn by a subterfuge the *Brandenburg* Division seized the bridge at Gennep. Similar attempts at Nijmegen and Roermond failed, but the road was clear for the 9th Panzer Division to spearhead the advance on 's Hertogenbosch.

The Dutch (III Corps) fell back from its delaying position, the Peel Line. On the Grebbe Line II and IV Corps put up a tougher stand. Meanwhile the vanguard of Giraud's Army had started on its dash towards Breda, and the BEF, astonished at being unmolested from the air, was moving up towards Brussels.

Germans advance down a Belgian street to aid the French poilu *whom they had just shot.*

German motorized units move south of Amiens in their ten-day sweep to the sea in May 1940.

Meanwhile on the Albert Canal the 7th Belgian Division had a disastrous day. The initial German attack was made by the 424-strong Koch Detachment, a specially trained glider-borne unit. Landing in the midst of the defenses the Germans seized the bridges at Veldwezelt and Vroenhoven, and prevented their demolition. At Canne where the ground favored them, the Belgians had time to blow up the bridge, and the Germans suffered heavy losses.

Eleven gliders landed on top of Fort Eben Emael and 78 assault pioneers, working to a detailed and thoroughly rehearsed plan, set about destroying strongpoints and gun positions by means of explosive targets. At about noon the garrison of 1500 surrendered to 51st Pioneer Battalion. It had suffered 100

casualties. The commander shot himself.

The Belgian 7th Division, deployed on an 11 mile front, was not able to mount counterattacks on the captured bridges. The least movement seemed to bring down the Stukas. By about noon, despite demolitions on the Maas, forward elements of the 4th Panzer Division were in touch with Koch.

Gamelin learned of the German onslaught at 0530 hours and confidently launched 600,000 men upon his *War Plan 1940* of 26 February. Meanwhile the tanks of *Panzergruppe Kleist* were thrusting forward through the Ardennes, while French reconnaissance units, armored cars and cavalry squadrons, probed forward to meet them.

The British Prime Minister, Neville Chamberlain, resigned and a Coalition

Government was formed by Winston S Churchill, hitherto First Lord of the Admiralty, who now became Minister of Defense as well as Prime Minister.

11 May
By the evening the Belgians were falling back from the Albert Canal to the Antwerp-Louvain line, and in so doing exposed Giraud's right flank.

The Allies lost 28 planes on this day and the next in vain attempts to knock out the bridges over the Albert Canal. Hearing of these dismal events General René Prioux, whose cavalry corps was covering the French First Army in the Gembloux sector said to General Blanchard that in his opinion: 'because of the weak Belgian resistance and the enemy superiority in the air, the Dyle maneuver seems difficult and it would be better to

Exhausted Wehrmacht troops rest on a Parisian street after their triumphal entry into the open city on 14 June 1940.

settle for the Escaut maneuver.' With this Blanchard agreed, but Billotte (1st Army Group), quite rightly, would have none of it. Having launched the Dyle-Breda maneuver it was scarcely possible to switch to the old Escaut Plan in the middle of it. Meanwhile the forward move of the BEF was going well, and to everyone's relief was not interfered with by the *Luftwaffe*.

In the Allied center French cavalry discovered that the Germans were coming through the Ardennes in force. The 2nd and 5th Light Cavalry were thrown back with severe losses. General Corap (Ninth Army) drew his cavalry back to the left bank of the Meuse, and in his noon bulletin General d'Astier de la Viferie, Commander in Chief of the air forces with 1st Army Group reported: 'The enemy seems to be preparing an energetic thrust in the direction of Givet.' Seven Panzer divisions, with 2270 armored vehicles, were about to descend upon 300 French tanks and armored cars. Under the circumstances the latter did well to fall back in good order.

12 May

At 1500 hours there was a conference at Château Casteau near Mons at which the following were present:

His Majesty the King of the Belgians	Belgium
M Daladier, Minister of National Defense	France
General Georges, Northern Group of Armies	France
General Billotte, 1st Army Group	France
General van Overstraeten, ADC and Chief Military Adviser to King Leopold	Belgium
General Champon, Head of the French Mission at Belgian HQ	France
Lieutenant General Henry Pownall (representing Lord Gort)	Great Britain
Brigadier Swayne, Head of the British Mission at General Georges' HQ	Great Britain

The main object of the meeting was to co-ordinate the Allied Armies in the northern sector – not before time.

Pownall described the successes of the fighters of the British Air Component, but said that these were already reduced to some 50 planes. Four more squadrons had been asked for, but only one had been promised.

General Georges spoke of the difficulty of co-ordinating the command of the Belgian Army, the BEF and the Seventh and First French Armies. His own HQ (La Ferté-sous-Jouarre) was too far away. He asked if General Billotte (HQ Folembray) would be acceptable as his representative, and this was willingly agreed to. But since the Second and Ninth French Armies also belonged to the 1st Army Group, Billotte was being asked to do too much. With the benefit of hindsight it would seem that these last two armies should, from the outset, have been formed into a separate Army Group.

The cavalry of Corap's and Huntziger's armies fell back across the

Warehouses are blown up along the Seine in Rouen after the Nazis took the city.

British troops surrender at Calais as the Dunkirk encirclement closed.

Meuse and in the afternoon blew up the bridges behind them. There was one snag. That evening the 7th Panzer Division reached Houx lock three and a half miles north of Dinant, where the 7th Motorcycle Battalion crossed a weir and, checked by a company of the 66th Infantry Regiment, established a small bridgehead. They were urged on to this exploit by their divisional commander. He was Major General Erwin Rommel.

13 May

By this time the situation on the Dutch front had become so grave that Queen Wilhelmina and her Government had reconciled themselves to the idea that they must leave the country. In view of the Belgian retreat Giraud, whose movements were hindered by the Stukas of VIII *Fliegerkorps*, did not venture to push forward to Moerdijk and Dordrecht.

The diary of Lieutenant General Pownall, Gort's Chief of Staff, gives a good idea of the state of affairs in Belgium.

'On our front things were pretty quiet during the day, no tank attacks only some small infantry ones easily held. On our right First French Army are pretty well up in line, in front of them the French Cavalry Corps fought a good delaying action. They found the Hotchkiss no good against German tanks but the Somua did very well....'

After some uncharitable remarks about King Leopold he goes on:

'The King seems completely to have lost his head. He was on the verge of blowing bridges that would have left some 70 Somua tanks of Giraud's DLM completely cut off. Only with great difficulty was he induced to delay the demolition until the tanks had got back. All the Belgians seem to be in a panic, from the higher command downwards. What an ally!' It is a passage which makes one sympathize with poor General Billotte in his role of co-ordinator!

During the night 12/13 May French 102nd (Garrison) Division, around Mézières, observed heavy columns of German transport making for Monthermé. They were pushing on boldly with their headlights on. This spectacle dismayed the French High Command rather less than it ought to have done. 'Crediting the enemy with our own battle methods,' wrote General Doumenc, 'we imagined that he would not attempt to cross the Meuse until he had brought up a considerable amount of artillery. The five or six days we thought he would need would give us time to reinforce our own

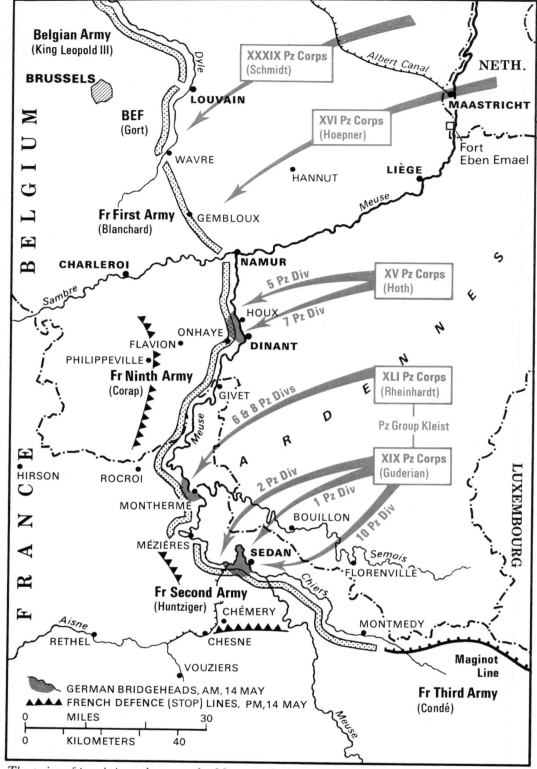

The point of breakthrough across the Meuse at Sedan on 14 May 1940.

river line, and infiltrated into the sector of 5th Motorized Division, who found by 0600 hours that it had lost touch with II/39, which indeed seemed to have vanished. At 0630 hours Boucher sent three mechanized squadrons towards Houx to try and regain contact. At 0730 hours further German progress decided Boucher to send his whole reconnaissance group to counterattack towards Haut-le-Wastia, but this never came to pass as the Germans were advancing too fast. And, of course, from dawn onwards the *Luftwaffe* had resumed its activities.

At 1000 hours Boucher detailed II/129 Regiment, supported by the reconnaissance group, to counterattack Haut-le-Wastia at 1300 hours. The regiment in fact crossed its start line at 1400 hours but was immediately pounced on by German aircraft and took to the woods. Bouffet, (II Corps) then ordered the 14th Mechanized Dragoons, an excellent unit, to carry out this counterattack, but as it was unable to reach its Start Line until 2000 hours the operation was postponed until the morning of 14 May.

South of Houx the 7th Regiment of riflemen – tried to cross at Bouvignes. They were stopped by 66th Regiment, and Rommel wrote: 'The situation was not very pleasant; the boats were destroyed one after the other by the flanking French fire, and the crossing had to be suspended.'

About noon General Martin (XI Corps) ordered two battalions of 39 Regiment (the 18th Division) with the support of tanks and artillery to recapture Surinvaux Wood and throw the Germans into the Meuse. H-hour 1930 hours Start Line: Foy Wood. Once more desire outran performance. Delayed by air attacks the regiment moved incredibly slowly. H-hour had to be put back half an hour, but though the supporting arms were ready by 2000 hours, the infantry had still not arrived. Dusk was falling and the tanks, after a 10 minutes bombardment, set off without them. Finding that Surinvaux Wood was not in fact occupied they pushed on to a little wood overlooking the Meuse, where they found some German motorcyclists, who, as the spirit moved them, either surrendered or departed.

No French infantry had followed up, so the tanks simply withdrew – one of them with seven POW riding on it. So ended XI Corps counterattack! The maghine gun carriers of the 1st Light Cavalry Division had taken part. They reported: 'The enemy is extremely cautious. Our small local counterattacks

defenses.' It was not to be. No sooner had the Germans reached the Meuse than they began the assault – at least two days earlier than the French thought such an operation possible.

At Dinant, Hoth (XV Panzer Corps) attacked the junction of two corps: II (Bouffet) and XI (Martin). II Corps comprised a single division: 5th Motorized (Boucher), which, thanks to its mechanization, was already in position. Martin had two infantry divisions of the

A Series: the 18th (Duffet) and 22nd (Hassler). Incredible though it may seem neither of these were properly 'set' in their positions when the French cavalry withdrew across the Meuse, and indeed the 22nd only arrived in the Givet sector during the early hours of 13 May.

At 0300 hours Rommel's motorcyclists, who had massed on the French bank, advanced rapidly, surprising some companies of II/39 Regiment, who were on high ground too far back from the succeeded and made progress without serious opposition. The Germans surrender easily. The Luftwaffe's bombing has only caused light losses and, on the whole, our men need not be unduly hindered by them.' The French infantry took a less optimistic view of affairs. Nevertheless the fact is that in the Dinant area by the night 13/14 May, the Germans had nothing but infantry on the left (French) bank of the Meuse, without a single tank or anti-tank gun.

During the morning the French at Monthermé observed the approach march of Reinhardt's Corps and shelled its columns, though, too intent on saving ammunition, they made insufficient use of their opportunities.

The Germans began their attack at 1500 hours, as planned, although the

Right: A wounded Highlander bemoans his capture after being separated from his unit.

Below: A German encampment prior to their drive southward down the Atlantic coast in the final stages of the French campaign.

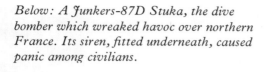

Below: A Junkers-87D Stuka, the dive bomber which wreaked havoc over northern France. Its siren, fitted underneath, caused panic among civilians.

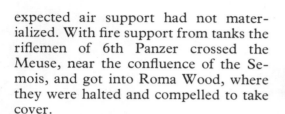

expected air support had not materialized. With fire support from tanks the riflemen of 6th Panzer crossed the Meuse, near the confluence of the Semois, and got into Roma Wood, where they were halted and compelled to take cover.

In the Sedan sector General Grandsard awaited Guderian's onslaught with confidence, despite the fact that on the previous day the Germans had taken the town, which is on the right bank, without firing a shot. 'What can the enemy do on the 13th?' he wrote. 'He can of course engage the defenses and close up to them. Will he attack? That depends on him. Will the attack succeed? The Corps Commander believes not, as the enemy has tanks and infantry to hurl against us, but he needs time to bring up his artillery and suitable equipment for the type of country, all this while being harassed by our artillery. Moreover, their tanks have an impassable object facing them, unless the infantry opens the way for them, and for this they require heavy fire support. What could give them this? Artillery? They have none yet! Tanks? Their guns are not good enough! Their air force? We have complete confidence in our fighters! Conclusion: on the evening of 12 May it seemed that the enemy was not in a position to attack on 13 May, provided that our air force did the same as on 12 May.' The Second Army's fighter group had done rather well on that day, intercepting some German squadrons which were bombing Sedan and French positions along the Meuse. They claimed to have shot down 30 planes for no loss.

The night was not a restful one for X Corps, because the 71st Division (Baudet) which had just arrived after a nine mile march was inserted into the center of the line, relieving the left of the 3rd North African Division (Chapouilly) and the right of the 55th Division (Laf-

ontaine). It would have been better to have kept the 71st Division in reserve in the Stonne-Bulson area. This would have precluded the disruption caused in the defensive layout of the other two divisions, and would have given the men of the 71st a night's rest.

'At dawn on 13 May,' Grandsard tells us, 'enemy activity appeared to be very great. In the whole area, from Vrigne-aux-Bois to Carignan, the enemy emerged from the forest. This was it! Observation-posts everywhere were signaling an almost uninterrupted descent of infantry, of armored vehicles and motorized infantry towards Donchery, the Iges peninsula, Floing, Balan, Bazeilles, and Messincourt. Our artillery reacted, but the battle by remote control was hampered by a break in telephone communications caused by the bombing and by the anxiety to spare the ammunition.' The French had plenty of artillery: there were 140 guns available to support the 55th Division alone. The Germans were splendid targets – for example, 200 tanks were spotted in the outskirts and center of Sedan – but, for fear of running out of ammunition, such targets, which should have been a gunner's delight, were simply sprinkled with shots of from 30 to 80 rounds gunfire. It is obvious that there was no clear policy as to the artillery tactics to be employed.

At about 1100 hours Baudet, whose 71st Division was still far from ready, expressed his concern to Grandsard, who assured him that the German ac-

tivity was simply 'the advance to contact before engagement of the enemy.' But Guderian meant to strike that very day.

During the morning German tanks and anti-tank guns, moving down toward the right bank of the Meuse began to engage the French pillboxes, firing at the loopholes and knocking them out in turn. The French artillery retaliated by knocking out several armored vehicles, but their fire slackened when, about 1100 hours the Stukas began to come over. And on this day no French fighters put in an appearance over Sedan.

The *Luftwaffe*'s attacks were not particularly heavy but they were continuous. Guderian's idea was that: 'The constant attack or threat of attack would paralyze the French batteries in their uncovered gun positions and force the gunners to look for cover from the real or supposed threat from an aircraft.' The moral effect on unprepared troops was all that he could have desired. 'The gunners,' General Edmond Ruby relates, 'stopped firing and went to ground, the infantry cowered in their trenches, dazed by the crash of the bombs and the shriek of the dive-bombers; they had not developed the instinctive reaction of running to their anti-aircraft guns and firing back. Their only concern was to keep their heads well down. They did not dare move. Five hours of this torture was enough to shatter their nerves. They became incapable of reacting to the approaching enemy infantry.

'Anyone who was not blind or deaf,' he writes, 'would have had to admit that an enemy attack was imminent.'

General Lafontaine was of the same opinion, and at 1500 hours warned Grandsard that the Germans were going to attack that evening without further support. Meanwhile at about 1400 hours Grandsard had prudently moved up his reserves. They were the 205th and 213th Infantry Regiments and the 4th and the

Top right: He-52 transport planes prepare to unload their parachutists, who created a spirit of defeatism among civilians.

Right and far right: A parachutist prepares himself and then executes his jump. Parachute units had little tactical use, although their propaganda effect was enormous.

Below: Another drive by German infantry into a forested area in northeastern France.

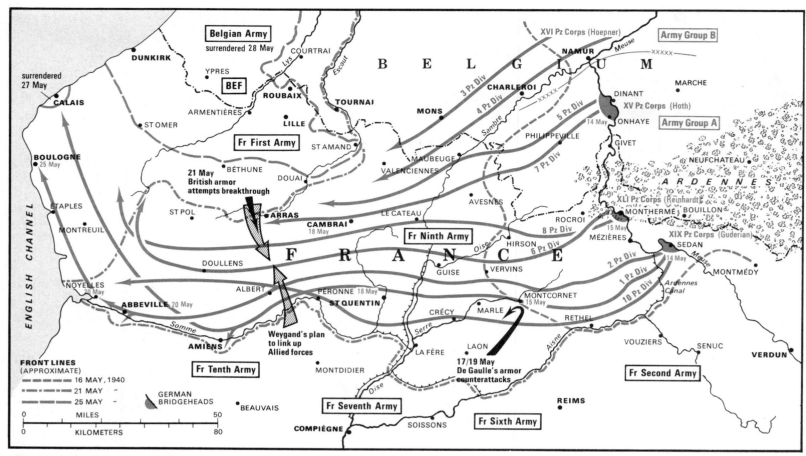

Above: A ten-day sweep to the sea.

Below: Triumphal Wehrmacht troops march forward.

7th battalions of FCM light tanks. The Corps Commander sent this force to prepared positions along the line Chéhéry-Minière Wood – Hayes Wood – Bulson – Gros Bois – Raucourt, which was, he considered 'the most favorable position either to stop the enemy, or as a firm base for a counterattack.'

At 1530 hours the infantry of 1st Panzer Division attacked. 'The assault,' writes Guderian with pardonable exaggeration, 'proceeded as if it had been a training exercise. The French artillery was more or less paralyzed by the ever-present threat of the Stukas and bombers. The concrete works had been destroyed by the anti-tank guns and the *flak*, and the French machine guns were neutralized by our own heavy weapons. In spite of the broad stretches of exposed ground our losses were small.' It was a dashing performance. According to Major Keilmansegg: 'Immediately after the last bombs, under a shower of falling earth, the first pneumatic boats reached the opposite shore. The riflemen, motorcyclists and infantry rushed and encircled the first pillboxes.'

The infantry of the 1st Panzer took the Iges peninsula and pushed on towards Frenois and Marfée Wood. By 1800 hours, according to General Ruby, 'the last flickerings of resistance were com-

pletely extinguished.' Although Keil-mansegg speaks of 'numerous casemates which defended themselves desperately,' it would be idle to pretend that the French infantry had distinguished itself. Nor did the artillery. Ruby tells us how at about 1800 hours, when the bombardment had ceased, General Lafontaine was surveying the situation from his Command Post at Fond-Dagot, south of Bulson, with a view to restoring the position. 'Suddenly a wave of terrified fugitives, gunners and infantry, in transport, on foot, many without arms but dragging their kitbags, swept down the Bulson road. "The tanks are at Bulson!" they cried. Some were firing their rifles like madmen. General Lafontaine and his officers ran in front of them, tried to reason with them, made them put their lorries across the road. . . . Officers were among the deserters. Gunners, especially from the corps' heavy artillery, and infantry soldiers from the 55th Division, were mixed together, terror-stricken and in the grip of mass hysteria. All these men claimed actually to have seen tanks at Bulson and Chaumont! Much worse, commanders at all levels pretended to have received orders to withdraw, but were quite unable to show them or even to say exactly where the orders had come from. Panic brooked no delay; CPs emptied like magic . . . the colonel commanding the corps' heavy artillery and the lieutenant colonel commanding the artillery group allocated to the 55th Division ordered their troops to retreat, and disappeared. (The former subsequently committed suicide.) In the mad flight most of the guns, more or less put out of action, were abandoned.' The Corps lost 800 guns, and the 55th Division had 500 killed on this day. It is not necessary to see in all this evidence that Communist anti-war propaganda had been at work in the ranks, though that has been asserted. It is simply what one may expect when unindoctrinated troops are exposed to the hazards of modern warfare, their minds unprepared for the sights and sounds of battle.

And so poor General Lafontaine was left practically on his own with a few reserve troops to hold out as best he could between the Bar and the Ennemane.

It was not only the troops that had panicked before a single German tank had crossed the Meuse. At 1830 hours, according to General Menu, someone on X Corps Staff had telephoned the 71st Division to say that the Panzers were at Chaumont and were reaching Bulson. By

nightfall the Germans had reached Marfée Wood. Colonel Pinaud, commanding the Frenois subsector, tried to eject them with 3/295 Regiment (55 Division), but, according to Grandsard 'the companies fell back before reaching their prescribed positions.' The Germans pushed on down into the valley of the Bar toward Chéhéry and Cheveges which they occupied, unopposed, at about 2300 hours. The defenders of Croix-Piot Wood, not wishing to be cut off, departed.

That X Corps had been subjected to a thoroughly unpleasant ordeal cannot be denied. At the same time, it should not have been impossible to mount a proper counterattack, and unquestionably Grandsard had enough troops at his disposal to have pitched Guderian's infantry back into the Meuse. But the French generals were not capable of abandoning the tenets of 1918 in a single day, and of coming to terms with the ideas of 1940.

At 2345 hours, Georges sent Gamelin his moderately accurate view of the situation. 'From Second Army: we are holding out east of the Bar; 213th Regiment on line Chémery – Maisoncelle and Villers. Our units fighting in Marfée Wood.(?) Elements of 3rd Armored Division arriving at Chesne as planned. Commander of 3rd Motorized Division preparing to engage. We are confident here.'

Meanwhile German pioneers had rebuilt Gaulier Bridge, and in the darkness of early morning the tanks began to cross the Meuse.

14 May
Rotterdam During the afternoon while General Rudolf Schmidt (XXXIX Corps) was parleying with the Dutch authorities for the surrender of the city, bombers of *Luftflotte* II came over and bombed it. It is said that 25,000 houses were destroyed and 78,000 people rendered homeless. At the time the dead were estimated at 35,000, a figure which has since dwindled to 900 without in any way reducing the horror of the bombing. Meanwhile the Dutch Army had been compelled to withdraw from the Grebbe Line.

Once more Pownall outlines the situation in Belgium. 'Bad news from down south. The Germans, inexplicably, have got across the Meuse in the neighborhood of Sedan and Mézières, . . . The Bomber Command is being turned on from home and . . . we are sending down three squadrons of fighters – no small gesture. Luckily we have just been rein-

A pillar of smoke rises from an ammunition dump destroyed by the British near Dunkirk.

forced from home ... The Air Ministry previously had been impossibly sticky.

'Gort was away from GHQ at Renaix for eight hours today – too long at difficult times, but he did well in heartening Corps Commanders and, especially, the King of the Belgians who like the rest of his Army is in a complete state of wind up ... There have been fights on our right, tanks reported breaking through at Gembloux but later the situation was reported easier. On the other hand at Dinant and Sedan the situation is worse. A defensive battle is a brute of a thing to fight despite Liddell Hart's saying that it is the "strongest form of warfare."'

At 0200 hours the 1st Hussars, raised in 1720 by the Comte de Bercheny, began to move up from Bayonville towards Chagny on its way to help in sealing the breach in the Sedan-Bulson sector. The Regiment was still a mounted one and, so as not to impede the columns that encumbered the road, moved along the verges and in the fields. About 0800 hours when it had just reached Chagny it was pushed on northeastwards to occupy positions abandoned by the infantry. It got to Omont about 1100 hours having marched 40 kilometers, entirely at the trot, in trying heat. The roads were encumbered by elements of the 55th Division, and notably by a column of every sort of vehicle, except guns, belonging to the 45th Regiment of Artillery. This was flowing rearwards in the greatest disorder: 'Few officers, men overexcited and insolent declaring that the Germans were on their heels, atmosphere of panic.' The Hussars and the 8th Chasseurs had to clear the way – *sabres au clair.*

At 0300 hours General Doumenc accompanied by Captain (later General) Andre Beaufre visited General Georges' HQ to find none of the confidence expressed in his midnight message to Gamelin. 'Our front has been broken at Sedan,' cried Georges, and flinging himself into a chair burst into tears. Alphonse-Joseph Georges, now 64, had been a tough battalion commander of World War I and had ended up on Foch's staff. He had been badly wounded when King Alexander of Yugoslavia was assassinated at Marseilles in 1934, and it seems he had never quite got over it. Doumenc did his best to encourage him and to suggest measures to counter the German onslaught.

During the night Corap gave out orders for containing the German bridgehead with a semicircular defensive line from the Meuse at Anhée to the Meuse at Anseramme. He intended to use the 4th North African Division, when it arrived for a counterattack, but in general the tone of his orders was very far from inspiring his troops with the idea of hurling the *Bosche* into the Meuse. Even so the day began with a tonic for French morale.

At 0445 hours Colonel Préaud staged the operation against Haut-le-Wastia, which had been postponed the previous evening. After a short mortar barrage II/14th Motorized Dragoon Regiment and the 1st Divisional Reconnaissance Group seized the village, and took 40 prisoners. 'The 14th Dragoons,' wrote Rommel, 'have given our motorcycle battalion some rough treatment.' But instead of exploiting this success the victors were withdrawn to Corap's 'line of containment.' The Germans were acting in very different fashion. The 28th Infantry Division, crossing the Meuse at Yvoir, took Warnant, Annevoir, and Bioul, enlarging the bridgehead and mopping up the river fortifications. Meanwhile Rommel was slowly assembling the 7th Panzer in the Bouvignes area, with a view to clearing the heights west of the river with his infantry, and then thrusting towards Philippeville.

A battalion of the 39th Regiment (18 Division), which was intended to attack Surinvaux Wood, had somehow got

Right: A French city in the glow of burning buildings on its outskirts. The city is probably Sedan, which was quickly taken in May.

Below: A German unit brings an artillery piece the hard way across the Seine estuary during their astonishing advance.

there during the night 13/14 May. In the morning Rommel's infantry captured it without difficulty. At Rostenne and Hontoire the 66th Regiment put up a respectable resistance, but was overcome. Thereafter the French line drifted back. 'The *Luftwaffe* raged relentless around the sector;' wrote Doumenc, 'communications were cut, orders could not be passed; it became impossible to control the battle.' Rommel pushed on against stiffening resistance in the villages from units of the 4th North African Division, 1st Light Cavalry and 18 Division. He took Anthée and Morville and then settled down for the night.

During the morning the German 32nd Infantry Division crossed the Meuse at Bac-en-Prince, north of Givet, and partly overran the 22nd Division, which fell back in disorder for about six miles, its morale shattered.

In the evening General Martin decided to redeploy XI Corps on a stop line, linking up with XLI Corps, and offering a firm base to 1st Armored Division, which Georges had promised to Corap. Martin summoned his divisional commanders, at about 2000 hours and ordered them to retire to the line Matagne – Chaumont – Oret, with the 22nd Division on the right; 4th North African in the center, barring the way to Philippeville, and the 18th on the left. Corap meanwhile was issuing orders for a general retreat to the defense line on the frontier.

The unfortunate 1st Armored Division was 'messed about.' On the morning of 14 May Billotte finally made up his mind that the main German thrust was against the Ninth rather than the First Army. In giving the division to Corap he hoped, somewhat unrealistically, to clear the Dinant pocket that same day. General Bruneau, its commander only got his orders at 1330 hours. He was then east of Charleroi, some 23 miles from the bridgehead. He called at Martin's Command Post at Florennes at about 1700 hours and was told to assemble in the area Ermeton – Flavion – Corenne – Stave so as to attack in the direction of Dinant as soon as possible. But what with bad staff work and crowded roads the division – less one regiment which lost itself – did not reach its assembly area until between 2000 hours at night and 0300 hours in the morning. Moreover the gasoline trucks, being at the rear of the column, had not yet appeared. General Bruneau was compelled to postpone his attack until the following day.

Meanwhile at Monthermé the 102nd

Above: The remains of Rotterdam after the destruction of the heart of the city on the afternoon of 14 May.

Right: Nazi occupation troops move through the ruins of a French town.

Division was still holding out against Reinhardt's Corps.

Turning to the Sedan sector we find that at 0130 hours Grandsard issued orders for a counterattack at dawn by two regimental groups, the whole under General Lafontaine.

Nobody was ready by dawn and H-hour was postponed to 0700 hours. By this time the 1st Panzer, whose leading brigade had crossed the Meuse between 0500 and 0600 hours, was moving on Chéhéry and Bulson, which meant that it was using the same axes as Lafontaine's columns.

LAFONTAINE

Left (West)	Right (East)
7th Tank Battalion	4th Tank Battalion
213rd Infantry Regiment	205th Infantry Regiment

The West Group started at 0700 hours and advanced unmolested, until half way between Chémery and Chéhéry it was assailed by a large number of Panzers coming from the direction of Connage. The 7th Battalion fought bravely and soon lost 50 tanks. The 1st Panzer Brigade then mauled 213rd Regiment whose survivors took cover in the north edge of Mont Dieu Wood.

After this rude experience Lafontaine called off the attack, deploying his right group along the northern edge of Raucourt Wood.

General Huntziger, the Army commander, now decided that he was too far forward, and moved his Command Post back to Verdun, a move which others will find, as did General Grandsard, 'premature and rather surprising in extent.' At about noon General Baudet (the 71st Division) moved his CP seven miles southwards from Raucourt-et-Flaba to Sommauthe. 'Thus,' as General Ruby remarks, 'he lost all contact with his troops, who, because they were left to themselves, dispersed without even being attacked.' The left of the 3rd North African Division was now exposed.

Early in the morning the 3rd Armored (Brocard) and 3rd Motorized Divisions reached Chesne, nine miles from the battlefield. They had been put under Huntziger so that he could make a serious counterattack at Sedan. At midnight the Second Army had issued its orders. General Flavigny (XXI Corps) was to contain the bottom of the pocket formed by Guderian's advance. Having done that he was to counterattack as soon as possible in the direction Maisoncelle – Bulson – Sedan, so as to clear the area between the Bar and the Ennemane. This operation was to be carried out 'with the utmost energy and disregard for losses.'

It is time to look at things from Guderian's point of view. Early in the morning the 1st Panzer signaled that they had gained ground during the night and were through Chémery. 'So off to Chémery I went. On the banks of the Meuse were thousands of prisoners. At Chémery the commander of the 1st Panzer Division [Kirchner] was giving orders to his subordinate commanders and I listened while he did so. There was a report of strong French armored forces moving up, and he sent the tanks of 1st Panzer Division into the attack towards Stonne to head them off.' Guderian returned to the Meuse bridge and ordered the 2nd Panzer Brigade to move across immediately behind the 1st.

The face of defeat; a British Tommy captured at Dunkirk.

The French attack, that of Lafontaine, was stopped at Bulson with the destruction of 50 tanks. Infantry Regiment *Gross Deutschland* took Bulson and then pushed on towards Villers – Maisoncelle. 'Unfortunately shortly after my departure German dive bombers attacked our troop concentration in Chémery, causing us heavy casualties.'

Near Donchery 2nd Panzer had crossed the Meuse and Guderian went to see how they were getting on. Finding all well he returned to the Meuse. 'There was now a most violent air attack by the enemy. The extremely brave French and English pilots did not succeed in knocking out the bridges, despite the heavy casualties that they suffered. Our anti-aircraft gunners proved themselves on this day, and shot superbly. By evening they calculated that they had accounted for 150 enemy airplanes. The regimental commander, Colonel von Hippel, later received the Knight's Cross for this.'

'Towards midday, to our general delight, the Army Group commander, Colonel General von Rundstedt, arrived to have a look at the situation for himself. I reported our position to him in the very

middle of the bridge, while an air raid was actually in progress. He asked drily: 'Is it always like this here?' I could reply with a clear conscience that it was. He then spoke a few deeply felt words in appreciation of the achievements of our gallant soldiers.'

Guderian now went back to see Kirchner again, who had his GSO1, Major Wenck, with him: 'I asked him whether his whole division could be turned westwards or whether a flank guard should be left facing south on the east back of the Ardennes Canal. Wenck saw fit to interject a somewhat slangy expression of mine, *Klotzen, nicht Kleckern* (the sense of it being to strike concentrated not dispersed—it might be translated roughly as 'Boot 'em, don't spatter 'em') and that really answered my question.' Guderian ordered the 1st and 2nd Panzer 'to change direction with all their forces, to cross the Ardennes Canal, and to head west with the objective of breaking clear through the French defenses.'

Next he visited the CP of 2 Panzer in the Château Rocan above Donchery. 'I was surprised that the French long-range artillery in the Maginot Line and

its westerly extension had not laid down heavier fire and caused us more trouble during our advance. At this moment as I looked at the ground we had come over, the success of our attack struck me as almost a miracle.'

Back at his own HQ that afternoon Guderian made his arrangements for 15 May. By evening the 1st Panzer was across the Ardennes Canal and had taken Singly and Vendresse in the teeth of strenuous resistance. The 10th Panzer had crossed the line Mainsoncelle – Raucourt-et-Flaba, and had reached the high ground south of Bulson and Thelonne, taking more than 40 guns. The village of Stonne had changed hands several times, and both the Infantry Regiment 'G D' and the 10th Panzer had seen hard fighting.

It is plain that if Huntziger was going to eject Guderian from his bridgehead it had got to be no later than 14 May. At 0500 hours Brocard, at Flavigny's CP had issued his orders for an attack in two groups. Start Line: Mont Dieu Wood. H-hour: 1100 hours. 'The enemy will be attacked with the utmost vigor and determination.' But due to the time it took to transmit orders and to refuel the tanks H-hour had been postponed to 1600 hours.

At 1530 hours Flavigny changed his mind. He had been talking to an officer of the shattered 7th Battalion, and had come to the conclusion that he had better do something about containing the bottom of the German pocket, and so, as General Roton tells us: 'he ordered the 3rd Armored Division to organize armored strong points along the whole of the Second Army's area on all the tracks and possible tank runs.' So Brocard had to disperse his tanks in penny packets over a front of 12 miles between Omont and Stonne.

What could be more imbecile?

Brocard may not have been a thunderbolt of war, but with ordinary luck two of the better French divisions, boldly handled, must have made *some* impression had they put in the attack as planned.

Flavigny's plan turned precious tanks into pillboxes.

15 May
At 0730 hours Monsieur Reynaud rang up Winston Churchill and said to him, in English: 'We are defeated.' This statement provoked an outburst of Churchillian prose, and a promise to visit Paris next day. Nevertheless Reynaud concluded as gloomily as he had begun: 'We are defeated; we have lost the battle.'

Above: A German soldier views the effect of an air raid on a northern French village. Below: A shell bursts over the head of a German soldier in eastern France.

Above: Wehrmacht troops move through a flimsy barbed wire defense in their rapid advance.

Below: A German flame thrower in action

At 0930 hours General Winkelman, anxious to spare Utrecht the fate of Rotterdam, signed the instrument of surrender for forces under his direct command. This excepted Zeeland. He had lost 2100 killed, and 2700 wounded. Queen Wilhelmina and her Government went into exile; her efficient navy fought on as well as a merchant fleet of nearly 3,000,000 tons and all her colonies. The French Seventh Army had now to extricate itself as best it could, falling back in some disorder to Antwerp, whence many of its troops were sent to reinforce Blanchard's Army.

Pownall confides to his diary that the Belgians 'simply are not fighting; long loads of very cheerful troops driving along roads west from Brussels.' The present writer, moving up with the 4th Division, recalls meeting a column of horse-drawn Belgian artillery withdrawing through Alost. They were not notably cheerful. Pownall tells us that at the British Embassy at Brussels, there was a conference of British Corps Commanders 'to discuss confidentially the ways

Above: The road of the vanquished, as millions of French refugees stream southward past a column of French prisoners.

Left: An anti-tank gun passes before the Arc de Triomphe in Paris during the occupation on 14 June.

and means of withdrawal if that comes about. It is highly probable that one side or another will give way on our flank. And we don't know which will do it first. With *one* weak flank one can take definite precautions. With two it's the devil to know what needs most doing. A most awkward situation. The day was quiet enough till about 1800 hours when there was a rare flare up. The *Boche* penetrated the division on our right on a 5000 yard front and to a certain depth, getting rather behind our right at Wavre. Barker [I Corps] got into a flat spin. . . .'

By this time the BEF was established on the River Dyle with three Divisions forward.

Two German corps attacked the BEF; X Corps at Louvain, which was held by the 3rd Division and the IV Corps near Wavre on the 2nd Division's front. The British got the better of the fighting and the German Sixth Army reported that

they had not succeeded in penetrating the Dyle position at any point.

On the 1st French Army front IV Corps (General Aymes) had repulsed the tanks of Reichenau's XVI Panzer Corps. But despite these successes both Gort and Blanchard were compelled to order a retreat on the evening of 15 May. Events on the Dinant – Sedan front demanded it. The swift withdrawal of the French endangered that of the VII Belgian Corps, but its commander, General Deffontaine, managed to extricate it. Meanwhile the forts at Liège and Namur were putting up a creditable resistance.

Billotte's chief concern was, of course, to restore the situation on Ninth Army's front, and at 0400 hours he telephoned to Georges: 'It is absolutely essential to put some life into this wavering army. General Giraud, whose vigor is well known, appears to me to be best fitted to take on this difficult task and able to effect the necessary re-invigoration.'

When Giraud reached Corap's CP at Vervins the situation was already beyond repair, largely thanks to his predecessor's incompetence. In the north the II Corps (5th Motorized Infantry Division) was still covering the southern flank of First Army and was no longer in

The railway carriage at Compiègne where the surrender was signed.

touch with the rest of Ninth Army. The XI Corps was in a horrible muddle, as some units had halted on Martin's 'stop line,' and others, obeying Corap's orders were on their way back to the French frontier. Others, it is said, had disbanded and gone home! The unfortunate 1st Armored Division, on the Ermeton-Flavion was out in front of the infantry, waiting for its gasoline. To the south XLI Corps was also cut off from Ninth Army.

At dawn General Bruneau (1st Armored) informed Martin that his refueling would be complete by noon, and asked what he was expected to do then. The Germans gave him his answer.

Hoth's Corps had advanced at dawn, in two divisional columns, the 5th Panzer (Hartlieb) on the right and the 7th Panzer (Rommel) on the left. Contact was made about 0900 hours while the French had just begun refueling from their gasoline tankers. Rommel's right approaching Flavion made the first attack. Bruneau, expecting a withdrawal, had sent five of his six batteries to the rear; but with the support of the remaining one the French tanks fought back. A squadron of Char Bs counterattacked. Despite this Rommel's main body pushed on towards its objective, Philippeville. By noon German tanks were reported approaching Florennes.

During the afternoon Bruneau tried to regroup on the Mettet – Oret road, facing southeast, but in the confused fighting that was going on, this proved extremely difficult. The French lost many tanks simply because they ran out of gasoline. They fought bravely and inflicted many casualties, but by evening when Bruneau withdrew he had only 50 tanks left.

Rommel meanwhile had occupied Philippeville, a disaster which sent the French reeling back to the frontier, where their commanders felt they had some hope of stopping their men. How remote that hope was, Martin tells us. 'The section of the line south of the Maubeuge fortifications (held by the 101st Garrison Division) had absolutely nothing: no occupying troops, no reception units. The first task was to get the engineers to open the doors of the concrete works!'

Still in the Solre-le-Château area, for which both Bruneau and Rommel were making, some pillboxes were opened and occupied that night. The trouble was that, because of the casualties and the confusion, there were not sufficient troops to hold the frontier position. The

Above: A German cemetery in France to commemorate those who fell during the six-week conquest of Western Europe.

Anor passage, for example, was allocated to 22nd Division, but it could only assemble a few hundred men.

Late in the afternoon General Giraud reached Vervins and at 0730 he reported to GHQ: 'No news of the IInd Corps! The 4th North African Division 'appears' to have some units west of Philippeville. No news of the 18th or the 22nd Divisions, which from all accounts are completely disorganized. The 61st Division had abandoned Rocroi ... Enemy tanks are probably at Rumigny and

Liart by now ... I have ordered General Martin to take charge of the defense line within our frontiers. Things look bad.' In the middle of the night it was reported that German tanks were at Montcornet, only 11 miles from Vervins. This was Reinhardt's Corps, which was taking advantage of XLI Corps withdrawal from the Mézières – Monthermé sector. At dawn General Libaud had received orders from Ninth Army to retire. But the 102nd Division had no transport, and that of the 61st Division was too far to the rear: it was compelled to abandon its heavy weapons. Pressed by the German armor these two divisions were soon overtaken. The majority threw down

at 1130 hours, the latter (CP: Senuc) gave out his orders to the GOCs of 3rd Armored and 3rd Motorized Infantry Divisions (General Bertin-Boussu). H-hour was to be 1500 hours. The plan was a methodical one with three objectives: (1) Chéméry, (2) Gros-Bois, (3) Marfée Wood. Two infantry regiments were to attack, with the tanks in support. They were to halt on each objective, take up defensive positions, and await orders before making the next bound. It was good old 1918 stuff, but even so it had a chance of success – even if rather less than on 14 May.

The trouble was that Brocard, with his tanks dispersed on a 12 mile front, could not assemble them in time. H-hour was postponed to 1730 hours. When the tanks still did not turn up Flavigny gave the order to attack with the tanks available at a time to be decided by Bertin-Boussu. Eventually, at about 1700 hours he canceled the order to attack. And so another day was wasted.

Guderian's chief difficulties came not from Huntziger's Army but from orders from von Kleist which asked for 'a halt to all further advance and to any extension of the bridgehead.' Guderian was not having this at any price and, after a heated exchange with his superior, got him to approve of the advance being continued for another 24 hours so as to make his bridgehead big enough to take the infantry corps that were following up.

This day saw some hard fighting on the Vendresse – Omont line. Bouvellemont was stoutly defended by the 53rd Infantry Division – two regiments from Normandy – reinforced by the 15th Dragoons and 3 Brigade of Spahis. The Spahis barricaded in La Horgne defied Kirchner for 10 hours. Their commander, Colonel Marc, was wounded.

In the early afternoon 15 or 20 tanks infiltrated between the 8th Chasseurs and the 1st Hussars, who knocked one of them out with a 25mm anti-tank gun. Then three Chars B compelled the rest to pull back, 'but this was the only action of the Chars B to profit the Regiment, as they disappeared about 1700 hours, called to other missions.' As we know they were due to take part in Flavigny's nonexistent counterattack.

At 1700 hours precisely the Germans hotted up their thrust towards Bouvellemont, after a violent bombardment of guns and mortars the 8th Chasseurs, defending itself bitterly, was compelled to give ground. The 1st Hussars endeavoring to close the breach destroyed

their arms. By nightfall XLI Corps no longer existed.

Guderian got to work early. At his HQ at 0400 hours he and General von Wietersheim discussed the relief by XIV Corps of the Panzers in the Meuse bridgehead south of Sedan. Then they visited the 10th Panzer near Bulson. General Schaal was up forward, but his excellent GSO1, Lieutenant Colonel Freiherr von Liebenstein, explained the situation and its difficulties, and patiently answered von Wietersheim's many detailed questions. The upshot was that the 10th Panzer and Infantry Regiment 'GD' were left under the latter's command so as to cover the

southern flank of XIV Corps along the Ardennes Canal. It was reinforced during the day by the 29th (Motorized) Infantry Division.

Next Guderian went to see the HQ of *Gross Deutschland* at Stonne. 'A French attack was actually in progress when I arrived and I could not find anyone. A certain nervous tension was noticeable, but finally the positions were held.'

At 0630 hours Georges, who had recovered somewhat, had formally ordered Huntziger to mount the counterattack that 3rd Armored Division should have made on the previous day. Huntziger, therefore, told Flavigny to make an offensive on the Bulson – Sedan axis, and, several tanks and scored a direct hit on a *minenwerfer* whose crew were seen sailing through the air. Infiltrating patrols were stopped by machine gun fire, and when night came the regimental front was quiet. Sporadic artillery fire could be heard from the direction of Louvergny and Chagny, and in a violent air battle six planes were shot down. A British pilot parachuted down and was welcomed at the CP of the Bercheny Hussars.

16 May

On 15 and 16 May 93 bombers of the Royal Air Force attacked industrial targets in the Ruhr, which was, no doubt, very irritating to the Germans in general and Hermann Goering in particular, but cannot have brought much comfort to General Billotte.

Pownall gives his usual realistic appreciation of the situation in Belgium:

'I Corps swung back last night successfully though with sharp fighting on right divisional front where the enemy must have followed up pretty closely. The Belgians on our left Louvain – Lier – Antwerp forts are quiet and our II Corps front is all right. We sent [Major General] Eastwood early this morning [0500 hours] to Billotte [at Laudry] to point out that now even a minor withdrawal on our part would leave a shocking salient at Louvain, which would have to be evacuated. This would affect, obviously, the Belgians whom also he is supposed to "co-ordinate." If, therefore, he meant to withdraw further, however little, he should let us know the policy and the timings at once, since we should have to make a big bound back to the Serre Canal.' At 1000 hours GHQ heard that the BEF was indeed to retire to the Serre that very night.

Pownall continues: 'The news from the south is very bad. German mechanized columns are getting deep into France towards Laon and St Quentin. I hope to God the French have some means of stopping them and closing the gap or we are *bust*.'

Early in the day Guderian motored through Vendresse to Omont to visit HQ 1 Panzer. 'The situation at the front was not yet clear.' Guderian pushed on to Bouvellemont and in the main street of the burning village found Lieutenant Colonel Balck, the tough commander of 1st Rifle Regiment, who described the events of the previous night. 'The troops were over-tired, having had no real rest since 9 May. Ammunitiion was running low. The men in the front line were falling asleep in their slit trenches. When

the officers had complained against the continuation of the attack, Balck had replied: "In that case I'll take the place on my own!"' He had moved off and his men had followed. Now, though the French machine guns were still firing down the street, the artillery had ceased fire. Guderian and Balck agreed that resistance was nearly at an end. The Corps Commander gave the tired men a pep talk, and then ordered them to return to their vehicles and carry on with the advance.

'The fog of war that had confused us soon lifted. We were in the open now, with results that were rapidly to be seen.' Guderian pushed on to Montcornet passing a column of the 1st Panzer.

'The men were wide awake now and aware that we had achieved a complete victory, a breakthrough. They cheered and shouted remarks which often could only be heard by the staff officers in the second car: "Well done, old boy" and "There's our old man," and "Did you see him? That was hurrying Heinz," and so on. All this was indicative.'

At Moncornet Guderian met General Kempff (6th Panzer) of XLI Corps and they agreed on a corps boundary and ordered that the advance should continue until the last drop of gasoline was used up. 1st, 2nd and 6th Panzer were pouring through the town, and Guderian's foremost units made 40 miles that day, reaching Marle and Crécy, 55 miles beyond Sedan. In Montcornet the Germans rounded up hundreds of prisoners from several units. Their 'amazement at our being there was plain to see on their faces.'

On this day the 1st French Armored Division found itself at Solre-le-Château. Its strength had fallen to 17. This Giraud evidently did not know for at 1700 hours he ordered them to move to Avesnes and La Capelle and clear the area. They reached Avesnes in the middle of the night and ran into Rommel's advanced guard. A sharp fight followed in which they were destroyed.

The 3rd Armored, whose commander, Brocard, had been dismissed the previous evening, was now found to be incapable for technical and mechanical reasons of launching its long-deferred counterattack, a fact which Huntziger reported at 0500 hours.

This then was the deplorable situation in the French center when in the afternoon Winston Churchill, accompanied by Generals Dill and Ismay, arrived in Paris. At the Quai d'Orsai, with Reynaud and Daladier present, a downcast

Gamelin outlined the situation. The German armor had broken through on a 50 mile front and was dashing forward at incredible speed. Whether it was making for Amiens or Arras or Paris was as yet unknown.

Not unnaturally Churchill asked what plans there were for a counterstroke. '*Où est la masse de manœuvre?*' to be told with a shake of the head and a Gallic shrug '*Aucune.*' Thus with a word General Gamelin destroyed his own reputation as a strategist.

So ended the first great battle of the 1940 campaign. The damage done was past mending.

Now that it was too late, Reynaud took various measures to save the situation. On 18 May he assumed the office of Minister of National Defense. He brought Marshal Pétain, the aged hero of World War I, out of retirement to be Vice-President of the Council, dismissed Gamelin, and recalled General Weygand from Syria to take his place (19 May). Weygand, though still energetic – at least in the morning – was even older than Gamelin. He could make plans which looked convincing on paper, but related to nothing that was actually taking place on the ground.

Meanwhile the Germans were rushing on. St Quentin fell on 18 May and Amiens on 20 May. Gort tried hard to improvise some resistance to their onrush, and managed to hang on to Arras until 24 May and even launch a counterstroke by two battalion groups supported by tanks (21 May). This had a sobering effect on Panzer Group Kleist. The spirited defense of Boulogne (19–25 May) and Calais (22–26 May) further delayed the German armor.

Von Bock's Army Group B kept up a steady pressure against the armies cut off in the North. General Billotte was mortally injured in a motor accident on 21 May and Weygand did not confirm Blanchard as his successor until 25 May. So to add to the confusion there was very little co-ordination. The Allies successfully held out on the Escaut from 19 May to 22 May when the BEF fell back to the Gort Line on the Franco-Belgian frontier. There followed the desperate battle of the Ypres-Comines Canal (27–28 May), in which General Brooke (II Corps) and General Franklyn (5 Division), who, fortunately had a captured copy of the German operation order, beat off an attack which could have dealt the *coup de grace* to the BEF and the First French Army.

The evacuation of Allied troops from

Dunkirk began on 26/27 May and did not finish until 4 June, by which time 338,226 men had been evacuated.

Belgium did not surrender until 28 May. Her relatively ill-equipped army had acquitted itself well under all the circumstances. Those who are inclined to be critical of their performance should take a look at the map, and consider what would have happened, if the Belgians had packed up on, say, 25 May.

On 23 May Colonel General von Rundstedt gave orders to the Fourth Army for a halt. Hitler agreed with this on the following day, but it was *not* his idea. It is true that the Dunkirk perimeter is unfavorable for tanks, but had the advance continued the plight of the BEF would have been even worse than it was. In the event the British got away with the nucleus of the armies which were to fight the Germans in Africa and Italy; in Normandy and Germany. One wonders whether upon reflection von Rundstedt may not have lived to regret the decision to order a halt on 23 May 1940.

The Battle of the Meuse, then, led inevitably to the Dunkirk evacuation, and the fall of France. To seal the breaches torn at Dinant and Sedan noth-ing could serve but prompt counter-strokes by armored divisions, and, as we have seen, the French, though they ordered counterattacks, made little practical effort to mount them.

It is easy to attribute the fall of France to a lack of courage on the part of her fighting men. And certainly it was not only the politicians that failed. But what is courage? In some fighting men it is simply a gift, but they are few. It is largely moral, partly physical. It is displayed not only by the dash, the thrust, that a soldier puts into his actions, but by the resolute tenacity with which he holds on in the bad times, and in war even the victor often has a bad time.

The commander must nurse the courage of his men. He must use his imagination in preparing the soldier for the ordeals that lie ahead. This is done by explaining to him the hazards unavoidable in any operation, so that he will not be surprised, and therefore liable to panic. It consists in hardening his body by marches and every sort of physical exercise. It consists in giving him tactical training, so that he will not throw away his life needlessly, and so that he will know how to take advantage of the enemy. It consists in making him a master with his weapon, so that, if he comes face to face with a group of the enemy, he will set about them with confidence. His training must be tough enough to give him a sense of achievement. Lastly he must be well indoctrinated so that he will cheerfully hazard himself in the cause he fights for, and so that he will close his ears to sedition and rumor. There were plenty of brave men in the French Army of 1940, but what had its commanders, from Gamelin downward, done to prepare the ordinary soldier, who may as easily become a coward as a hero, for the ordeal that lay ahead? The Allied soldiers, who fell in 1940 were a sacrifice to the conservatism and complacency of Gamelin and the French High Command, as much as to their political masters.

The Germans had every reason to be pleased with themselves for their brilliant passage of the Meuse. But thereafter they had more than a fleeting chance to destroy the personnel as well as the *materiel* of the BEF. Had that been achieved it is not impossible that they would have won the war.

Below: British dead on the beach at Dunkirk after the Germans had taken the port.

THE BATTLE OF BRITAIN 1940

On 2 July 1940 Adolf Hitler authorized the preparation of provisional plans for the invasion of Britain. It marked the culmination of a remarkable string of German military successes. Since 10 May the army and air force, in a brilliant display of mutual support, had overrun France and the Low Countries, forcing the British Army to withdraw from Europe in such haste that the bulk of its equipment and a significant proportion of its manpower had been left behind. The next logical step was the conquest of Britain itself, thus securing the western flank of the new German Empire preparatory to the main assault upon the USSR. On paper the idea was both feasible and tempting, for the Channel, less than 22 miles wide at its narrowest point, appeared to be little more than a large river, the British Army was clearly beaten and the German forces were at a fever pitch of morale.

But in wartime things are rarely as simple as they seem, and this was no exception. Hitler himself, although aware of the importance of destroying Britain as a future base for the re-invasion of Europe, was preoccupied with his projected campaign against ideological enemies in the East and imagined that some sort of peace settlement could be made with the British government. If this failed, then the most he would plan for was a very swift victory which would release troops and equipment for the war against Russia. This posed problems. The German Naval Staff, under Grand Admiral Erich Raeder, was dubious about the ability of its force to ferry sufficient troops across the Channel to establish a viable bridgehead in southern England, expressing deep fears not only about the Royal Navy, as yet virtually untouched by the war, but also about the Royal Air Force, enough of which had survived the French campaign to mount telling attacks upon vulnerable shipping. In addition, the Army itself had neither the experience nor the equipment to carry out a seaborne invasion, having never foreseen such a contingency and lacking even the

most mundane items such as landing craft or troop-carrying barges. In the end only one man expressed overwhelming confidence, and that was Hermann Goering, Commander in Chief of the Luftwaffe. An ex-fighter pilot of World War I with 22 credited air victories to his name, he was convinced that, given a period of fine weather and the necessary political backing, he could destroy what remained of the RAF, gain air superiority over the Channel and southern England for the duration of the invasion and even, if permitted to go that far, destroy Britain and her will to resist through aerial attack.

Nor was this an entirely idle boast, for there was no doubting the efficiency and power of the Luftwaffe. Denied an air force by the terms of the Versailles Treaty in 1919, members of the German army, with political support, had laid the foundations for future expansion as early as the 1920s, exploiting a loophole in the peace settlement which permitted the establishment of a civil airline. Lufthansa was set up in 1926 and used extensively as a cover for the training of military pilots, some of whom were sent to Soviet Russia and Italy to gain experience. At the same time experiments with aircraft design were carried out by German engineers in Sweden, and as early as 1928 the prototype of a dive bomber – the forerunner of the Ju 87 Stuka – had been successfully tested. In 1933, when Hitler came to power, the terms of Versailles were gradually undermined or openly flouted, and when Goering was appointed Air Minister the embryonic Luftwaffe was allowed to blossom. By the mid-1930s it had developed into one of the most modern air forces in existence, sporting an impressive mix of fighters, dive bombers and medium bombers. All it lacked was combat experience.

That came in 1936, when a special 'Condor Legion' was sent to Spain to aid the Nationalist forces under General Franco. Its success was stunning, contributing decisively on more than one occasion as Ju 87 dive bombers, co-

Above: Me-110s after take-off from a French field on their way to Britain. Even the shorter flying time did not enable Luftwaffe planes to remain over their targets for more than a few minutes.

Above: A Hawker Hurricane IIB, one of the two principal fighting aircraft used by the RAF in the Battle of Britain.

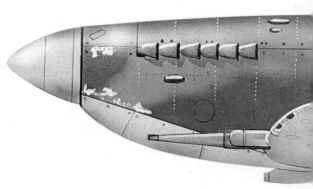

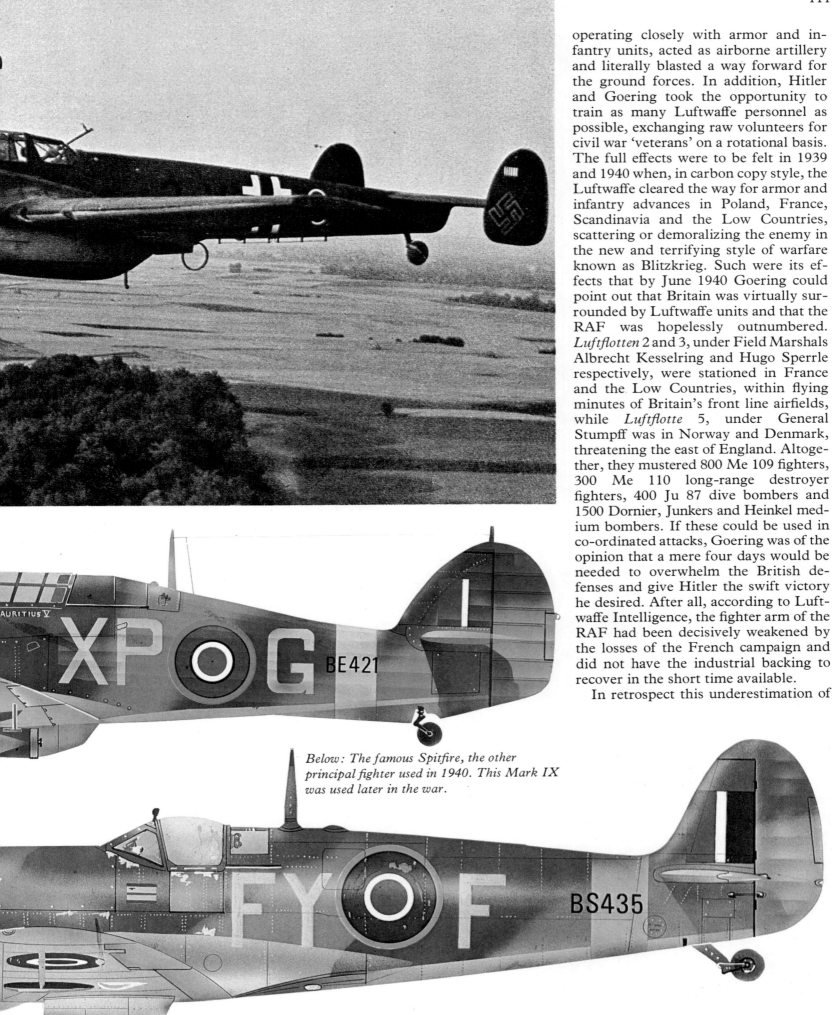

operating closely with armor and infantry units, acted as airborne artillery and literally blasted a way forward for the ground forces. In addition, Hitler and Goering took the opportunity to train as many Luftwaffe personnel as possible, exchanging raw volunteers for civil war 'veterans' on a rotational basis. The full effects were to be felt in 1939 and 1940 when, in carbon copy style, the Luftwaffe cleared the way for armor and infantry advances in Poland, France, Scandinavia and the Low Countries, scattering or demoralizing the enemy in the new and terrifying style of warfare known as Blitzkrieg. Such were its effects that by June 1940 Goering could point out that Britain was virtually surrounded by Luftwaffe units and that the RAF was hopelessly outnumbered. *Luftflotten* 2 and 3, under Field Marshals Albrecht Kesselring and Hugo Sperrle respectively, were stationed in France and the Low Countries, within flying minutes of Britain's front line airfields, while *Luftflotte* 5, under General Stumpff was in Norway and Denmark, threatening the east of England. Altogether, they mustered 800 Me 109 fighters, 300 Me 110 long-range destroyer fighters, 400 Ju 87 dive bombers and 1500 Dornier, Junkers and Heinkel medium bombers. If these could be used in co-ordinated attacks, Goering was of the opinion that a mere four days would be needed to overwhelm the British defenses and give Hitler the swift victory he desired. After all, according to Luftwaffe Intelligence, the fighter arm of the RAF had been decisively weakened by the losses of the French campaign and did not have the industrial backing to recover in the short time available.

In retrospect this underestimation of

Below: The famous Spitfire, the other principal fighter used in 1940. This Mark IX was used later in the war.

112

No 85 Squadron of Hawker Hurricanes of the RAF take to the skies to defend Britain.

RAF pilots scramble to reach their planes as another wave of German bombers approaches.

German photograph of an attack on an RAF base as Spitfires are destroyed on the ground.

RAF potential assumes crucial importance, but in the context of the time it was understandable. For much of the peacetime period, while the Luftwaffe was being formed in secret, the RAF had suffered from two major problems which cast serious doubts upon its war capabilities. On the one hand, as the country experienced severe economic crisis, it was kept desperately short of money, competing for funds not only with the more urgent needs of society at large, but also with the army and navy, neither of which was entirely convinced about the necessity for an independent air service. This produced the second problem, for in an attempt to justify their independence, successive Chiefs of the Air Staff stressed the importance of a strategic bombing fleet, capable of hitting the enemy homeland so hard at the beginning of a future war that his bombers would be unable to attack England. This argument implied in turn that neither side would be stopped by air-defense systems – a consideration given a degree of official credence in 1932 when the Prime Minister, Stanley Baldwin, openly announced that 'the bomber will always get through.' In such circumstances, fighter development obviously suffered, and at a time when the Germans were producing the prototypes of their modern machines, England was still defended by obsolete bi-planes. Admittedly the Spitfire and Hurricane first flew in 1934 and 1935 respectively, but without the dedication and enterprise of their manufacturers, financial stringency and official preference for bombers could easily have prevented their evolution. As it was, in 1938 at the time of the Munich Crisis, out of 30 operational RAF fighter squadrons, only one was equipped with Spitfires and five with Hurricanes. The air defense of England was clearly a very flimsy structure, and when the losses in France between 10 May and 4 June were taken into account some 430 front-line fighters – there appeared to be little to prevent an easy victory for Goering and his battle-hardened flyers.

But the picture was incomplete on a number of counts. A massive rearmament program immediately after Munich had rushed the Spitfire and Hurricane into mass production, so that by July 1940 only one squadron in England was still operating biplanes, and although some front line aircraft such as the twin-engine Blenheim and turret-armed Defiant were poorly designed for interceptor work, Fighter Command was a revitalized force. In addition, in-

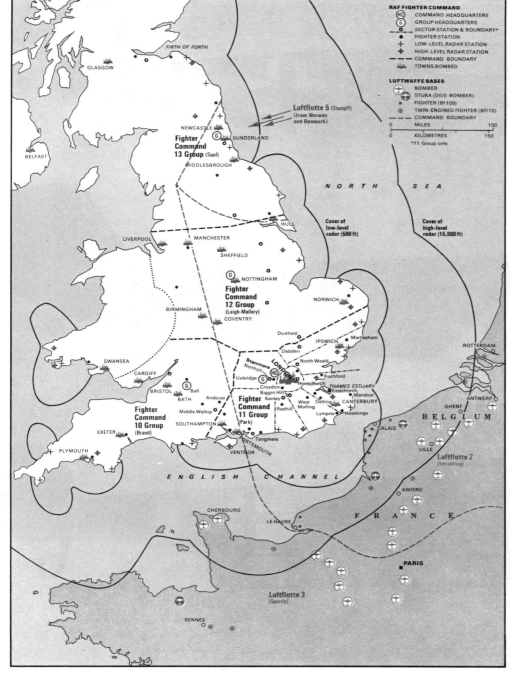

Above: The British defensive posture and the location of forward airfields in German hands.

Below: Dornier-17 bombers over West Ham in London in September 1940.

dustrial back up had been much improved, particularly when, in May 1940, the Canadian-born Lord Beaverbrook was appointed Minister of Aircraft Production by the new Prime Minister, Winston Churchill. Beaverbrook's 'vital, vibrant energy' cut through the red tape of existing industrial plans and achieved remarkable results. In the month before his appointment 256 fighters were produced – a figure quite close to that put forward by Luftwaffe Intelligence in their estimation of RAF replacement rates – but by September, at the height of the battle, this had risen to the staggering figure of 467. The losses in France could therefore be replaced in a far shorter time than the enemy imagined possible, although it is worth noting that if Churchill had not prohibited the transfer of more squadrons to the continent as early as 19 May, the problem could have been far worse.

Fighter aircraft are only a part of any air defense system, however, and in 1940 the British had other advantages unknown to the enemy. The elaborate measures introduced to counter the Gotha and Giant raids of 1917–18 may have been allowed to lapse during the interwar period, but the experience counted for much. Indeed, when Air Chief Marshal Sir Hugh Dowding was appointed in 1936 to build up Fighter Command and take charge of the entire defensive structure, he merely reintroduced many of the ideas from World War I, creating anti-aircraft barrage lines, fighter patrol areas, observer stations, searchlight companies and balloon sites. As World War II approached, he also gained a weapon which Major General Ashmore would probably have given his right arm to possess in 1918, and that was radar. Developed by British scientists under Robert Watson-Watt, who discovered that radio beams could be bounced off approaching aircraft, giving fairly accurate readings of height, numbers and direction, the first radar masts were built on the southern coast of England in 1938. The Germans expressed interest, even sending one of the old Zeppelin airships to investigate in 1939, before the war began, but monitoring instruments failed to discover the true nature of the masts and they were dismissed as unimportant. It was to be a decisive oversight. With early warning of this kind, Dowding was able to prepare his defenses, particularly in the crucial area of southeast England, as the Germans approached, stationing interceptors above the expected line of attack to achieve

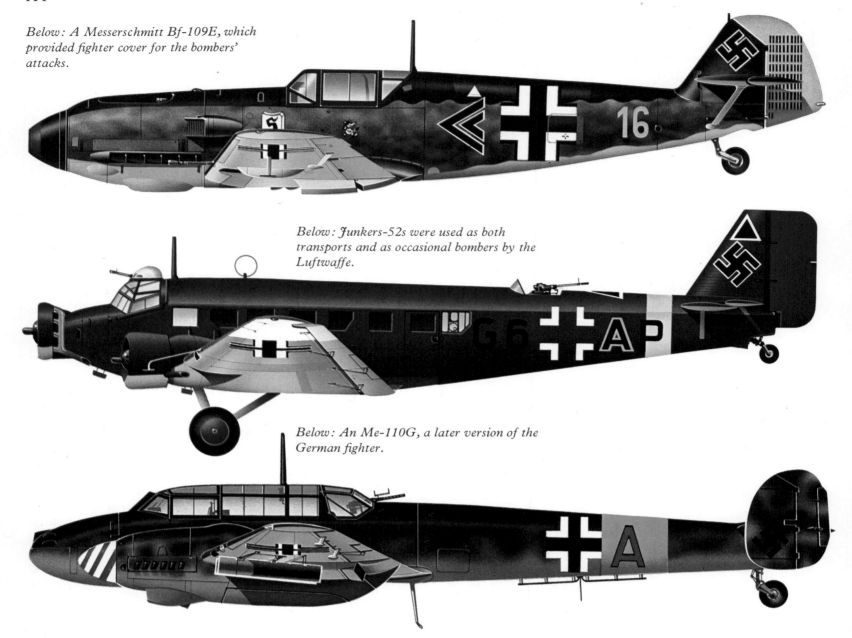

Below: A Messerschmitt Bf-109E, which provided fighter cover for the bombers' attacks.

Below: Junkers-52s were used as both transports and as occasional bombers by the Luftwaffe.

Below: An Me-110G, a later version of the German fighter.

surprise. As the RAF could muster only 600 front-line fighters in early July, less than a third of which were actually in the southeast, the advantage was clearly important.

Even so, with 3000 fighters and bombers available, the Luftwaffe should have been able to overwhelm the British defenses if it had been concentrated in a single blow. But this was not to be, for from the start of the battle Goering wasted his resources. On 10 July, confident of easy victory but lacking political support for an all-out attack, he opened hostilities by ordering his airmen to destroy British shipping in the Channel. A convoy was selected and in the early afternoon a force of some 70 aircraft put in their assault. The RAF reacted cautiously, relieved that the English mainland was not the target but mindful that it could be a trap designed either to lure Fighter Command away from the main

attack or to tempt it into a fatal war of attrition. Nevertheless, Air Vice-Marshal Keith Park, commanding No 11 Group in the southeast, could not ignore the convoy attack entirely, and ordered a mixed force of 26 Spitfires and Hurricanes to intervene. A dogfight ensued, during which the convoy escaped and the Luftwaffe lost four aircraft to the British three: a victory for the RAF which merely served to worry Dowding and Park. If losses continued even at that rate, it would not be long before the Luftwaffe achieved air superiority purely through an advantage of numbers. The choice was clear – either the ships using the Channel had to make do with a token protective screen or the battle would be lost before it had really begun.

The decision not to hurl No 11 Group *en masse* against the Luftwaffe attacks was difficult and, inevitably, unpopular with the fighter pilots who were keen to

see action, but in the event it proved wise. Goering was only testing British defenses and attempting to lure the Spitfires and Hurricanes into combat over relatively unimportant targets. But he persisted in this policy for over a month, leaving radar stations, airfields and aircraft factories in southern England untouched, enabling Dowding to complete his defensive structure and build up a useful reserve of newly-manufactured fighters. During this period the Luftwaffe was not completely devoid of success – on 25 July elements of *Luftflotte* 2 sank five ships and crippled a further six, following it up two days later with the destruction of two destroyers – but they suffered disproportionate losses whenever the RAF appeared. Both the Spitfire and Hurricane proved to be more maneuverable and better armed than their adversaries, and although the Me 109 had advantages of speed and a

Above: Supermarine Spitfires cruising at 300mph at 6000 feet over East Anglia.
Right: Hugh 'Stuffy' Dowding, the unsung hero of Fighter Command in the Battle of Britain.

better rate of climb, Luftwaffe losses mounted. By 23 July 85 aircraft of *Luftflotten* 2 and 3 had failed to return from attacks upon targets which were, in the final analysis, of peripheral importance to Goering's stated aim of achieving a swift and total victory.

The need for a change of tactics was discussed by the Luftwaffe chiefs as early as 30 July, when the *Luftflotten* were first put on the alert for *Adlertag* or Eagle Day, a code name for concerted assaults upon southern England which were 'to destroy the flying units, ground organizations and supply installations of the RAF and the British air armaments industry.' But definite orders were delayed, chiefly by Hitler's refusal to issue specific instructions for the invasion, and in the meantime the convoy attacks continued as before, with both sides gradually committing larger forces. Then, on 12 August, the Luftwaffe suddenly changed tack, concentrating upon radar stations and front-line airfields. The RAF was caught unawares, and for a time it looked as if the assault would achieve damaging results as the radar station at Ventnor on the Isle of Wight was destroyed and the crucial airfields at Manston, Hawkinge and Lympne came under sustained attack. Once again, however, Goering's lack of a definite plan was apparent, for by the afternoon of the same day it was the convoys that were suffering. With 31 aircraft destroyed to the RAF's 22, the Luftwaffe had successfully warned Dowding of future trends and lost the important element of surprise. The effects were to be felt within 24 hours, when Goering finally decided to instigate Eagle Day. It was to be an anticlimax.

Orders for the sustained attack were sent to *Luftflotten* 2 and 3 late on 12 August, demanding a full-scale commitment of available bombers with fighter support, the idea being to force the RAF into a major battle with the Me 109s and 110s while the Junkers, Dorniers and Heinkels hit the ground defenses. Unfortunately 13 August began with bad weather, and although the orders were canceled, not all the squadrons were told in time. By 1730 hours a force of over 70 Dornier 12s was in the air looking for fighter escorts which had been recalled, and when they went on alone they were pounced upon by Hurricanes, losing five of their number within as many minutes. At the same time a force of Junkers 88s, briefed to attack the research and development establishment at Farn-

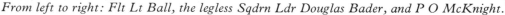

From left to right: Flt Lt Ball, the legless Sqdrn Ldr Douglas Bader, and P O McKnight.

Group Captain Leonard Cheshire.

borough, lost its way in low cloud, missed the target entirely and was forced to fight its way home, leaving two if its number behind. Later in the morning, in a reverse of the earlier error, 30 Me 110s, intended as an escort for bombers which never turned up, were routed by two squadrons of Spitfires, losing five machines in six minutes. A pause ensued, but Goering refused to accept defeat. In the afternoon 90 heavily-escorted bombers tried to overwhelm the southern defenses by attacking airfields as well as the docks at Southampton. It was a tall order, reflecting the foolish optimism of the Luftwaffe chiefs, and little was achieved. By early evening, having flown a total of 1485 individual sorties for the loss of 45 aircraft, the German attacks fizzled out. As the RAF had lost only 13 fighters, Eagle Day had failed to live up to expectations.

This proved to be only the beginning, however, for the true test of RAF defenses had yet to come. After a 24 hour respite, Goering ordered all three *Luftflotten* to attack simultaneously, on the assumption that the only way the RAF could replace reported losses was to concentrate a dwindling fighter force in the southeast. By attacking from Scandinavia, as well as France and the Low Countries, the defenses would be stretched to the point of collapse as squadrons were rushed round the country in answer to threats. In theory it was a fair argument, but Goering did not have access to

the RAF loss figures (reported losses on both sides were always far higher than actual losses, as in the *melée* of an air battle more than one pilot would claim the destruction of an enemy machine) and did not know about Beaverbrook's successes with aircraft production. Furthermore, Dowding had always made it a policy to leave each of his four Groups – No 10 in the southwest, 11 in the southeast, 12 in the Midlands and 13 in the north – as intact as possible, regardless of pressure upon any one of them. The Luftwaffe then came across squadrons of fighters as yet untouched, piloted by men who were eager to join a battle which they felt was passing them by.

The effects of this miscalculation were felt on 15 August by *Luftflotte* 5, when a force of 65 Heinkel 111s, escorted by 34 Me 110s, took off from Norway and Denmark to attack airfields in Yorkshire and the northeast. They were tracked by radar as they crossed the North Sea, enabling Air Vice-Marshal Richard Saul of No 13 Group to scramble every available aircraft in good time. Three squadrons of Spitfires, one of Hurricanes and even one of Blenheims intercepted the enemy 30 miles off the coast, attacking out of the sun to destroy eight of the bombers and seven of the escorts without loss to themselves. Further south, about fifty Ju 88s, also of *Luftflotte* 5, fared slightly better, breaking the defenses and bombing an airfield at Great Driffield in southern Yorkshire, but they too experi-

enced the full effect of untried squadrons, this time of Air Vice-Marshal Trafford Leigh-Mallory's No 12 Group. Eight of the bombers failed to return, increasing German losses to 23 aircraft; a fact which persuaded Stumpff to pull out of the battle. *Luftflotte* 5 never again attacked England during the hours of daylight.

Such a victory obviously did wonders for British morale, but in the south the battle continued. While *Luftflotte* 5 suffered, the aircraft of *Luftflotten* 2 and 3, in a rare example of complete cooperation, concentrated upon the major airfields of No 11 Group. In mid-morning 40 Ju 87s, escorted by 60 Me 109s and 110s, attacked Lympne and Hawkinge, important sector stations on the Kent coast. Lympne was devastated and although Hawkinge escaped the worst, two radar stations in the vicinity were completely destroyed. An hour later 12 Me 109s strafed Manston to the north, knocking out two Spitfires on the ground, and at 1500 hours Martlesham Heath near Ipswich was hit by Ju 87s. Meanwhile, to the west, airfields in Hampshire and Wiltshire were assaulted by 250 aircraft of *Luftflotte* 3, and it began to look as if the Luftwaffe at last had picked upon a definite strategy. Dowding was understandably worried, particularly as the attacks continued into the evening when Kenley, Biggin Hill and West Malling, on the direct air route to London, became targets. The Luft-

London docks and Tower Bridge after the first major air raid on 7 September 1940.   *Below: Anti-aircraft gun crews.*

waffe even kept up the pressure after nightfall, and although the 70 bombers involved did little damage, they did represent a new and perplexing trend of concentration which had been missing so far.

By 16 August, therefore, Goering was feeling satisfied, in spite of the setbacks in the north. According to the calculations of his Intelligence officers the Luftwaffe losses of the previous day were well worth sustaining, for despite the failure of 75 aircraft to return, the RAF was almost finished, having lost a reported total of 770 fighters since the beginning of the battle. A little more pressure, and victory would be assured. But once again, the calculations were wrong. Dowding had in fact lost about 220 of his machines – a figure which was more than canceled out by industrial replacements – and was far more worried about a lack of trained pilots. Even in this respect he enjoyed an important advantage, however, for the majority of British airmen who survived having their aircraft destroyed parachuted down onto friendly soil and could be back with their squadrons in a matter of hours. Their German rivals faced nothing but a prisoner of war camp for the duration of the conflict. Almost imperceptibly, the odds were stacking up against the Luftwaffe.

Two further factors contributed to this gradual loss of initiative. On the one hand, after another 71 German aircraft had failed to return from raids on Eng-

Fires break out during an air blitz by the Luftwaffe near St Paul's Cathedral, London.

lish airfields on 18 August, Goering insisted that his fighter pilots pay more attention to the close protection of bombers, a policy which successfully restricted the Me 109s at a time when they could have played a decisive role. After all, although Dowding had nearly 600 Spitfires and Hurricanes to pit against the 700 Me 109s of *Luftflotten* 2 and 3, he still insisted on keeping a proportion outside the area of Park's command, leaving only about 200 actually in the southeast. If the battle had been just between fighters, the Luftwaffe would have been far more effective; Goering's order of 18 August merely took away one of the dwindling number of advantages he had left. At the same time, any plans for a sustained assault upon Britain had to be temporarily shelved when, between 19 and 23 August, poor weather imposed a halt upon all operations. Dowding took the opportunity to rest and re-equip his tired force, and awaited a resumption of hostilities.

The Luftwaffe attacked again on 24 August, using new tactics. In the early morning the radar screens of southern England showed a force of about 100 aircraft gathering over Calais for what looked like an attack on Dover. Squadrons were scrambled and defenses alerted, but the force evaporated. The fighters came down to refuel, only to be caught on the ground by a series of small, sharp attacks upon forward airfields, the worst of which hit Manston, where a squadron of Defiants was decimated. Manston itself was abandoned. The pattern was repeated thereafter for over a week, in a campaign which seemed to offer almost certain victory to the Germans. Airfield after airfield was attacked, with special attention being paid to Biggin Hill, a sector station essential to the defense of London from the south. By 6 September Dowding's defenses were reeling and the battle seemed to be going Goering's way. But at the last moment he made yet another change of policy. Realizing that, regardless of Intelligence estimates, Fighter Command was not being wiped out and victory was not going to be achieved in four days or even four weeks at the present rate of progress, the Luftwaffe leader made what many commentators regard as his cardinal error. He called off the airfield attacks and ordered a complete concentration upon London.

Hitler had, up to now, prohibited direct attacks upon the English capital, partly to prevent a strategic bombing campaign which could only result in the

Above: St Paul's Cathedral during the blitz.   *Below: German bomber crew receives its instructions.*

German fighter pilots don their parachutes.

Above: Stukas prepare to strike, although they were ineffective in the Battle of Britain.
Below: German bomber crews study maps and determine their next targets.

RAF hitting German cities in retaliation, and partly because of his continuing hope for a peace settlement which would allow him to concentrate on Russia. Unfortunately, his arguments were undermined considerably when, on the night of 24/25 August a group of ten Luftwaffe bombers, briefed to attack oil-storage tanks at Thameshaven, were confused by the British defenses and, in something of a panic, dropped their bombs over London itself. The attack was almost certainly a mistake, but to the British government it looked like the beginning of the city-destruction campaign they had feared since the first day of the war. Bomber Command, formed specifically to reply to any such campaign, was ordered to bomb Berlin, and any reservations felt by either side about strategic bombing promptly disappeared. By 6 September Goering had received the go ahead for the aerial bombardment of London around the clock, it being planned that the RAF fighters would be forced into a massive air battle which they could not hope to win.

Goering was so convinced that this was to mark the culmination of his assault upon Britain that on 7 September he traveled by special train to Cap Gris Nez in northern France to view proceedings. While standing on the cliffs, with the English coast clearly visible across the Channel, he watched 300 bombers and 600 fighters fly toward London, nearly 70 miles away. Late in the afternoon this force hit the East End docks, causing considerable damage and, once more, the initiative seemed to swing in favor of the Germans. Dowding, caught unawares by this sudden change of target, had put his fighters up to defend the southern airfields and they had been unable to attack the bomber stream on its way in. Forty-one Luftwaffe aircraft had been destroyed by early evening, with the RAF losing 28, but the damage to London and to British morale had been significant. The situation was not helped when *Luftflotte* 3 took up the assault after nightfall for, in a repetition of the problems of 1917–18, London's anti-aircraft guns proved ineffective and night-flying skills were poor.

This pattern was repeated, day after day as the weather permitted, for nearly two weeks, with the largest raid being mounted on 15 September – a date chosen by the British after the war to mark the climax and turning point of the battle. On that morning the radar screens in Park's command post at Uxbridge showed a large enemy force, estimated to consist of 100 bombers and 400 fighters, aiming for London. Clearly the Germans, convinced that Fighter Command was in its death throes (their intelligence estimates were now proclaiming nearly 2000 RAF machines destroyed since early July – a larger number than Dowding had ever possessed, even with replacements) were intent upon a major air battle. Park made sure they were not disappointed, scrambling 11 of his 21 squadrons and calling upon No 10 Group to help out. At the same time Douglas Bader, the famous legless fighter ace, received permission to try out an experiment with 60 aircraft, organized into a huge 'Wing,' which would fly down from No 12 Group. Spitfires were ordered to go for the Me 109s, leaving the bombers to the Hurricanes.

The German attack went in at noon, and although some bombers managed to get through to Central London, it was against amazing opposition. All the way there and all the way back, squadron after squadron of British fighters tore into the Luftwaffe units until, over Kent, Bader's 'Wing' came tearing out of the north, sweeping all before them. It was the biggest shock experienced by the Luftwaffe so far in the battle, and the heart went out of their attack. Another force of 100 bombers and 300 fighters returned in the afternoon, to be intercepted with almost equal force, but to the most casual observer it was obvious that the Germans had suffered a major defeat. Sixty of their aircraft lay burning on the route to London, together with 26 of the RAF, but the initiative had passed

People of Coventry after the destruction of their city.

to the British. By 16 September Hitler, for one, had recognized this, for he postponed the invasion until 1941 – a fact which those closest to him realized was tantamount to cancellation: from now on the USSR was to be the enemy.

Poor weather between 17 and 23 September seemed to underline the British victory, for no German raids were put in, but this did not mean that Goering had given up. Angry that his boast of a quick victory had turned into something of a nightmare, he ordered yet another change of tactics, this time deciding upon selective attacks upon aircraft factories in the south. On 24 September, when the weather cleared, the Spitfire plant at Southampton was hit by Me 109s, some of which had been converted to a bombing role, and 24 hours later a factory at Bristol suffered the same fate. The trend was worrying, for if RAF losses could not be replaced, the battle might still be lost. But Dowding's fears did not last, for on 27 September there was a switch back to the earlier tactics of escorted day bombing of English cities when 80 Ju 88s, He 111s and Do 17s, with fighter support, headed for Bristol and 100 for London. The RAF swung into action as before, reinforcing their earlier success by destroying a further 55

enemy machines. Goering seemed intent upon demoralizing the British people by the razing of major cities: a policy which could only favor Fighter Command. As airfields, radar stations and aircraft factories escaped attack, the defenses as a whole could be strengthened and expanded. The Luftwaffe tried to escape by bombing from greater and greater altitudes – by mid-October the air battles were taking place at 30,000 feet, the limit of RAF fighter ceiling – but the only effect was a loss of accuracy. By early November, after an abortive and rather farcical attack upon London by elements of the Italian Air Force which resulted in the British destroying six aircraft for no loss to themselves, the daylight raids were phased out, to be replaced by a night-time campaign against all British cities, starting with Coventry on 14 September. The Battle of Britain was over – the 'Blitz' was about to begin.

Reviewing the course of the Battle, it is apparent that the Germans lost eventually because of their lack of concentration upon specific targets. By the beginning of October, after 12 weeks of fighting, the Luftwaffe had tried everything, but had never maintained their assault upon worthwhile tactical or strategic targets for long enough to be de-

The Elephant and Castle underground station was a makeshift air raid shelter.

cisive. Between 10 July and 12 August, in a parade of strength over the Channel, they had wasted the element of surprise and given Dowding time to build up his defenses. This had been followed, between 13 August and 6 September, by the sustained assaults upon Fighter Command airfields which understandably worried the British, but just when the defenses were reeling, the target was shifted to London. The small, sharp raids on aircraft factories three weeks later seemed equally perplexing, but once again, the Luftwaffe moved elsewhere before a decision could be forced. It was almost as if Goering, in a stubborn display of optimism, could not understand why the enemy did not give up as soon as the Luftwaffe appeared, and this was manifested not only in his inability to find a policy and stick to it, but also in his refusal to accept that his force was perhaps not suited to this type of warfare. After all, the Luftwaffe had been formed originally to support the army in its Blitzkrieg operations and was not designed to win or even maintain basic air superiority in the face of organized opposition. Its bombers were useful when it came to blasting poorly-defended localities in front of advancing armor, but lacked the armament, speed

A mobile YMCA canteen on an anti-aircraft site.

and maneuverability to fight their way through hordes of interceptors. They had therefore to be protected by their own fighters – a policy which tied down the only Luftwaffe aircraft which stood any chance at all of meeting the Spitfires and Hurricanes on equal terms. Add to this the poor Intelligence information available to the Luftwaffe commanders, the brilliant, unflappable leadership of Dowding and Park and the sheer bravery

of the RAF fighter pilots – the fabled 'Few' – and the eventual outcome of the battle is clearly understandable. It was undoubtedly a turning point in World War II, leaving Britain unconquered as the Achilles Heel of the new German Empire, but it was also important as the first real proof that the conclusions of the interwar theorists were wrong: air space could be defended – the bomber did not always get through.

PEARL HARBOR 1941

Brigadier General William (Billy) Mitchell was an air theorist of some importance during the interwar period. After service in France in the latter part of World War I as Aviation Officer in the American Expeditionary Force, he was convinced that the future of modern warfare lay inextricably with the airplane, particularly in its strategic role. He was an admirer of Lord Trenchard, the British Commander of the Royal Flying Corps on the Western Front who had become Chief of the Air Staff when the RAF was formed in 1918, and envious of the independence gained by the British air arm. In an attempt to achieve a similar state for the American air services, split as they were between the Army, Navy and the Marine Corps, he put forward the argument that, so far as the United States was concerned, air power was the most important form of defense applicable to the future. Armies were expensive and took time to ship out to trouble spots; navies were inflexible and extremely vulnerable to air attack. His attempt to prove the latter point was dramatic and, as it turned out, alarmingly prophetic.

In 1921 Mitchell received permission to try out a series of experiments involving the bombing of capital ships. After trials with dummy bombs, which proved nothing, he was allowed to go one stage further, using the supposedly unsinkable German battleship *Ostfriesland*, surrendered to the Allies in 1919 and by now little more than a hulk. Stationing the vessel some 60 miles off the Virginia coast, a squadron of Martin bombers, armed with specially designed 2000lb bombs, attacked on 21 July 1921. Within a matter of minutes, the ship had turned turtle and sunk. Detractors immediately pointed out that the experiment would have had a different outcome against a fully-armed and protected battleship, able to take evasive action, and the event was conveniently dismissed as a publicity stunt for Mitchell's campaign of revolutionary thinking. As Mitchell himself was to be court-martialed four years later for an ill-judged attack upon

the 'incompetence' of the War Department over the loss of the dirigible *Shenandoah*, it was easy to regard him as something of a crank. But this ignored the most important aspect of the *Ostfriesland* sinking. A new era of naval warfare had arrived, and although it undoubtedly needed technological improvement, the advent of the naval aircraft, capable of attacking capital ships from above, spelt the end of the huge, expensive and vulnerable battleship as the central feature of fleet organization. Mitchell provided the lesson, but it was not to be appreciated for another 20 years, when the Japanese, using their naval air power based upon aircraft carriers, dealt a stunning blow to American prestige at Pearl Harbor.

War between the United States and Japan seemed inevitable for much of the 1930s. Ever since Japan, intent upon territorial expansion to ease domestic pressures caused by rapid industrialization and a population explosion, had moved into Manchuria in 1932, encroachments upon the American spheres of influence in China and the Pacific had threatened to escalate into open hostility. But for much of the decade the traditional isolationism of the United States had forced her political leaders to take a conciliatory stance. Even in 1937, when Japan attacked China on a broad front and abrogated a Naval Limitation Treaty signed with America and Britain in 1921 – a treaty which had allowed the Japanese to build only three capital ships for every ten constructed in the West – protests had been the full extent of American reaction. However, by early 1940, with Japanese forces established along the entire Chinese coast and Chiang Kai-shek's Nationalist armies driven inland, the Americans felt obliged to act. Consequently, on 26 January President Roosevelt canceled a Treaty of Commerce with Japan and tried to impose economic sanctions. This had little effect, and as the Japanese became progressively more aggressive, allying themselves defensively to Germany and Italy in September 1940, concluding a

Above: General Tojo on an inspection of army units in Japan after his becoming premier in 1941.

Right: A Nakajima 'Kate' B5N2 carrier bomber, one of the type used at Pearl Harbor, was introduced in 1937 and served throughout the war.

Above: President Roosevelt and his Cabinet aboard the USS Indianapolis, *later sunk by Japan in 1945.*

Right: The Japanese aircraft carrier Akagi *in 1939 at Sukumo Bay.*

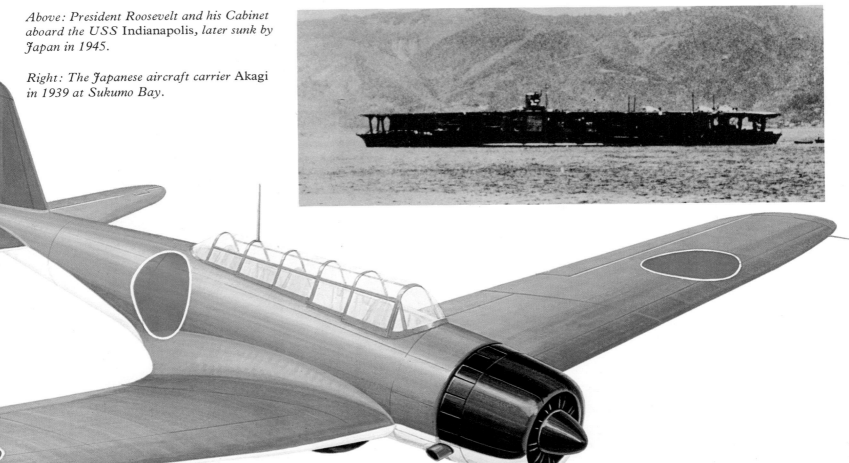

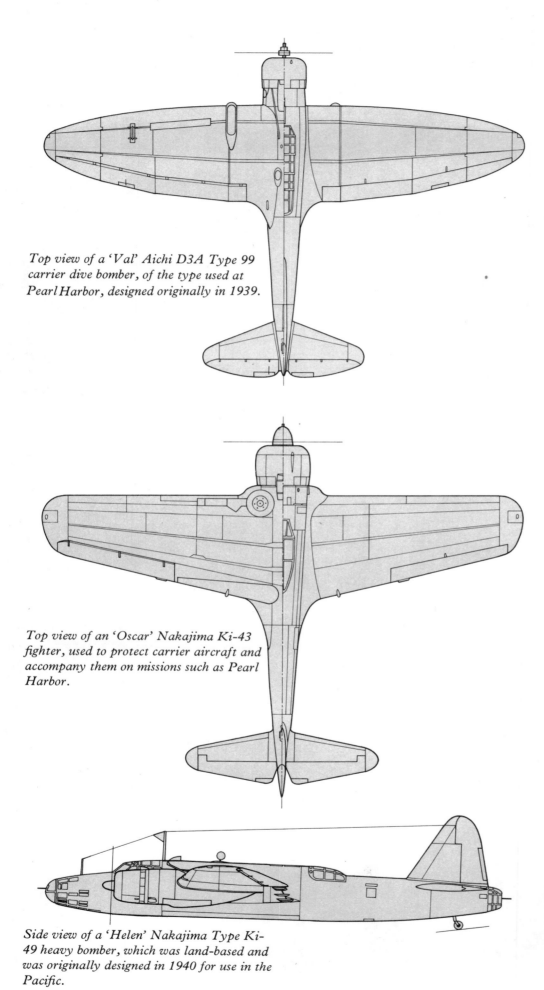

Top view of a 'Val' Aichi D3A Type 99 carrier dive bomber, of the type used at Pearl Harbor, designed originally in 1939.

Top view of an 'Oscar' Nakajima Ki-43 fighter, used to protect carrier aircraft and accompany them on missions such as Pearl Harbor.

Side view of a 'Helen' Nakajima Type Ki-49 heavy bomber, which was land-based and was originally designed in 1940 for use in the Pacific.

non-aggression pact with Russia in April 1941, and actually moving into French Indo-China (now Vietnam) three months later, Roosevelt went one stage further. In July 1941 he 'froze' all Japanese assets in the United States, an act which effectively dried up, for want of cash, all supplies of oil to Japan and forced the Tokyo government to react. Oil was a key commodity, entirely absent from Japanese national or occupied territories. To replace American supplies Japan would either have to give in and accede to Washington's demands for a full withdrawal of forces from China and Indo-China, or attack southward to the oil-rich Dutch East Indies. With a militarist party in power in Tokyo, the choice was obvious: an attack was the only honorable way out.

Plans for such an assault, with the establishment of an economically self-sufficient 'Great East Asia Prosperity Sphere,' had been laid down long before 1941. They owed their origin to a National Defense Policy, formulated as early as 1909. This, for the purposes of fleet maneuvers, had stipulated the United States as a purely hypothetical enemy, but had increased in relevance as the century progressed. It centered upon the assumption that the Americans would take the offensive in the Western Pacific – that is, virtually in Japanese home waters – as soon as hostilities began, and planned the destruction of the US fleet somewhere between the

Admiral Yamamoto, Japanese naval C in C.

Marianas and Marshall Islands. In other words, the Americans would sail straight into a carefully-laid trap. But things had changed since 1909, particularly so far as Japanese aspirations were concerned, and by the late 1930s revisions were desperately needed. They were provided by Admiral Isoroku Yamamoto.

Appointed Commander in Chief of the Japanese Combined Fleet on 30 August 1939, Yamamoto recognized immediately that existing war plans were unsatisfactory. They were based upon a defensive stance, waiting for the Americans to appear, whereas if hostilities began the exact opposite was intended, with a southward thrust to gain the Dutch East Indies and their essential oil fields before the British, Dutch and Americans could react. This necessitated a concentration of Japanese naval and military power away from the area of intended fleet action, leaving the route to Japan itself dangerously exposed, particularly as the Americans, in May 1940, had moved their Pacific fleet from the West Coast to Pearl Harbor in the Central Pacific island of Oahu, a part of the Hawaiian chain. A westward thrust by this fleet could be decisive, threatening Japan and cutting the vulnerable lines of communication with forces attacking the Dutch East Indies. This led Yamamoto to the conclusion that if war was inevitable, the first Japanese action should be an attack upon Pearl Harbor to destroy the US Pacific fleet in its base. He began

Zero fighters take off from the deck of the carrier Akagi, *7 December 1941.*

to work for this from the start of his command.

At first he had to tread carefully in the face of entrenched opposition from the Naval General Staff, gradually pushing the area of intended fleet action eastward until it included the waters around Hawaii. This was accepted in principle, but as the main part of the Japanese fleet was already earmarked for the protection of the southward push, it seemed a hollow victory. It was then that Yamamoto introduced his trump card – the use of naval aircraft, taking off from a carrier force stationed near Hawaii, to bomb the Americans in a surprise attack. The idea was revolutionary and immediately opposed, but Yamamoto was convinced of its viability. He had always been in-

terested in the capabilities of air power, recognizing it as a crucial new element of naval strategy as early as 1927, and when he was appointed to the aircraft carrier *Akagi* in 1928 he had devoted himself 'to the practical problems involved in the developing theories of air warfare.' By 1937 he was sure in his own mind that attacks by torpedo-carrying aircraft could destroy any battleship then afloat, and that the key to naval supremacy in the future lay with the aircraft carrier and its long-range strike potential. If a force of carriers could approach Hawaii in secret, the war could commence with a powerful aerial strike upon the US fleet in Pearl Harbor, destroying battleships and shore installations to a crippling extent.

The two waves of attack which devastated Pearl Harbor.

Battleship Row on Pearl Harbor Day.

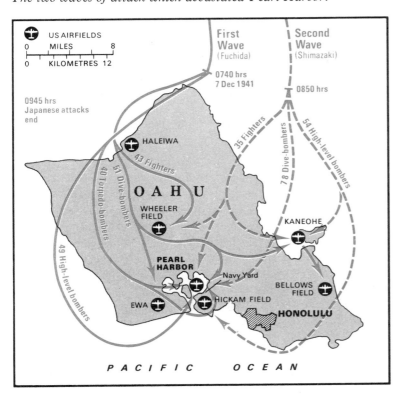

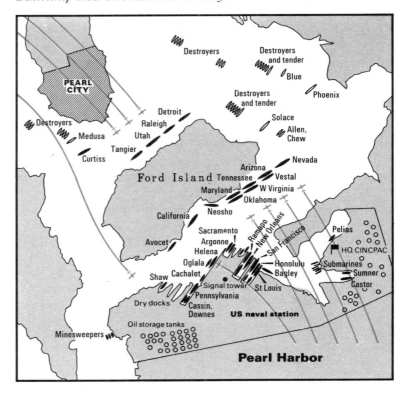

Preparations for such an assault began in late 1939, well before the Naval General Staff had given its blessing, with Yamamoto insisting upon a high standard of proficiency in carrier-based attacks throughout the naval air arm. In addition he managed to persuade his superiors to increase the carrier-building program and to authorize the introduction of new naval aircraft. By the end of 1940 Japan was well-stocked in both respects. Four carriers – the *Akagi*, *Kaga*, *Hiryu* and *Soryu* – were immediately available, with two others – the *Shokaku* and *Zuikaku* – expected to be ready by August 1941; long-range flying boats, capable of carrying 2000lb bomb loads over 800 miles had been introduced into service, and a new fighter aircraft, the A6M Zero, had been put into production. A torpedo bomber, the Nakajima B5N2 (later code named 'Kate' by the Allies), already existed, while the Aichi D3A1 ('Val') dive bomber, although approaching obsolescence, was still an adequate machine, capable of inflicting the necessary degree of damage. Taken together, equipment was clearly no problem, but Yamamoto still had to gain permission to mount his *coup de main*.

Approaching the problem cautiously, he began by building up support from among his own staff, confiding firstly in his Chief of Staff Admiral Shigeru Fukudome and then in Rear Admiral Takajiro Onishi, Chief of Staff of the land-based 11th Air Fleet. It was the latter who introduced Yamamoto to Commander Minoru Genda, a brilliant and experienced naval airman, and it was at this point that the plan started to assume its final form. After ten days of careful study, Genda came to the conclusion that the projected operation was 'difficult but not impossible,' provided that certain changes were made. To begin with, he did not agree with Yamamoto that the main target should be the American battleships, preferring to aim for the destruction of carriers, particularly as three such vessels – the *Enterprise*, *Lexington* and *Saratoga* – were known to be with the Pacific Fleet. Similarly, he favored far more concentration of force than Yamamoto had envisaged, with all six Japanese carriers taking part, their aircraft making more than one attack if circumstances allowed. Onishi passed these comments on to the Commander in Chief, and Genda was requested to draw up a detailed plan.

This began to take shape towards the end of March 1941 under the code name

A Nakajima 'Kate' torpedo bomber takes off from a carrier for Pearl Harbor.

Operation Z, with Genda gradually expanding the scope of the attack. According to his ideas, a special task force of twenty *I-class* submarines and five two-man midget submarines would approach Hawaii before war was declared, the former stationing themselves around Oahu to catch any American ships that tried to escape, with the latter actually entering Pearl Harbor to add to the chaos caused by the aerial strike. Meanwhile the main force of six carriers, protected by destroyers and cruisers, would take a circuitous route, well away from known shipping lanes, and approach Hawaii from the north, where least expected. A total of 360 aircraft, comprising torpedo bombers, high-level bombers and fighters, would be launched about 230 miles from Oahu, to arrive over Pearl Harbor just after dawn, preferably on a Sunday when the American fleet, following peace-time training routines, would be in harbor with only skeleton crews on board. Once over the anchorage, if surprise was complete the torpedo bombers would attack first, followed closely by the high-level bombers and then the dive bombers, with the fighters providing a protective air umbrella. If surprise had been lost, the fighters would go in first to gain control of the air over the targets, clearing the way for the bombers. Either way, the assaults, to be delivered by two waves of aircraft, would be expected to last no more than two hours all told.

Yamamoto accepted this scheme without reservation, organizing training schedules and making sure that technical problems were solved on time. After sailing round the coast of Japan to find a suitable training area, he chose Kagoshima Bay, south of Kyushu, a spot

which bore a striking resemblance to Pearl Harbor, and it was here that his naval pilots, as yet unaware of their projected task, practiced the necessary skills. They quickly attained a very high standard, with dive bombers reducing their release-point to 1500 feet and high-level bombers achieving 80 percent accuracy against stationary targets. At the same time existing torpedoes were modified to take account of the shallow nature of Pearl Harbor (it was only 40 feet deep) and special bombs, capable of cutting through the armor plate of battleships, were introduced. By late October 1941, each pilot, in a series of special briefings on board the *Akagi*, had been assigned to individual targets; Commander Mitsuo Fuchida, an experienced air leader, had been chosen to command the air attack on the day; and the entire force had been placed under Rear Admiral Chuichi Nagumo. All that was missing was permission to go ahead.

This came eventually on 3 November, when Yamamoto and his entire staff threatened to resign unless a decision was made. Even then, there was a continuing possibility of a last-minute cancellation, for the Japanese Emperor was determined to continue diplomatic negotiations with the Americans for as long as possible, in the hope that some kind of compromise could be worked out to prevent his militaristic government going to war. The chances of this occurring seemed fairly remote, however, and Yamamoto took the opportunity to draft his final orders. On 6 November a full-scale dress rehearsal of the attack took place, involving all six carriers, and 350 aircraft staged a successful mock attack on a target 200 miles from the launching

Zeke fighters prepare for take-off from a Japanese carrier on Pearl Harbor Day.

zone. Twenty-four hours later Nagumo was informed that Y day – the day of attack – would be Sunday, 7 December (Hawaii time) and ordered to assemble his fleet at Tankan Bay on Etorofu, the largest of the Kurile Islands, by 22 November. The ships began to leave their bases on 17 November, the submarine force set out for Hawaii between 18 and 20 November, and by 22 November all six carriers, together with two battleships, two heavy cruisers, one light cruiser, nine destroyers and eight fleet tankers, were ready to go. They set sail before dawn on 26 November, following

a northerly route in overcast and stormy conditions, hoping to avoid American detection for the whole of their 12 day voyage.

In retrospect, the maintenance of secrecy is surprising, for since August 1940 the Americans had been able to read all Japanese diplomatic communications, having cracked the relevant code. But there was never any direct mention of Operation Z, and so long as negotiations continued in Washington, the possibility of a sudden Japanese attack seemed remote. Even if this had not been the case, there was no reason to suppose that Pearl

Harbor would be a primary target. It was a long way from Japan, necessitating the formation of a naval force which did not appear to exist (US Intelligence, fooled by false wireless traffic, reported all Japanese carriers to be 'still in home waters' as late as 27 November), and seemed contrary to known Japanese aspirations towards the Dutch East Indies. An aura of complacency gradually emerged, to be reflected tragically in a total lack of defensive preparations in Hawaii. By the weekend of 6/7 December the fleet was still following peacetime routines, aerial reconnaissance was restricted to sea areas to the south and west, torpedo nets across the mouth of the harbor were rarely kept in place, and security was lax. Even when one of the Japanese midget submarines was spotted and sunk by the minesweeper USS *Condor* at 0635 hours on 7 December, no one in authority showed any interest. Pearl Harbor was wide open to attack.

The midget submarine was, in fact, one of three which approached the American base, acting upon orders received by the entire Japanese force on 2 December, after the Emperor had finally decided that war was unavoidable. The other two entered Pearl Harbor before dawn on 7 December, taking advantage of American neglect to close the torpedo nets across the harbor mouth between 0600 hours and 0840 hours. Meanwhile, Nagumo's force had reached the launch-

USS West Virginia, *which was severely damaged during the Pearl Harbor raid.*

Aerial view of Pearl Harbor, Ford Island and Battleship Row 30 October 1941.

Above: Admiral Thomas Hart, in charge of
US naval operations in 1941.
Below: Battleship Row as the bombs fell.

Above: Admiral Husband E Kimmel
(center), C in C Pacific Fleet.

ing zone, 230 miles due north of Oahu, and the decision to go ahead had been made, despite reports that the American carriers were absent from their usual anchorages. In fact, *Saratoga* was undergoing repairs on the West Coast of the United States, the *Lexington* was ferrying aircraft to Midway in preparation for war, and the *Enterprise* was returning to Pearl Harbor from Wake Island, but with a reported nine battleships, seven cruisers, three submarine-tenders and 20 destroyers at anchor, with no visible defensive screen, the opportunity seemed too good to miss. In the event, the count was not exact – only eight battleships were present and some of the other vessels had been wrongly described – but the discrepancies were minor. Fortunately for the Americans, the absence of carriers was to prove the difference between short-term disaster and long-term defeat.

Fuchida roared off the deck of the *Akagi* at precisely 0600 hours on 7 December, and within 15 minutes the first wave of the attacking force, comprising 43 fighters, 49 high-level bombers, 51 dive bombers and 40 torpedo bombers, had been successfully launched. Following a direct route at approximately 200 mph, the aircraft crossed the Oahu shoreline at 0740 hours to achieve complete surprise. Visibility was excellent, enabling the Japanese airmen to see American fighters and bombers lined up in neat rows in front of their hangars and the fleet at anchor, apparently deserted. Fuchida transmitted the radio message 'Tora, Tora, Tora' – a prearranged code to signify to his superiors in Japan that surprise had been achieved and all was well – and signaled his pilots to follow the first of their practiced plans, whereby the torpedo bombers would go in first, followed by the high-level bombers, leaving the dive bombers and fighters to bring up the rear. As it happened, in the confusion and excitement of the attack, such order rapidly disappeared, but this merely served to add to the surprise and chaos on the ground. At 0755 hours, the first bombs began to fall.

From the beginning of Yamamoto's planning, the fear of a positive American reaction in the air had been uppermost in Japanese minds, particularly when it was estimated that 455 aircraft would be stationed on Oahu at the time of the attack, and for this reason the initial assault was put in against the various Hawaiian airfields. 'Val' dive bombers, with Zero fighter support, concentrated upon Hickam Field and Ford Island, as

Battleship Row after the strike, with (left to right) the capsized Oklahoma, *the sinking* West Virginia *and the burning* Tennessee.

Above: USS Shaw *and* Nevada *(right) ablaze.* Nevada *was run aground to keep from sinking in the main channel. Below: A burned out plane at Wheeler Field.*

well as the Wheeler air base. At the latter, American fighters were lined up as if awaiting inspection, and in the first few minutes 20 P-40s and P-36s were destroyed. At Hickam, some 70 bombers – of which 12 were newly-delivered B-17s – were burnt out, and similar pictures emerged at Kaneohe, a flying-boat base, and Ewa, an uncompleted Marine Corps airfield. Within a very short time, American air defense potential had been virtually wiped out – there being, in fact, only 231 aircraft in the Hawaii region – and the Japanese had gained complete air supremacy, enabling the other portions of Fuchida's force to attack the fleet with relative impunity.

The assault upon the battleships began shortly after 0800 hours, with 'Kate' torpedo bombers, divided into two groups, making three successive low, fast runs against minimal opposition. An enormous amount of damage was done. In the first attack the battleships *California*, *Oklahoma* and *West Virginia* were hit; in the second the cruiser *Helena* was struck and the minelayer *Oglala* capsized; in the third the cruiser *Raleigh* and the aged battleship *Utah*, recently used by the Americans as a target ship, were torpedoed. At the same time the dive bombers plummetted down, making eight attacks from different points of the compass. Their aim was good – a product of the intense training at Kagoshima Bay – and the results were catastrophic. The battleships *Nevada*, *Maryland*, *Pennsylvania* and *Tennessee* all caught fire, while the *Arizona*, hit in the forward magazine and boilers, blew up and capsized, showering huge fragments of debris over the harbor. Four hundred seamen were trapped in her upturned hull. Permitting no respite, Fuchida himself led the high-level bombers into the attack, organizing all 49 into a single column and passing over the harbor at 12,000ft. By now the Americans had recovered sufficiently to put up anti-aircraft fire, and as Fuchida's force wheeled round for a second run, two bombers were shot down and a third forced to ram its target. Unperturbed, the bombers made a third and final run, pouring their armor-piercing bombs onto the burning ships, before climbing to 15,000ft and making way for the second wave. It was 0840 hours.

By this time all seven front-line battleships were on fire, and when the second wave of 170 aircraft arrived, led by Lieutenant Commander Shigekazu Shimazaki of the *Zuikaku*, their task was not made easy by billowing clouds of smoke. Nevertheless, a force of 80 'Val' dive bombers, briefed to hit the absent American carriers, mounted a furious assault upon the battleships, concentrating upon those which were still capable of putting up anti-aircraft fire. The *Nevada* tried to escape by slipping anchor and making for the harbor mouth, but was pounced on and torpedoed in mid-channel. Wallowing dangerously and threatening to sink in the middle of the anchorage, blocking it to all traffic, she had to be nursed to the shore and beached. Meanwhile the high-level bombers of the second wave had revisited the air bases, destroying surviving aircraft and installations at Hickam, Wheeler, Ford Island and Kaneohe. At the latter they were joined by 31 Zero fighters, whose original task of acting as a protective air umbrella had proved unnecessary. At 0945 hours, after nearly two hours sustained assault, the Japanese withdrew.

Fuchida's first wave aircraft reached their carriers at 1000 hours, to be followed two hours later by the last of Shimazaki's force, and when it was found that only 29 machines had been lost out of the 353 committed, the pilots were understandably ecstatic, demanding permission to mount another attack. This would have been quite feasible, but Nagumo, worried that the missing American carriers were even then steaming to intercept him, refused. The task force turned for home, transmitting Fuchida's report – 'Four battleships definitely sunk, and considerable damage inflicted on the airfields.' It looked like a crippling blow.

Few people on Oahu at the time would have argued against this assessment. By noon on 7 December eight battleships, three cruisers, three destroyers and eight auxiliary craft – totaling some 300,000 tons – had been immobilized; Hickam, Wheeler, Ford Island and Kaneohe had been destroyed, together with 96 of the 231 aircraft in Hawaii (in fact only seven of the remaining machines were immediately airworthy); and over 3400 people had been killed or wounded. The only success had been against the midget submarines, all of which had been sunk before they could inflict any damage, but this was minor compared to the sheer shock and force of the Japanese assault. In what looked like a treacherous pre-emptive strike – because of translation problems the actual Japanese severance of negotiations was not delivered to President Roosevelt until after the attack had finished – the US Pacific fleet had been virtually wiped out, enabling the enemy to advance into the Southwest Pacific, free from American interference.

But the Japanese victory was in fact far from complete. The fatal flaw was that the stroke had missed the US carriers entirely, so sparing a weapon which was to have decisive effects upon the future conduct of the war. American admirals, denied their traditional dependence upon the battleship, were forced to tear up existing plans and, of necessity, concentrate their attentions upon the role of naval air power. Because the *Saratoga*, *Enterprise* and *Lexington* escaped Pearl Harbor, the carrier had to replace the battleship as the central feature of fleet organization, rapidly becoming the principal naval weapon. The Americans were quick to learn, using their carriers successfully at the Battles of Coral Sea, Midway, Philippine Sea and the Leyte Gulf to beat the Japanese at their own game. In addition, Fuchida's airmen had failed to destroy the oil tanks, machine shops and other installations on Oahu and, despite the depressing picture on 7 December, Pearl Harbor itself was quick to recover from the blow of the eight battleships attacked, all but two were later raised and repaired, as were many of the smaller ships, and in the end the catalog of total destruction contained the names of the *Arizona*, *Oklahoma* and two destroyers only. Even so, if the lesson provided by Mitchell in 1921 had been heeded, there might have been no need for a catalog at all.

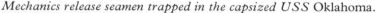

Mechanics release seamen trapped in the capsized USS Oklahoma.

CORAL SEA 1942

Admiral Chester W Nimitz.

3–8 May 1942

The Battle of the Coral Sea heralded a revolution in naval warfare. It was the first in which the capital ships of either side did not so much as catch a glimpse of an opponent. The damage was all done by aircraft, the new artillery of the sea. The battle was one of those, in which the right thing, if it happened at all, usually happened for the wrong reason. It was the first great seafight of the Pacific War, the greatest naval war of all time, fought with, for its prize, the mastery of the Pacific.

The Japanese Navy had not fought a fleet action since Tsushima in 1905. Until January 1936 when Japan had withdrawn from the Washington Naval Limitation Treaty, the details of her naval construction had been known to the Western powers. Thereafter the Japanese went in for a program of naval expansion, but nobody knew precisely what they were building. In fact between 1921 and 1941, while Great Britain and the USA made modest increases to their navies, the Japanese doubled their combat tonnage. By 1941 their navy was more powerful than the Pacific fleets of their opponents, which were not, of course, combined.

The Japanese ships were well-designed and well-armed. Their fleet was well worked-up, and thoroughly efficient both technically and tactically. The Japanese qualities of discipline, toughness and diligence, were apparent in every department.

Two monster battleships were added in 1940: *Yamato* and *Musashi*, each of 63,000 tons and with 18-inch guns. By that time a comparison of the Japanese and the US Pacific Fleets shows a very considerable advantage to the former:

	Japanese	United States
Battleships	10	9
Carriers	10	3
Heavy cruisers	18	12
Light cruisers	17	9
Destroyers	111	67
Submarines	64	27

It is an interesting illustration of the way in which a wealthy democracy, while knowing who its potential opponents are, can allow itself to be outstripped in those warlike preparations, without which there can be no guarantee of peace.

Admiral Isoroku Yamamoto had been interested in naval air warfare since the 1920s, indeed he was the leading light in the small group of officers, who believed in aircraft, and perceived that the days of the battleship were numbered. It takes real courage to peer into the future and predict that a well-loved 'weapon' is obsolescent. Yamamoto was appointed commandant of a naval school, and he supervised the training of many pilots. This is not to say that his views appealed to the more conservative Japanese admirals, who successfully resisted reform of the fleet as a whole. At the same time, arriving at a typically Japanese solution, they formed an extra and separate fleet oriented toward air tactics. This development went unnoticed by the intelligence services of the Western Powers. It was thought that there were few skilled Japanese naval pilots – an illusion which was shattered at Pearl Harbor.

The Japanese Navy, as we have seen, was conservative in its views. The Army on the other hand had involved Japan in its tremendous Chinese adventure, and was in any case deeply involved in the government. With Pearl Harbor the Navy too became involved, though

Below: A Type 99 Aichi 'Val' D3A carrier dive bomber, like those used against US carriers in the Battle of the Coral Sea.

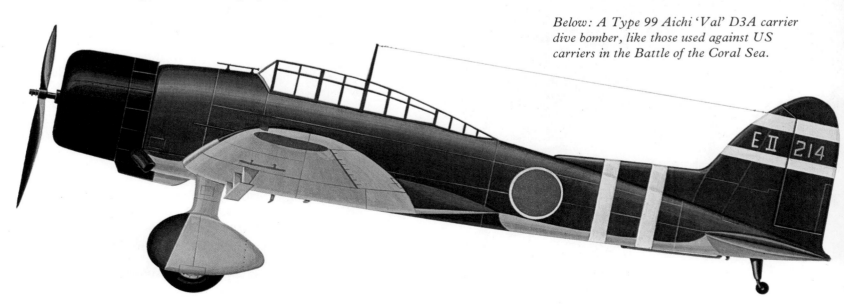

USS Yorktown *in happier days in 1937; she was seriously damaged in the Coral Sea.*

The Japanese carrier Shokaku *at Yokosuka in 1941 prior to the outbreak of war.*

Dauntlesses on the deck of the Yorktown *during the Battle of the Coral Sea.*

Yamamoto himself had only consented to war because economic sanctions had rendered Japan's position so desperate. With the spread of the war to Southeast Asia and the South Pacific the Japanese Navy had its own Theater in which it was paramount. Yamamoto's plan had been to destroy the US fleet at Pearl Harbor, before it could sail and attack the Japanese in the Western Pacific. Oddly enough the Japanese had not concealed the fact that they did not exclude such an attack from their plans, but with wellnigh incredible complacency the United States had ignored the possibility. It is not generally known, moreover, that the Japanese had given the Americans 30 minutes warning of the attack, an attempt to observe the usages of war, but the message had not got through. Yamamoto's six carriers had put the American battleships out of action, but by a great stroke of good fortune three carriers, which were out on an exercise, had escaped undamaged.

The Japanese, as it turned out, now had two years in which to consolidate their position, or to make peace. By the spring of 1942 they had taken Wake Island, Guam, Hong Kong, the Philippines, Malaya, the Dutch East Indies and most of Burma. Resistance had, generally speaking, been ineffectual; occasionally, as at Singapore, quite inept. Their casualties had been light, and the Japanese became so elated that there seemed no limit to their potential conquests. A second offensive was decided upon.

The proposed strategy of this new campaign may be summarized as follows. The Japanese would first seize Tulagi in the Solomon Islands and Port Moresby in Papua (New Guinea). This would give them air control over the Coral Sea. The Japanese Combined Fleet would then sail on across the Pacific to seek out and destroy what remained of the US Pacific Fleet, besides capturing Midway and the Western Aleutians. They would consolidate their conquests by a 'ribbon defense,' with impregnable fortresses on Attu, Midway, Wake, the Marshalls and the Gilberts. The invasion of New Caledonia, the Fiji Islands and Samoa, would isolate Australia and New Zealand. It was felt that, with their fleet destroyed and the ribbon defense established, the Americans would tire of the war and come to terms.

This strategy had been conceived as early as 1938, and formed part of the Japanese Basic War Plan. In 1942 the

Above: Rear Admiral Frank Fletcher.

timetable was speeded up, and the major fleet action with the Americans was added.

Easy successes had given the Japanese a contempt for the Americans. They had become infected, as the perceptive and intelligent Rear Admiral Chuichi Hara was to admit after the war, with Victory Disease. It is always a mistake to underrate the enemy, and now the Japanese were falling into this error. Moreover, Japan's resources were simply inadequate for the manifold tasks her strategy imposed. The Japanese merchant navy had neither the tonnage nor the organization to supply her far-flung outposts. Nor had Japan the industrial capacity, or even the manpower, to build up a fleet sufficient to protect her long lines of communication. For sea power, as she

herself proved, now meant carrier-borne air forces. And her early successes, due to superior pilots, planes and techniques, had not been won without loss. It is estimated that by April 1942 Japan had lost 855 naval planes, 315 in combat and 540 lost 'operationally.' These losses, were of course, replaced, but there was a decided fall in the quality of air crews. That Yamamoto was right to insist that the US Pacific Fleet must be destroyed by 1943 is certain. He knew very well that the United States with its tremendous economic and industrial capability could outbuild Japan. But would this second offensive overstrain Japan's military potential? That was the question.

In April 1942 the Japanese made a foray into the Indian Ocean, which effectually neutralized the small British for-

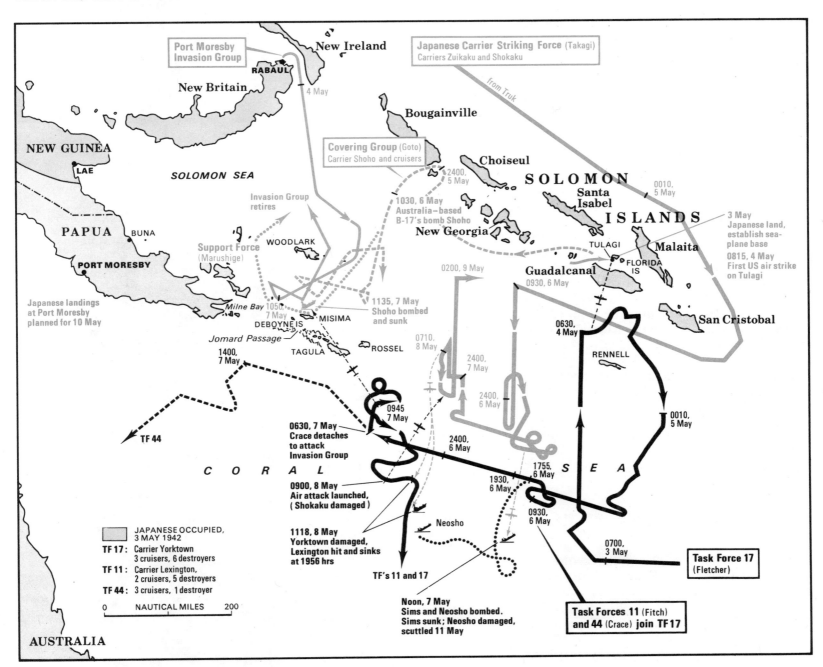

ces in those waters. This done they turned their attention to the first objective of the new strategy. The Coral Sea is bounded on one side by New Caledonia, the New Hebrides and the Louisiades, on the other by the Great Barrier Reef.

The Coral Sea was vital to Australian security. Early in the year the Japanese had established a big base at Rabaul, from which the operation was to be mounted.

The Japanese believed that the Americans had only one carrier in the South Pacific. They thought up a complicated plan in which five forces, following different routes, but adhering to a set timetable would surprise the enemy and engage them in an unequal fight. What they did not know was that American intelligence had actually broken their codes before the war, and could decipher many of their fleet messages. By 17 April the American Pacific Fleet had already unraveled the outline of the Japanese plan.

Vice-Admiral Inouye, Commander in Chief of the Fourth Fleet was the overall commander. It was hoped that with Port Moresby in their hands Japanese aircraft could attack Australian ports and airfields, and perhaps even compel Australia to quit the war.

Operation Mo: Coral Sea
Overall Commander: Vice-Admiral Shigeyoshi Inouye

Groups	Ships	Commander
Port Moresby Invasion Group	11 transports	Rear Admiral Tanaka
Tulagi Invasion Group: set up seaplane base		Rear Admiral Shima
Covering Group: for Tulagi Group and then Port Moresby	Light carrier Shoho 4 Heavy cruisers 1 destroyer	Rear Admiral Goto
Support Group: establish seaplane base in the Louisiades	2 light cruisers seaplane tender	Rear Admiral Marushige
Striking Force	Carriers Shokaku Zuikaku 2 heavy cruisers 6 destroyers	Vice-Admiral Takagi

Port Moresby was vital to General Douglas MacArthur's plans. It was to be the major air base from which he would counter the Japanese threat to Australia, and a springboard for his return to the Philippines.

Admiral Chester Nimitz, Commander in Chief of the Pacific Fleet, concentrated all available forces to foil Inouye's threat.

Task Force 17	Carrier Yorktown, etc	Rear Admiral Frank Fletcher
Task Force 11	Carrier Lexington, etc	Rear Admiral Aubrey Fitch
Task Force 44	2 Australian cruisers 1 American cruiser 2 Destroyers	Rear Admiral Crace, RN

Top right: Anti-aircraft battery on a US carrier after having repelled a Japanese attack.

Right: Flight deck of Yorktown *after the first Japanese strike when a bomb hit the funnel.*

Fletcher was to be the overall Allied commander. Task Force 17 was already in the South Pacific; Task Force 11 was sent from Pearl Harbor. Task Force 44 was what was called 'MacArthur's Navy.' Fletcher's three forces put together were somewhat inferior to Inouye's fleet, if only because the latter had one more carrier, albeit a small one, *Shoho*.

American strategy at this juncture was defensive. Its object was to protect the Hawaiian Islands and communications with Australia and New Zealand *via* Palmyra, Samoa, Fiji and New Caledonia. MacArthur was organizing the few Australian and American troops of South West Pacific Command for the defence of Papua and northern Australia.

MacArthur, who had an impressive record from World War I, and had been Chief of Staff of the US Army, had been on loan to the Philippine Commonwealth at the outbreak of World War II, and had commanded the futile attempt to save the Philippines. It would be idle to pretend that he saw eye to eye with President Roosevelt, or with General Marshall, the Army Chief of Staff. But their differences were as nothing compared to the intense rivalry which quickly sprang up between MacArthur and Nimitz, a rivalry which, for ill or good, was to affect the whole strategy of the Pacific War. That MacArthur was 'difficult' there can be no question. President Truman was to find that during the Korean War, but where his relations with the US Navy were concerned all the blame cannot be laid at MacArthur's door. The Navy had an ethos all its own. At a time when the United States was pursuing its foreign policy of isolation, the US Navy, self-sufficient and self-contained, was pursuing its own similar policy; secure in the knowledge that it had its own air force, and a Private Army, the US Marine Corps, the élite of the American fighting men. In war the enemy were only marginally more hostile than the army with which the US Navy so reluctantly co-operated! Rivalry between services is not altogether unhealthy: in this case it had been carried rather too far.

1 May

Shima set sail from Rabaul.

Task Forces 11 and 17 rendezvoused north of new Caledonia.

2 May

Reconnaissance plane sighted Shima's force, but the reports which reached Fletcher were not clear. So Fletcher moved northwest with Task Force 17.

Then the Japanese were sighted approaching Tulagi, from which island the small Australian garrison withdrew.

3 May

In the evening, one of MacArthur's reconnaissance planes reported Japanese disembarking on Tulagi. Fletcher in the *Yorktown* made for Tulagi.

4 May

A dawn strike on Tulagi by over 40 American planes sank one destroyer, three small mine sweepers and destroyed five seaplanes. Inexperienced pilots gave glowing reports of this modest score. Fletcher moved south to rendezvous with Fitch. Crace joined Fitch. Takagi's carriers, delivering nine fighters to Rabaul, were still out of range, far from Coral Sea.

5 May

Fletcher concentrated his task forces, and refueled from the tanker *Neosho*. Reconnaissance reports produced a confused picture. Fletcher decided in the evening to set course northwest toward probable route of Port Moresby Invasion Force.

Takagi's Carrier Striking Force rounded San Cristobal and turned northwest into the Coral Sea. Neither admiral had any real idea of the size and position of his opponent's fleet.

6 May

Awaiting intelligence Fletcher turned southeast while refueling. In the morning, Takagi set a southerly course, which he hoped would bring him into contact with Fletcher, but he did not send out any reconnaissance planes! A plane from Rabaul spotted Fletcher's force, but this report did not reach Takagi until the next day. American reconnaissance, due to low cloud, failed to locate Takagi, who was only 70 miles from Fletcher's task force.

7 May

Takagi launched an air search at dawn, when he and Fletcher were some 200 miles apart. At 0736 hours, a report reached Takagi of one carrier and one cruiser, 200 miles southsouthwest. Takagi thought this was the *only* US carrier in the South Pacific, and launched a major strike: 36 'Val' dive bombers, 24 'Kate' torpedo bombers, 18 Zeroes as cover. The target turned out to be the tanker *Neosho* and the destroyer *Sims*, which were duly sunk. Reconnaissance planes from one of Goto's cruiser's reported the true position of the American carriers. Fletcher decided to detach Crace, who was to wait south of the Jomard Passage in order to block the route of the invasion convoy. The American carriers turned north and launched a major air search, but the Japanese fleet was still concealed by bad weather. By 0815 hours, planes from the *Yorktown* accidentally reported two heavy cruisers and two destroyers as two carriers and four heavy cruisers 175 miles northwest of the American force. (This was actually Marushige's support group.) Fletcher assumed, not unreasonably, that this was the main Japanese force and launched a major strike.

	Lexington	Yorktown	Totals
Dauntless divebombers	28	25	53
Devastator torpedo bombers	12	10	22
Wildcat fighters	10	8	18
	50	43	93

Above: The USS Lexington *(CV 2) shortly after she was launched. Note the 8-inch gun turrets which were removed in July 1941 for coastal defense.*

Below: A TBD-1 Devastator lands as a Wildcat comes in behind to land on USS Lexington. *Note the damaged port forward gun battery.*

Thus, like Takagi, Fletcher had sent a major strike against a minor target, and was himself vulnerable to shore or carrier-based attack. Another plane reported a Japanese carrier and other ships in the same target area, so Fletcher did *not* recall his strike (This second force was Goto's covering group, protecting the Port Moresby Invasion Force.) At 1100 hours, attack groups from the *Lexington* sighted Goto and attacked the *Shoho* by dive-bombing from 18,000ft. Japanese Combat Air Patrol shot down one Dauntless, and lost eight fighters. The *Shoho* was sunk in ten minutes, and the strike leader signaled: 'Scratch one flattop.'

At 1338 hours, the *Lexington*'s force returned from their mission having lost three planes. Admiral Inouye at his headquarters in Rabaul, informed of Crace's position, and of the loss of the *Shoho*, ordered Shima to hold the Port Moresby Invasion Force at a safe distance north of the Louisiades, so Goto followed Shima.

In a mix-up over identification three of MacArthur's B-17s from Townville, Queensland, attacked Crace, who managed to beat them off!

Then Task Force 44 came under attack from 31 Japanese shore-based bombers, but Crace handled his ships brilliantly, and not one was hit. Japanese

report the destruction of two battleships and a heavy cruiser.

In the late afternoon Takagi sent out a search-mission: 12 'Vals' and 15 'Kates.' (No Zeroes as they were not capable of night operations.) The search proving fruitless they jettisoned bombs and torpedoes and made for home. Their course took them over Fletcher's fleet, which got 20 minutes warning from radar. His Combat Air Patrol of Wildcats shot down eight 'Kates.' 'Vals' shot down two Wildcats, for the loss of one.

At dusk, three Japanese aircraft attempted to land on the *Lexington* and three on the *Yorktown*, because they had lost their way. Only seven of the 27 Japanese planes landed safely back on their carriers.

Above right: Lexington *lists to port prior to sinking as a destroyer moves in to take on survivors.*

Right: A Douglas SBD-5 Dauntless dive bomber used on aircraft carriers.

Below right: Lexington *at about noon on 8 May shortly before the explosions which sank her.*

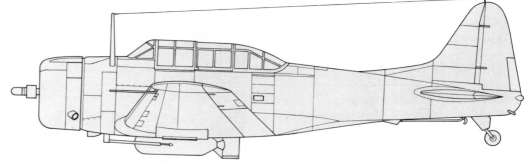

Below: Lexington *under aerial attack. Note the 'Kate' bomber off the carrier's bow.*

Takagi, after considering an attempt to bring on a night action with his cruisers, decided that with the loss of the *Shoho* he must give the Invasion Force air protection. He turned north. Both admirals now had a good idea of the strength and position of their opponents. Each gave tactical command of his fleet to the most experienced carrier officer of flag rank. These were Rear Admiral Aubrey Fitch and Chuichi Hara.

8 May

At the crisis of the battle the two carrier groups were fairly evenly matched:

	Japanese	*United States*
Planes	121	122
Carriers	2	2
Heavy Cruisers	4	5
Destroyers	6	7

Hara decided to launch an early search 200 miles southeast and southwest. At dawn in heavy rain squalls Hara launched a strike force of 33 'Vals,' 18 'Kates' and 18 Zeroes. It was airborne by the time the air search reported the American force 180 miles south, with its own air search launched.

A reconnaissance plane from the *Lexington* spotted the Japanese fleet soon after.

At 0915 hours, a strike force from the two US carriers made for the Japanese fleet, composed of 46 dive bombers; 21 torpedo bombers and 15 fighters. At 1057 hours 41 planes from the *Yorktown* attacked the *Shokaku*, while the *Zuikaku* was hidden in a rain squall. A Dauntless landed a 500lb bomb on the *Shokaku* so that planes could no longer be launched from her flight deck.

The *Lexington*'s attack group was disorganized by the rain clouds, and many planes, unable to find the target, turned back. But four Dauntless and 11 Devastators went into the attack, scoring one bomb hit, killing 100 men, and starting a fire in the *Shokaku*. The strike cost the Americans 13 planes: five dive bombers, five torpedo bombers and three fighters.

Meanwhile the Japanese strike force, almost 70 planes, caught the American Combat Air Patrol low on fuel. Despite 20 minutes warning from radar, nine Wildcats did not have the altitude to meet the attack with advantage. The Japanese courageously pressed home their attack against unpracticed Amer-

Above: Lexington *listing to port shortly before the end after the Coral Sea battle.*

Above: US ships quickly rescue survivors from the Lexington *as fires spread aboard her.*
Below: The remaining crew abandons the sinking Lexington. *Dozens of men leaped into the sea.*

ican Ack-Ack gunners, in action for the first time. Surrounded by torpedo tracks the *Lexington*, unable to take avoiding action against them all, received two torpedo and two bomb hits. The *Yorktown*, with a shorter turning circle, received a bomb on her flight-deck, which, however, remained serviceable. By noon the battle was over.

The *Yorktown*, with 66 men killed by a single bomb was still in fighting trim, and her planes were still landing. The *Lexington*, listing seven degrees to port, was containing three major fires, but her power plant was intact.

At 1247 hours violent internal explosions shook the *Lexington*, resulting from gasoline fumes and finally threatened the ready bomb storage. The fires soon raged uncontrollably and at 1707 hours orders were given to abandon ship.

At 1853 hours using five torpedoes, a destroyer sank the *Lexington* with 35 planes still aboard her. Inouye, frightened at the prospect of intensive allied air activity, postponed the Port Moresby invasion, so the Allies had achieved their objective. Takagi withdrew to Truk and then Yamamoto ordered him south to 'annihilate' the remnants of the enemy.

With the Port Moresby invasion foiled Admiral Nimitz ordered Fletcher to withdraw so that the *Yorktown* would be available for the defense of Midway.

Thus the battle ended. It was in terms of profit and loss a draw. Indeed the Japanese had lost the little *Shoho* while the Americans had lost the *Lexington*.

The *Yorktown* had to go to Pearl Harbor for repairs, while the *Shokaku*, heavily damaged, had to limp back to Japan, for repairs which took two months. The *Zuikaku* had so few planes left that she had to go home for replacements. The Japanese had lost 75 percent of their bomber pilots and planes.

The battle showed that the Japanese pilots were not the men of Pearl Harbor. They were, moreover, unaccustomed to night operations. The 'Kate' was a lumbering old kite and the lack of radar had been a serious disadvantage to the Japanese. Yamamoto was always alert in keeping abreast of technological advances – indeed it is practically a principle of war that one should do so. Still at a time when the despised British had been using radar for two years, and the Germans knew all about it, the Japanese persisted in ignoring it. One could even assert that they could have won this battle had they previously adopted radar. Oddly enough the Germans had sent two radar sets to their ally by submarine. For some reason, lack of technicians perhaps, the Japanese were unimpressed. Co-operation between Germany and Japan was in fact minimal.

So one could say that the Battle of the Coral Sea was a draw. But that is not really so. It was a battle that the Japanese might have been expected to win, but in which the Allies, with their inexperienced pilots, had held their own. Admirals Fletcher, Fitch and Crace had really deserved well of their countries!

The Americans emerged from the or-

deal with clearer ideas on the tactical use of carriers. This was, of course, to serve them well at Midway and thereafter. More to the point, Coral Sea marked the high water mark of Japanese southward expansion. It was their first repulse. The level-headed and experienced Yamàmoto found in it confirmation of his views that the further acquisition of territory, so far from helping Japan, would merely squander her exiguous resources.

Fortified by the prestige he had won at Pearl Harbor Yamamoto, quite correctly, now convinced his more conservative colleagues, that the paramount object of the Japanese Fleet must be to complete the destruction of the United States' Pacific Fleet. This thinking led naturally to the next great battle – Midway.

Coral Sea was a tactical draw, but, strategically, it saved Port Moresby, the gateway to New Guinea, and Australia. The relatively good news raised morale, when the fall of Corregidor could have had a really bad moral effect in the United States.

Thirty-six years have passed since Fletcher led forth his hastily assembled and relatively untrained force to counter the very serious threat to Port Moresby. It was a heavy responsibility, which, bravely supported, he discharged most nobly against a tough and vigorous foe.

The main interest of Coral Sea, however, is that it ushers in a new era in the history of naval warfare: the paramountcy of the aircraft carrier.

Right: Admiral Nimitz awards Admiral Thomas C Kinkaid the Distinguished Service Medal for his action in the Coral Sea.

Below: Lifeboat bearing survivors from the abandoned Lexington, *which finally sank in the early evening, 8 May.*

MIDWAY 1942

4–6 June 1942

Midway Island is a flyspeck in the vast Pacific Ocean, about halfway between Pearl Harbor and Japan. It is, in fact, an atoll – two tiny islands almost entirely surrounded by a barrier reef. In the center of the atoll is a lagoon with a narrow ship channel leading to it, on the western edge an open harbor. A few insignificant bits of coral – but in June 1942, they were to become the object of one of the greatest naval battles of World War II.

Admiral Isoroku Yamamoto, Commander in Chief of the Japanese Combined Fleet, had presented his plans for the campaign to the General Staff at the beginning of April 1942. It called for luring the remnants of the American Pacific Fleet to the defense of the solitary outpost, forcing it into a decisive battle, and destroying it.

The Naval General Staff agreed that a decisive battle was necessary at that point in the war, but was not convinced that Midway, only 1136 miles west-northwest of Pearl Harbor, was the best place to fight it. Instead, many members advocated cutting the lines of communication between the US and Australia by advancing on the islands of Fiji and Samoa. In addition, II Fleet objected on the grounds that it was not ready; IV Fleet, which was detailed to look after logistical problems following the occupation of the island, claimed it could not guarantee its ability to carry out this function even if the operation was successful; and I Air Fleet wanted to postpone the campaign to gain some time for rest and refitting after extensive operations in the Indian Ocean. Others pointed out that if the battle took place as planned, Japan's two most powerful carriers, the *Shokaku* and *Zuikaku*, would have to be left behind.

But Yamamoto stood firm. One of Japan's greatest military geniuses, with the rare ability both to devise original ideas and translate them into action, he had never been entirely confident about his island country's ability to wage war

against an industrial giant like the United States. Before the war he had warned the Premier, General Hideki Tojo, that 'If I am told to fight . . . I shall run wild for the first six months or a year, but I have utterly no confidence for the second and third years.' His outlook was not improved by the success of the Japanese attack on Pearl Harbor; he wrote to his sister, '. . . in spite of all the clamor that is going on we could lose [the war]. I can only do my best.' He now felt that success at Midway was not only vital strategically, but essential to Japan's survival. Eventually the General Staff gave in.

Just at this time, on 18 April, 16 B-25 bombers led by Lieutenant Colonel James Doolittle carried out a surprise attack on Tokyo from the aircraft carriers *Enterprise* and *Hornet*. They inflicted very little physical damage, but the psychological impact of this first attack on the Home Islands themselves was enormous. The Japanese had no idea where the raid came from (Roosevelt's comment that it had come from Shangri-La was not very helpful), and many suspected that it had originated from Midway. To the major goal of the Midway campaign – the destruction of the American fleet and subsequent mastery of the Pacific Ocean – was added another purpose: capture of the island would protect the Emperor from the indignity of being bombed again. It would also mean the elimination of an important refueling base for US submarines and provide a base for future raids on Pearl Harbor.

On 5 May, then, Imperial General Headquarters issued the order: 'Commander in Chief Combined Fleet will, in co-operation with the Army, invade and occupy strategic points in the Western Aleutians and Midway Island.'

By that time the first phase in the great Japanese offensive – the campaign to achieve control of the Coral Sea by seizing Tulagi in the Solomon Islands and Port Moresby in Papua – was well underway. The Battle of the Coral Sea, which began on 5 May, was a portent of

the trend in naval battles. For the first time in history, two fleets fought at a range of more than a hundred miles, without ever seeing each other. It was aircraft carrier against aircraft carrier while the great obsolete battleships proved to be of little use.

The opposing forces in that battle were more or less evenly matched; the Japanese V Carrier Division under Rear Admiral Chuichi Hara contained the two carriers *Shokaku* and *Zuikaku*, while Task Force 17 and 11 contained the two American carriers *Lexington* and *Yorktown*. Tactically, the action could be called a draw. The Japanese sank one heavy carrier – the *Lexington* – and heavily damaged *Yorktown*. On the other hand the Americans did achieve their aim of preventing the occupation of Port Moresby and, in addition, gained good experience in the tactical use of carriers. The Americans inflicted their share of damage as well: the *Shokaku* was so badly damaged that she was forced to retire for two months for repairs, while the *Zuikaku* lost so many crews and planes that she too had to return to Japan to be refitted. Overall, the Japanese pilots showed themselves unused to night operations and not all up to the high standards demonstrated at Pearl Harbor; over three-quarters of their bombing planes and pilots were lost. But the setback in the Battle of the Coral Sea – the first the Japanese had suffered – confirmed Yamamoto in his belief that

Admiral Nimitz inspects a bunker on Midway Island in June 1942.

top priority had to be given to the destruction of the rest of the American Fleet. Thus, the stage was set for the Midway campaign.

Yamamoto's battle plan, modeled on Hannibal's strategy at Cannae and Ludendorff's at Tannenberg, was a complicated one, utilizing the diversionary tactics and division of forces that were always integral parts of Japanese strategy. The standard Japanese pattern was to lure the enemy into an unfavorable tactical position, cut off his retreat, drive in on his flanks, and then concentrate forces for the kill.

Midway was no exception; Yamamoto's plan called for a strike on 3 June against Dutch Harbor in the Aleutians. Destruction of the American base and occupation of the western islands would not only secure the northernmost anchors of Japan's proposed 'ribbon defense,' but would, he hoped, lure the US Pacific Fleet northward. While the Americans were rushing to defend the Aleutians the Japanese would bomb and occupy Midway by 5 June. Then when the American fleet returned, before 7 June, Japanese planes based on the island and on carriers would mount an intensive bombing offensive. Any ships that escaped would be sunk by the Japanese battleships and cruisers.

Surprise was the key element in Yamamoto's plan; there was to be no challenge from the Americans until after Midway had been occupied. Even if the enemy did not take up the Aleutian challenge, they could not get to Midway before 7 June. And even if they did not contest the occupation, the pressure from Midway on Pearl Harbor would soon force them to counterattack.

The Japanese force was divided into five sections. An Advance Force of 16 submarines would harass the Americans as they approached Midway from either the Aleutians or Pearl Harbor. The Northern Area Force under Vice-Admiral Hosogaya consisted of the light carriers *Ryujo* and *Junyo*, along with two heavy cruisers, a destroyer screen, and four transport ships carrying troops for occupying the Aleutian islands of Adak, Attu, and Kiska.

The most power lay with Vice-Admiral Chuichi Nagumo's Main Striking Force: the four big carriers *Akagi*, *Kaga*, *Hiryu*, and *Soryu*, and their screen of destroyers and cruisers. Nagumo's task was to launch air strikes against Midway, to soften it up for Admiral Nobutake Kondo's Midway Occupation Force. Kondo had two bat-

tleships, six heavy cruisers, and many destroyers to support the 12 transports carrying a 5000-man occupation force.

Yamamoto was 300 miles behind Nagumo and Kondo, with the Main Body – a force composed of nine battleships and two light carriers, with their attendant cruiser and destroyer screen. He was flying his flag in the newly-constructed *Yamato* which, with its nine 18-inch guns, was the biggest and most powerful battleship in the world. There was little chance that the battleships, with a maximum range of only 40 miles, would play much part in the battle; some of Nagumo's younger officers claimed caustically that the battleship fleet was

Right: Cartoon drawn by a Marine and sent to Admiral Nimitz after the Battle of Midway.

Below: Admiral Chuichi Nagumo, C in C of the carrier fleet which struck at Midway.

holding a naval review in the Pacific. But Yamamoto, despite the great importance that he gave to aircraft and carriers, still felt it necessary to compromise with the conservatives who still advocated big ships and big guns.

The Japanese Fleet contained almost the entire fighting force of the Japanese Navy – 162 ships including four heavy carriers, four light carriers, 11 battleships, 22 cruisers, 65 destroyers, and 21 submarines.

To counter the blow that Yamamoto was planning, the Americans had three carriers – the *Enterprise*, *Hornet*, and *Yorktown*, eight cruisers, and 15 destroyers. There were no battleships; they rested on the bottom of Pearl Harbor, except for a few stationed on the West Coast that were too old and too slow to be of any real use in modern warfare. But even that small force was more than Yamamoto had thought the Americans could assemble. He believed that the *Yorktown* had been sunk in the Battle of the Coral Sea along with the *Lexington*, when in fact she had managed somehow to limp back to Pearl Harbor. Much has been made of the fact that the carrier was repaired and reprovisioned in three days and three nights, when the job would normally have taken 90 days. But it would be far from accurate to imply that the repairs were anything other than rough jury-rigging. The hull was patched and damaged compartments were braced with timbers. But only a few of the watertight doors were fixed and three superheated boilers that had been knocked out were not even touched. The ship would never be able to make a speed better than 27 knots.

The island of Midway itself served as a base for 54 Marine Corps planes (including 25 obsolete Brewster Buffalo fighters, 32 Navy Catalinas, and 23 Air Force planes (including 17 B-17s and six brand new Navy Avenger torpedo bombers). In addition to its planes, the island had two good search radars, was dotted with

artillery, and had almost 3000 men in Army and Marine units dug in and protected by bombproof shelters throughout the island. The actual invasion never took place, but if it had there is no certainty it would have succeeded. Midway's defenses were as carefully prepared as Tarawa's would be later in the war, and Kondo's force of 5000 was not nearly as impressive as the American force that eventually took Tarawa.

Admiral Chester Nimitz, Commander in Chief of the Pacific Fleet, was the man charged with containing the Japanese threat. Nimitz was a 57 year old Texan who had served in a variety of commands, including a stint in the submarine service during World War I, since his graduation from the US Naval Academy. He had made Rear Admiral in 1938, had been promoted to admiral in 1941, and was given command of the Pacific Fleet following the raid on Pearl Harbor. His calm, confident manner and refusal to bring in new staff gradually

rebuilt shattered morale, and even with the meager forces at his disposal he was able to organize raids on Japanese bases in the Marshall Islands, New Guinea, and New Britain during the spring of 1942.

Rear Admiral Frank Jack Fletcher, the spare, leathery veteran of the Coral Sea, was in tactical command of the forces mustered to defend Midway. Fletcher – 'Black Jack Fletcher' to his men, though his hair was blond and his eyes blue – was the commander of Task Force 17 built around the patched-up *Yorktown*. He had no control over the Midway-based forces, the submarines operating in the area, or the force sent to defend the Aleutians. Nor did he exercise much control over Task Force 16, which was centered on the *Enterprise* and the *Hornet*, under the temporary command of Rear Admiral Raymond Spruance; Rear Admiral William Halsey (mistakenly nicknamed 'Bull' by a confused journalist) was in the hospital being treated for a skin disease.

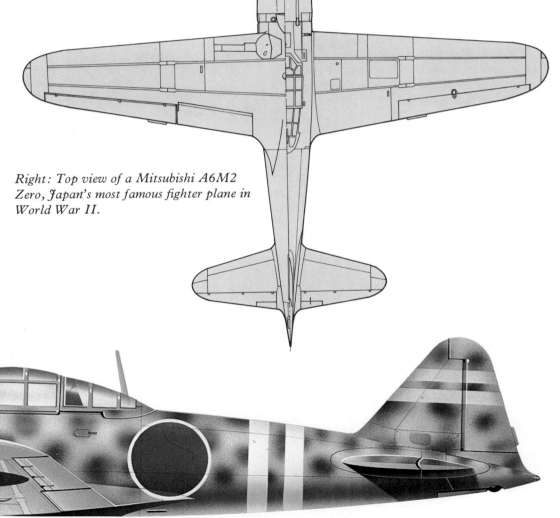

Right: Top view of a Mitsubishi A6M2 Zero, Japan's most famous fighter plane in World War II.

Below: Side view of a Zeke (Zero). Zeke was the nickname used when a Zero operated from a carrier.

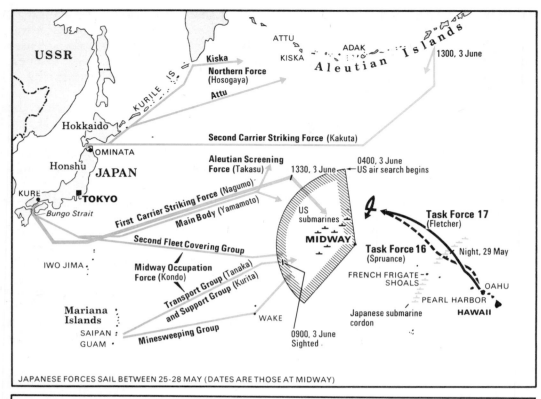

Map labels (top):

USSR

ATTU
ADAK
KISKA
KISKA
1300, 3 June
Aleutian Islands

Kiska
Northern Force
(Hosogaya)
Attu

Hokkaido

Second Carrier Striking Force (Kakuta)

OMINATA

Honshu
JAPAN

Aleutian Screening Force (Takasu)
1330, 3 June

0400, 3 June
US air search begins

KURE
TOKYO
Bungo Strait

First Carrier Striking Force (Nagumo)
Main Body (Yamamoto)

US submarines

MIDWAY

Task Force 17
(Fletcher)

Second Fleet Covering Group

Midway Occupation Force (Kondo)

Task Force 16
(Spruance)
Night, 29 May

IWO JIMA

FRENCH FRIGATE SHOALS

Transport Group (Tanaka)
and Support Group (Kurita)

OAHU

Mariana Islands

WAKE

PEARL HARBOR
HAWAII

SAIPAN

0900, 3 June
Sighted

Japanese submarine cordon

GUAM
Minesweeping Group

JAPANESE FORCES SAIL BETWEEN 25-28 MAY (DATES ARE THOSE AT MIDWAY)

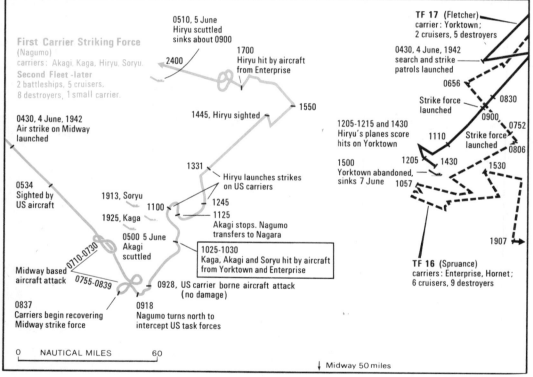

Map labels (battle detail):

First Carrier Striking Force
(Nagumo)
carriers: Akagi, Kaga, Hiryu, Soryu.
Second Fleet -later
2 battleships, 5 cruisers,
8 destroyers, 1 small carrier.

0510, 5 June
Hiryu scuttled
sinks about 0900

2400

1700
Hiryu hit by aircraft
from Enterprise

1445, Hiryu sighted

1550

TF 17 (Fletcher)
carrier: Yorktown;
2 cruisers, 5 destroyers

0430, 4 June, 1942
Air strike on Midway
launched

0430, 4 June, 1942
search and strike
patrols launched

0656

Strike force
launched

0830

0900
0752

1110

Strike force
launched

0806

1205-1215 and 1430
Hiryu's planes score
hits on Yorktown

1331

Hiryu launches strikes
on US carriers

0534
Sighted by
US aircraft

1913, Soryu

1100

1245

1205

1430

1530

1500
Yorktown abandoned,
sinks 7 June

1057

1925, Kaga

1125
Akagi stops. Nagumo
transfers to Nagara

0710-0730

0500 5 June
Akagi
scuttled

1025-1030
Kaga, Akagi and Soryu hit by aircraft
from Yorktown and Enterprise

1907

Midway based
aircraft attack

0755-0839

0928, US carrier
borne aircraft attack
(no damage)

0837
Carriers begin recovering
Midway strike force

0918
Nagumo turns north to
intercept US task forces

TF 16 (Spruance)
carriers: Enterprise, Hornet;
6 cruisers, 9 destroyers

0   NAUTICAL MILES   60

↓ Midway 50 miles

The strike forces attacking Midway (top) and the battle itself (above). Below: The remains of the Japanese carrier Kaga.

In one sense Yamamoto had done the US Navy a favor at Pearl Harbor by effectively forcing America into the new age of carrier warfare. Although in 1941 the Navy was still wedded to the notion that battleships and big guns engaging in epic Jutland-style battles constituted naval warfare, they were forced by the destruction of Battleship Row to make full and exclusive use of their real power – the carriers and the fighter planes, with their bombs and airborne torpedoes. Nimitz and his subordinate officers were adept at meeting the new situation, while Yamamoto had to contend with the highly conservative staff of the Japanese Navy, many of whom found his interest in naval air warfare anathema.

With the vast area of the Central and South Pacific to defend and with only modest forces at his disposal, Nimitz would have found himself in difficulties many times had not American intelligence come to his aid. The Japanese codes had been broken long before the war started, and as a result the Pacific Command usually had enough information from decoded fleet messages to form a reasonably accurate picture of Japanese intentions.

By 10 May intelligence had already confirmed Nimitz's suspicions about the next Japanese objective – Midway. He even had the major details of Yamamoto's plan, along with his approximate schedule and routes. Nimitz was familiar enough with Yamamoto's philosophy and style to predict a full attack on the island, with the destruction of the American carriers as one of the primary objectives, even though some of his officers feared that it was all an elaborate deception designed to cover another attack on Pearl Harbor or the West Coast.

The North Pacific Task Force – two heavy cruisers, three light cruisers, a destroyer division, a nine-destroyer strike group, six S Class submarines, and numerous other craft – was formed by 17

May and placed under the command of Rear Admiral Robert ('Fuzzy') Theobald. Theobald did not get to Kodiak, off the Alaskan coast, to take command until 27 May, however; and the main body of his fleet was still assembling when the Japanese attacked Dutch Harbor on 3 June.

Meanwhile, on 24 May, Fletcher received a high-priority, top secret message at Tongatabu in the Friendly Islands where he was refueling and repairing what damage he could after his pounding on the Coral Sea. 'What it said,' he later recalled, 'was simply this: Get the hell back here, quick.' Fletcher hoisted anchor almost immediately; 26 May marked the *Yorktown*'s hundredth day at sea without proper replenishment – a record unequaled by any other modern American warship up to that time – and on 27 May she was steaming up the channel to Pearl Harbor to the accompaniment of whistles, sirens, and cheers. On 28 May, the *Hornet* and *Enterprise* left to take up their stations; *Yorktown* followed on 30 May. Fletcher and Spruance had received their orders: to '... inflict maximum damage on the enemy by employing strong attrition attacks' (in other words, heavy air strikes). A further letter of instruction directed them to be 'governed by the principles of calculated risk.'

Nagumo's Japanese carrier force left their home base on 26 May, followed by Yamamoto and the Main Body on 28 May. Neither commander was feeling very happy; Yamamoto was suffering from stomach cramps caused by tension, and Nagumo was worried because his carriers and crew had had barely a month for maintenance and refresher training. He later commented, 'We participated in the battle with meager training and without knowledge of the enemy.' Morale among the men in the fleet was high, however. Meanwhile, Japanese submarines were taking up stations east of Midway to intercept any American ships sent out to relieve the island.

As they approached Midway from the west the Japanese Main Striking Force was shielded from patrolling American search planes by the many storms and fogs that occur in that area in May and June. Aboard his flagship, the carrier *Akagi*, Nagumo went over his plans for the last time. He decided to send 100 planes against Midway on 4 June and to hold back an equal number, including some torpedo planes, for a second wave. Of his many long-range scouts, which included cruiser and battleship float

planes with a range of over 600 miles, seven would be detailed to keep a lookout for an enemy task force while Midway was being hit. They would cover an arc from due south to northeast; in the unlikely event that an American force should appear, the second wave could be sent against it instead of against the island.

Starting on 30 May, Nimitz began taking precautions to ensure against a Japanese sneak attack. The 22 Navy Catalina patrol bombers on Midway were sent on daily sweeps 700 miles out, and the Midway B-17s flew on daily search-attack missions to the area where the enemy was expected.

The waddling Catalinas were both the joy and despair of American pilots. They climbed, flew, and landed at almost the same speed (about 65 knots) and were armed only with .30 caliber machine guns in side blisters. The rumbling amphibians were death traps when cornered by Japanese fighters, but their redeeming feature was that they could fly almost all day long without refueling.

Just before noon on 2 June Task Forces 16 and 17 – the *Yorktown* and her escorts, and the *Enterprise*, *Hornet* and their escorts – rendezvoused at 'Point Luck' about 325 miles northeast of Midway, and Fletcher took command of the combined fleet.

The Battle of Midway opened at 0300 hours on 3 June, more than 1000 miles

Below: SBD Dauntlesses over Midway Island, which was a fourth US 'aircraft carrier.'

USS Yorktown *(CV. 5) was repaired in a weekend and was ready for action at Midway.*

Grumman fighters take off from the carrier Enterprise *at the start of the Midway battle.*

A Douglas SBD-3 Dauntless warms up aboard the Yorktown.

from the atoll itself, with the diversionary attack in the Aleutians. Theobald had deployed his force 400 miles south of Kodiak, fearing an attack on the American base at Dutch Harbor. Hosogaya's force slipped by the Americans easily in the fog and rain, however, and the base in the Eastern Aleutians was heavily bombed. The undefended islands of Attu and Kiska were occupied by the Japanese by 7 June, but the Army P-40s on Unmak convinced Hosogaya to bypass that island.

At 0843 hours the first sighting report was received from a Midway-based Catalina pilot, who continued to shadow the 11 Japanese ships he had found until 1100 hours. Fletcher concluded rightly that they were not the large carrier force he was expecting; in fact, they were probably Kondo's Midway Occupation Force. Nine Army B-17s took off from Midway to attack the convoy, but made no hits. Fletcher, who was 300 miles eastnortheast of Midway (and some 400 miles east of Nagumo), was certain that the Japanese carriers would approach the island from the northwest and strike the following day. Assuming that his presence was – and would remain – unknown, he hoped to be in a position to launch an attack against the carriers from their left flank as soon as the enemy planes had begun their strike against Midway. At 1931 hours on 3 June, he altered course to the southwest, which would bring him to a point some 200 miles north of Midway by morning. Through the night of 3–4 June the two carrier forces sailed toward each other on converging courses.

At 0430 hours on the morning of 4 June, 15 minutes after some 11 Catalinas had taken off from Midway to make another attempt to find the Japanese carriers, the *Yorktown* sent up ten dive

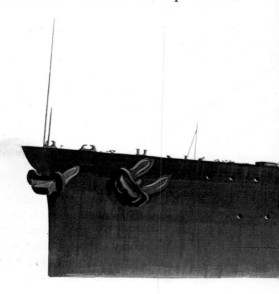

bombers on a 100-mile search, as a routine precaution against the possibility of surprise. At the same time, 215 miles to the west, Nagumo was launching his first strike against Midway: 36 Nakajima B5N2s (Kates), 36 Aichi D3A2s (Vals), and 36 Mitsubichi A6M3s (Zeros) rose from the decks of their four carriers. At 0500 hours the 108 Japanese planes were in formation, flying on a steady course for Midway.

Along with this first strike wave, Nagumo also sent up seven float planes to make a 300 miles reconnaissance. But no one in command really expected the American fleet to be anywhere near the area, and their overconfidence must have been transmitted to the search planes. Even though a seaplane from the heavy cruiser *Chikuma* passed almost directly over the US force and had an indecisive encounter with one of the *Yorktown*'s Dauntless dive bombers, it failed to either spot the American ships or to report the engagement, which would have been a sure sign of the presence of an American aircraft carrier in the vicinity.

At 0530 hours one of the Catalina pilots spotted the Japanese carriers through the heavy cloud cover and radioed a report back to Midway; the message was intercepted by the *Enterprise* and relayed to Fletcher on *Yorktown* at 0534 hours. A few minutes later, at 0545 hours, a second PBY radioed another message, without even bothering with code: 'Many planes headed Mid-

way, repeat, Midway . . . .' The Pilot then continued to shadow the Japanese ships, dodging the fighters that had been sent up to intercept him, until he was joined by other Catalinas who kept the carriers under constant surveillance from then on.

As soon as Fletcher had an approximate position for the Japanese force he signaled Spruance to proceed southwest with the *Enterprise* and *Hornet* and 'attack the enemy carriers when definitely located.' The *Yorktown* would wait to recover her search planes and obtain further information. At the same time (about 0530 hours) every plane on Midway was being ordered into the air in response to the Catalina's warning; by 0600 hours the only plane left on the ground was an old Grumman single-float biplane. Most of the interceptors were elderly, slow, Marine Corps Buffaloes – no match for the efficient new Zeros. But anti-aircraft fire on the island was good and about a third of the Japanese strike force was shot down. They had inflicted a fair amount of damage on the ground installations – barracks, mess halls, oil tanks, even the hospital. But casualties were light and the runways remained

useable. Six new Navy Avenger torpedo bombers and four Army B-26s streaked after the recent attackers to counterattack, and 16 B-17s already in the air were also ordered to turn north and attack the Japanese carriers.

Nagumo's second strike force (93 planes) was waiting on its flight decks, armed with bombs and torpedoes, in case enemy surface forces appeared. But the returning planes from the first strike reported that the island would require another attack – a point that was emphasized by the appearance of the ten American planes from Midway even though they were not able to score a hit.

At 0715 hours Nagumo ordered the second wave planes taken below and rearmed with incendiary and fragmentation bombs for an attack on the island, clearing the decks for the return of the first wave; the entire process would take about an hour. Although in retrospect the order appears to have been a colossal blunder, at the time it seemed a reasonable move; Japanese scout planes had found no sign of an American surface force in the area, and Midway obviously had to be struck again since planes from the island had just attacked Nagumo's own ship.

But not quite 15 minutes later, at 0728 hours, the Admiral was amazed to re-

Right: The Japanese battleship Fuso *displaced 34,500 tons and carried twelve 14-inch guns. She was finally sunk in the Surigao Strait during the Battle of Leyte Gulf in 1944.*

ceive the worst possible news from the *Chikuma*'s scout plane – a vague report that an 'estimated ten ships' had been sighted in the northeast. Nagumo paced the bridge for another 15 minutes, then asked the reconnaissance plane for more specific information and ordered the second planes to be rearmed with torpedoes. At 0809 hours the scout plane reported that the enemy force consisted of five cruisers and five destroyers; at 0820 hours the pilot added that they were accompanied by 'what appears to be a carrier' (the *Yorktown*). Nagumo's worst fears had been realized, but he could not send his second wave off; the flight decks had to be kept clear to recover the first Midway strike force.

Following the first attack by the Avengers and B-26s the Japanese carrier force had been subjected to a series of attacks, first by the Army B-17s, then by a flight of 11 old Vought SB2U Vindicators piloted by Marines, and finally by the submarine *Nautilus*, which had intercepted early reports of the Japanese position. Without fighter cover, however, all the planes were beaten off without scoring a single hit and the submarine was only able to fire one ineffective torpedo before she had to run for her life under a heavy Japanese depth charge attack. At this point Nagumo had been attacked by 52 American planes and one submarine, and had not been touched; his fleet was intact while over half of the aircraft on Midway had been knocked out. As far as he knew he had only to launch one more strike at Midway and deal with one American carrier. But Spruance had already decided on a strategy and launched his own attack forces.

Spruance had originally intended waiting until 0900 hours when he would be about 100 miles from the enemy, but after discussions with his Chief of Staff, Captain Miles Browning, he decided to launch his planes early in hopes of catching the carriers while the Japanese attack planes were being rearmed and refueled. He sent up almost every operational plane he had – 67 Dauntless dive bombers, 29 torpedo bombers, and 20 Wildcats – holding back only 32 Wildcats for combat air patrol. The pilots were given orders based on the assumption that Nagumo would continue on his course toward Midway until his strike planes were recovered at about 0900 hours.

Fletcher, in the *Yorktown*, had lost sight of Task Force 16 soon after he had sent it dashing on ahead; the two functioned almost as independent units

Torpedo bombers on the deck of the USS Enterprise *during the Battle of Midway.*

A Dauntless ditches near a heavy cruiser at Midway after running out of gas.

Yorktown *under heavy attack at Midway which finally sank her.*

through the rest of the battle. After he recovered his search planes he held back his own attack force for a time, waiting to see if any additional sighting reports would come in. When none did, he sent up his own planes at 0906 hours – 12 torpedo bombers, 17 dive bombers, and six Wildcats. Above his ship flew the Japanese scout plane, now joined by another float plane, the *Tone*, beaming a homing signal to be used later to guide a strike force directly to the carrier. From that moment the *Yorktown* was a marked ship.

Recovery operations had begun aboard the four Japanese carriers at 0837 hours, as they steamed toward Midway in a loose box formation – *Hiryu* and *Kaga* to the east, *Soryu* and *Akagi* to the west – inside a screen of two battleships, three cruisers, and 11 destroyers. But Nagumo was growing increasingly nervous as reconnaissance reports told him of a large force of carrier planes approaching; before his recovery was complete he turned eastnortheast to contact the enemy carriers, while his crews worked hastily (and thus, somewhat carelessly) to rearm and refuel the planes.

Fortunately for the Japanese, this change in course caused 35 dive bombers and ten fighters from the *Hornet* to miss them completely; all of them eventually ran out of fuel and either made forced landings on Midway or ditched. The torpedo squadron from the *Hornet*, however, had ignored their orders and set off on their own course; at 0925 hours they spotted smoke from the Japanese ships and swooped down to attack in the face of heavy anti-aircraft fire and a large number of Zeros. Without air cover they had no chance – all 15 planes were shot down and 29 of the 30 pilots were killed. At 0930 the 14 torpedo bombers from the *Enterprise* arrived, also without fighter cover; ten were shot down and the remaining four were so badly battered they could hardly make their escape. At 1000 hours Torpedo 3 from the *Yorktown* arrived with six Wildcats, who were quickly driven off by about 15 Zeros in the only fighter plane action to take place over the Japanese fleet. Only five of the 12 torpedo planes and three of the Wildcats survived the attack. No hits had been registered by the 47 aircraft, only six of which returned.

Meanwhile, 37 dive bombers from the *Enterprise* had been searching vainly for the Japanese force when the leader of the Wildcat fighter squadron radioed that he was over the enemy fleet, but that he was

Yorktown *ablaze after the first Japanese assault.*

A 'Kate' bomber turns away from the Yorktown *after missing the first strike.*

Crewmen cautiously examine damage aboard the Yorktown *during the battle.*

short on fuel and was heading home. This was the first news that Spruance and Browning had had of their strike, and Lieutenant Commander Clarence McClusky, leader of the squadron, could hear Browning screaming, 'Attack! Attack!' over the radio. Replying 'Wilco, as soon as I find the bastards,' he headed toward the carriers. At 1002 hours the dive bombers raced down from 14,000 feet toward the *Akagi* and *Kaga*.

The Japanese ships had been forced to take violent evasive maneuvers to escape the torpedo attacks and had not been able to launch more defensive fighters, while those already in the air were at a low altitude and could not climb high enough to meet this new attack. The *Akagi*, with 40 planes refueling on deck, sustained three hits within two minutes; one of the bombs fell on a hangar containing stored torpedoes and another struck the fueling planes on the flight deck. At 1047 hours Nagumo reluctantly transferred his flag to the light cruiser, *Nagara*; by 1915 hours that evening the fiercely burning carrier had been abandoned. The *Kaga* took four hits; one killed everyone on the bridge, including the captain, while others started fires in the bomb and gasoline storage areas. She, too, was soon abandoned and sank at 1925 hours.

While the planes from the *Enterprise* were attacking *Akagi* and *Kaga*, 17 dive bombers from *Yorktown* were swooping down on the *Soryu*. Despite starting out nearly an hour and a half later than the other attack groups, they had arrived at the same time, thanks to smart navigating advice from Hubie Strange (the weatherman) and Oscar Pederson (the air group commander) aboard *Yorktown*. Attacking in three waves at one-minute intervals, they dropped three 1000lb bombs on *Soryu*'s flight deck. The ship burst into flames and had to be abandoned within twenty minutes. Damage control parties had the fires under control by 1145 hours, but then the submarine *Nautilus* re-entered the fray and put three torpedoes into the carrier, restarting the fires. At 1610 hours the *Soryu* broke in half and slipped beneath the waves.

After the attacks the dive bombers

Above: A Douglas SBD Dauntless used by pilots of the US Marines on the Yorktown.

headed back to their carriers. Most made it – some on literally their last gallon of gasoline – but a few had to ditch, owing to a miscalculation of the carriers' position. Three Japanese carriers had been left in flames, but the *Enterprise* had lost 14 of 37 dive bombers, ten of 14 torpedo bombers, and one Wildcat. The *Hornet* had lost all her torpedo bombers and 12 Wildcats, while her dive bombers had missed the battle entirely. *Yorktown* was down seven of 12 torpedo bombers, two dive bombers, and three Wildcats. Fletcher launched a search mission to find the fourth carrier; the *Hiryu* had been far ahead of the other three carriers, and had been missed by the first wave of American dive bombers.

Since he still had *Hiryu*, with a full complement of planes, Nagumo decided to carry on the battle, reasoning that the Americans had only one or two carriers which had already used most of their planes. He sent a message to Yamamoto: 'Sighted enemy composed of one carrier, five cruisers, and six destroyers at position bearing ten degrees 240 miles from Midway,' then he headed for the *Yorktown*.

The first Japanese attack group, composed of 18 Vals and six Zeros, was launched at 1100 hours, followed by a second group of ten Kates and six Zeros at 1331 hours. At the same time Admiral Kondo, who had intercepted the message to Yamamoto, signaled that he was coming north to support the carrier force, while Yamamoto ordered the light carriers *Ryujo* and *Junyo* south from the Aleutians to help.

By flying low, the Japanese planes managed to stay under the straight line beam of the *Yorktown*'s crude radar, and

were not detected until they were only 46 miles from the ship. At noon the carrier began taking evasive action; the heavy cruisers *Astoria* and *Portland*, as well as the destroyers *Hammann*, *Anderson*, *Russell*, *Morris*, and *Hughes*, formed a defensive ring around her; the 12 Wildcats that were airborne as combat air patrol went out to intercept, joined by several Wildcats rushed over from *Hornet*. The first wave of 24 Japanese planes arrived at 1210 hours. In a dogfight to end all dogfights, the badly outnumbered interceptors knocked out ten Vals and three fighters, while anti-aircraft fire accounted for two more dive bombers. But three of the remaining six planes managed to score a hit. The first bomb damaged the boilers, the second started a fire that was put out by flooding, and the third exploded on the flight deck, resulting in another fire and many casualties. Fletcher transferred his flag to the *Astoria*, since *Yorktown*'s communications equipment had been knocked out; but by 1340 hours repair parties had the carrier running at 18 knots again. The fighters were on deck refueling at 1630 hours when the second attack group was picked up on the radar. There were 12 Wildcats on combat air patrol, but the Kates and Zeros slipped by them and scored two torpedo hits which ruptured most of the fuel tanks on the port side, cut of all power, jammed the rudder, and caused a

17° list. Afraid that the *Yorktown* would capsize, and unable to repair the damage, Captain Elliott Buckmaster gave the order to abandon ship at 1500 hours.

'Old Yorky' stayed afloat, however, and on 6 June Fletcher sent a salvage party over on the destroyer *Hammann* to attempt to get her back to port. But the *Yorktown* had been sighted by a Japanese reconnaissance plane, and Submarine *I-168* commanded by one of Japan's great daredevil sailors, Commander Yahachi Tanabe, slipped through the destroyer screen. *I-168* put one torpedo into *Hammann*, which sank within four minutes, and two more into the *Yorktown* before escaping through a heavy depth charge attack to wind up what had been one of the greatest submarine exploits of the war. The *Yorktown* finally sank at 0500 hours on 7 June.

The *Hiryu* was finally spotted by one of the planes Fletcher had sent out just prior to the attack on the *Yorktown* and at 1630 hours 24 dive bombers from *Enterprise*, including ten refugees from the *Yorktown*, took off – without fighter cover, since all operational Wildcats were flying defensive formations. The group found the *Hiryu* at 1700 hours and

Above right: A firefighting detail aboard the Yorktown.
Right: The Yorktown *lists to port shortly before sinking as a destroyer draws by to rescue survivors.*

Below: Yorktown *lies dead in the water after the first attack as F4F Wildcats remain helplessly on deck.*

scored four solid hits, losing only three of their number. B-17s from Midway made another attack about an hour later, but – with their usual bad luck – made no hits. Another group of five Vindicators and six dive bombers took off from Midway at 1900 hours, but could not locate the carrier. The *Hiryu* was abandoned by all hands except her captain at 0230 hours the next morning, and finally sank at 0900 hours.

For all intents and purposes, the Battle of Midway was over. Yamamoto, who had been several hundred miles north-west of Nagumo during the carrier battle of 4 June, considered joining up with Kondo's Midway Occupation Force and the Aleutian force and engaging the Americans in a traditional naval battle. Nagumo, who disagreed, was summarily relieved of command. But as reports came in revealing that the Americans still had two operational carriers, while all four Japanese carriers were either sunk or abandoned, Yamamoto realized that a dawn air attack was more probable than a night gun battle. He therefore reluctantly ordered his forces to turn west.

Spruance, meanwhile, had quite rightly decided that a night engagement with a large Japanese force, far better equipped than he for night fighting, would not be to his advantage. He turned east and headed away from the battle area until midnight.

Midway was the first defeat ever suffered by the Japanese Navy, and news of the debacle was completely suppressed in Japan. All papers concerning the event were classified top secret and destroyed in 1945, so that the Japanese public only learned of the events at Midway in the 1950s when published accounts began to appear.

Japan lost four heavy carriers, one heavy cruiser, 322 planes, and 3500 men at Midway, against one heavy carrier, 150 planes, and 307 men for the Americans. Though Yamamoto blamed the disaster on the failure of his advance screen of submarines to locate and harass the Americans, in fact the responsibility for deploying the submarines in the wrong place was his. It was also Yamamoto who divided his huge fleet and then devised for it a rigid, highly complicated battle plan that was entirely based on what he assumed the Americans would do. The Americans did not follow the script, and the Japanese commanders were not trained to adapt rapidly to radically different situations.

But without the complete and accurate intelligence reports gathered by the

Survivors of the Yorktown *assemble on the deck of a cruiser that rescued them.*

Japanese heavy cruiser Mikuma, *abandoned and sinking, on the afternoon of 6 June. She was sunk by dive bombers from the* Enterprise.

Americans, the Japanese plan might well have succeeded. These reports, which gave Nimitz the time and the knowledge to correctly dispose his forces, were probably the crucial factor in the American victory.

The Battle of Midway is worthy of note in the history of naval warfare, in that it marks the end of the transition period between the eras dominated by battleships and by carriers. Even more than Coral Sea, Midway demonstrated the central role of the carrier plane. Despite a fleet that remained largely intact and immeasurably superior fire power, Yamamoto was forced to retire without firing a shot once he lost his air cover.

Midway saw the debut of the Zeke, or Zero-3 fighter plane. The original Zero had been far more maneuverable and had a rate of climb three times greater than its American counterparts, and the new Zero was a vast improvement. But the Japanese pilots proved to be inferior to the Americans, an indication of the deterioration of the Japanese air arm and the growing shortage of well-trained pilots since Pearl Harbor. On the American side, the Dauntless dive bomber, which was to become the most successful carrier plane of the war, performed superbly, while the Devastator torpedo bomber proved so disappointing that it was taken off the list of naval combat planes and replaced with the new Avenger.

The Battle of Midway did not decide the entire course of the Pacific War in a moment, nor did it end with the utter destruction of one of the combatants. Its importance lies in the fact that it broke Japan's naval superiority and restored the balance between the two navies. Once that had happened, as Yamamoto foresaw, it was only a matter of time until economic mobilization allowed America to overwhelm Japan.

Japanese carrier Hiryu *burning on 5 June.*

A TBF Avenger, the sole survivor of its squadron after Midway.

GUADALCANAL 1942

Immediately after the Battle of Midway, the central point of the war in the Pacific moved back to the Southwest Pacific Area again. The Japanese wished to strengthen their hold in that area, and decided to temporarily give up the plan to disrupt communications between the Australians and Americans. Japanese planners decided on a two-fold maneuver, beginning with an overland campaign from the north coast of New Guinea to capture the vital supply base at Port Moresby, and at the same time consolidating their position in the Solomons.

Meanwhile, American interest in the southern Solomons was picking up considerably. The two overall commanders were Admiral Chester Nimitz and General Douglas MacArthur, men who were not used to being on the defensive. The pressure was now off Hawaii for the moment and the time was ripe for a limited offensive against the Japanese. The important question was where to strike and who would command the offensive. This was settled by a Joint Chiefs of Staff directive on 2 July 1942, ordering a parallel advance upon Rabaul, up the Solomons and along the New Guinea coast. It was to be accomplished in three stages: the seizure of the Santa Cruz Islands, then Tulagi and the adjacent islands; the occupation of the Solomons, with Papua and New Guinea up to the Huon Peninsula; finally, the capture of Rabaul and the remainder of the Bismarck Archipelago. The initial phase of this operation was code named Watchtower. Also the boundary between the Southwest Pacific and Pacific Ocean Commands was moved slightly so that some of the Solomons came under Nimitz's sphere of operational control. MacArthur was to oversee the completion of the final two phases.

On 5 July 1942 reconnaissance aircraft confirmed the reports of the Australian coastwatchers that the Japanese had transferred large troop concentrations from Tulagi to the nearby island of Guadalcanal, and were building an airfield of unknown proportions. This news

threw a monkeywrench into the entire operations, if the Japanese were allowed to complete an airfield unopposed, they would be able to launch fighters and bombers at all Allied attempts to move into the Solomons and the Coral Sea. The all important objective was now to seize Guadalcanal and the strategic airstrip at Lunga Point, later to be renamed Henderson Field, and consequently the Santa Cruz portion was dropped from the agenda.

Guadalcanal was no paradise as the Marines who fought and died there could attest. It was a hell hole, an island forgotten in time. Ninety miles long and 25 miles wide, a mixture of rain forests, stinking malarial swamps, thick grasslands and undergrowth, and steep, treacherous mountains; that was Guadalcanal, a strategic objective for a few months on a general's map which later as the war progressed would be forgotten and returned to its semi-primeval state of existence. The 'Canal' as it became known to the Marines who fought on it and to the American people who read about it in their daily papers, was situated in the southern half of the Solomons group, which comprises many islands running for 600 miles in a southeast direction from Rabaul, Buka and Bougainville. The remaining islands and atolls form a double chain separated by a deep channel which was given the name of 'The Slot.'

In the weeks which followed, plans were thrashed out, differences settled, troops gathered and an overall strategic commander selected, Vice-Admiral Robert Ghormley. The amphibious force was commanded by Rear Admiral Richmond Kelly Turner. Rear Admiral Frank Fletcher, who commanded the carrier task force at the Battles of the Coral Sea and Midway, was in command of the carriers off Guadalcanal and provided air cover for the operation. The air support force was composed of the carriers *Enterprise*, *Saratoga* and *Wasp* screened by the new battleship *North Carolina*, six cruisers and 16 destroyers. The convoy of transports consisted of

Below: Bomb damage on the USS Enterprise (CV.6) received in the Battle of the Eastern Solomons in August 1942.

Bottom: A PT boat of the kind introduced in the Solomons and subsequently used throughout the world by the US Navy during World War II.

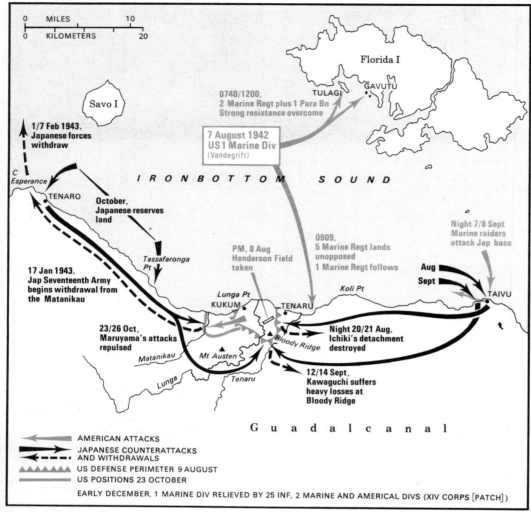

The long fight on land for Guadalcanal.

four cruisers and 11 destroyers, and was to carry the 1st US Marine Division. The Marine force was commanded by a crusty old fighter, Major General Alexander Archer Vandegrift. The convoy was screened by Rear Admiral Victor Crutchley with a force of three Australian and two American cruisers (HMS *Australia*, *Canberra* and *Hobart*, USS *Chicago* and USS *San Juan*).

The operation was being supported by land-based aircraft from airfields in Fiji, New Caledonia and New Hebrides, and also from army aircraft under Mac-Arthur's command. There were to be two landings, the first on the larger island of Guadalcanal and the second on the much smaller island of Tulagi.

Although these preparations seemed quite thorough, in fact, the organization behind the operation left much to be desired. Vandegrift had been given very little time to train his men and get them acclimatized. Although the 1st Marine Division had a core of seasoned veterans, most of the men were new recruits with no fighting experience. The Operation was nicknamed Operation Shoestring because it had been so hastily put to-

gether. Vandegrift pushed the target date back by a week for a landing on 7 August but could not get a further extension. Thus much equipment and materiel was left on the docks at Wellington, New Zealand. The amphibious force set off on 22nd July and met the air support task force south of Fiji; after a four day practice on a remote island of the group, they set sail for the 'Canal' on 31 July. The force was undetected in its approach because of heavy haze and intermittent rain squalls. On 7 August the initial landings were made on Red Beach at Guadalcanal near Lunga Point and on Tulagi. There was no opposition on Guadalcanal as all the Japanese technicians had fled into the jungle and by nightfall 11,000 Marines were ashore. On the next day, the airfield was secured and the Marines put out scouts to ascertain what the Japanese were planning. On Tulagi the situation was not as clear-cut, the Japanese were better prepared, and the three battalions of Marines met stiff resistance. By 8 August Tulagi was completely under Marine control, the casualties were 108 Marines dead and 140 wounded. The Japanese garrison of

1500 troops was practically exterminated to a man. Meanwhile, it had taken only 48 hours to gain the initial foothold on the 'Canal,' but it would be another six months of intense and bitter fighting before it could be secured. The scene was now set for one of the cruellest hardest fought campaigns in the Pacific.

Japanese actions were swift: immediately after the US landings, a striking force from the 25th Air Flotilla was dispatched from Rabaul. On 7 and 8 August, Japanese bombers attacked the transports lying off Lunga Point and would have caused heavy damage, except for the timely warnings given by the Australian coastwatchers. The attacks were intercepted by US aircraft from the naval carriers but two destroyers were hit and one transport was lost. The Marines were digging in around Henderson Field and prepared for a major Japanese attack.

When the news of the landings reached Rabaul, Admiral Gunichi Mikawa was in the middle of preparing for a major offensive against Port Moresby. He immediately guessed American intentions and decided to send all available ships to attack and destroy the US naval forces off Guadalcanal, and then to reinforce and exterminate the Marine landing force on the island. By 7 August, five heavy and two light cruisers were sailing towards the 'Canal.' To make matters worse, Imperial General Headquarters issued orders to reinforce the garrison of the island and a convoy carrying 500 additional troops, with a destroyer escort were *en route*. Shortly after setting sail one of the transports was torpedoed by a US submarine, so the convoy was recalled to Rabaul.

On the beaches itself, the supply and logistics problems were mounting for Vandegrift, who was trying to keep to his original timetable. At 1400 hours, he ordered the 1st Battalion, 5th Marines to advance westward to Alligator Creek and dig in for the night. By 1600 hours Vandegrift was ashore and had established his forward command post. During all this the Japanese were far from idle, they had launched two air strikes. The first was at 1320 hours and consisted of 24 aircraft of the Japanese 25th Air Flotilla. Warning was received from an Australian coastwatcher and a welcoming party was arranged. Twelve Japanese aircraft were shot down by Wildcats from the *Saratoga*, but the USS *Mugford*, a destroyer was hit and 22 men killed. Two hours later there was an attack by ten Aichi E16A1 dive bombers

Above: Major General A A Vandegrift of the Marine Corps in his tent on Guadalcanal.

Above right: Rear Admiral Kelly Turner organized the transport of Marines.

Above far right: Admiral Turner and General Vandegrift aboard the McCawley.

Right: The anti-aircraft guns of the Enterprise *in early 1943.*

but no serious damage was recorded. The First Marine Combat Group 'B,' commanded by Colonel Clifton Cates had been ordered by Vandegrift to proceed to Mount Austen but they were held up due to the terrific heat and tropical undergrowth. Vandegrift realized that Mount Austen would not be reached that day; so he changed his plans accordingly. The Marines were to secure their positions and dig in for the night. The next morning the Marines would push forward towards the Lunga and bypass Mount Austen, occupying the airstrip from the south. The 5th Marines were to advance on Lunga also and then continue to Kukum. There were many shaky Marines on the first night but the Japanese did not make the expected counterattack. On Saturday, 8 August, the 1st Battalion, 5th Marines, supported by the 1st Tank Battalion, succeeded in crossing the mouth of Alligator Creek. The Marines believed that this was in fact the Tenaru River, but it was in reality the Ilu. The 1st Battalion, 1st Marines, acting on orders swung west away from Mount Austen and began to advance. This unit moved very slowly

and had difficulty crossing one of the numerous creeks in its path. The other units, the 2nd and 3rd Battalions made faster progress through the jungle than their counterparts in the 1st. The day was extremely hot and humid to say the least and by the end of the day the 1st Battalion had passed the airfield, but the 2nd and 3rd Battalions had in their turn slowed down and were still south of the airfield when the order came to dig in for the night.

The 5th Marines made good progress and managed to take a few Japanese prisoners. It was gathered from information sweated out of the enemy that no Japanese resistance would be encountered within the next 48 hours. Vandegrift took immediate advantage of this situation and ordered the 5th Marines to advance more rapidly. The regiment crossed the Lunga over the main bridge, and by skirting the airfield to the north, it took Kukum along with large quantities of supplies.

Meanwhile the situation on the beach was not going according to plan and after another attack by Japanese Betty bombers escorted by Zero fighters, Fletcher's fighter strength was being gradually thinned down. From 99 aircraft, he was now down to 78 and was also dangerously low on fuel reserves. Fletcher decided that he was putting his entire Task Force 61 in jeopardy if he remained off Guadalcanal any longer and asked Ghormley for permission to withdraw his carriers. Ghormley was not too happy with this request but because he was too far removed from the scene felt that it would be unreasonable to deny such an urgent request. This decision was the most controversial made during the entire Guadalcanal campaign. The main points being that only 50 percent of the supplies for the Marine force had been unloaded; Fletcher still had enough fuel for at least 72 hours and the Japanese air attacks had been beaten off; and the majority of ships were undamaged. Also unbeknown Mikawa was steaming down 'The Slot' making for Guadalcanal. US aircraft had sighted the Japanese squadron on the evening of 7 August but due to a belated report, giving the wrong information and bad weather, the enemy was not located again that day. Therefore, Mikawa was able to make his approach down 'The Slot' undetected.

Turner summoned Rear Admiral Crutchley and Major General Vandegrift aboard his flagship the USS

Left: USS Roper *(DD.147) in 1942.*

Tanambogo Island, the scene of an attempted landing in August 1942, after an attack by planes of the US Navy.

McCawley, and relayed the information to them that Fletcher was pulling out and taking their air cover and supplies with him. Vandegrift's response to this was not recorded, but he must have been very angry. While Turner was expanding on the details, Mikawa's force sailed right past the picket destroyers and turned their guns to bear point blank at the unsuspecting *Canberra* and *Chicago*. The *Canberra* was hit so hard that she had to be abandoned but the *Chicago* was more fortunate, and received no crippling damage. The Japanese did not wait to see the result of their surprise attack but sailed out of range and towards the northern patrol group. The southern patrol group was so confused that no warning was sent to the northern group. The northern fared even worse than its southern counterparts. The Japanese sunk the USS *Astoria*, *Vincennes* and *Quincy* in less than an hour. Mikawa had taken the US Navy by surprise and the result was an astounding victory which would have been even more resounding if he had taken the initiative and destroyed the unprotected transports. It is only conjecture but the entire campaign on 'The Canal' would have changed, and possibly the war in the Pacific taken a different turn if the transports had been eliminated.

This disaster, and disaster is exactly what it was, confirmed Fletcher's belief that he must remove his task force from

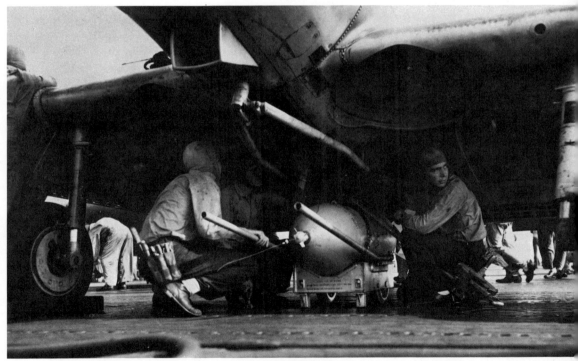

Crewmen load a 500lb demolition bomb on an SBD Dauntless aboard the Enterprise.

the danger zone. The 9 August was spent in preparation for departure and by sunset Task Force 61 was steaming away. The Marines under Vandegrift were now completely on their own. The situation was not very inviting. The US Navy had lost control of the seas in the Solomons. The nearest air support was in Espiritu Santo in the New Hebrides. Supplies were already beginning to run out, and morale was not very high after

what most Marines thought was naval desertion. Vandegrift realized that he was in no position to attack, so his schedule stressed defense. His most important operational concern was to make the airstrip functional at all costs. An extended perimeter defense was established around the airfield. The Marines set up .30 and .50 caliber machine-guns, backed up by 37mm guns and 90mm AA guns all around the defensive perimeter.

The feeling of being abandoned was considerably lessened on 14 August when the Navy ran the gauntlet of enemy aircraft and surface ships to bring supplies of ammunition and fuel, as well as the bare essentials to the Marines at Guadalcanal. Vandegrift decided to make a small foray against the Japanese by driving them across the Matanikau. This action was successful but did not allay the doubts in his mind of the ability of his men to sustain and repulse a heavy attack from the numerically superior Japanese force on the island. The major thing which aided the Marines was the Japanese confusion over exactly what to do – the Japanese believed that the US would eventually get tired of the 'insignificant' island and withdraw. Japanese intelligence showed that the Marines were digging in and this put a whole new picture on the screen. Plans were made to expel the Marines from Guadalcanal. Lieutenant General Haruyoshi Hyakutake, 17th Army Commander was ordered to retake Tulagi and Guadalcanal before setting out on the all important mission of securing Port Moresby. Hyakutake had over 50,000 men in his 17th Army but he had a slight problem, they were spread out all over the Pacific. Undaunted, he believed that if he could send one really crack unit into the islands that the Marine force could be driven into the sea and utterly destroyed. He chose Colonel Kiyanao Ichiki's 28th Infantry from Guam to accomplish the task. At the time, he appeared to be the ideal man for the task at hand but events proved him to be impetuous and rash. On 18 August he was to take 900 men on six destroyers and land at Taivu Point, around 20 miles from the Marine positions. The remainder of his 2500 men outfit would join him within the week.

Vandegrift was being kept up to date by his native coastwatchers and knew that Japanese forces were building up in the east. Captain Charles Brush set out on a patrol on 19 August with Marines of Abel Company, 1st Marines and headed toward Koli Point. At noon Japanese troops were sighted, Brush sent his executive officer, Lieutenant Joseph Jachym round to flank them and put them in a cross-fire between the two marine columns. The result was 31 out of 35 Japanese dead. From the documents and maps taken from the bodies it was discovered that they were army personnel and not navy men who had previously been fighting the Marines on Guadalcanal.

Ichiki attacked the Marine positions on the mouth of Alligator Creek on the Ilu River (still called the Tenaru by the US), early on 21 August. He recklessly decided that the 900 men he had brought with him would be sufficient and he need not wait for the rest of his 2500 man force. The Japanese made two attempts: the first at 0240 hours and the second at 0500 hours, both attacks were repulsed with heavy casualties to the attackers. Some of the Japanese were caught on the far bank of the river and Colonel Gerald Thomas, Divisional Operations Officer, recommended to Vandegrift to counter-attack immediately and drive the survivors into the sea. Vandegrift ordered the reserve battalion, Cate's 1st Battalion, 1st Marines under Lieutenant Colonel Creswell to cross the river and drive all Japanese troops downstream. Meanwhile Pollock's men provided a heavy and continuous fire from the other side of the river. Also to insure total success a platoon of light tanks were brought up and Marine aircraft would be utilized to strafe the entire affected area. Needless to say, the operation was a complete success. In Vandegrift's own words 'the rear of the tanks looked like meat grinders.' By 1700 hours, the Battle of Tenaru (Ilu) was finished. The Marines had killed over 800 Japanese, taken 15 prisoners and of the survivors, most of these died in the jungle. Colonel Ichiki survived the battle but upon reaching Taivu, he shot himself after burning his regimental colors.

The Battle of Tenaru was an American victory but there was still a great deal to be done before Vandegrift's position on Guadalcanal could be called secure. The Japanese became even more determined than ever to drive the Marines off the island. To make the airfield serviceable, US Marine Corps engineers utilized captured Japanese equipment, as their own was still on board the transports. On 12 August the aide to Rear Admiral John McCain flew a Catalina flying boat onto the airfield for an inspection of the runway. McCain was responsible for land-based air operations. The strip was only 2600ft long, with no drainage and no steel matting coverage, and finally there were no taxiways. The aide was a realistic man and passed the field as fit for fighter aircraft operations. The airfield was named Henderson Field after a hero of the Battle of Midway. The first aircraft arrived on 20 August; 12 Dauntless dive-bombers commanded by Major Richard Mangrum and 19 Marine Wildcat fighters under Captain John Smith.

The Japanese had gathered two task forces consisting of three aircraft carriers, eight battleships, four heavy cruisers, two light cruisers, 21 destroyers and other vessels, with air cover provided by the 25th Air Flotilla at Rabaul. To meet this small armada, Fletcher had at his disposal three aircraft carriers, one battleship, four cruisers and ten destroyers. The resulting battle became known as the Battle of the Eastern Solomons and was very like Midway, except that the result was a stalemate. Dogfights were now a matter of daily routine for the Marines. But without these pilots and the support crews of the 'Cactus Air Force' as it became known, Vandegrift's Marines might not have held their beach-head in the black days of August and September 1942. These Marine pilots lived in tents and dugouts, their staple diet was rice and spam but they were the actual front line of

US Marines leave on their rafts for a landing on Guadalcanal in August 1942.

resistance at the 'Canal.' Still at the beginning of September, Vandegrift's position was not very reassuring to say the least. His battle-weary troops were hungry, stricken with dysentery and jungle rot and by October malaria would also take its toll. The Marines could not get an uninterrupted night's sleep because of the Japanese night prowler aircraft nicknamed 'Louie the Louse' and 'Washing Machine Charlie.' Morale in the American camp was falling. Tension mounted as the Americans had to wait for the Japanese to act.

Admiral Raizo Tanaka managed time after time to run the gauntlet with nighttime runs to reinforce Guadalcanal. This became so regular that the Marines called it 'The Tokyo Express.' Vandegrift was in desperate need of reinforcements with the Japanese landing more and more troops to both the east and west of his perimeter. He transferred troops from Tulagi to Guadalcanal, including the experienced Edson's Raiders. The Marines kept making occasional thrusts into the Japanese held areas to keep the enemy on their toes and to gather intelligence information. On 10 September, one of Vandegrift's urgent requests was granted; down to only 11 out of the original 38 Wildcats, Ghormley sent an immediate 24 replacements. Colonel Edson moved his command post and his mixed force of Raiders and Parachutists to a ridge one mile south of Henderson Field and not far from Vandegrift's own headquarters. This ridge was 1000 yards long, running northwest to southeast, and surrounded by steep undulating thick jungle growth. This was to be renamed Bloody Ridge in a few days.

Edson deployed his 700 men in the prime locations for a possible Japanese penetration attempt. The Jungle was cleared out and barbed wire strung out between the trees to give it the appearance of a perimeter. In direct support of Edson's men were 105mm howitzers and the 2nd Marine Battalion, 5th Marines. On 12 September the long-awaited Japanese attack was at last launched. It started off with an intense naval bombardment of the Marine positions, followed up immediately by heavy mortar and artillery and then an all-out infantry attack by Kawaguchi's troops. The Marines were displaced from their positions but through faulty communications and the disorientation of their men, the Japanese attack lost impetus and stopped. The Marines under Edson then charged and retook their former positions along the ridge. Now

US Marines search for snipers on Guadalcanal in September 1942.

Marines ready to jump from their landing boats on Guadalcanal in August 1942.

Kate torpedo bomber attacks a US aircraft carrier in the Battle of Santa Cruz in October.

Below: USS Buchanan *(DD.484) was a fast destroyer used in the Pacific in World War II and was eventually sold to Turkey in 1949.*

started the long process of redigging in, laying more barbed wire and getting ready for the next attack which would surely come. The noise was intense, again naval bombardment, artillery and mortar barrages and the follow up infantry but Kawaguchi threw 2000 men across the slope on 13 September. This mass wave of men was something which the Marines had never experienced before, as fast as they cut them down, their comrades just climbed over their dead bodies. The Marines were at the breaking point when 'Red Mike' Edson took the front himself and urged his weary men to smoke down all the enemy. Edson called for increased artillery support and practically brought it down to his own positions. Another stalwart was Major Kenneth Bailey who kept screaming at the top of his lungs the traditional Marine Corps cry 'Do you want to live forever.' Between the intense and accurate fire coming from the Marines on the ridge and the perfect artillery support, the Japanese were being decimated.

By 14 September the Japanese were defeated and Kawaguchi knew it. The remainder of his force were retreating to Matanikau. The result of Bloody Ridge was an ocean of dead and wounded. Japanese dead totaled over 700 with an additional 600 wounded. US casualties were 59 dead and 204 wounded. The US Marines had won another total victory but this was to be overshadowed again by a defeat at sea.

Admiral Turner was keeping his word and was rushing reinforcements to Guadalcanal. This was the 7th Marines which he had picked up at the New Hebrides after their stint of duty on Samoa. The task force and its carrier escort force was sighted on 14 September by a Japanese aircraft. Turner remained on course until nightfall and then withdrew *McCawley* and the six precious transports and its cargo of 4000 Marines. The carriers *Hornet* and *Wasp*, the battleship *North Carolina* and various escort destroyers continued on course. On 15 September, at 0220 hours,

the Japanese submarines *I-15* and *I-19* attacked the carrier force. The result of this attack was devastating: the *Wasp* was abandoned and sunk by the *Lansdowne*, the *North Carolina* had a 30 by 18ft gaping hole put in its side below the waterline and the destroyer *O'Brien* was also sunk. This naval action was off the Santa Cruz islands and again the US Navy had suffered another blow by the Imperial Navy. Turner's decision to withdraw was vindicated by his safe arrival at Guadalcanal and the landing of the 4000 men and some supplies. There was a brief lull in the fighting while both sides experimented and probed with the enemy's defensive positions. The Marines lost a few skirmishes and won a few but it was not until November that the offensive really got under way. The US were determined not to lose its hold on Guadalcanal. But as the struggle reached its climax, President Roosevelt ordered the Chiefs of Staff to send all available equipment, supplies and troops to the two priority theaters – the Pacific and

North Africa – even if this meant drastically reducing strategic commitments elsewhere. Admiral King, CNO, could not send any carriers to the South Pacific, but he diverted a sizeable force to SOPAC, including a battleship, six cruisers, 24 submarines and 130 naval aircraft. General George Marshall, Army Chief of Staff, also sent an additional 75 army aircraft from Hawaii to reinforce the southwest Pacific but would not increase the troop commitment to the area, especially with the pressure on from Operation Torch, the Allied landings in North Africa. However, reinforcements were stripped from the other island bases and sent to the 'Canal.' On 4 November two regiments from the 2nd Marine Division were landed and a further 6000 officers and men were landed on 6 November from Noumea and Espiritu Santo (the latter were troops of the American Division). The two convoys were commanded by Rear Admiral Turner, and were escorted by two squadrons, the first under Rear Admiral Nicholas Scott and the second under Rear Admiral Daniel Callaghan. This force was shadowed by a task force formed around the hastily refit *Enterprise* and the two battleships *Washington* and *South Dakota*. The Japanese were still no less determined than the US Marines to gain complete control over Guadalcanal, and November saw another major attempt to reinforce the island and force the Marines out once and for all. Their plan was basically no different from all previous attempts. Bombardment by two naval squadrons of Henderson Field, followed up again by artillery and mortar fire and a massive infantry breakthrough. The only difference this time was that a 3rd squadron was escorting the rest of the 38th Division from Rabaul, while a 4th squadron gave support. This was by far the largest planned general offensive to date.

Unknowingly, the US convoy, escorted by Rear Admiral Scott's squadron, arrived off Lunga Point early on 11 November and was joined by Callaghan's squadron on 12 November. Just a few hours later, a strong Japanese naval force, including the battleships *Hiei* and *Kirishima*, was sighted steaming down 'The Slot.' Turner, nonplussed, calmly finished unloading the transports of all troops and supplies and then sailed in convoy for Espiritu Santo, only escorted by three destroyers. The remainder of the combined escort forces commanded by Rear Admiral Callaghan stayed behind to engage the enemy fleet,

The USS Wasp *was torpedoed on 15 September 1942 and she sank following a fire.*

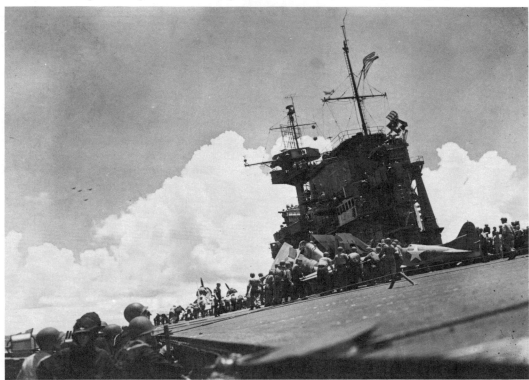

Plane handling crews at work on the Enterprise *during the Battle of Santa Cruz trying to save the Wildcats on deck. Note a formation of Wildcats on the left.*

Japanese transports burn close to the shore after the second naval battle of Guadalcanal on 16 November 1942.

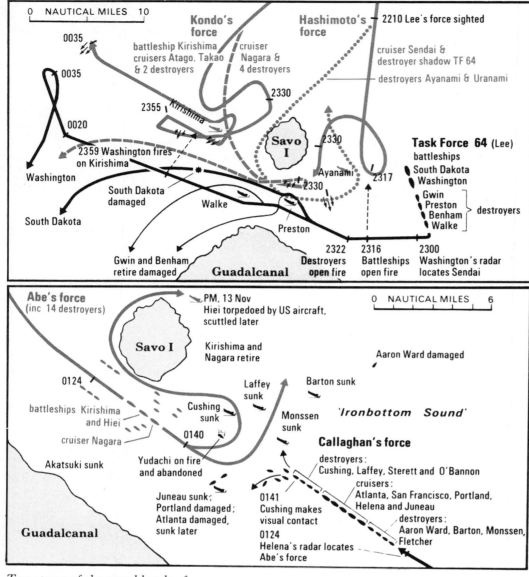

Two stages of the naval battle of Guadalcanal.

heavily damaged that she had to be scuttled; and one Japanese and three US destroyers had been sunk. The *South Dakota* was damaged but remained afloat. At daylight on 15 November, the four remaining Japanese transports were spotted by the Marines aground and helpless; shore batteries opened up and aided by aircraft from Henderson Field turned them into blazing hulks. Out of 10,000 troops which sailed with the ill-fated expedition, only 4000 arrived and they were without equipment or rations. The three-day battle of Guadalcanal was the first decisive US victory since the beginning of the Solomons campaign.

At the end of November the Japanese tried once more to reinforce Guadalcanal, but Halsey sent out a squadron of five cruisers and four destroyers to intercept it. On 30 November, this cruiser squadron encountered eight Japanese destroyers attempting to bring supplies and reinforcements to the garrison at Tassafaronga. Only one Japanese destroyer was sunk, but the US Navy had four of its cruisers hit by torpedoes. This was the last of the midnight encounters in the narrow waters of the South Solomons. On the last day of 1942, Japanese Imperial General Headquarters decided to abandon Guadalcanal and fall back to a line of defense based on New Georgia. On 9 December General Alexander Patch relieved Vandegrift and during the next two months the 1st Marine Division was withdrawn for a much needed rest to Australia. It was relieved by the 25th US Division on 31 December. On 4 January 1943 the 2nd Marine Division Headquarters and 6th Marine Regiment arrived from New Zealand, bringing the strength of the Guadalcanal garrison to 50,000 men. The Japanese on the other hand were down to 25,000 effectives. They were underfed and disease-ridden, but were still willing to fight to the last man. General Imamura, Commander in Chief, 8th Area Army ordered them to Cape Esperance, from where they were to be evacuated during the first week in February. Exactly six months after the first US Marines landed at Red Beach, on Guadalcanal, the last Japanese had been safely evacuated from 'The Canal.' General Patch was left in undisputed control of the island. Fortitude, courage, failure to give in and belief in the ultimate victory carried the Marines through one of the most arduous campaigns of their history. This was the first US land victory achieved in World War II and marked the limits of Japanese territorial expansion.

although outnumbered by superior Japanese forces, he did so to cover Turner's withdrawal.

After escorting the transports clear of the anchorage, Callaghan steered west to engage the enemy. It was an extremely dark and dismal night with no moon. In the early hours of the morning of 13 November, both forces practically collided before opening fire. The battle which followed lasted only 24 minutes and must go on record for being one of the most furious sea engagments ever fought. The Japanese lost two destroyers. The battleship *Hiei* was critically damaged, and left dead in the water for the US aircraft to finish off the next day. The US task force lost two light cruisers and four destroyers; both Rear Admirals Callaghan and Scott were killed in the battle and casualties were heavy. Callaghan's action accomplished his main objective allowing the task force time to intervene. The following after-

noon, naval aircraft from the carrier *Enterprise* sank a cruiser and severely damaged other surface ships of the Japanese cruiser bombardment force. Furthermore, aircraft from Henderson Field inflicted grave damage to the transports unloading on the north side of the island and sunk seven out of 11. The Japanese heavy bombardment force was now reorganized and reinforced to cover the transports. It was composed of the battleship *Kirishima*, four cruisers and nine destroyers. Vice-Admiral 'Bull' Halsey, who had relieved Ghormley on 18 October, sent Rear Admiral Willis Lee with the battleships *Washington* and *South Dakota*, and four destroyers to attack it. Lee led his small squadron around the southeast tip of Guadalcanal and just after midnight engaged the enemy in the narrow channel south of Savo Island. This battle was fought at a longer range than the preceeding one, but the fighting was just as intense. The *Kirishima* was so

EL ALAMEIN 1942

23 October–5 November 1942

One of the best known battles of World War II, and one which must be considered a major confrontation of the 20th century, was the Battle of El Alamein. Operations opened in late August 1942 with Rommel's final bid to capture Egypt and the Suez and were finally resolved with Montgomery's counteroffensive two months later.

As in many battles, it is not so much the occurrences during as what preceded the battle which seem to determine the ultimate outcome. At the battle of El Alamein three main issues acted as factors which shaped the final results and directly influenced the outcome of the war in the North Africa theater. The first of the pre-battle decisions was made in April 1942 when Hitler vetoed a proposal to seize the British naval instal-

lation at Malta. Rommel himself had proposed that a mixed German and Italian parachute and amphibious assault take place to ensure that Axis supply lines across the Mediterranean remain intact. Hitler balked at the suggestions. As had become his habit, he felt that the Luftwaffe could handle the Malta situation. Furthermore, he was reminded of the heavy losses which were incurred when such an assault was mounted for the capture of Crete. Although Hitler was not unsympathetic to Rommel's cause, and promised to review the plan at a later date, he bought Rommel off by promising him more tanks and supplies for the continuing of the attack on Tobruk. Later, after Rommel's victory there, Hitler again bought him off with the presentation of a Field Marshal's baton; which is not to say that Rommel did not deserve the promotion. The

laying of the blame must fall to Hitler, in allowing Rommel to strike out against Egypt and the British without securing the logistic lines which were the life support of the Afrika Korps.

The second effective pre-battle decision was made by the British. Chief of the Imperial General Staff, General Sir Alan Brooke, persuaded Churchill to accompany him on a tour to assess the situation in the Mediterranean, especially that of the British forces in the Middle East. After several days there, Churchill decided that new blood had to be injected into the British Eighth Army. Something was needed to put a spark into the troops and into all aspects of the organization, from logistics to planning, and most importantly the Staff. A definite correlation between Churchill and the American Civil War President Lincoln can be seen. Lincoln needed to find the right man to lead his Army of the Potomac, and after much trial and error he found General Grant. The same can be said for Churchill in the North African situation, yet fate played a much larger part in his ultimate selection.

Churchill had lost confidence in General Auchinleck and replaced him as Commander in Chief of the Middle East with General Alexander. He also decided to appoint Lieutenant General William

British troops advance through barbed wire as they moved forward on a narrow front close to the sea toward Alamein in the spring of 1942.

Gott as Commander of the Eighth Army. Gott was an old hand at the desert war and had fought in all of the major battles since its beginning. It was here that fate took a hand in the affair; while flying to Cairo to assume command of the army, Gott was killed when his transport aircraft was shot down by Luftwaffe fighters. In that moment of confusion the man whose name has become synonymous with the Eighth Army, Lieutenant General Bernard Montgomery, was chosen as the new commander. With Alexander making the strategic decisions and Montgomery carrying them out tactically, the British had finally discovered a winning combination with a hope of defeating the Afrika Korps.

It is at this point that the two main characters, Montgomery and Rommel, must be interjected. Field Marshal Erwin Rommel was the source of a myth which had grown around his Afrika Korps and himself. He stood as the main adversary who had pushed and been pushed, crossed and recrossed the desert, but had always managed, regardless of the odds, to bounce back and inflict a resounding defeat on his enemies.

Right: Indian troops in British uniform at Alamein.

Below: Me-109s of the Luftwaffe over the desert sands of Cyrenaica in 1942.

Perhaps most of all Rommel knew from where to command; and that was from the Front. He was known to scoff in amusement at the British generals' attempts to command their battles from the rear with only a second hand knowledge of the action. The German soldiers of the Afrika Korps did not find it unusual to see their commander racing across the desert in his armored command post, or flying overhead in his light observation aircraft. It was that form of familiarity which Montgomery later applied and which worked so successfully with the Eighth Army. Rommel also 'took the risks.' However he was not the same Rommel of the early days in North Africa, but a man who was seriously ill and in need of a rest. Although his physician maintained that he could still command, he stressed that the Field Marshal needed medical attention and a period of respite if his health was ever to improve. Finally, on the night of the beginning of the battle of Alam El Halfa on 30 August, Rommel's physician and Chief of Staff sent a message to the German High Command informing them that Rommel was suffering from a chronic stomach and intestinal catarrh, nasal diphtheria, and considerable circulatory problems. In their opinion Rommel was not fit to continue in command and the state of his health had an undoubted effect on the course of events.

General Montgomery, who could hardly be considered a new lad in camp, set about picking up the reins of the Eighth Army. Montgomery's true virtue lay in two directions. The first was his extroverted character, which made him popular with his men and the public. The second, and by far more important aspect was his experiences of World War I. As a junior officer in that war he knew what it was to fight a battle of attrition. He remembered with horror the lives which seemed freely and carelessly thrown away. He himself was wounded and spent the remainder of the war on the British Staff. It was undoubtedly these two factors which made Montgomery the right man at the right time. He gave organization to a staff which reeked of inefficiency and he was not willing to have troops needlessly wasted in battles which he might never hope to win.

To return to the outline of the situation, the third critical decision was made by Montgomery. After he had succeeded in turning Rommel back, and stabilizing the front, he would engage the Axis forces only on his terms and when he was ready. In Sir William Jackson's account of the battle of El Alamein, he pointed out that Montgomery emphasized ten points in his reconstruction policy for the Eighth Army. Although all ten were very important, several stand out more than the others and were the key to his success. First, he wanted to ensure that the Eighth Army was always ready to move and fight, and prepared to take the advantage in any situation which might arise on the battlefield. He proceeded to form what he dubbed the 'Corps de Chasse.' That Corps was to be made of the Eighth Army's X Corps which, with its heavy armor complement, would be able to fight the Afrika Korps on its own terms. In adopting such a policy Montgomery forced his staff to be looking ever toward victory. He even went so far as to have all the withdrawal plans done

away with and the vehicles normally kept in reserve for troops withdrawal sent to the rear areas to help with the movement and logistics problems.

His next step was to demand no further failure from either the logistical or

Italian aircraft set ablaze by the British as they advanced through Libya on their way to Egypt.

Bir Hacheim under attack in June 1942, where the Free French made their gallant stand.

A General Grant tank moves up past the wreckage of captured enemy vehicles south of the El Alamein sector after the first battle of June 1942.

General (later Field Marshal) Montgomery and his staff after he took over the Eighth Army.

German flak guns on the Alamein front where the Afrika Korps fought their 'hopeless' battle.

The famous 88mm cannon in use at Alamein in June 1942.

operational aspects through poor co-ordination or mismanagement. Training and enthusiasm also ranked high on his list of relevant factors and he forced commanders to rehearse operations until they were as familiar to the troops as their own names. Montgomery believed that every man, regardless of position or rank, should know the operation and its objectives and how best he could help to fulfill each. Much like Rommel, Montgomery encouraged enthusiasm by getting out among his troops and allowing the men to know him, know what he wanted, and know that he too was amid the action.

Finally, Montgomery passed down a policy which curtailed future 'belly-aching.' Those who did not live up to his professional standards, or who were incompetent, were removed from their positions as rapidly as possible. 'Monty' let it be known that if any one of his staff could not 'cut it' he would find someone else who could. He stressed that orders were orders and that he would give them with the expectation of having them carried out, not questioned.

At midnight on 30 August Rommel commenced his attack against the British position drawn around Alamein, Ruweisat Ridge, Ragil Depression, and Alam El Halfa Ridge. His attack was intended to be a sweeping maneuver from the south, with the objective of pushing his force as deep as possible, then swinging north to the sea, cutting British lines of communication, avenues of retreat, and trapping much of the Eighth Army. This move came as no great surprise to Montgomery, and in fact was almost a welcome relief. He had guessed, shortly after assuming command, that Rommel would attempt just such a maneuver and had prepared the Eighth Army accordingly. As has been stated, the Rommel of August 1942 was not the Rommel of earlier times, and the attack lacked the creativity which had been seen in his order of battle in Africa.

As the attack unfolded Rommel hoped that his drive would continue all the way to Gabala before dawn. As a result of the difficulties encountered in clearing the British minefields there was a large consumption of fuel used in the attempts to maneuver around those obstacles and Rommel found that he had to abort his main objective and turn his force north long before he was ready. In doing so Rommel felt that he would save himself from calling off the attack. Perhaps the lesser gains would be sufficient to throw the Eighth Army off balance and gain him some type of respectable victory.

As dawn broke German tanks were moving directly toward Alam El Halfa Ridge, playing directly into Montgomery's hands. With daylight RAF fighters took to the air and delivered heavy blows to the German units. Also, Montgomery's concentrated armor, which had been dug in at the Ridge, took a heavy toll of the German armor throughout the day. British artillery pounded the German position, and according to one German source every round a German artillery piece fired was answered by ten British rounds.

For three days Rommel and the Afrika Korps tried desperately to gain some advantage along the front, but to no avail. On 3 September Rommel called off the assault and began pulling his troops back to the line from which they had begun. One of the major factors which frustrated Rommel during that engagement was Montgomery's prohibiting British tanks to swing out and engage the German tanks in a running battle. By keeping his tanks in their dug-in positions the British had taken minor casualties to their armor, few to the artillery pieces, and minimal troop injuries. The German and Italian forces' losses were devastating. To compound the aggravation of the situation Rommel, who had always been able to inflict heavy losses against British armor as they counterattacked, was denied that privilege because of Montgomery's unwillingness to pursue his enemy with anything more than the harassing attacks of aircraft. With the conclusion of the battle at Alam El Halfa Ridge Montgomery realized that he could apply himself to the serious business of training and preparing his troops for Operation Lightfoot which would be recorded as the Battle of El Alamein, though it was in fact the second Battle of El Alamein.

Even this modified plan seemed a little too big a bite to many of the corps commanders. Once again, as at so many other times in the history of the Eighth Army, all of the commanders went to Montgomery to complain about the timetable. The armor commanders particularly complained that the break in for the infantry consisted of two successive night attacks through which the infantry would have time to clear the minefields. Montgomery believed that it would only take one night and told them not to worry, that their tanks would not be caught in the open during the daylight. Although they continued to protest, Montgomery cut them off sharply and

refused to alter the plan any further.

For the Germans two issues had become very apparent. First, the logistics situation was critical. Second, German losses in the Battle of Alam El Halfa had taken a far greater toll on both equipment and personnel than Rommel could afford. Because of that his defense lines were strengthened with an elaborate minefield network, nicknamed 'Devil's Garden.' They were not merely the usual minefields which littered the front at that time, but almost all the fields and most of the mines were booby-trapped so that they could not be removed to deter sapper teams. Behind the elaborate minefield system came the infantry and anti-tank positions. To steady the Italian units German troops were interspersed with them. Next in the line were the artillery defenses, backed by small groups of German and Italian armor intended for use in plugging holes should a breakthrough occur. Although

The British offensive at Alamein in October.

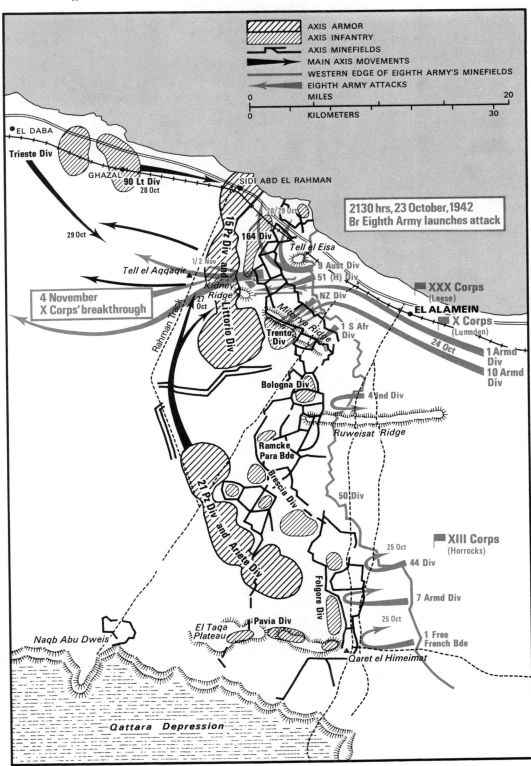

German bombers were devastating though in short supply at Alamein. The Russian Front came first on the priorities list.

Rommel did not like having his armor in multiple small groups, he could not afford to keep them in a large mobile reserve due to a lack of fuel and the threat of the RAF air superiority. He did manage to keep one reserve division. That was the ever faithful 90th Light, grouped with the Italian Trieste Mechanized Division. These units were kept along the coastal road so that Rommel could maintain his main supply avenues, and to reduce the chance of a surprise amphibious landing behind the German lines.

There was nothing more that Rommel could do but wait, and since German Intelligence reports were predicting that the British attack would not begin until the end of November, Rommel was sent to Germany for a rest and recuperation period. A Panzer general, General Stumme from the Eastern Front, was brought in to replace him and General von Thoma took command of the Afrika Korps. True to habits formed in the earlier campaigns in the desert, Stumme's staff advised him to begin the preparation of the southern sector for the upcoming British attack.

Operation Lightfoot was not very different from other operations conceived by previous British commanders in Af-

German Panzer in Egypt. Rommel was starved of tanks and could get no replacements.

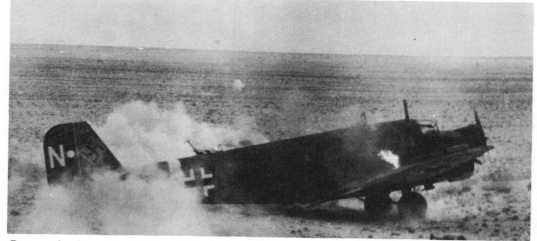

Cannon fire hits a Ju-52 forced down on a British airstrip. Its starboard engine is on fire and a crew member lies face down near the shattered plane.

rica. It was based on the belief that in order to crush the Afrika Korps one first had to destroy Rommel's armored units. If able to accomplish that, then and only then could the rest of the army be brought to the point of collapse. Lightfoot did have one novel twist however. Rather than striking out from the south, moving parallel to the enemy forces, reaching the rear, then heading north to the sea and entrapping the German forces, Montgomery decided that his main attack would take place in the north. His newly formed Corps de Chasse would straddle Rommel's lateral lines of communication and supply, forcing the Germans to commit their armor to recapture that much needed link. Again British tanks in a defensive position would be able to destroy the Axis armor, with the ultimate aim of making it completely ineffectual.

To accomplish all of that Montgomery decided to attempt two breaches in the German defenses. One attempt would be in the north with Lieutenant General Leese's XXX Corps, made up of four infantry divisions, making the initial and main breakthrough assault. Once their objective, known as Report Line Oxalic, was gained a highly specialized group of engineers attached to the 1st Armored Division, along with the 10th Armored Division, would push through to grab their objective. Known as Report Line Skinflint that objective was set along a slight rise of ground beyond the Rahman Track and south through Tel el Aqqaqir. It was at that position, with its rise in elevation, that the British armor was to make its stand to destroy the Korps' tanks as they pushed forward against the British maneuvers in that area.

The second breach attempt was to be made in the south by Lieutenant General Brian Horrock's XIII Corps, and had no real objective other than as a diversionary attack to keep the Axis forces in the southern sectors pinned in their positions and unable to swing north to support the defense against the British main force.

Although the plan seemed sound, as the weeks wore on Montgomery became concerned about whether or not his troops were properly trained to execute such an ambitious plan. He finally decided to modify his scheme. Basically it developed into a three-part program. First would come the infantry 'break in.' After the infantry had opened a path through the enemy defenses and cleared lanes through the minefields for the armored units, the second phase would

British soldier takes cover behind a wrecked vehicle during a dive-bombing attack.

Enemy shellfire out of range this time in June 1942 at the start of the Alamein struggle.

begin. This was to be an intentional 'dogfight' stage. During that phase both infantry and armor were to destroy the enemy's defensive positions and carry out carefully planned attacks against the enemy's rear defenses, with support from both artillery and RAF units. Finally, once the Afrika Korps was on the verge of collapse the British armor units would deliver the final blow by a break out, not only destroying the enemy's rear area but cutting off their avenues of retreat.

Thus, the stage was set, and with Rommel out of the way everything must surely have tilted the balance in the British favor, but Montgomery was not to be rushed as he prepared himself and his troops for Operation Lightfoot. Days passed, then weeks, and still Montgomery would not be pushed into action. Stumme, who had no experience of desert conditions, continued to have German troops prepare positions and the minefields and booby traps of Devil's Garden were increased with every day.

Finally, on 23 October 1942, at 2140 hours, the entire front erupted with an artillery barrage which lasted for 15 minutes. The British had massed so many guns for the offensive that several of the German Staff likened the bombardment to the all-out assault which was often seen on the Eastern Front. That 15 minute artillery preparation was primarily to disrupt Axis forces, but also to destroy known positions of artillery and anti-tank weapons. By using the vast number of guns it was also hoped that a possible path through Devil's Garden would be cleared. Suddenly, the British guns went silent, and for five minutes not a sound could be heard across the desert. Again, at 2200 hours the guns opened up and the German outposts all along the front radioed back to the next echelon of command that the long expected offensive had begun.

The skies on that night were clear and it was a perfect night on which to begin the offensive. In the desert very few landmarks truly exist and navigation for moving from one known point to another is accomplished much as navigation at sea. Bearings and compass readings are taken, and stars are used to ensure that the proper direction or course is being followed. Because of the need to keep a proper course, light anti-aircraft weapons were employed by the British to fire tracers on predescribed readings across the skies. Although it was more difficult, night was the best possible time for the clearing of the minefields and moving of

Rommel confers with a colleague about plans for the British attack en masse.

armor across the field of battle.

Throughout the night one delay after another plagued the British troops. Specially designed Flail tanks, known as Scorpions, which were used to clear the minefields, broke down almost every 100 yards. The infantry, whose job it was to secure paths and clear them of mines, found it almost impossible, not only because of the large number of mines but also because a large number of them were booby trapped. In some cases they even found mines on top of mines, which would have triggered the second should they attempt to remove the first. The process of mine clearing slowed to a snail's pace since the electronic devices usually employed could not detect booby traps and all the work had to be done by manual probing.

By dawn on 24 October the British 1st

Armored Division in the northern corridor was only half way to its objective, while the 10th Armored Division in the south had almost managed to clear four routes to one of their prime targets, Miteirya Ridge. Unfortunately for the 10th Division, the other side of the ridge had also been mined.

All along the front Montgomery was receiving reports from his irate field commanders that the break-in phase had not succeeded. After studying the situation he decided to extend the break-in stage for another 24 hours with the hope that once darkness fell on 24 October his losses due to German artillery and anti-tank fire would not be too disastrous. To keep pressure on the Axis tank units held in reserve, the RAF, and for the first time US Army Air Corps planes, flew over 1000 missions together and managed to

A 5.5in Long Range gun raises a cloud of sand round the gunners' feet.

Australian troops move through the gap made by Montgomery's forces in early November 1942.

2200 hours, while both RAF and Luftwaffe aircraft dropped flares over the battlefield, a German aircraft was hit by anti-aircraft fire and lost its load of bombs directly over the vehicles of the 10th Armored Division. The explosions and flames, which lit up the desert skies, drew the fire of every German gun in the area and completely disorganized the 10th Division and its Headquarters.

With so much seemingly going wrong, Montgomery's staff approached him to break off the battle. The armor commanders feared that their tanks would be caught in the open when morning came, and all along the front troops were preparing to give up and fall back. It was at that instant that Montgomery made the decision which was to affect the outcome of not only that battle but the entire North African theater. He issued orders that Object Line Pierson would be taken in the morning by his armored units. He firmly believed that a battle consisted of not only men and machines but of opposing wills. He intended to show the Germans and his own army as well that his was the greater will. Montgomery informed his commanders once again that if they could not obey orders he would find men who could. For the first time the Eighth Army knew just where it stood with its commander and that Montgomery was truly the master.

As the sun rose once again British armor fought its way through the open, managed to link up with the forward infantry units, and began the dogfight stage of the operation. Even though the break-in phase had not been completely successful, Montgomery felt he could not waste any more time and decided to continue his plan as best he could.

The dogfight phase was in motion. All along the line both infantry and tanks engaged their enemy. The apparent British superiority with longer-range tanks seemed to be stacking the odds ever more in their favor. Logistically the Eighth Army had to maintain its forward troops by driving vehicles through many as yet uncleared minefields. Although both the northern and southern sectors seemed to be showing signs of making headway, casualties and losses were high among the New Zealand and 10th Armored Divisions in the south. Montgomery decided to swing the main British effort behind the northern corridor.

At midday British forces of the northern sector swung in two directions. One was toward Kidney Ridge and the other went north toward a sector known as Point 29. The Australians managed to

destroy several armor columns as they jockeyed for position.

For yet another time fate seemed to go against the Axis as General Stumme, who like Rommel believed that it was impossible to conduct operations from the rear, went forward with some of his staff to appraise the situation. After entering an area of heavy fire, his driver apparently became disoriented and drove straight into a barrage of British machine gun fire. Stumme's Chief of Intelligence was killed instantly and Stumme, who had fallen from the vehicle, died of an apparent heart attack. It would be several days before any of the German command learned of his fate and General von Thoma assumed command in the commander's absence on 24 October.

Thoma was convinced by his reports that Montgomery had underestimated

the German defense and that a breach was impossible for the British to accomplish in one day, but he had to wait to see whether or not the Allies would continue the attack or break off. He hoped that he could guess the main attack, whether from the north or south, and reinforce the proper area. Thoma was applying every caution and hastened to inform Hitler and the German General Staff that if at all possible Rommel should return immediately to resume command. Hitler himself called Rommel several times and with both apologies and regrets asked him to return to Africa to command the Afrika Korps. Rommel would return on the night of 25 October to his old headquarters.

With nightfall on 24 October British sappers and engineers began work on clearing the minefields once again. At

British artillery softens up the German positions which eventually forced their retreat.

capture Point 29, which was considered key in the Axis defense of the coastal road. Once again fate intervened and two German officers were captured by Australian patrols with maps showing not only defenses of Point 29 but the route through the minefields. In a very neat, swift action on the night of 25 October Australian troops captured the sector with little trouble. The Axis defenses in the north were beginning to crumble.

Yet another day opened and Montgomery still did not feel that his army was making any headway. The 26 October was Rommel's first day back with his Korps, and he began it by re-evaluating the situation after Thoma reported that the front was deteriorating more rapidly than it had ever done in any previous desert engagement. Rommel knew that Point 29 had to be recaptured in order to stabilize the northern front. More importantly he had to open the coastal road for supply purposes and as a possible avenue of withdrawal. As Rommel reconsidered his army's plight he plotted a counter-offensive.

Montgomery realized that if he was to follow through with his final break-out phase he would have to create a new reserve, as his Corps de Chasse – his principal strike force – had already been committed. Making one of the most crucial decisions of the battle, Montgomery decided to allow the Australians of the 1st Armored Division, supported by the Highlanders Division, to continue holding the north while he readjusted the

entire Eighth Army, allowing the New Zealanders and the 7th and 10th Armored Divisions to move back to constitute a new reserve strike force. Although Rommel tried a haphazard attempt at recapturing Point 29 before he committed his reserves, British troops with RAF and artillery support showed him that it would take a full-fledged attack if results were to be achieved.

Rommel put the 21st Panzer Division together with the 90th Light and the Trieste, already in the north, and decided to attack both Point 29 and Kidney Ridge. He knew that everything depended on the success of that mission and he secured every available German aircraft from the German Chief of the South, Kesselring, for a Blitzkrieg style attack. He was fairly confident of success since that tactic had never failed him in the desert, and many incidents were recorded when defeat had turned into victory through its use.

Throughout the day and into the evening the Australians and the 1st Armored Division were hammered on Kidney Ridge and Point 29, but British tank crews and gunners stood their ground and by early evening the German attack was totally broken. For the first time in the North Africa campaign the British had not only physically but psychologically defeated their enemy. With the few tanks and vehicles left to them the Axis forces retreated across the desert.

With the failure of his attack Rommel realized that he could no longer hope to

win the battle, but he was determined to draw it into a stalemate and deny the Eighth Army its long awaited victory. As a precaution he ordered a reconnaissance of a position known as Fuka, where he felt a final delaying action could be made if it became necessary. That defense line was more than 50 miles west of his current position and Rommel knew that if he had to opt for that defensive line it would mean leaving his non-mechanized units behind. Before resorting to that course Rommel decided to make one last attempt to prove to the British that the continuing of the battle would be far too costly.

On the nights of 28 and 29 October Australian units made a desperate attempt to push the German 90th Light out of their defensive position to capture the coastal road. Although initially the Australians caught the Germans off guard, they were halted well shy of their objective. On 29 October Headquarters in Cairo and London began to put pressure on Montgomery to show positive results for this great expenditure of ammunition and equipment. Churchill was so frustrated that a victory had not already been gained that he had thoughts of choosing a new commander and relieving Montgomery on the spot.

It was at that point that Montgomery revealed his final operation: Supercharge. His idea was to strike out from the Australian position along the coastal road, making that the key to his break-out phase. General Alexander was not pleased and thought the plan was a strategic disaster. He was convinced that Supercharge was nothing more than a scaled-down version of Lightfoot and that it should be employed further south, away from the main Axis defenses. Although Supercharge was scheduled to begin as soon as possible, all manner of delay and confusion surrounded it and it was postponed until 1 November.

However, on 30 and 31 October the Germans were again to fall victim to ill fortune. On those two days Australians tried once again to breach the coastal road defenses. Rommel, believing that the Australians were the spearhead of Montgomery's break out, threw everything he had against them. In so doing he misrouted the mass of his troops against a false objective. The fighting that ensued was some of the fiercest since the German attack against Point 29 and Kidney Ridge, but in spite of heavy losses the Australians managed to hold.

On 1 November, in a well-planned artillery and bomber attack which dis-

A German periscope.

Italian prisoners are marched into captivity after the battle.

rupted the Afrika Korps' lines of communication, Operation Supercharge began. Everything seemed to be going well for the British. By midnight the New Zealanders had made their objective and the armor columns following up were well on the way to achieving theirs. By the time the lead units had reached Rahman Track, Axis forces had managed to put together a fairly strong defense. Instead of running up against the weaker, disheartened Italian units, British tank units found themselves fighting a combined effort from the remaining units of the 15th and 23rd Panzers. Although fighting was heated and furious, the 9th Armored Brigade of the 1st Armored Division managed to hold against the Afrika Korps' last bid for a stalemate.

The situation seemed to crumble rapidly for the Axis defenders. Rommel continued to misjudge British tactics, and believing that the main thrust would come from the Australians he sent Thoma to prepare to defend against the assault. It was not until the following morning that he realized his mistake and sent Thoma to the area that had previously been breached, around Tel el Aqqaqir. However, Thoma's attempts were in vain and 117 Axis tanks were lost in his two efforts. British Armored Car Squadrons were beginning to slip through the lines in several areas, and were not only disrupting Axis lines of communication but were destroying supply units in the rear areas. In spite of

A British 25pdr fires a round during a night action.

German troops inspect a knocked-out British tank.

all of this Montgomery still could not get a complete upper hand.

By nightfall on 2 November, although Thoma had somehow managed to check the British advance, Rommel knew that the battle was over. With less than 35 tanks Rommel decided to pull back to Fuka and attempt to withdraw as many of his troops as he possibly could before the British realized that the Axis Front was crumbling away.

On 3 November Rommel had begun to move the remains of the Afrika Korps, organizing a defense along the coastal road as his army withdrew. Although British units noticed a slacking of pressure along the front, Rommel managed to maintain enough pressure to keep the British convinced until evening that the Korps was still stable. However, in the afternoon of that day the final blow was struck. Hitler sent a message to Rommel that he must hold as relief was on the way. He ended his message with the statement; 'as to your troops, you can show them no other road than to victory or death.' Hitler was sure that while the British assault was strong, the will of the Afrika Korps was stronger. Rommel was destroyed by that message. Although hesitant, he attempted to obey the command, but in vain. His Panzers were gone and the Italians were on the verge of complete collapse. Montgomery sensed something of a crisis and increased the assault against the Afrika Korps in both the west and southwest throughout the day.

On 4 November the Battle of El Alamein was truly over. During the afternoon the Axis forces finally snapped and the cohesion of units all along the front disintegrated. Even Thoma, who tried one last-minute attempt to stem the British advance, was captured. Rommel decided that the situation was totally hopeless and ordered his mechanized units to fall back immediately to Fuka, abandoning his infantry to the oncoming British.

Although the battle continued for two more days the Eighth Army was physically and mentally exhausted. Their supplies were low and they had not been able to really destroy the Afrika Korps. On 6 November Rommel slipped through their fingers as a heavy rain bogged down British tanks in their bid to cut him off by crossing the desert.

The Battle of El Alamein, although considered one of the most decisive battles of World War II, was not unlike many of the engagements in the desert. Although Montgomery is credited with

One of the men of the Afrika Korps who could not make his escape from Alamein.

The Eighth Army advance after the Afrika Korps was swift and without opposition for miles.

A British soldier captures an Italian and his tank.

winning the battle he failed to stop the driving force – Rommel – and the war in the African theater would continue for some time. It would end only with the destruction of the Afrika Korps by a combined Anglo-American effort, converging from two directions and decimating the Korps once and for all.

In terms of cost, Rommel had lost nearly every tank in the Panzer Army, some 30,000 men as prisoners, had abandoned more than 1000 guns on the battlefield, and had only 20 of his original 500 tanks still in full operational order. It was a war of attrition, which the British had so feared, which had won the day. Montgomery had also helped in an indirect way to prove the foolishness of Hitler's strategy in North Africa. The issue of Malta, which the German Command chose to ignore, showed a lack of long-range planning. Perhaps of greatest importance was the factor of Rommel's health. His physical condition was becoming too much for him to bear and was affecting his performance to no small degree. Finally, the war in Africa was only a sideshow for Hitler and the German General Staff. The total war picture did not hinge for them on the victories in North Africa and as such Hitler did not adequately support Rommel nor concern himself with the true problems of the area. By the same token the war in Africa was everything to the British. It was their first experience of a war of attrition since World War I. Perhaps of greater significance was the fact that the Allies needed to have a place to which they could point and say, 'the Germans were defeated here.' At El Alamein the British put their feet on the road which would lead to the ultimate defeat of the Axis powers. Their exuberance can best be described in the words of Winston Churchill, who after the Battle of El Alamein stated, 'Before Alamein we never had a victory. After Alamein we never had a defeat.'

Scottish soldier has a smoke.

STALINGRAD 1942-43

Stalingrad, one of the bloodiest, bitterest battles of World War II, was the decisive battle on the Eastern Front. When it began in the fall of 1942, the hitherto unbeaten Germans held a 2300-mile front deep in Russian territory and were mobilizing to annex the oil-rich fields of the Caucasus. Some five months later the 'hinge of fate' had turned. Nearly two million men, women, and children were dead, but the German tide was on the ebb. The myth of German invincibility was shattered and the Russian behemoth gathered itself for the westward push that would take it to Berlin.

The irony is that neither side intended it to be so. Hitler did not see Stalingrad as a key objective at first, nor did Stalin plan to defend it so fiercely. Both sides spent the first months of 1942 laying plans for the summer – plans that underestimated their opponent's capacities and overestimated their own.

The Soviets struck first, launching the first of three separate offensives in March 1942. In the Crimea an effort was made to relieve the siege of Sevastopol, in the north an attempt was made to restore communication and transportation links between Moscow and Leningrad, and in the south a major campaign was launched to recapture Kharkov and regain control of the Donets Basin.

All three efforts failed. The ambitious offensive in the Kharkov area was the greatest disaster. Beginning on 12 May the huge Red Army dashed through south of the city, but by 18 May the Germans had recovered from their surprise and launched their own planned offensive on the overstretched Soviet lines. By 23 May German forces surrounded Marshal Semyon Timoshenko's Army, capturing some 241,000 men and over 600 tanks. In the last analysis, the Russian offensive proved to be the most important factor in clearing the way for the German advance.

With the Russian offensives stymied and a good part of their resources wiped out, the Germans were ready to launch their own campaign. Hitler's economic experts had told him (erroneously as it turned out) that Germany could not continue the war much longer unless they obtained control of the Caucasus. In view of his limited resources he decided to place German forces in the northern and central areas of the Front on the defensive and reinforce Army Group South for the big drive down the corridor between the Don and Donets rivers.

After they had crossed the lower reaches of the Don, Army Group A – under the command of Field Marshal List – would strike for the Caucasus while Army Group B – under Field Marshal von Bock – would secure the left flank. Troops from Hungary, Italy, and Rumania would be used to assist Army Group B in maintaining the long vulnerable line along the Don from Voronezh to Stalingrad. It was a bold scheme and it worried the German generals. Not only did the thought of making such a deep advance on only one flank violate every principle they had learned in staff college, but they were more realistic than Hitler about Germany's ability to mount such an action. They were even more nervous at the thought that the only thing preventing the German forces from being squeezed between the Red Army and the Black Sea would be a thin line of auxiliary troops. But Hitler overrode all their objections, and in the end the generals gave way.

At this point in the planning, Stalingrad was little more than a name on the map. Although Hitler had originally toyed with a grandiose scheme that involved capturing Stalingrad to open the way for a northward sweep to outflank Moscow, his Chief of Staff, General Halder, had managed to dissuade him. The German Army would advance east past Stalingrad only as far as was necessary to provide cover for the left flank. Commanding as it did the narrow neck of land between the Don and the Volga, it did have some strategic importance, but if it proved difficult to capture, Stalingrad could simply be bombarded to rub-

ble to prevent its functioning as a communications center.

The Germans began their advance in June 1942. On the right was the Seventeenth Army which, with the Eleventh Army in the Crimea and the First Panzer Army further north, comprised List's Army Group A. Bock's Army Group B on the left consisted of the Fourth Panzer Army, the Sixth Army, the Second Army, and the Second Hungarian Army. The offensive was to be staggered; the units farthest on the left would move first while those on the right waited for them to come up before trying to advance. The First and the Fourth Panzer Armies backed up by the infantry armies would strike first from Kharkov and Kursk against the most advanced Russian positions.

The main offensive began on 28 June, following diversionary offensives in the Crimea and in the Izyum sector. The Soviet forces, still retreating after their defeat in May, managed to put up a stiff fight for several days before their reserves ran short and the Fourth Panzer Army broke through between Kursk and Belgorod. General Hoth and his tanks swept easily and rapidly across the hundred miles of open, rolling plain towards Voronezh and the Don. Once at the river the Second Hungarian Army came up to relieve the Fourth Panzer Army, which then wheeled southeastward down the corridor between the Don and the Donets. The Panzers were followed by the Sixth Army, which was charged with taking Stalingrad.

Meanwhile on the right wing General Kleist's First Panzer Army moved out of the Kharkov sector and drove rapidly eastward to Chertkovo, on the railway line between Moscow and Rostov. Turning southward they then continued their spectacular sweep down to Rostov. The city was quickly captured by the right wing, thus cutting the oil pipeline from the Caucasus and leaving Russia with only the oil that could be brought up the Caspian Sea and via the new rail route that ran along the steppes next to it.

Impressive as it seemed, however, this offensive was not nearly as effective as earlier ones in 1941. The German tank troops were not so well trained; in addition, the reorganization of the Panzer Groups into Panzer Armies, with a proportionate increase in infantry and artillery support, tended to make the new units more unwieldy and much slower.

Left: Exhausted German motorcyclists pause to check their maps on the race to Stalingrad.

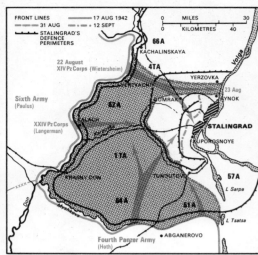

General (later Field Marshal) Paulus and his staff before the gates of Stalingrad.

The encirclement of Stalingrad.

So, although large bodies of Russian troops were overrun and temporarily isolated, many were able to fall back to the northeast before they could be taken prisoner. This took them, naturally, to the area in and around Stalingrad.

Encouraged by their success, the First Panzer Army turned southward, crossed the Manych River, and fanned out on a wide front. By 9 August the right column was in possession of the great oil fields around Maykop, though much of the equipment had been destroyed by the retreating Soviets. The center column, 150 miles to the east, was already in the foothills of the Caucasus Mountains and the left column was moving toward Bud-envosk in the east. Then the great rush suddenly slowed down. In brief, there was too little fuel and too many mountains; in addition, the action at Stalingrad soon began to siphon off a large part of the forces.

The Germans could obtain no fuel from the wrecked oil fields they had captured, and delivering a sufficient supply to such a wide front by air and rail was virtually impossible. The mountains cramped their style by channeling their advance, and as they drove deeper into the Caucasus resistance stiffened. Here they were fighting troops that had been recruited locally; men who were not only familiar with the terrain, but who were fighting to defend their own homes. Throughout September and October the Germans battered themselves against the mountain barrier to no avail, as the Battle at Stalingrad in the north drained away their reserves.

During the last part of July, the Sixth Army, under General Paulus, pushed down the north side of the Don-Donets corridor. It made excellent progress at first, but as it began to outrun its supply lines, and as more and more troops had to be detached to guard the northern flank, progress slowed. A series of determined Soviet stands further sapped the Army's strength. Paulus was forced to by-pass several Soviet positions in the Don bend – a move that was to have disastrous consequences in November.

The narrowed Front limited German

The Germans took Rostov to protect the right flank of Paulus' advance on Stalingrad.

maneuverability and it took Paulus more than three weeks to establish bridgeheads across the river. Once across, the Sixth Army drove relentlessly for the Volga north of the city; on 23 August the forward units supported by some hundred tanks reached the west bank of the river north of the village of Rynok, and infantry, motorized, and Panzer divisions poured through the five-mile-wide corridor.

The stage was set, with Paulus poised to begin the final stages of the offensive. As planned it would be a pincer attack, with the Sixth Army moving in from the northwest and Hoth's Fourth Panzer Army coming up from the southwest to envelop the Russian Sixtysecond and Sixtyfourth Armies.

That evening the Luftwaffe launched a mammoth raid on the town; some 2000 bombers rained death and destruction, killing thousands, and leaving the huge city enveloped in flames. Response to the raid, however, was precisely opposite to what the Germans had intended. As in England, the effect of the attack was to strengthen resistance, not dissipate it in panic and confusion. General Chuikov, who was to emerge as one of the vital personalities in the defense of Stalingrad, described the city's reaction to the raid.

The soldiers and citizens replied by closing their ranks. The famous Barrikady and Krasny Oktyabr factories and the power station became bastions of defense. The workers forged guns and fought for the factories alongside

A Russian KV-1 heavy tank, with the T-34 a mainstay of the Russian defense.

the soldiers. Gray-haired veterans ... foundrymen and tractor engineers, Volga boatmen and stevedores, railwaymen and shipbuilders, officeworkers and housewives, fathers and children – all became soldiers, and each and every one turned out to defend their city.

The fighting in the outskirts grew more and more intense. The Soviets, with the two-mile-wide river at their backs, were fighting desperately to keep the arms of the pincers apart – and were succeeding. The Germans mounted an offensive from the west to complete the semi-circle and attack followed attack, but for gains that were measured in yards instead of miles.

The psychological importance of the battle grew daily, for both sides. In this respect it has been likened to the Battle of Verdun in 1916 – but with an important difference. At Verdun the adversaries cut each other down at long range with artillery or machine gun fire; Stalingrad was virtually a battle of individuals. At Stalingrad, too, the very name of the city was a symbol – one that inspired the Soviets and infuriated Hitler.

The Führer, in fact, soon lost all sight of strategy and committed his Armies to the one kind of battle in which they were at a disadvantage. Hoth's Panzers were taken from the vast steppes where they traveled unencumbered, and swung into a jungle of brick and concrete, where the makeshift barricades at every intersection proved insurmountable. Germany's superiority in fire power was of no use in the channelized, hand-to-hand, house-to-house fighting that followed.

Bitter battles were waged over every house, every water tower, every pile of rubble. Enemies cursed each other across a street, or even across a corridor. Men fought for a room with pickaxes and clubs. Try as they might to break out of the close fighting, the Germans were trapped in a form of barricade warfare in which the Soviets far surpassed them.

The German supply position also worsened rapidly. Their repetitive attacks would have had more effect if Stalingrad had been isolated from outside help. But the city had all of the USSR behind it, and although there was a serious shortage of material and equipment, Soviet manpower reserves were much greater than Germany's. The German Front widened; the supply lines became longer and more difficult to maintain; Paulus was forced to bring up reinforcements by depleting the forces guarding his left flank; and every engagement in that battle of attrition reduced his already limited reserves still further.

In the first week of September, Hoth's tanks broke through to the Volga in the southern sector, splitting the Soviets in two. This put the Soviet Sixty-second Army, already badly mauled in the fighting west of the Don, in an especially bad position. Defending the northern half of the city they found themselves outnumbered three to one; at one point the Germans got to within machine gun range of the Volga ferries' central landing stage. Still the Soviets held on, defending their sectors with sheer tenacity and sometimes little else. In the inner city the street fighting continued, if anything, more bitterly than in the suburbs.

On 11 September General Vasily Chuikov was summoned to Stalingrad Front Headquarters at Yamy on the east bank of the Volga to see Comrade Nikita Krushchev, the Communist Party representative on the Front Military Council, and General Andrey Yeremenko, Commander of the front. Making his way across the Volga, he arrived at Yamy at midnight, only to spend the next two hours searching for the Headquarters. Eventually he chanced upon someone who knew where it was; however, by that time everyone had gone to bed, and he was forced to wait till morning to discover the reason for his summons.

His orders, when they came, were

Top and side views of a German Pzkw-IV of the type used at Stalingrad.

short and simple. General Lopatin, Commander of the beleaguered Sixty-second Army, had lost faith in his ability to hold the city, and had been withdrawing his troops. Chuikov was to take command of the Army, and hold the city at all costs.

Chuikov was ready and more than willing to take on the task. During the preceding weeks he had been analyzing German tactics, and had seen a definite pattern: a tank attack with air support from the Luftwaffe, followed by an infantry attack. He had also come to the conclusion that Germans intensely disliked close fighting. He decided, therefore, that by forcing the Germans to fight at close quarters he could gain an important psychological advantage as well as deprive them of their trump card – their Air Force, who could not risk bombing their own troops. Stalingrad was made to order under those conditions. There

was, then, some room for hope in a situation that must have appeared quite hopeless to others than Lopatin.

During the next three weeks it became obvious that Paulus' offensive had been brought to a standstill, and that major strategic revisions were necessary. But the Germans were trapped by their own propaganda machine, which had been steadily building up the importance of the battle. More importantly, Hitler's determination to capture Stalingrad had become a full-fledged obsession. Day after day the Chief of the General Staff, Halder, urged him to abandon the offensive, while the Führer became increasingly angry and sure that the 'old generals' on the staff were holding back his magnificent schemes. And so at the end of September Halder departed, breathing an inward sigh of relief. He was replaced by Kurt Zeitzler, a much younger officer whom Hitler felt would

In happier days Wehrmacht troops on the march through the Ukraine in the summer of 1942.

be more amenable to his schemes. At first Zeitzler was as malleable as Hitler might have wished. Later, however, he too began to try to argue that maintaining the front at Stalingrad was impractical. Hitler did not like this advice any better the second time around, and by 1943 Zeitzler too found himself being increasingly ignored.

On 3 October Paulus launched a head-on strike at the Soviets' strongest point – the triple complex of the Tractor factory, the Barrikady ordnance plant, and the Krasny Oktyabr (Red October) steel works. The decision to mount the offensive was dictated not so much by tactical considerations as by personal ones: Paulus had recently received a visit from General Schmundt, Chief of the Army Personnel Office, who had strongly hinted that he was being strongly considered for a 'senior post,' but that Hitler was anxious to see the Stalingrad operations

brought to a successful conclusion first.

The ensuing battle proved to be the fiercest and longest of the five that were fought in the city. The German lightning attack struck and fizzled out, with no gain. Both sides fought ferociously for three days and then stopped for four, with the lines, in many cases, only a few yards apart. Both sides showered the city with leaflets: the German ones showing the hopeless situation faced by the defenders and the Russian ones containing stories of individual heroism and exhortations to stand fast. The Volga ferries plowed back and forth – for the most part under fire – with men and supplies.

On 12 October Chuikov launched a counterattack against the German main group in the western outskirts of the Tractor factory. It was a calculated risk, based on the premise that it would be better to force the Germans to fight before they were quite ready rather than

wait for them to throw their full strength into an attack.

The 14 October 1942 and the next three days were the most critical moments of the battle. By midnight, Paulus' troops had surrounded the Tractor factory on three sides and were fighting in some of the workshops, following their biggest operation in the city so far. On 15 October fresh forces were thrown into the battle and the Sixty-second Army was split in two; on the morning of 16 October a determined German attempt to crush the encircled northern group was barely stopped. The battle raged on, with the center of the fighting shifting from the Tractor factory to the Barrikady factory and toward the Krasny Oktyabr factory. By the end of the month the Russian positions had been reduced to a few pockets of rubble, most less than 300 yards deep, on the edge of the Volga. Krasny Oktyabr had fallen to the Ger-

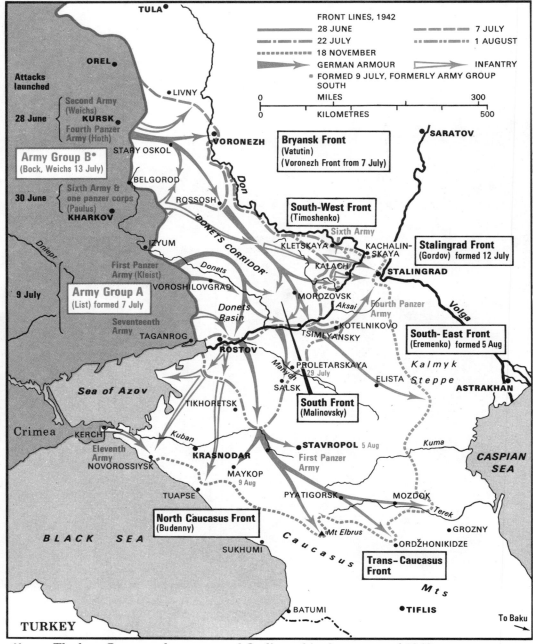

Within the map:

FRONT LINES, 1942
28 JUNE — — — 7 JULY
22 JULY — · — · 1 AUGUST
18 NOVEMBER ········
GERMAN ARMOUR ▶ INFANTRY ▷
● FORMED 9 JULY, FORMERLY ARMY GROUP SOUTH

MILES 0 — 300
KILOMETRES 0 — 500

TULA
OREL
LIVNY
Attacks launched
Second Army (Weichs)
28 June
KURSK
Fourth Panzer Army (Hoth)
STARY OSKOL
VORONEZH
Army Group B* (Bock, Weichs 13 July)
BELGOROD
Don
SARATOV
Bryansk Front (Vatutin) (Voronezh Front from 7 July)
30 June
Sixth Army & one panzer corps (Paulus)
KHARKOV
ROSSOSH
IZYUM
DONETS CORRIDOR
Donets
KLETSKAYA
Sixth Army
KACHALIN-SKAYA
KALACH
STALINGRAD
South-West Front (Timoshenko)
Stalingrad Front (Gordov) formed 12 July
First Panzer Army (Kleist)
VOROSHILOVGRAD
9 July
Army Group A (List) formed 7 July
Donets Basin
MOROZOVSK
Aksai
Fourth Panzer Army
Volga
Seventeenth Army
TAGANROG
TSIMLYANSKY
KOTELNIKOVO
South-East Front (Eremenko) formed 5 Aug
ROSTOV
Sea of Azov
Manych
PROLETARSKAYA 29 July
SALSK
ELISTA
Kalmyk Steppe
ASTRAKHAN
South Front (Malinovsky)
Crimea
KERCH
Eleventh Army
NOVOROSSIYSK
Kuban
TIKHORETSK
STAVROPOL 5 Aug
First Panzer Army
Kuma
CASPIAN SEA
KRASNODAR
MAYKOP 9 Aug
PYATIGORSK
MOZDOK
Terek
GROZNY
North Caucasus Front (Budenny)
TUAPSE
ORDŽONIKIDZE
BLACK SEA
SUKHUMI
Mt Elbrus
Caucasus
Trans-Caucasus Front
Mts
TURKEY
BATUMI
TIFLIS
To Baku

Above: The long German advance toward Stalingrad in the summer of 1942.
Below: Wehrmacht troops approach the city, and the fighting became more fierce.

mans; only three splinter groups fought on in the Tractor factory; in the Barrikady Germans at one end faced Russian machine gunners in the foundry ovens at the other. But things were not quite as desperate as they appeared on the surface. The battle for the factories had finally drained the offensive strength from the German Army; its morale had been shattered by its growing frustration, its enormous losses, and the coming of winter, and the overstretched flanks had been stripped of their reserves.

The dark, towering buildings had become charred houses – shards of glass from skylights littered the floors, blood smeared the walls. The Germans slowly penetrated the giant complexes, around the machines, through the offices. In cafeterias Germans and Russians fought around and over tables and chairs while cannon shells and tracer bullets ricocheted through the rooms. Five thousand of the 8000 commandos of General Zholudev's Thirty-seventh Guards were killed during one 48-hour period in the Tractor factory.

A young German lieutenant wrote of the ... 'ceaseless struggle from noon till night. From storey to storey, faces black with sweat, we bombarded each other with grenades in the middle of explosions, clouds of dust and smoke, heaps of mortar, floods of blood, fragments of furniture and human beings. Ask any soldier what half an hour of hand-to-hand struggle means in such a fight. And imagine Stalingrad: eighty days and eighty nights of hand-to-hand struggles . . . . Stalingrad is no longer a town ... it is an enormous cloud of burning blinding smoke; it is a vast furnace, lit by the reflection of the flames . . . . Animals flee this hell; the hardest stones cannot bear it for long; only men endure.'

The Soviets perfected the art of house-to-house fighting; the streets and squares were virtually deserted much of the time. Their basic tactic was active defense; to defend by attacking whenever possible, to further wear down the enemy. No German soldier was safe from the Russian snipers; no building or sector, once occupied, could ever be considered secure from counterattack or re-occupation.

The basic unit for these tactics was the 'storm group' – a battle unit adapted to the needs of city fighting. Although it could vary in size from eight to 80 men, a storm group typically consisted of an infantry platoon (from 20 to 50 soldiers) plus two or three guns, a squad of

A wrecked German fighter outside Stalingrad. Goering was unable to keep up air supply.

The military council of the Russian Sixty-second Army; General Chuikov is second from the left.

Chuikov in his bunker across the Volga when most of the city was taken by the Nazis.

sappers, and some chemical warfare men. Each man in the group had a tommy gun and many had hand grenades.

The men (and women) in a storm group were usually sub-divided into an assault group, a reinforcement group, and a reserve group. The assault group contained six to eight soldiers, lightly armed with tommy guns, grenades, dagger and spade. This group would break into the building first, and wage battle against the enemy inside.

As soon as the assault groups were inside the building, members of the reinforcement group would enter simultaneously from different directions. They carried heavier arms – heavy machine guns, mortars, anti-tank rifles and guns, crowbars, picks, and explosives – as well as tommy guns and grenades. Their job was to seize the firing positions and hold off any attempts to assist the beleaguered garrison from outside.

The reserve group supplemented the assault groups, guarded the flanks, and also acted as a blocking party when necessary.

Timing and surprise were the storm troops' most important weapons, though individual pieces of artillery or single tanks were sometimes used to provide covering fire. Tactics were based on a sudden charge, rapid action, and a wide sense of initiative on the part of every soldier. Much time was spent before the storming of any building, studying the building and the daily routine of its occupants, and preparing the men so that each soldier knew precisely where he would launch from, how he was going to enter the building, and what his responsibilities were when he got there.

Two weeks later – in mid-November – the Germans still had not been able to conquer the last few pockets of resistance, even though delivery of supplies to the Russians had been stopped for some days because drifting ice on the Volga had rendered it unnavigable. For the last two months, however, Chuikov had been sent just enough reinforcements and supplies to keep him going; everything else that fall was committed to the great counteroffensive that the Russians were preparing in the east and west. Chuikov and the Sixtysecond Army had been the bait for a gigantic and terrible trap.

The counterstroke, a triumph of military strategy and psychology, was devised by three brilliant members of the Russian General Staff: Generals Zhukov, Vasilievsky, and Voronov. It

Above: The famous T-34/76, manufactured in large numbers east of the Volga which saved Russia.

Left: A weary German soldier in the Stalingrad railway station.

was launched on 19 November – after the first frosts had hardened the ground enough to permit rapid movement, but before the heavy snows slowed everything to a snail's pace. Psychologically it caught the Germans at the height of their exhaustion, when they were experiencing the most frustration at not being able to attain the final victory as well as depression at the thought of the coming winter.

A pair of pincers, each with several prongs, was to be driven into the German flanks on either side of the salient at whose tip was Stalingrad. The attack would take place at locations where the flanks were held by Rumanian troops. The principal Russian commanders were General Vatutin (Southwest Front), General Rokossovsky (Don Front), and General Yeremenko (Stalingrad Front).

German Intelligence had realized that something of the sort was in the air, but both the Wehrmacht and the Luftwaffe grossly underestimated its scale. On 19 November the Russians threw six fresh armies, 450 new T-34 tanks, and a 2000-gun artillery barrage against a few tanks and a relatively small number of very tired men.

Northwest of Stalingrad the Russian prongs pushed down the banks of the Don to Kalach and the railway line that ran back to the Donets Basin. Southeast of the city, spearheads of the left pincer pushed west to cut the railway line that

Russian factory workers defend the Krasny Oktyabr plant as the Germans stormed the city.

ran to the Black Sea, while others moved up to Kalach to complete the encirclement. The Germans, long considered the unrivaled practitioners of the encirclement maneuver, were now – for the first time in the war – doubly trapped. Not only were the Sixth Army and a Corps of the Fourth Panzer Army completely surrounded, but they were forced to continue attacking – not to get in, but to get out!

Meanwhile, another Russian force burst across the Don at Serafimovich and spread out in the Don-Donets Corridor, moving south to link up with elements of the left pincer, moving on from Kalach. This outer circle was of vital importance, for it upset the German base of operations and cut off the direct routes by which Paulus might have been relieved.

For two nights no one on the Sixth Army's staff slept as they desperately tried to regroup their precious Panzers and pull their infantry out of the maze of Stalingrad to protect their crumbling flanks. In the rear, everything was confusion. A platoon of engineers had prepared the bridge at Kalach for demolition, and were waiting in case orders came through to destroy the only land route for Paulus' supply trains. At 1630 hours on 23 November, tanks approached from the west; since the first three were Horch personnel carriers with 22nd Panzer Division markings, the lieutenant in charge ordered the barrier lifted. Once on the bridge, 60 Russian

tommy-gunners leapt from their captured vehicles and killed or captured the entire platoon. They removed the demolition charges, and that evening 25 tanks rolled across the bridge. The weapons had changed but the tactics were virtually the same as in the Trojan War.

Paulus fired off a series of urgent telegrams to Hitler, requesting freedom of action: there was still one route out open in the south, over the frozen Don, but he would have to move fast. Ammunition was in short supply and he had supplies for only six days. Finally on 24 November, he received a reply: the Sixth Army was to hold Stalingrad 'at any price.' There would be no withdrawal.

Isolated German pockets had, of course, held out during the preceeding winter, supplied by airlift. So, when Goering claimed that the Luftwaffe could land the 500 to 700 tons of supplies needed daily to keep the Sixth Army going, Hitler had chosen to believe him – despite protests from Zeitzler and others that an operation on that scale was beyond their capability.

The newly appointed commander of 'Army Group Don,' Field Marshal Erich von Manstein, was ordered to carve a corridor to the Sixth Army so that supplies could be delivered by land – but nothing was said about bringing them out of Stalingrad. His only other instructions were to work with the Commanders of Army Groups A and B, to protect the flanks of the troops in the Caucasus.

Manstein, with his hooked nose and silver hair, was a legend to ordinary German soldiers. Generally regarded by his colleagues as the ablest strategist on the General Staff, he had devised the plan for Germany's invasion in the West. Now he had to arrive at one that would enable him to achieve his primary purpose with the scanty resources under his command: the encircled Sixth Army, Hoth's battered Fourth Panzer Army, and the shattered remains of the Rumanian divisions, now scattered about the steppes.

Assuming that Goering's airlift could keep Paulus' army alive for the time being, Manstein planned a two-pronged attack. One prong would be a diversionary move against Kalach in the west. Hopefully, this would divert Russian troops from the main attack which would start at Kotelnikovo, 73 miles southwest of Stalingrad. The Kotelnikovo offensive would not have to cross the Don itself. Only two of its tributaries, the Aksai and the Myshkova rivers, were in the way, and beyond the Myshkova were 30 miles of open steppe. Once his troops crossed the Myshkova, Manstein would expect Paulus' men to break out and link up with them. Hoth's men would never be able to break through the Russian ring on their own, and this simultaneous sortie by Paulus on receipt of the code signal *Donnerschlag* (Thunderclap) was necessary to the success of the operation.

Another vital factor was the ability of an improved defense force led by Colonel Walter Wenck to stall the Russians south of the Don. The colonel realized the importance of keeping the enemy from Rostov, but had neither troops nor equipment to do it with. In order to put together his impromptu army (later named Operational Group Hollidt) he was forced to resort to rather unorthodox methods. He showed movies at intersections; the soldiers who stopped to watch were rounded off and sent off to form one of his ad hoc units. He rode the highways collecting stragglers. One of his officers found an abandoned fuel dump and put up signs that read 'To the Fuel-Issuing Point.' Hundreds of vehicles – cars, trucks, and tanks – drove in, only to form part of the new army.

Manstein, meanwhile, had been collecting supplies in a more conventional manner. The 6th Panzer Division – 160 tanks and their elite crews – arrived in Kotelnikovo. The 25 tanks that were left in the 23rd Panzer Division limped in. Also expected were the 17th Panzer and

16th Motorized Divisions, but these never arrived. The 17th Panzer Division was pulled off the trains carrying it to Kotelnikovo to act as reserves for an expected Russian attack and the 16th Motorized Division was ordered by Hitler to stay where it was.

On the surface, the Sixth Army was functioning smoothly inside the encirclement. Fuel and food were distributed in an organized, efficient manner; hospitals operated without confusion; the highways were kept clear of snow. But by 11 December it was obvious that the Luftwaffe had failed. The best they had been able to average was 84.4 tons a day – less than 20 percent of what was needed to keep the Sixth Army alive. Manstein was Paulus' only hope.

The next day, 12 December, the white tanks of the 6th Panzer Division roared out of Kotelnikovo. Manstein's relief mission had begun. The attack took the Russians by surprise and at first met little resistance; after the first few days of fighting, however, it had slowed to a crawl. Paulus, pressed to begin his own breakout operations, refused to do anything until he had more supplies. He had only enough fuel to go about 20 kilometers (12 miles), and had no confidence in his ability to hold the breakout once it had been achieved.

By this time both the regular telephone and radio-telephone links between Paulus and Manstein had been destroyed, and the teletype was the only means of communication at their disposal. Using this unsatisfactory medium, Manstein continued to press for a breakout. Paulus continued to follow Hitler's orders: he stayed where he was. Hoth's Panzers could not remain poised on the steppe for long, although Manstein kept them there longer than was safe in order to cover the air lifeline to the doomed army. Over Christmas Russian pressure gradually pushed him back, destroying the last prospect of relief for the Sixth Army.

On 16 December the Russians began yet another outer-circle maneuver as General Golikov, Commander of the Voronezh front, sent his left wing against the Eighth Italian Army on a 60-mile front between Novaya Kalitva and Monastyrshchina. A pre-dawn artillery barrage followed by tank and infantry attacks sent the defenders reeling back through blinding snowstorms toward Millerovo and the Donets. Vatutin's forces were moving southwestward from the Chir toward the Donets at the same time. Within two weeks Russians had

Russian big guns fire their salute across the Volga on 8 January 1943.

German tanks seized by the Soviets.

Field Marshal Paulus after his capture.

The red flag is raised in triumph after the recapture of Stalingrad.

retaken almost all of the Don-Donets corridor, 60,000 prisoners had been taken, and all the German armies in the Caucasus were threatened.

Continued snow and stubborn resistance on the part of German troops at Millerovo and other cities held the Russians off temporarily, but Hitler finally realized that his dream of conquering the Caucasus was doomed to failure. In January 1943 they were ordered to retreat and, almost miraculously, managed to extricate themselves before they were cut off.

In Stalingrad on New Year's Eve the Sixth Army battled on against starvation, the cold, the snow, the vermin – and the sixty-second Army. The Volga had frozen over, and supplies were flowing in to Chuikov and his troops. Now it was the Germans' turn to stubbornly defend building after building, often to the last round, as the Russians relentlessly pushed them back.

Violinist Mikhail Goldstein came to Stalingrad with a group of entertainers for the New Year celebrations. Now living in the West, he recalls going out alone to play for the troops in the trenches. Since it was a holiday he risked including some forbidden German music in his program, and as he played, shooting from the German trenches stopped. When he stopped absolute silence reigned for a few moments and then from a loudspeaker a voice pleaded in broken Russian, 'Play some more Bach. We won't shoot.'

On 8 January General Rokossovsky offered Paulus a chance to surrender. Paulus, on orders from the Führer, refused. On 24 January he was forced to dismiss a similar offer; although he warned Hitler that further resistance was useless, he was told 'Surrender is forbidden. The Sixth Army will hold their positions to the last man and the last round....'

On 31 January Paulus – the new Field Marshal Paulus – was taken prisoner with the rest of his staff when his bunker in the basement of the Univermag Department Store was captured. After more than four months the desperate, bloody battle for Stalingrad was over.

The reasons for Germany's defeat – the greatest her armies had suffered since the Napoleonic Wars – are many. Hitler's obsession with the 'City of Stalin' led to a great strategic error: the concentration of his attacking forces in a single, very limited area where they had no room for maneuver, and their subsequent entrapment in the urban jungle of Stalingrad for which they were singularly ill-equipped. Just as 'strategic overstretch' had led to Napoleon's downfall, so Paulus' overextended lines were a decisive influence on the outcome of the battle. Later, of course, the Luftwaffe's failure, for whatever reasons, to supply the encircled garrison sounded its death knell. The Red Army, on the other hand, had many problems to contend with – but it did not have to worry about strung-out lines of communication and supply. In addition, Russia had far greater reserves, especially in terms of manpower, and when the time came to counterattack they had the vast steppes in which to maneuver and outflank their enemy.

Hitler argued – with some justification – that the Sixth Army's desperate stand had been to some advantage. It tied up enough Russian troops long enough to allow Kleist's troops in the Caucasus to effect their narrow escape. Without Stalingrad to divert their attention Manstein could never have stemmed the flood of Russian troops that would have poured down the Don to Rostov.

Still, German strength in the East would never recover from the blow dealt it at Stalingrad. It is impossible to do more than make an educated guess at the magnitude of the losses sustained by both sides. The greatest damage to Germany, however, was psychological. Quite apart from the resounding blow to morale as the hitherto invincible German Army was stopped, trapped, and finally soundly defeated, Stalingrad would henceforth work as a subtle poison in the minds of many German commanders, undermining their confidence in the Führer's infallability and in the orders he gave them. The next great battle in the East was Kursk: the greatest tank battle in World War II.

Russians move into the smoking ruins of their city.

A soldier's grave in the burned-out ruins of Stalingrad.

SCHWEINFURT RAIDS 1943

The theories of Billy Mitchell were not confined merely to the effect of aircraft in a naval context. His experiments in 1921 were only a part of his overall belief that the future of warfare lay in the element of the air, and were designed to convince his peers and superiors that aircraft, acting with freedom from the constraints of tactical support of either armies or navies, could win wars on their own. In common with the Italian theorist, Giulio Douhet, he based his ideas upon the apparent successes of the Gotha and Giant raids against England during World War I, and concluded that bombing attacks upon an enemy's homeland could destroy both his industrial capacity to wage war and the will of his civilian population to support it. As late as 1930, five years after his court-martial, Mitchell was still pursuing this line of argument, writing that 'the advent of air power, which can go straight to the vital centers and entirely neutralize or destroy them, has put a completely new complexion on the older system of war.' But despite growing interest and support from men like Henry Arnold and Carl Spaatz, both of whom were to hold high air posts during World War II, such ideas fell upon stony ground for much of the interwar period, providing the Americans with neither an independent air force nor an official strategic bombing policy.

Immediately after World War I American isolation and a determination to regard the aircraft as nothing more than a ground-support weapon had combined to limit both the size and importance of the air arm. In 1921 the Air Force Reorganization Act made the US air service completely subordinate to the army, subject to the control of corps commanders, leaving the navy to organize and equip its own separate air arm. The Lassiter Board in 1923 recommended the evolution of a force capable of carrying out independent bombing missions, while two years later the Lampert Committee even went so far as to suggest the creation of a separate air force, of equal rank with the army and navy, but

nothing was done. President Coolidge stepped in to find a compromise, and later in 1925 the Morrow Board advised against air force independence, recommending instead that the army's air arm should be redesignated as an Air Corps, with representation on the General Staff. This was accepted by Congress, to the disgust of Mitchell, and the subordination of air power to the older forms of war was complete.

This did not prevent the gradual evolution of strategic potential, however, for throughout the 1930s, under a variety of pretexts, both the weapons and techniques of long-range bombing were introduced. In 1931 it was agreed that the Air Corps should undertake responsibility for the land-based air defense of the United States and her overseas possessions: a decision which opened the way for the development of strategic aircraft, capable of traveling long distances at relatively high speed with large bomb loads. The immediate result was the B-10 twin-engined, all-metal monoplane, an aircraft with a top speed of over 200 mph, an operational ceiling of 28,000ft, well out of range of existing anti-aircraft defenses, and a capability of long-distance flying which Arnold, then a lieutenant colonel, displayed in 1934, when he led a force of them nonstop from Alaska to Seattle. A year later the Boeing Company produced a four-engined machine, test-flown by the Air Corps as the B-17, and this set new records, flying the 2100 miles from Seattle to Dayton nonstop at an average speed of 232 mph. The General Staff showed little enthusiasm, preferring a smaller aircraft which could be used for ground support, but when in 1939 President Roosevelt called for an immediate strengthening of air services because of the worrying situation in Europe, opposition was withdrawn. A total of $300,000,000 was voted in order to build up the Air Corps to over 5000 aircraft, a significant proportion of which would be bombers, and on 1 September the defensive role of the force was extended to cover the whole of the Western Hemisphere, including Latin

America and the Caribbean. Long-range bombers became essential weapons, permitting the introduction of the B-17 into squadron service and the development of another four-engined machine, the Consolidated Air Corporation's B-24 (Liberator), with an even larger bomb-load capacity and longer range.

But the evolution of the weapons was only half the picture, for it was no good going into a war without knowing how they were to be used. It was here that Mitchell's arguments began to take a hold. As early as September 1938, the newly-promoted Major General Arnold, a supporter of Mitchell's views, was appointed Chief of the Air Corps, and when Roosevelt began to express anxiety about future American involvement in a European war, he was on hand to advise upon air potential. In June 1940 Arnold was appointed to command and co-ordinate the newly-established Army Air Forces, and at the same time preliminary talks took place in London between British and American representatives to determine possible areas of co-operation should the United States enter the war. It was decided that the Atlantic and European theaters were 'decisive' and that American bombers should be based in Britain for offensive action 'in collaboration with the Royal Air Force against German military power at its source.' This was, of course, purely hypothetical – it was to be over a year before the Japanese attack upon Pearl Harbor catapulted America into the war against the Axis powers but the principle that strategic bombing should take place had been laid down.

Once this decision had been made at a political level, the actual techniques to be employed were left to the Army Air Force leaders under Arnold, and they expressed a unanimous preference for daylight raids upon precise targets of integral importance to the enemy's war economy. At first sight, this appears rather strange, for by late 1940 both the Germans and the British – the only two countries then involved in strategic bombing – had switched from day to

night attacks to counteract heavy losses sustained by their forces. The lesson seemed to be that the bomber could not survive in daylight against the interceptor fighter and anti-aircraft defenses, but the Americans were unconvinced. They laid great stress upon the ability of their aircraft to defend themselves – the B-17 was known as the 'Flying Fortress' because of the large number of guns it carried – and to breach German defenses by sheer speed, altitude and numbers. By 1940 a liquid oxygen system had been perfected, allowing crew members to operate at altitudes beyond the maximum ceiling of anti-aircraft guns, and a special bombsight, named after its inventor C L Norden, had been developed, whereby bombs could be dropped from extreme height with impressive accuracy. Indeed, in tests at Muroc, California, bombs had regularly landed within 50ft of the intended target, leading to claims that the B-17s could hit a pickle barrel from 20,000ft! In addition, as the B-17 was faster than any of the American fighters in operational service at the time of its initial flight in 1935, the need for any additional protection, either by way of escort aircraft or the cloak of darkness, was deemed entirely unnecessary.

Thus, when the Americans entered the war in December 1941, a great deal was expected from strategic bombing. According to the advocates, fleets of B-17s would be able to 'fly over Berlin and drop bombs with city-block accuracy,' untroubled by enemy fighters which lacked the speed to engage the fast-moving bombers in running dogfights. Such optimism led inevitably to two significant conclusions. On the one hand, fighter escorts were neither required nor advisable – 'Why should a fighter go with a Fortress when the Fortress is better equipped to defend itself than the fighter?' – on the other, that the American aircraft would be able to bomb Germany with virtual impunity. As so often in war, reality was a far crueller business, culminating in the two raids upon Schweinfurt in 1943, when a total of 120 B-17s and 950 airmen were lost in a tragic attempt to prove the argument.

To begin with, however, optimism prevailed. Within days of the Pearl Harbor attack, President Roosevelt and Prime Minister Churchill met in Washington and agreed upon the desirability of a combined Anglo-American bombing offensive in Europe, setting the seal to the preliminary talks of 1940. On 14 January 1942 it was further decided that

Generals Ira Eaker and Carl Spaatz meet at US headquarters in London in 1943.

Flying Fortresses drop their bombs on a smoke marker on a mission over Germany.

A Republic P-47 fighter takes off from an English airfield to protect the bombers on a mission.

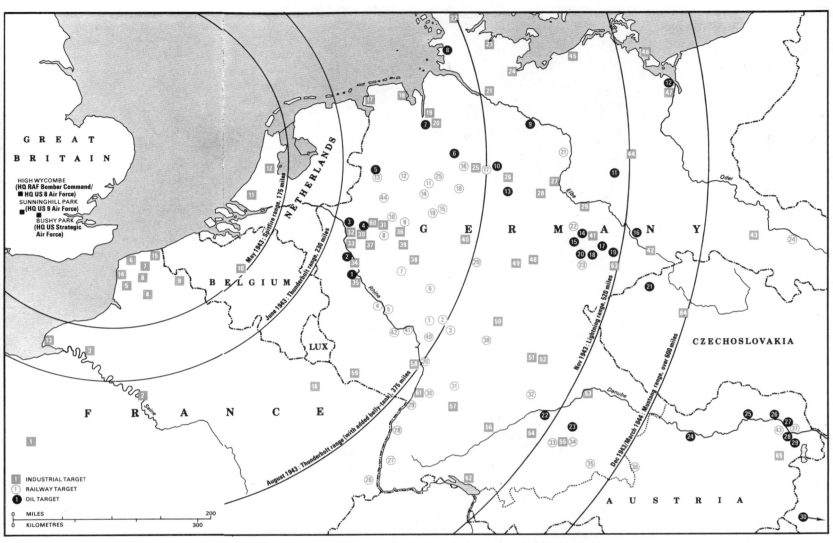

HIGH WYCOMBE
(HQ RAF Bomber Command/
■ HQ US 8 Air Force)
SUNNINGHILL PARK
■ (HQ US 9 Air Force)
BUSHY PARK
■ (HQ US Strategic
Air Force)

NETHERLANDS

BELGIUM

LUX

FRANCE

GERMANY

CZECHOSLOVAKIA

AUSTRIA

Oder

Elbe

Rhine

Seine

Danube

May 1943: Spitfire range, 175 miles
June 1943: Thunderbolt range, 230 miles
August 1943: Thunderbolt range (with added belly tank), 375 miles
Nov 1943: Lightning range, 520 miles
Dec 1943/March 1944: Mustang range, over 600 miles

☐ INDUSTRIAL TARGET
◯ RAILWAY TARGET
● OIL TARGET

0   MILES   200
0   KILOMETRES   300

As the range of Allied aircraft extended new targets came into bombsight; Schweinfurt is No 50.

the US Army Air Force units, under the command of Major General Carl Spaatz, another of Mitchell's disciples, should proceed to Britain without delay. To be known as the 8th Army Air Force, these units would be divided into four commands – Air Service, Ground Air Support, Fighter and Bomber – with Brigadier General Ira Eaker in charge of the bombers. His units would be subdivided into Bombardment Wings (each of three groups), Groups (each of four squadrons) and squadrons (each of 12 aircraft). He was directed to carry out a daylight, precision campaign in co-operation with the RAF.

This produced the first problem, for co-operation was, in the context of the time, impossible. After two years of war and heavy bomber losses, the RAF had not only switched from day to night attacks but was also in the process of a further switch, from precision to area raids. The British campaign in early 1942 was therefore diametrically opposite to that proposed by the Americans and was unlikely to be changed. But

The wreckage of a munitions works in Peenemünde after a raid in 1943.

Flying Fortresses over England on their way to a mission over Germany.

Spaatz and Eaker, following Arnold's lead and intent upon proving that their views upon strategic bombing were correct, remained convinced that 'one bomb dropped by daylight is as effective as many bombs dropped by night,' even concluding that 'the British objective should be to join us in day raids as soon as possible.' As a result, far from a combined offensive bringing increasing pressure to bear upon the enemy, two entirely separate and unconnected campaigns were carried out. The Americans regarded British bombing as a waste of effort; the British thought the Americans suicidal; the Germans were merely thankful that the Allies had apparently forgotten the military maxim about concentration of force.

It is against this confused background that the decision to attack Schweinfurt in 1943 must be seen. At first, American efforts to destroy the enemy were poor. It took time for the 8th AAF to be organized in America and even longer to ship it over to Britain and begin operations. The first fully American bombing mission did not take place until 17 August 1942, when 12 B-17s with RAF fighter escorts hit marshaling yards at Rouen, but the problems were by no means over. Weather patterns were different to those experienced in California, often causing projected raids to be canceled at the last minute as cloud or fog closed in; crew morale suffered and bombing accuracy declined. In one raid on Lille in early October, for example, 108 B-17s and B-24s set off, but 39 were forced to return because of bad weather or mechanical trouble and only nine bombs fell within the stipulated 500 yards of the target. Eaker's claims that his aircraft could land 90 percent of their bombs around a target, with the other ten percent within 100yd of the actual aiming point were beginning to look rather suspect. On top of this, by late 1942 – after a year of active participation in the war – not one bomb had been dropped by the Americans upon Germany itself.

B-17s in formation over the English countryside.

Below: Side view of a B-24 Liberator bomber.

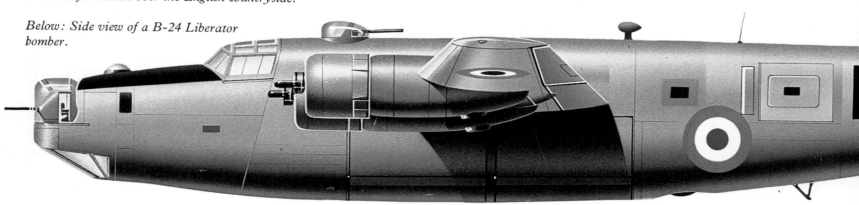

Crew of the famous Memphis Belle *after their 25th operational mission in their B-17.*

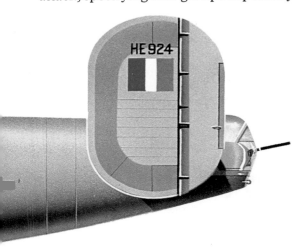

The situation was not helped by a further political call for co-operation between RAF and American bombers at the Casablanca Conference of January 1943. A Directive talked of 'the progressive destruction and dislocation of the German military, industrial and economic system, and the undermining of the morale of the German people to a point where their capacity for armed resistance is fatally weakened,' and even listed the types of target to be attacked, in order of priority (submarine construction yards, the aircraft industry, transportation, oil plants and 'other industrial targets.' This was exactly what the 8th AAF had been formed to do, and Eaker had little choice but to accept it, despite the problems with which he was faced. By 1 May he had drawn up a draft plan of attack, specifying four groups of primary targets (submarine construction, the aircraft industry, ball-bearings and oil) and two of secondary targets (synthetic rubber and military transport vehicles), but had been forced to add an intermediate objective 'second to none in priority' – German fighter production. The reason for this became obvious as the year progressed, for as the Americans, intent upon contributing to the bomber offensive, sent their B-17s and B-24s on deep-penetration raids into Germany itself, the theory of the self-defending bomber came under increasing pressure. On 17 April 115 aircraft attacked the Focke-Wulf assembly plant at Bremen, losing 16 of their number shot down, with a further 44 damaged. Two months later, 22 out of a force of 60 B-17s failed to return from a mission against Kiel, and the trend reached a peak between 24 and 30 July (the so-called 'Blitz Week'), when 88 aircraft were lost in a series of raids. This represented 8.5 percent of the committed forces, a figure which, if allowed to continue, would effectively wipe out the 8th AAF in less than a month. As the majority of losses were caused by interceptor fighters, German production of such machines had to be curtailed before the daylight attacks could begin to take effect.

But the RAF was not interested. Its night-time area raids, designed to destroy entire urban complexes, were not accurate enough to hit precise industrial locations, and the RAF commanders saw little profit accruing from selective bombing. This was reflected in the Pointblank Directive of 10 June 1943, which was supposed to lay down the guide-lines for a Combined Bomber Offensive. In the event, all it did was to reinforce the existing RAF aim of a 'general disorganization of German industry,' leaving the 8th AAF to carry out the plans put forward at Casablanca and to destroy German fighter production. The Americans had been maneuvered into a corner. If their prewar claims were correct, the B-17s and B-24s should have been able to pick precise targets of prime importance to enemy aircraft production and hit them with ease. But if Eaker went ahead, the problems already experienced suggested heavy losses, which in turn would cause a political backlash in America against future air force independence.

There was only one way out of the dilemma, and that was to choose areas of German industry which were absolutely crucial to the manufacture of fighters, force a way through to them, accepting inevitable casualties, and hit them so hard that recovery would be impossible. Toward this end, a number of plans were put forward, including the possibility of raids against the Rumanian oil fields at Ploesti (Operation Tidalwave) and the Messerschmitt works in southern Germany at Regensburg and Wiener Neu—stadt (Operation Juggler), which would involve not only the 8th AAF from Britain but also the 9th from the Middle East. These were eventually carried out –

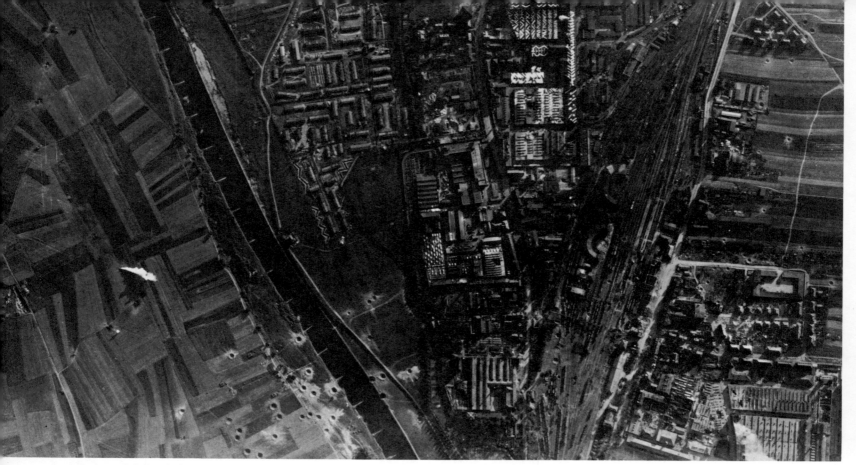

Aerial view of Schweinfurt during the first raid of 17 August 1943.

although the 8th could not participate because of weather problems – and it was in this context that the Bavarian town of Schweinfurt was suggested as a target. As this was a center for the production of ball bearings, and as ball bearings were essential in the manufacture of air frames, engines and almost every piece of modern fighting equipment (to take just one example, a Ju 88 air frame, exclusive of engines, required 1056 anti-friction bearings, each of which had to be precisely tooled), this seemed to be exactly the sort of target the Americans were looking for. Once the Pointblank Directive had been issued Eaker planned an attack at the earliest opportunity.

In outline, the raid appeared to be relatively straightforward, although the distances to be covered, particularly over enemy-occupied territory, were immense. B-17s of the 4th Bombardment Wing, 8th AAF, were detailed to attack Regensburg before flying on, over Italy and the Mediterranean, to air bases in Algeria – a trip of 1500 miles. As they entered Europe it was presumed that they would become an immediate focus for enemy interceptors and that these interceptors would be forced to land and refuel as soon as Regensburg was hit, preparatory to following the bombers on their southward journey. If the 1st Bombardment Wing, also from Britain, could be briefed to follow the 4th and attack the more important target of Schweinfurt on

a strict time schedule, it could put in its raid at the precise moment when no interceptors were in the air. In addition, as the 1st was to return to its bases in England – a round trip of some 800 miles – the German defenses might well be confused and pursuit minimal. After delays, caused yet again by weather, the raid was set to follow this pattern on 17 August – the first anniversary of American involvement in the bombing campaign.

The days immediately before the mission augured ill for its success. On 1 August 175 unescorted B-24s from the 9th AAF base at Benghazi carried out a raid on Ploesti: only 92 returned safely, with a further 19 limping into other Allied airfields, and 532 crew members were lost. On 12 August 25 out of 243 8th AAF bombers were destroyed in a daylight raid on the Ruhr, and 24 hours later an attack by the 9th on Wiener Neustadt's alerted defenses in southern Germany. In normal circumstances, reason would have demanded cancellation, but Eaker was committed to proving once and for all that unescorted deep-penetration daylight raids upon precise targets could shorten or even win the war.

The first Schweinfurt raid was threatened by disaster from the start, and problems continued to emerge on the day itself. When the 383 B-17s were ready to go on 17 August, a last minute

change of plan had to be introduced. Early-morning mist shrouded the bases of the 1st Bombardment Wing in East Anglia, yet cleared from those of the 4th, situated nearer the coast. As the 4th had to take off as early as possible in order to reach North Africa in daylight, no delay could be permitted so far as it was concerned, and its aircraft set off as planned. But the 1st had to wait until the mist had cleared, thereby destroying the time schedule so carefully laid down. The Regensburg raid, instead of forcing the German fighters to refuel while the Schweinfurt attack was carried out, would now merely alert interceptor controllers and give them time to build up fighter strength to counter the second wave. The Schweinfurt force was flying into a trap.

Further delays occurred off the coast of East Anglia, where the Bombardment Wings were supposed to assemble, for some units milled around, wasting precious fuel, waiting for others to arrive. In addition, fighter escort, provided as far as Aachen, did not always materialize due to poor liaison, and at least one Combat Group started out unprotected. All the time of course, the German radar was tracking the bombers and any element of surprise was quickly lost. The results were tragic. Of the 167 B-17s committed to the Regensburg attack, 24 were lost, but did not succeed in drawing the teeth of the German defenses. As

The results of the first bombing assault.

Below: The second raid on Schweinfurt took place in October 1943.

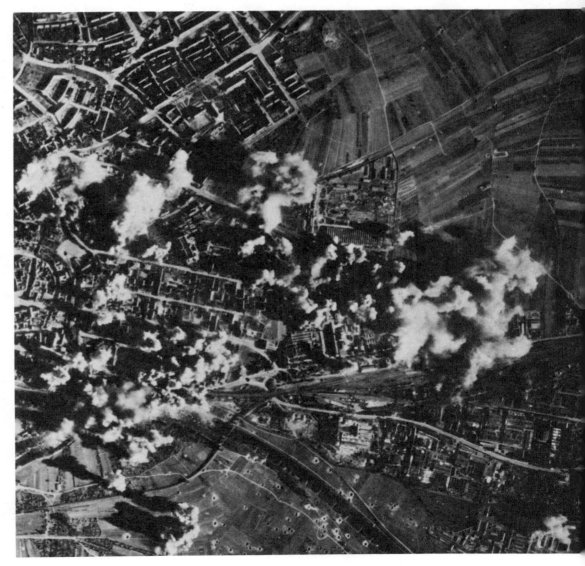

soon as the Messerschmitt works had been hit, the fighters ignored the 4th Bombardment Wing entirely, allowing it to fly on to North Africa unmolested. Instead they refueled and concentrated their strength against the Schweinfurt force, attacking in carefully controlled relays all the way from Aachen, where the escorting Spitfires and P-47s withdrew for lack of fuel, to the target. Twenty-one of the 216 B-17s involved were destroyed in this phase of the battle. Once over the factories of Schweinfurt, the bombers had to contend with anti-aircraft fire, which shot down another B-17, before wheeling round and fighting all the way back to Aachen and the replacement escorts. The Germans used everything at their disposal, committing not only the normal interceptor fighters such as the Me 109 and FW 190, which attacked the bombers from every conceivable angle, but also night-fighters like the Me 110 and Ju 88, which stood off from the American formations and lobbed rockets into their midst. By the time the English coast had been regained, a further 12 B-17s had been destroyed, with another two being forced to ditch in the Channel. The remainder struggled thankfully to their bases, but with many showing distinctive signs of air combat and some barely able to fly, it was obvious to all that a disaster of some magnitude had taken place.

In all, out of the 383 aircraft which had taken off, 60 had failed to return and some 350 airmen were missing. This represented a loss rate of about 16 percent (it rose to 19 percent if the Schweinfurt mission was taken alone) and left the American commanders with the unenviable task of justifying the whole affair. This they attempted to do by stressing two factors, arguing on the one hand that the damage inflicted upon both Regensburg and Schweinfurt was extensive, contributing decisively to the destruction of German war potential in key areas, and on the other that, despite the heavy American air losses, those of the enemy – reported to be 228 fighters destroyed – were much worse. Both claims were grossly exaggerated. Albert Speer, the German Armaments Minister, noted an immediate drop of 38 percent in ball bearing production after 17 August, but was able to organize repairs so quickly that normal rates of manufacture were resumed within four weeks. He also began a systematic process of dispersing the industry away from Schweinfurt, locating factories in remote areas that Allied Intelligence found impossible to trace. Similarly, on the air battle side, the original figure of German losses had to be amended after a strict cross examination of surviving B-17 gunners, being reduced to 148 aircraft destroyed and 100 damaged, although this was still an exaggeration – the Luftwaffe actually lost only 25.

The first raid was therefore a failure, achieving little of long-term value and calling seriously into question the future of unescorted daylight raids. But the process could not stop there, for the Americans were fully committed to their

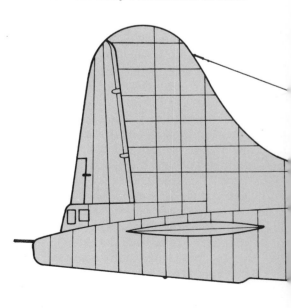

strategy. Politically and militarily, they were forced to power their contribution to the bombing of Germany, however disastrous that might be, and were in no position to change their methods. The use of fighter escorts was a possibility, but none existed with the necessary range for deep-penetration raids; a return to short-range attacks was merely retrogressive; and a switch to night bombing unthinkable. The argument which emerged was that selective targets had to be bombed more than once if they were to be knocked out entirely, and that the raid of 17 August was just a beginning. Tactical errors were admitted – the splitting of forces between Regensburg and Schweinfurt and the long overrun to North Africa were recognized as counter-productive – but the basic aim of the American campaign was not altered. A concentrated return visit to Schweinfurt, designed to prevent a full recovery of ball bearing production and to deal another blow to the already weakened Luftwaffe, was all that was needed to prove the viability of precision daylight attacks.

Unfortunately, another raid could not be launched immediately. The losses of 17 August had to be replaced and a political decision to mount a series of short-range, cross-Channel missions throughout late August and early September, designed to persuade the Germans that invasion was imminent, involved the 8th AAF elsewhere. Even when raids upon Germany were resumed, the old pattern quickly re-emerged. On 6 September an attack upon factories at Stuttgart was extremely costly, with 45 B-17s failing to return, and in raids on three successive

days, 8–10 October, the 8th lost a total of 88 bombers. But the return to Schweinfurt could not be delayed indefinitely. President Roosevelt, conscious of growing civilian unease about bomber losses, was pressing for some sort of decisive action, while a sudden increase in German fighter strength in Europe emphasized the need to destroy the enemy's aircraft industry. Ball bearings were still regarded as crucial, and if their production could be curtailed by a second visit to Schweinfurt, faith in deep-penetration raids by self-defending bombers would be restored.

The second Schweinfurt raid was set to take place on Thursday, 14 October, when 360 B-17s and 60 B-24s, escorted by Spitfires and P-47s as far as possible, were to attack in a concentrated body. But the old problems reappeared. On the day, it was not possible to muster 360 B-17s because of recent losses, and only 324 set out. In addition, the weather was again unfavorable, and before the force had even left England the B-24 contribution was canceled. Only 25 of the Liberators had reached the rendezvous point, so they were sent instead on an uneventful and wasteful diversionary raid to the Frisian Islands. Meanwhile, the main B-17 force had dwindled to 294 because of mechanical problems, the German radar had begun to track the bomber stream, and a formidable interceptor defense had been set up. Once again, the scene was set for a major tragedy, with events bearing a frightening resemblance to those of 17 August.

In many ways the mission was a repeat of the first raid, for as soon as the bombers left the English coast, the German attack began. The escort fighters

provided good protection as far as Aachen, but as soon as they withdrew the bombers began to suffer. In the long flight from Aachen to the target, the enemy interceptors, again with support from rocket-firing Me 110s and Ju 88s, put in a series of intense assaults. Single-engined fighters acted as a screen for the twin-engined aircraft to get close in for rocket attacks; synchronized onslaughts from all angles were mounted by the Me 109s and FW 190s; there was even an attempt to use the obsolete Ju 87 dive-bombers to swoop down and break up the American formations. It was estimated that between 200 and 400 aircraft took part in these attacks, and the results were inevitable. Even before Schweinfurt was reached, 36 B-17s had been shot down, with a further 34 turning for home because of damage. Instead of a concentrated blow delivered by 420 heavy bombers, the attack was put in by 224 B-17s only.

German anti-aircraft defenses around Schweinfurt had been increased after 17 August, and by the time the second raid went in, the bombers had to face a barrage from over 300 88mm flak guns. In the event, none was shot down, but many were damaged and the combat formations, designed to provide mutual protection, were broken up. Meanwhile, the fighters had taken the opportunity to refuel, and as soon as the B-17s turned for home the whole process of air attack began all over again. Fighters and rocket-firing aircraft repeated their earlier tactics, anti-aircraft guns added to the chaos, and there were even reports of medium bombers flying above the American units, dropping bombs into their midst. As one B-17 pilot remarked,

Far left: These men were responsible for maintaining contact between the plane and the control tower.

Below: Side view of the B-17 Flying Fortress bomber.

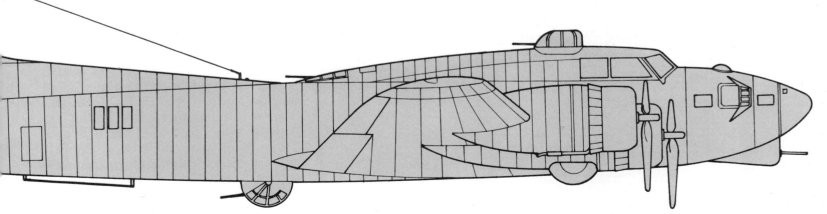

'the scene was similar to a parachute invasion, there were so many crews bailing out'; a comment which was understandable when it was discovered that a further 24 bombers were destroyed (two of them by flak) on this return journey. Yet again, the surviving B-17s limped into their English bases, and yet again, the signs of disaster were apparent. A total of 60 bombers failed to return, with a further five crashing on the airfields as they tried to land: a staggering loss-rate of 25 percent. In addition, 12 of the surviving aircraft were fit only for scrap and 121 needed repairs of some de-

scription. Out of nearly 300 bombers, only 62 were completely unscathed. Six hundred men were missing.

The Americans christened 14 October 'Black Thursday,' a name which became even more apt when it was seen as the culmination of a disastrous week, for since 8 October the 8th AAF had lost the appalling total of 148 aircraft and 1480 airmen. The results were similar to those of 17 August. Despite exaggerated claims that the B-17s had destroyed three-quarters of the ball bearing industry at Schweinfurt, as well as 288 Luftwaffe aircraft during the air battles,

Speer was able to accelerate his repair and dispersion programs, productive capacity was reduced for only six weeks, and the Luftwaffe reported a mere 35 aircraft lost. The second raid conclusively proved what the first had suggested: that long-range penetration flights by unescorted bombers were impracticable. The Americans had no choice but to review their strategy.

The initial reaction was to put a stop to deep-penetration raids – with one third of the 8th AAF destroyed, there was little alternative – but this was only temporary. Reviewing the two Schweinfurt raids together, there did appear to be another possibility in the long term, for it was apparent that during the times when escort fighters were available, bomber losses declined. Therefore, if escorts could be provided all the way, the disasters of 1943 could be avoided, with the added bonus of forcing the Luftwaffe into a sustained battle of attrition which it could not hope to win. Existing escorts were obviously of little use – even with drop tanks, Aachen was the limit of their range – but there did seem to be possibilities with the recently-introduced P-51 Mustang which, when equipped with a Rolls-Royce engine and drop tanks, could fly well beyond targets such as Schweinfurt. By the end of October 1943, Arnold had recognized the need for change, ordering all P-51s to be reserved exclusively for the 8th as long-range escort fighters. They rapidly proved their worth and by early 1944 were beginning to establish the air supremacy over Europe which daylight bombing raids required. The myth of the self-defending bomber had been destroyed, but at a cost which seemed to suggest that strategic bombing was not as instantly decisive as the interwar theorists had foreseen. Furthermore, the time wasted in learning the lesson had delayed the evolution of a Combined Anglo-American Bomber Offensive, which did not even begin to approach reality until late 1944, after the invasion of Europe by Allied armies. By then the war was entering its final phase, leaving very little time in which to prove or disprove strategic bombing theory. The overall lesson appeared to be that the aerial bombardment of the enemy homeland was not a straightforward affair, but was fraught with a myriad of practical problems. This was reinforced by the British experience, culminating in the disasters of late 1943 and early 1944 which were known as the Battle of Berlin.

SERGEANT N. C. JACKSON V.C.

905192 SERGEANT (now Warrant Officer) Norman Cyril JACKSON, Royal Air Force Volunteer Reserve, No. 106 Squadron, Bomber Command.

This airman was the flight engineer in a Lancaster detailed to attack Schweinfurt on the night of 27th April, 1944. Bombs were dropped successfully and the aircraft was climbing out of the target area. Suddenly it was attacked by a fighter at about 20,000 feet. The captain took evading action at once, but the enemy secured many hits. A fire started near a petrol tank on the upper surface of the starboard wing, between the fuselage and the inner engine.

Sergeant Jackson was thrown to the floor during the engagement. Wounds which he received from shell splinters in the right leg and shoulder were probably sustained at that time. Recovering himself, he remarked that he could deal with the fire on the wing and obtained his captain's permission to try to put out the flames.

Pushing a hand fire-extinguisher into the top of his life-saving jacket and clipping on his parachute pack, Sergeant Jackson jettisoned the escape hatch above the pilot's head. He then started to climb out of the cockpit and back along the top of the fuselage to the starboard wing. Before he could leave the fuselage his parachute pack opened and the whole canopy and rigging lines spilled into the cockpit.

Undeterred, Sergeant Jackson continued. The pilot, bomb aimer and navigator gathered the parachute together and held on to the rigging lines, paying them out as the airman crawled aft. Eventually he slipped and, falling from the fuselage of the starboard wing, grasped an air intake on the leading edge of the wing. He succeeded in clinging on but lost the extinguisher, which was blown away.

By this time, the fire had spread rapidly and Sergeant Jackson was involved. His face, hands and clothing was severely burnt. Unable to retain his hold, he was swept through the flames and over the trailing edge of the wing dragging his parachute behind. When last seen it was only partly inflated and was burning in a number of places.

Realising that the fire could not be controlled, the captain gave the order to abandon aircraft. Four of the remaining members of the crew landed safely. The captain and rear gunner have not been accounted for.

Sergeant Jackson was unable to control his descent and landed heavily. He sustained a broken ankle, his right eye was closed through burns and his hands were useless. These injuries, together with the wounds received earlier, reduced him to a pitiable state. At daybreak he crawled to the nearest village, where he was taken prisoner. He bore the intense pain and discomfort of the journey to Dulag Luft with magnificent fortitude. After 10 months in hospital he made a good recovery, though this hands require further treatment and are only of limited use.

This airman's attempt to extinguish the fire and save the aircraft and crew from falling into enemy hands was an act of outstanding gallantry. To venture outside, when travelling at 200 miles an hour, at a great height and in intense cold, was an almost incredible feat. Had he succeeded in subduing the flames, there was little or no prospect of his regaining the cockpit. The spilling of his parachute and the risk of grave danger to its canopy reduced his chances of survival to a minimum. By his ready willingness to face these dangers he set an example of self-sacrifice which will ever be remembered.

LONDON GAZETTE DATED 26th OCTOBER, 1943.

KURSK 1943

After Stalingrad the war on the Eastern Front was different. The Russians were certain they would win and most Germans – with the notable exception of Hitler – faced up to the strong possibility of defeat.

Although it is an easy fact for American and British historians to overlook, 'the war' to Germany meant the war in the east. Most of the German forces were deployed on the Eastern Front, where success might well have given them the time and resources to counter American assaults in the west and fight the Allies to a standstill. But it was clear not only to the Germans, but to most military analysts, that defeat on the Russian steppes meant eventual defeat in the entire war.

If Stalingrad marked the turning point in the war on the Eastern Front, the mammoth, but often underplayed, Battle of Kursk banished any lingering doubts about its eventual outcome, or about the long term survival of the Soviet Union.

But if the outcome could be predicted, the Germans were still far from beaten.

They continued to hold the Ukraine, the Crimea, the Donets Basin, much of Central Russia, and the Baltic states. In the north Leningrad was still threatened, and several deep salients pushed toward Moscow. They had been badly bruised, but their strength was still massive.

During the end of January and beginning of February 1943, action on the southern wing of the front entered a new and violent phase. The Hungarian Second Army and the Italian Eighth Army had already been defeated in a Russian drive southwest toward Kharkov. While attention was focused on this offensive, the Russians moved west from Voronezh on a wide front, hoping to reach the southern reaches of the Dnieper before the winter snows melted. An offensive against Army Group Center by the armies of the Kalinin, Western, and Bryansk Fronts was planned for mid-February.

The Russians had become masters at alternating the pattern and rhythm of their offensives, to place the greatest possible strain on the Germans' already overstretched resources. Another characteristic was their fondness for indirect attack. The first moves in a new offensive were never aimed directly at the place they were actually threatening, but were rather intended to make that place untenable, or at least cripple it so that it was no longer of any strategic value.

The Germans' task meanwhile was to stop the Red Army's advance and throw it back to the Don – or at least stabilize the front in a way that would be most advantageous when the summer campaign began.

At first the Soviet offensive went well. Izyum fell into their hands on 5 February, Kursk on 7 February, and Belgorod on 9 February. By the time General Fillipp Golikov captured Kharkov on 16 February, the Germans had been pushed out of the northeastern Donbass region, and the forward divisions of the Russian Southwestern Front had reached the Dnieper at Dnepropetrovsk, while in the south the front had been pushed to the Mius River, some 55 to 90 miles further westward.

During the second half of February, however, the Russian advantage began to pass. It was the old problem of overstretched lines again: while the Germans

Lt General Rotmistrov, commander of the Fifth Guards Tank Army, and Army Chief of Staff Baskakov discuss the Kursk situation with Lt Col Dokukin just prior to the battle.

САМООТВЕРЖЕННЫМ ТРУДОМ
ОБЕСПЕЧИМ КРАСНУЮ АРМИЮ
И ВОЕННО-МОРСКОЙ ФЛОТ
ВСЕМ НЕОБХОДИМЫМ
ДЛЯ ПОБЕДЫ НАД ВРАГОМ!

НАРОД И АРМИЯ НЕПОБЕДИМЫ!

Russian propaganda poster urges factory workers to help their comrades in arms on the front.

were falling back nearer to their main supply base, the Russians were drawing ever farther away from theirs. When the Stavka (the Red Army's equivalent of Joint Chiefs of Staff) and the Russian General Staff had planned the winter offensive they had found that there was not enough transport available to carry even half of the minimum amount of fuel, food, and munitions needed for such a vast undertaking. They decided to go ahead anyway, counting on obtaining most of their supplies from the Germans. At first many supply depots were captured in each breakthrough and the policy worked well. But as the German lines stiffened the captures became fewer, and serious interruptions in supplies of all kinds became more frequent. The rail routes ran at angles that favored the Germans, who were also now fighting on a front 600 miles shorter than it had been eight months before.

By the beginning of March, the Germans had launched a counteroffensive

General Nikolai Vatutin.

General Vasiliy Chuikov.

that regained Kharkov and Belgorod by the end of the month. And then the spring thaw came, and with it the mud. The entire front became a thick, deep sticky morass in which nothing moved. Both sides settled down to wait for the ground to dry up, and to plan their spring and summer campaigns.

In German headquarters Field Marshal Erich von Manstein was advocating a defensive operation; one which would force the Soviets to do the attacking and then, when the Russian force was spent, allow the Germans to strike back.

Hitler, however, had temporarily lost

An 88mm cannon used throughout the Russian campaign.

interest in the Eastern Front following the defeat of Stalingrad. He allowed Zeitzler, his Chief of Staff, to plan his own decisive battle. By retaining Orel and regaining Belgorod, the Germans would be in an excellent position for a pincer movement against the Russian-held salient around Kursk. Pinching off the salient would open a great hole in the Russian lines, through which he could pour his Panzer divisions. More and more Zeitzler began to see an early breakthrough at Kursk as essential to stem the Red Army's advance.

The German armies were under pressure on all fronts. In North Africa German forces teetered on the edge of destruction, and the prospect of an Anglo-American attack against southern Europe was more than probable. The U-Boat blockade of Britain had demonstrably failed. Mussolini was in deep trouble in Italy and the political situation there was deteriorating rapidly. In the Balkans, Germany's allies – Rumania, Hungary, and Bulgaria – were more than a bit unhappy about the fiasco at Stalingrad and were worried that the war would soon be on their doorstep.

In the east, two great offensives had already failed. Although the USSR had always enjoyed an advantage in men and machinery, superior German tactics had been enough to offset it. Now it was obvious that the USSR had quality as well as quantity – and her production was increasing at a rate Germany could never hope to match. It was essential to lure the Red Army into committing most of its forces to one great battle and to deal it a crippling blow so that German troops could be spared for other theaters.

Not all the generals shared this view; Generals Ewald von Kleist and Heinz Guderian, among others, had doubted that such a victory in the East was possible at all. Manstein, Walther Model, and many others joined them in begging Hitler to abandon the offensive. They pointed out the dangers of the plan: the overstretched lines and the commitment of reserves that could well be needed in Italy and France, not to mention the risk involved in postponing the summer campaign until a large enough force could be gathered. Hitler vacillated; some days he seemed to be accepting their arguments. But in the end he stood by Zeitzler and rejected the advice of the 'old generals,' thus staking everything he had on the battlefield at Kursk. The offensive was given a name: Operation Citadel.

Once Hitler had taken this decision, plans for Operation Citadel moved ahead, though still subject to delay on the part of the Führer, who failed to realize that the success of the operation depended on an early start. The main attacks were to come from Model's Ninth Army in the north, which would move in southeast from the area south of Orel toward Kursk. Three Panzer corps would make the major effort in the

Left: Vatutin on the Voronezh front.

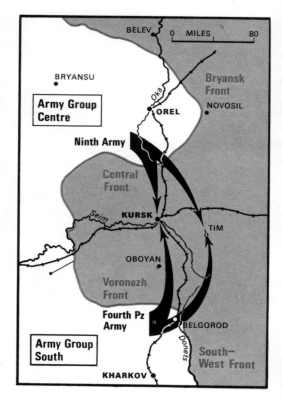

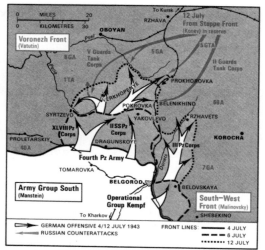

The Russians, meanwhile, were under no illusions about the German plans. In this regard, much has been made of their superior intelligence network, and particularly of the master-spy 'Werther' who supposedly held a confidential position within the German High Command itself. No doubt this efficient espionage ring was of great value, but to give it sole credit is to denigrate the expertise and far-sightedness of Marshal Georgi Zhukov and other Russian generals, to whom the Kursk salient was an obvious German objective.

The Stavka had to decide how to meet the German threat; with a preemptive strike of their own, or a defensive battle from prepared positions followed by a counter attack. At first, the Russian General Staff seemed to favor striking first; Russia's many offensive successes since Stalingrad made taking the initiative look that much more attractive. On the other hand, past experience (including Marshal Semyon Timoshenko's disastrous offensive against Kharkov in May 1942), as well as the example of Field Marshal Bernard Montgomery's victorious defensive tactics at El Alamein, pointed up the advantages of a defensive battle.

Eventually the Soviets opted for the latter course of action. Especially during the latter part of February, as they moved away from their supply dumps, they had been consistently outfought and outmaneuvered in open warfare. In defense, however, the Russian soldier

had displayed a tenacity, bravery, and self-sacrifice that made him a formidable opponent. The Soviet High Command, then, played on its strengths, and during the spring and early summer huge quantities of men and materiel were moved into the Kursk salient.

The three commands in the salient – the Central, Voronezh, and Steppe (Reserve) fronts – began their elaborate preparations for a defense in which the primary purpose would be to bleed the Germans white and render them susceptible to a counteroffensive. Clusters of anti-tank strong points and areas, including minefields, were sited in depth. The strong points, which were centrally controlled and mutually supporting, each included three to five 76mm anti-tank guns, about five anti-tank rifles, and at least five mortars, with support from infantry and engineer units. The minefields covering them were designed to channel German tanks into 'killing zones' where they could be overwhelmed. The six main defensive belts within the salient were 110 miles deep, and a further defensive network stretched back to the Don. The men on the Central Front dug 3100 miles of trenches.

By the time battle commenced the Red Army had laid minefields with an average density of about 2200 anti-tank and 2500 anti-personnel mines per mile of front. Behind them waited some 1,337,000 soldiers and 3300 tanks, with another Tank Army in reserve. There were also more than 20,000 pieces of

attacks. They would link up with General Hermann Hoth's Fourth Panzer Army, which was operating as part of Army Group South under Manstein. Hoth's forces were to attack toward Kursk from the area north of Kharkov. After smashing through the defensive lines manned by the Soviet's Voronezh Front and joining up with the Ninth Army, they would be able to turn and destroy the encircled Red Army forces. Operational Group Kempf would cover the Fourth Panzer Army's eastern flank and would pursue offensive operations against the left wing of the Voronezh Front.

Altogether the Germans had some 900,000 men, 10,000 artillery, and 2700 tanks and assault guns, with 2500 supporting aircraft, concentrated around the salient by the end of June.

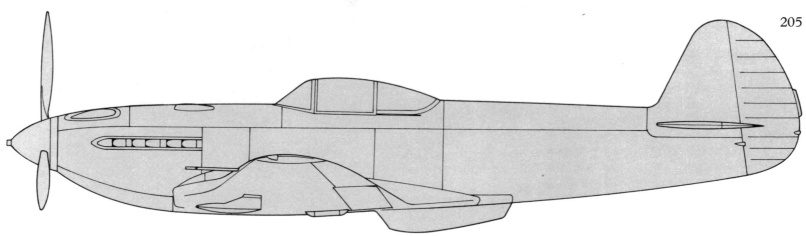

Above: A Yak-3, one of the Russian fighter aircraft used in the Battle of Kursk.

Left: Il-2 fighter aircraft of the Russian Air Force pursue the attacking Me-109s.

Far left: The German attack on Kursk.

Right: A Russian heavy gun in action during the battle. Stopping the German offensive at Kursk meant a complete collapse of the entire Eastern Front for the Nazis. The long march back to Berlin had begun.

artillery, including 6000 76mm anti-tank guns and over 900 devastating Katyusha multiple rocket-launchers. The only area in which the Germans were not dangerously outweighed was in the air; the Russians had deployed about 2600 aircraft.

The Germans naturally knew of these preparations and were concerned, but not dismayed. Considering that the Russians had never been able to withstand a concentrated frontal attack, and that the attacking pincers only had to cover 60 miles, German planners still had faith in their Army's ability to fulfill its mission.

Some changes in tactics were called for, however. In the north, Model decided that instead of sending his Panzers out ahead of the infantry, he would use the infantry and artillery to drive a wedge through the Russian defenses and feed his tanks through the breach. This strategy had worked well for Montgomery at El Alamein – but he had not been faced with such great in-depth defenses, and he had had a marked numerical advantage in terms of men and equipment. Even so, the British attack in the desert had only just succeeded.

In the south Manstein decided to use a flying wedge to pry open the defenses in a series of thrusts. It would be composed of eight of Germany's best armored divisions along a 30 mile front, backed up by infantry divisions who would, in turn, be followed by the artillery and mortar support. At the top of the wedge the newest heavy German tanks, the

Tigers, would be concentrated, while the medium and lighter weight tanks – the as yet untried Panthers and faithful Pzkw-IVs – followed in their wake. In order not to destroy the momentum of the attack, tanks would be ordered not to stop to support their disabled fellows.

The Russians awaited the battle with confidence that they could stop and throw back the German attacks. Their concentrations of artillery, in accordance with Stalin's edict 'Artillery is the god of war,' were tremendous. For weeks, Party officers and experienced tank commanders had been training troops in anti-tank tactics, to innoculate them against the notorious 'tank panic' and ensure a tenacious defense. Secure in the knowledge that their factories could easily replace their losses, the Russians were ready for a battle of attrition, in which they would sacrifice any amount of men and equipment to the elimination of German armor in the east.

But in war the best laid plans almost invariably go astray; the German plans went badly wrong, while on the other hand the Soviets still came close to losing the battle, since their deployments were not precisely correct. The balance of the Russian deployment favored General Rokossovsky's Central Front, since the Red Army expected that the main German attack would come from Orel in the north. In fact, the opposite was true; Model had only three Panzer divisions to Manstein's eight. Thus the German offensive in the north would be stopped

and held fairly quickly. In the south, however, German gains would be more pronounced, inflicting heavy damage on General Vatutin's Voronezh Front. The decision would be delayed and thus the simultaneous Russian counterattacks in the north and south would not be synchronized, so that both the great encirclements would fail.

Operation Citadel was scheduled to begin on 5 July with simultaneous attacks in the north and south. Sporadic skirmishes, however, had been breaking out for some days; both sides were patrolling the fronts and clashes were inevitable, especially on 4 July when German engineers were out clearing their own wire and minefields for the attack. On the same date, the Fourth Panzer Army launched an early attack in the south; Manstein wanted to make tactical gains that would give him command of the high ground and thus a better startline.

In the north, 4 July was a scorching hot, quiet day. As evening fell the Soviet camp grew tense; the troops had been kept on constant alert, and impatient queries were coming in from Stalin. Then, at 2200 hours, a Russian patrol captured a German engineer who told them that the German attack was scheduled to begin at 0330 on 5 July. (Nights are short in Central Russia in July; darkness begins to retreat around 0200 hours.) Rokossovsky responded and devised a nasty surprise for the Germans.

At 0220 hours a great roar burst out as

206

Soviet artillery and mortars began hurling their shells and rockets at German positions. The Germans were not able to reply until 0430 hours, provoking a second Russian bombardment which, though heavier than the first, was not as effective. At about 0530 hours some tank probes were sent out and quickly repulsed by heavy fire.

Two hours later the armor – Tigers, Panthers, and Ferdinand self-propelled guns – moved forward, to serve as battering rams for the infantry divisions.

The heavy Tigers, with their powerful 88mm guns, had already been tested in battle. No one was sure about the Panthers – elegant, medium-weight (45.5 tons) tanks with a length of 29 feet, frontal armor of 80 to 100mm, and a top speed of 34 miles per hour. Technical problems had precluded even a proper test period, let alone time for formation drill and individual training; the final drives were installed while the tanks were being carried by train to the Eastern Front. As they moved into their starting positions, bursts of flame came from their exhaust pipes and some even caught fire. These first Panthers were to continue to suffer teething problems throughout the battle, but later models would prove to be much more effective.

The Ferdinand was an aberration that would not be used again after Kursk. It was a formidable monster of a machine weighing 72 tons, with armor up to 200mm thick. Two Maybach engines produced current for two electric motors, each of which independently drove one of the two caterpillar tracks. In spite of its size it could attain speeds of up to 20 mph and was armed with the trusty 88mm gun. The Ferdinand had two major faults however. First, its drive was too weak and its tracks too vulnerable, which meant that it was relatively easy to

A burned-out column of German transports is attacked and destroyed by Soviet aircraft on the Voronezh front.

A Mk-IV tank is inspected at the Prokhorovka bridgehead at Kursk.

Below: The Mig-3 fighter aircraft of the Soviet Army was an invaluable though early tool used to repel the Luftwaffe.

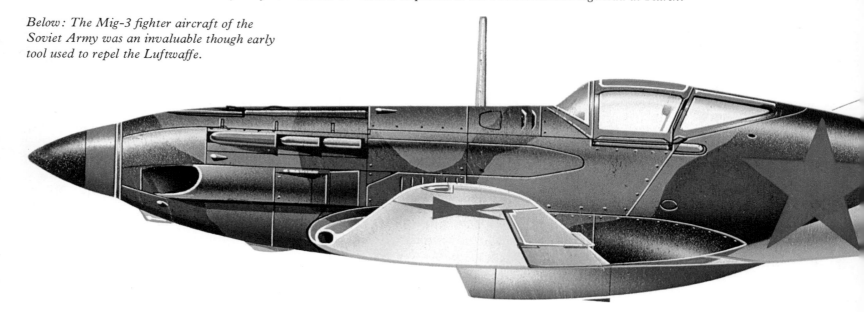

immobilize. Second, it was completely helpless in close combat; aside from the rigidly mounted cannon there were no other armaments. Some crews carried an MG-42 machine gun on board, to fire through the gun barrel when things got really bad – needless to say, it was not a very satisfactory solution. Many Ferdinands were able to break through the Russian lines, but the five or six infantry men who rode on a plank wired to the stern were easily picked off, leaving the great steel monsters to roll on, quite alone, through enemy territory.

By the afternoon of 5 July it was obvious that Russian resistance in the north was much stronger than the Germans had anticipated, and that things were not going at all well. At one point a German breakthrough of about three and a half miles had been achieved against two divisions of the Red Thirteenth Army, but there was little return for the amount of armor and manpower that had been committed. Small-arms fire from Soviet infantrymen who had remained crouching in their well-concealed fox holes as the tanks rumbled by had forced the German infantry to take cover, so that the armor became isolated and enmeshed in the Russian defense lines. More than 100 tanks were lost in the minefields, harassed by Soviet airplanes and anti-tank guns.

Intense fighting during the night enabled the Germans to clear the first Russian lines, and on 6 July Model was able to make about the same depth of penetration as on 5 July. The assault was most successful on the right flank, where it was eventually halted at a low line of hills north of Olkhovatka. Unfortunately for the Ninth Army, little progress was made in the center or on the left that could protect or support the right. Although Rokossovsky sent three tank

One of the first Mk-VI Royal Tiger tanks destroyed by the Russians in the Kursk salient.

Russian tankmen inspect a Tiger tank they put out of action.

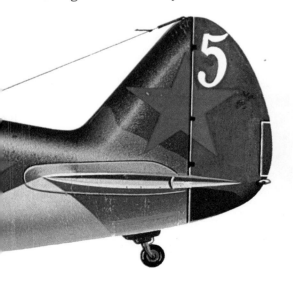

Major General Balkanov addresses his troops at Kursk in July 1943.

corps from his armored reserves to the endangered areas, he kept most of his reserve forces facing the German left flank.

Both sides dug in and the battle lines remained essentially the same through four days of close-quarter fighting and ferocious tank clashes. Wave after wave of Germans struck at the Russian stronghold atop the Olkhovatka ridge. The village and the heights finally fell on 8 July, but the Germans could not consolidate their gain. The ridge was to change hands six times in the course of the battle. By 10 July, then, the northern sector of the salient had been stabilized and the exhausted Germans halted for the moment.

In the south the forces were more equally balanced, and the Russians were hampered by their lack of knowledge about the German plans. Three Panzer Corps – Operational Group Kempf – were concentrated southwest of Belgorod, on the German right flank where, if they were to attack, they could roll up the defenses from the east. The five Panzer divisions of Hoth's Fourth Panzer Army were massed north of the city where they were in a position to strike directly at Kursk via either Oboyan or Korocha. The Russians had to decide which of these alternatives – or any of the others open to the Germans along the 50 miles front – was most likely. The Stavka and the High Command of the Voronezh Front decided that the direct approach, a move toward Oboyan, was most probable. To meet the threat the Sixth Guards Army was deployed north of Belgorod on the left of the Voronezh Front to block the way to Oboyan, while the Seventh Guards Army held the center of the front, east of Belgorod. The Sixth Guards Army was backed up by the First Tank Army, with its more than 1300 armored vehicles. Immediately facing Hoth, along the road to Oboyan, were the Russian 67th and 52nd Guards Rifle Divisions; behind them the III Mechanized Corps guarded the Kharkov-Oboyan-Kursk highway and the feeder road from Butovo. Hoth, however, was a cunning, methodically efficient commander who, after studying the terrain and aerial reconnaissance reports of Russian troop dispositions, devised a plan to sidestep the defenses. After breaking through the initial defenses his troops would wheel northeast. Instead of moving directly on Oboyan and Kursk he would engage the Red Army midway between Oboyan and Korocha at Prokhorovka, a place where

Soviet armored units press forward at Kursk as the Wehrmacht was forced to withdraw.

Russian mine-sweepers search for traps as the pursuit of the enemy continues after Kursk.

A German strongpoint is captured in the swift pursuit of the Wehrmacht after Kursk.

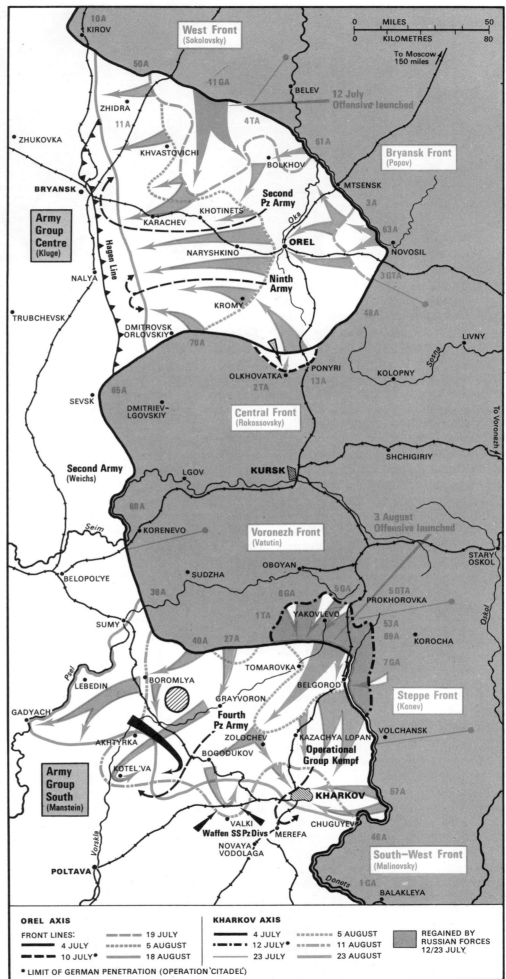

any Russian reserves would have to de-train. Thus the Russians were off balance to some extent in the south before the battle even began; when it did open, things began to go badly for them almost immediately.

Early on the morning of 5 July some 800 German aircraft – Stukas, Messer-schmitts, bombers, ground-support air-craft, and tank-busters – were moving into position for take-off on 16 airfields around the Kharkov area. The Soviets planned a precisely calculated, pre-emptive air strike by the Seventeenth Air Army to destroy the German planes while they were still on the ground and rob Manstein of his third dimension – air cover. The Germans, however, had in-stalled radar in the area, which detected the Russian formations, complete with direction and altitude, when they were still 60 miles away. It gave the Germans about ten minutes lead time – enough for the leaders of the fighter formations, acting on their own initiative, to get their machines into the air. At altitudes of 6000 to 10,000 feet the Messerschmitt fighters were clearly superior to the So-viet Migs, Yaks, and American-made Airacobras. The Russians lost 120 planes in the first few minutes of the attack; the number grew to more than 400 by the

Below: A T-34/76 used at Kursk along with its variant, the T-34/85, which had greater firepower.

end of the day, and to over 600 24 hours later. Far from being destroyed, the Germans had achieved command of the air in the south. Some 2000 sorties were to be flown in support of the German ground attack.

Manstein's method, which committed most of his armor from the outset, proved fairly successful. On 4 July XLVIII Panzer Corps broke through the 67th Guards Rifle Division in a broad and deep penetration of the Russian defenses, to head for the Psel River crossings and Oboyan. To the east the II SS Panzer Corps overran the 52nd Guards Rifle Division and moved toward Pokrovka. But Operational Group Kempf, which was facing the Russian Seventh Guards Army, made very slow progress toward Rzhavets, exposing the III SS Panzer Corps' right flank; in addition the three SS Panzer Corps that had broken separate holes in the Russian lines were unable to link up. Manstein, too, was experiencing many of the same problems that were to beset Model: the dangerous separation of armor and infantry, and the tendency of the Panthers to break down and catch fire.

On the Russian side, Hoth's tactical surprise and the loss of their forward positions put the outcome of the battle in the balance. Held up on 5 July by torrential rains and a re-organized Russian defense, Hoth resumed the offensive on 6 July. Despite a small local counterattack against the 3rd Panzer Division, the XLVIII Panzer Corps had penetrated to Syrtzevo; by the end of the day they had forced the Russians out of most of their positions along the Pena River. The II SS Panzer Corps had managed to advance four miles more on the right, and attempts to join up began. On 8 July German forces began to cross the river. At the forefront of the attack the Ar-

mored Reconnaissance Battalion of the extremely strong SS *Grossdeutschland* Division ran into a counterattack by 40 T-34s from the III Mechanized Corps. Three hours later 35 Russian tanks had been knocked out and the remaining five badly crippled.

In the five days since fighting in the south had begun, the Germans had broken through the first two Russian defensive lines, and the *Grossdeutschland*, on the right flank of XLVIII Panzer Corps, had cracked the third line. The 3rd Panzer Division wheeled south from the Pena and crushed the Russian 71st Guards Rifle Division on 10 July to secure the German left flank. Hoth's next move was to regroup and move toward Prokhorovka, to meet the reserves Stalin had ordered up from the Steppe Front.

To the south a Russian move by a combat group of the II Guards Tank Corps had been made against the flank of Hausser's SS Panzer Corps, near the village of Gotishchevo on the Belgorod-Oboyan highway – the main supply route for the German Corps. Sixty T-34s and several rifle battalions were spotted by German reconnaissance aircraft and a historic battle began: for the first time in military history a large armored formation was opposed and defeated from the air alone. The Germans called up a force of Henschel Hs-129 armored ground-support aircraft – flying anti-tank guns, each armed with a machine gun and a 30mm cannon. Flying in separate *Staffel* – formations of nine planes – the attackers swooped down at the tanks from all sides, cannons blazing. In between, Focke-Wulf ground-support aircraft peppered the infantry columns with high-fragmentation bombs. At the end of the hour-long battle of machines, 50 tanks lay burnt out

or badly damaged on the battle field.

The German XLVII, II and III SS Panzer Corps now faced four Russian armies, including the fresh troops and unworn equipment of the Fifth Guard and Sixth Guard Tank Armies. On the morning of 12 July about 700 German tanks met about 850 Russian tanks – mostly T-34s – in a head-on clash. The two armored avalanches, in clouds of dust and smoke, thundered into the narrow neck of land. The bursts of gunfire from individual tanks merged into a continuous mighty roar. Soviet tanks were able to burst into German formations at full speed, to get in close where the Tigers' big guns and massive armor were no longer an advantage. With their shorter barrels, the guns on the T-34s were very often able to get the critical first shot. There was no longer any protection in armor; all over the battlefield giant wrecks burned like torches, adding clouds of dense black smoke to the dust and exhaust fumes that already filled the air. Soviet and German airmen in fighters, bombers, and ground-support aircraft flew over the battle, unable to see enough to help their comrades. Furious battles raged in the sky as well, as dogfight followed dogfight in seemingly endless succession.

Operational Group Kempf's role in the operation should have been to come up from the south and attack the Russian flank. If they had succeeded, they might well have tipped the scales in Germany's favor. But although the 6th Panzer Division did eventually manage to capture Rzhavets, they could not get to Prokhorovka in time. At the end of the grueling eight-hour battle the Russians found themselves in possession of the black, scorched field. Each side had lost about 300 tanks, but the reduction in strength hurt Hoth much more than it

Street fighting in Belgorod during the Soviet counter attack.

hurt the Russians. He had less than two full-strength divisions left, and the exhausted *Grossdeutschland* had to go back into action to assist the 3rd Panzer Division.

The Red Army had also launched a counterattack in the north against the northern part of the Orel salient. Some 490,000 troops and 1000 tanks and assault guns were almost encircled, but Rokossovsky's attack was weaker than it should have been and Model was able to disengage his forces from a possible encirclement.

On 13 July Hitler decided to abandon Operation Citadel. The two Russian counteroffensives, the enormous number of men and machines that had already been lost, and the hopelessness of the situation in the Orel salient in the north were major factors in his decision. Also, Anglo-American forces had invaded Sicily three days before, and it was already clear that the Italians were not prepared to offer very stiff resistance; only by sending armor from Russia to Italy could the Allies be held in check. Field Marshal Gunther von Kluge, commander of Army Group Center and Model's superior, agreed with the Führer.

Manstein, however, was shocked at the very idea of calling off the operation when victory in the salient was – in his view – still possible. His ardor cooled a bit when he heard of Model's predicament, but he persisted in maintaining that victory in the southern sector was within his grasp. He believed that the Russians had used all of their reserves and would crumple under a continued German onslaught. (Here, he was wrong. The Soviets still had three unused armies in reserve in the south while four armies, including two tank armies, remained intact in the north.)

Russian artillerymen move up during the closing stages of the Kursk double encirclement.

Soviet troops pursue the rapidly retreating Wehrmacht.

Hitler hit on a compromise; Manstein was given permission to continue fighting in the south with his own forces while Model kept as much of the Red Army tied down in the north as he could.

In the Orel salient the stubborn German defenders were inexorably pushed back, through the elaborate field fortifications that had been constructed during their two-year occupation of the area. Most of the Russian gains averaged only four to six miles, but relentless pressure on the ground and continual harassment from the air kept the Germans in retreat. Orel fell on 5 August. Although the German forces got safely behind the Hagen Line – a defensive line across the neck of the salient – in good order, Army Group Center ended up losing 20 percent of its strength.

In the south, Hoth, in co-operation with Operational Group Kempf, continued the offensive, striking a number of successful blows. But on 17 July Hitler ordered the SS Panzer Corps to the Italian front, and two other Panzer divisions to be transferred to Army Group Center in the north. The Russians were attempting an encirclement from southeast of the battlezone, and the German position deteriorated rapidly. A massive Russian infantry attack on 3 August, employing over 650,000 men, 12,000 guns, 2400 tanks, and 1200 aircraft overran the German defenses, and Belgorod fell on 5 August. Reinforcements, combined with masterful handling of his armor, helped Manstein beat off the first Russian advance on Kharkov, which Hitler was determined to hold, on 12 August. But the fall of the city was inevitable; on 23 August Manstein – contrary to orders – abandoned the smouldering ruins that had already changed hands five times, and retreated to the Dnieper Line.

The last great German offensive in Russia was at an end. The reserves, built up over many laborious months, had been decimated. German offensive strength – particularly the cherished Panzer divisions – had been broken for a long time to come.

The Red Army too had changed. Its reorganized armored forces could depend upon an industry that could easily out-produce the Germans. The new SU assault guns, mounted on self-propelled carriages, were introduced at Kursk. The control of troops and reserves during the battle demonstrated that strategies and tactics had improved beyond recognition. Essential speed was supplied in large part by American standard

Top: A Russian gun crew in action at Kursk.
Above: Russian T-34s pass a knocked-out tank as the Kursk battlefield is swept clear.

army trucks, which were shipped by the hundreds of thousands to the Soviet Union after the summer of 1942. Morale, too, had taken a dramatic upswing; the new slogan of the Fatherland War was more effective than the earlier goal of World Revolution.

By 1943 the German Army's outmoded picture of the Red Army as a group of illiterate, technically incompetent peasants hounded by brutal, fanatical commissars was far from accurate. In fact, the literacy rate and the level of technical knowledge of the soldiers had risen dramatically under the stimulus of war and the tutelage of those self-same commissars who, by 1943, had come to be respected by fighting men and their commanders as valuable members of the team.

Kursk has gone down in history as the biggest tank battle in World War II – or any war to date. Together the two sides employed about 13,000 tanks and self-propelled guns; at one point some 3000

were on the move at the same time. These were in addition to the more than 4 million men, 69,000 field guns and mortars, and 12,000 aircraft that took part in the 50 days of heavy fighting for the Kursk and Orel salients. Losses are difficult to ascertain; but probably run to about 900,000 casualties on each side, not to mention the huge losses in tanks, aircraft, and other equipment.

The battle has often been played down – sometimes virtually ignored – by Western historians, while their Russian counterparts as often tend to tout it as proof of the complete superiority of the Soviet military, economic, social, and political systems. The truth, of course, lies somewhere in between.

It is certainly true to say that Kursk was one of the great battles of history, exceptional in its size, scope, and tension. It was also one of the most decisive battles of World War II, ushering in a new stage in the conflict between the Soviet Union and Nazi Germany. Kursk signaled not only the demise of the once all-conquering Panzer arm, but also the beginning of the end of the Third Reich's dreams of glory.

BERLIN RAIDS 1943-44

'We can wreck Berlin from end to end if the USAAF will come in on it. It will cost us 400–500 aircraft. It will cost Germany the war.' Thus did Air Marshal Harris, Commander in Chief of RAF Bomber Command, express his belief in the British mode of night-time, area bombing in November 1943. Conscious of American failures at Schweinfurt, and convinced that he had forged a weapon of such power and proven technique that other forms of bombing were unnecessary, he announced his intention to raze the German capital to the ground, in strict accordance with the Pointblank Directive of the previous June. If Berlin could be destroyed, he argued, the war would be shortened or even won outright as industry and administration in Germany collapsed and civilian panic made the government of the country impossible. In short, his bombers would take out the heart of the enemy, leaving the rest of the body to die. Military operations against the peripheral organs – the armed forces – would be unnecessary and the war would be won.

This rather neat argument was classic strategic bombing theory which both Mitchell and Douhet would have immediately recognized, but in fact it owed its origins to the British reaction to the Gotha and Giant raids of 1917–18. The Smuts Committee, with its twin conclusions that aerial attacks upon the enemy homeland were likely to become 'the principal operations of war' in the future, and that the only viable form of defense was a counteroffensive of equal or greater power, had led to the formation of the RAF in 1918, principally as a strategic bombing force. But its raids upon Germany were few and far between before the end of World War I, and once the peace treaties had been signed, there seemed little reason for its maintenance as an independent force. Politicians and military leaders pressed for the abolition of the RAF as a peacetime luxury, the existence of which might be construed as overtly offensive, and the British air chiefs had to fight very hard indeed to retain their independence. The fact that they succeeded was due almost entirely to the arguments of one man – Hugh, Lord Trenchard. Despite his opposition to the idea of strategic bombing during World War I – as Commander of the Royal Flying Corps on the Western Front he had viewed it as a dangerous dissipation of air strength – he became one if its most ardent advocates when, as Chief of the Air Staff between 1919 and 1929, he saw it as a useful means of securing RAF autonomy. His ideas were never codified into a definite theory – he was too much of an organizer and administrator for that – but three main points characterized his thinking to produce overall conclusions which were surprisingly similar to those of Mitchell and Douhet.

To begin with Trenchard, like Smuts, was an ardent believer in the air offensive, basing his argument upon the premise that air space above a homeland, was impossible to defend absolutely. It would therefore always be possible to hit the enemy homeland, just as it would be possible for him to retaliate: some of the bombers would be destroyed, but sufficient numbers would survive to hit industrial centers and cause civilian panic. For this reason, to devote aircraft and men to air defense seemed a waste of time; far better to concentrate resources into bombing to ensure that attacks upon the enemy were instantly crippling, or, in a peacetime context, to build up a bombing force of such power that potential enemies would be effectively deterred. This led Trenchard on to his second point, for as the majority of Britain's potential enemies were situated a long way off, the only way to make the deterrent force credible was to compose it entirely of long-range bombers. Finally, as there was little room within such plans for tactical co-operation with either the Army or the Navy, a completely independent RAF had to be maintained. Trenchard never actually stated that his bombers would end the war without the need for military or naval campaigns, but the implication was there. It was to be taken up and emphasized during the 1930s as Trenchard's successors at the Air Ministry came under renewed political pressure.

Their new arguments took two distinct forms. Firstly, from the belief that air defense was useless emerged the expression, used by Prime Minister Baldwin in 1932, that 'the bomber will always get through': something which Trenchard had never categorically stated. Secondly, in an effort to show that strategic bombing was not only viable but also essential – a point which, if

Major General William Kepner and Lt General Carl Spaatz at Fighter Command Station.

believed, guaranteed air force independence – the air chiefs began to increase their claims. Referring back more and more to the Gotha and Giant successes of World War I (the unfortunate casualties of the school in Poplar on 13 June 1917 were a favorite example), it gradually became acceptable to argue that strategic bombers, operating by day, would be able to hit enemy cities with impunity, destroying selected targets of vital economic importance and rapidly undermining the morale of the civilian population. This produced unforeseen consequences, within Britain itself – by 1939 people were convinced that the Luftwaffe was preparing a devastating attack upon London, so much so that on the day war was declared an estimated two million people fled the city – but in general terms the theory bore a striking resemblance to that put forward by both Mitchell and Douhet. When World War II began, the RAF was in possession of exactly the same sort of ideas about bombing as the Americans were to be two years later.

But these ideas could not be put into practice immediately. The RAF may have had a theory all worked out, but it lacked the necessary weapons and had no experience upon which to base a course

of action. In addition, the British did not wish to be the initiators of a strategic bombing campaign, partly because they did not wish to be seen as aggressors, a stance which might well alienate opinion in neutral countries, particularly America. To begin with, therefore, the activities of Bomber Command were limited to daytime attacks upon German shipping and night-time excursions over Germany itself, dropping nothing more lethal than leaflets. The results were interesting and crucial to the future direction of the bombing offensive. On the one hand, the shipping strikes, carried out by twin-engined Wellington bombers of No 3 Group, were disastrous: twice, in September and December 1939, the sorties suffered over 50 percent casualties as the slow moving, ill-armed bombers met interceptor fighters and anti-aircraft defenses. The British air chiefs began to realize, as their American counterparts were forced to do after Schweinfurt, that the air bombers could not survive in daylight on their

Right: B-17 Flying Fortress unloads its bombs over Germany in 1944.

Below: Bombers being checked on a flight line in eastern Holland before their Berlin raid.

own. This was reinforced in their minds by the apparent success on the other hand of the night-time leaflet raids, carried out against minimal opposition by Whitley bombers of No 4 Group. As a result, by May 1940 night bombing raids were becoming more frequent, and by the fall of that year daylight attacks had virtually ceased.

In retrospect, knowing the traumas which the Americans were to experience later, in discovering this flaw in prewar theory, the ease of the British switch might well be applauded, but in fact it produced more problems than it solved. The use of darkness to mask the bombers intentions may well have prevented the complete destruction of Bomber Command, but that same darkness blinded the British pilots and navigators to the extent that raids achieved very little. Standards of bomb aiming and navigation declined dramatically, and during this early period it was extremely fortunate if the bombers found their allotted target, let alone destroyed it. This was seen as early as 19 March 1940, when a group of 50 bombers was briefed to attack a German seaplane base on the island of Sylt. Most of the crews were later convinced that they had found the target and placed their bombs accurately, but reconnaissance photographs the next day showed no sign of damage whatsoever.

This unsatisfactory state of affairs continued until August 1941 when Lord Cherwell, the Prime Minister's Scientific Adviser, alarmed at the lack of results from the bombing campaign, instigated an investigation into its accuracy. His chosen investigator, a civil servant by the name of Butt, looked at some 600 air photographs taken by night bombers as they released their loads during June and July 1941. His findings were startling. Taking into account the necessarily selective nature of his evidence – after all, not all the bombers had returned to deliver their photographs – Butt's overall conclusion was that of the bomber crews who thought they had hit an intended target, only about a third had got to within five miles of it. Thus the target area, far from being an imaginary circle 1000yd around an aiming point – the maximum that precision bombing could allow – was in fact a territory up to five miles in radius. Understandably, when these findings were released, the old pressure for an end to strategic air power quickly re-emerged, with some very cogent arguments being put forward for an immediate transfer of heavy bombers to tactical support and naval co-operation. A revision of bombing policy was essential.

The Chief of the Air Staff, Air Marshal Sir Charles Portal, produced such a revision in early 1942, when he suggested the substitution of area for precision bombing so that, in the case of a city or large town, the entire urban complex, and not just the industrial areas within it, would be hit. This had two advantages. On the one hand it would normalize the results already being achieved, for if Butt reported that targets were being missed by five miles, then the simplest answer was to make the targets five miles square. On the other, it might achieve the desired aim of disrupting war production not by hitting the factories (although if this was done, all well and good) but by destroying housing, demoralizing and killing the working population. The new Bombing Directive was issued on 14 February 1942, effectively standing the prewar theory of strategic bombing on its head. Instead of being an offensive of precision bombing by day, practical problems, unforeseen by the interwar theorists, had swiftly turned it into one of area bombing by night.

But the problems were by no means over. If it was intended to hit huge urban complexes night after night – something which was essential if the workers were to be demoralized to the extent that factories no longer operated – a very large bomber fleet was needed, and this was not available in early 1942. Furthermore, even if the aircraft existed, little was likely to be achieved until the bombers could be guaranteed to find the target in the dark and, once over it, deposit their loads in concentrations which would swamp the civil defense services and destroy large areas of urban housing or industrial plants. Bomber Command was clearly in no condition to carry out the new policy in February 1942: a great deal of work needed to be done before the Area Bombing Directive could even begin to approach reality.

Right: RAF personnel inspect their equipment after a mission over central Germany.

Below: The Soviet encirclement of Berlin after the Berlin air raids had softened it up.

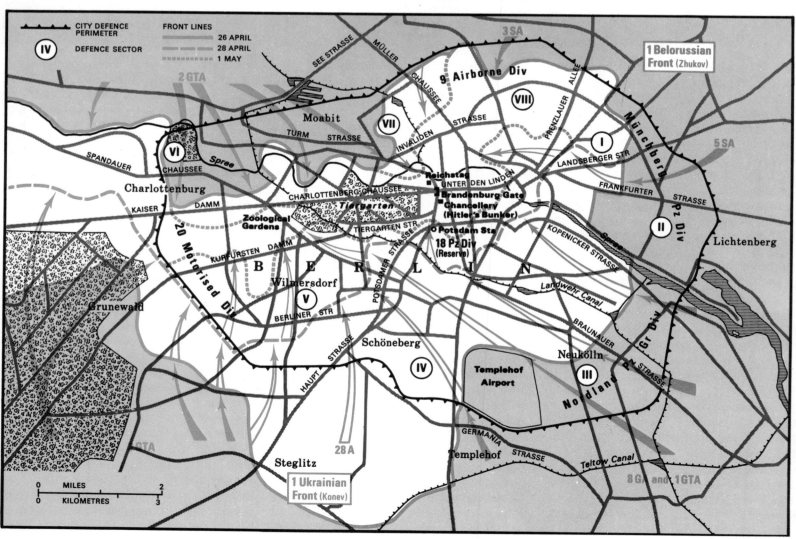

As it happened, this work began very quickly, for on 22 February 1942, only eight days after Portal's new orders, Harris was appointed Commander in Chief. He was wholeheartedly in favor of area bombing, dismissing the American preference for selective attacks as 'panacea-mongering,' but was aware that if something was not done soon to convince the detractors that bombing was not a waste of effort, his command would gradually disintegrate. He desperately needed to mobilize public opinion behind the bombing offensive, thereby undermining political opposition to it, and the method he chose was to mount the biggest possible strike against a German city. The result was the 1000 bomber raid on Cologne, carried out by the entire front line as well as the majority of the reserve of Bomber Command – 1046 aircraft – on the night of 30/31 May 1942. It was a tremendous gamble, for if anything had gone wrong, the British offensive would have come to an abrupt and inglorious end, but in the final analysis it paid off. Casualties were surprisingly small – 44 aircraft, 3.9 percent of the committed force, failed to return – and although the long-term damage to Cologne was slight, public approbation successfully vaporized official opposition to the bombing campaign. In addition, it reinforced Harris' belief that large-scale area attacks were the means to victory, and ensured that he devoted his energies to improving the size and potential of his force.

So far as equipment was concerned, he was fortunate in the fact that improvements in aircraft design had been taking place before his appointment as Commander in Chief. By early 1942 the twin-engined, short-range Whitleys and Wellingtons had been largely replaced by purpose-built, long-range bombers like the Stirling and Halifax. This development trend culminated in the introduction of the Lancaster, the first of which were available for the Thousand Raid on Cologne. Developed from an abortive twin-engined design known as the Manchester, this was undoubtedly the best British bomber of the war, well-suited to night operations. Its four Rolls-Royce engines were powerful, enabling it to fly relatively fast with large bomb loads over long distances, and although it was by no means a self-defending bomber – its .303in machine-guns lacked the range to deter or destroy German night-fighters – it was popular with the aircrews. By late 1943, when the average front line strength of Bomber Command had risen

A B-17 hurtles down toward Berlin after being hit on 6 March 1944.

A Martin B-26 Marauder plunges toward its doom over Berlin.

to nearly 1000, the vast majority were Lancasters. At the same time, the Mosquito 'light bomber' was introduced, contributing a unique combination of speed, versatility and striking power (in 1943 it was possible for a Mosquito to carry 4000lbs of bombs to Berlin – more than a B-17) which Harris was not slow to recognize and use.

But these aircraft, although providing Bomber command with the means to do the job, were unlikely to have a great deal of effect so long as the problems of navigation and bomb aiming remained. Fortunately the air scientists had been working on these, and before the Area Bombing Directive was issued the first steps had been taken to improve these aspects of the campaign. So far as navigation was concerned, a range of radar

inventions, extending the knowledge that had been so crucial during the Battle of Britain, helped the bombers to find the target in the dark. The first of these was *Gee*, introduced in 1942, enabling a bomber's navigator to fix his position by consulting an instrument in the aircraft which received special signals from three separate stations in England. The instrument worked out the time difference between the receipt of these signals, and from that information gave an instant 'fix.' It did suffer from defects of range, however, being unable to operate beyond 400 miles from England because the curvature of the Earth blotted out the signals, so its use was restricted. The same was true of the second new device – *Oboe* – which appeared in December 1942, for this too was dependent upon radar beams, preset to establish a track along which the bomber could fly to the selected target. It was not until January 1943, when a third invention – H₂S was introduced that the navigator could be provided with a radar map of the ground over which he was traveling, and although this also had its deficiencies, being most effective only when a direct contrast between land and water could be made, it did ensure a higher standard of target fixing.

The full effects of these innovations were not felt until the techniques of night bombing had been altered to take them into account. The first step in this direction was the decision, in May 1942, for the bombers to attack in a 'stream' rather than individually or by squadron. Initially the idea was introduced to counter the German defensive system known as the *Kammhuber Line* – a series of radar posts, anti-aircraft sites and night-fighter bases stretching from Denmark to Northern France – which, by dividing the defended area into a series of 'boxes' and stationing night fighters in each, had led to the destruction of many individual bombers. When the Thousand Raid gamble was contemplated, it was realized that one way to defeat this system was to concentrate the bombers and swamp selected boxes. It worked for the Cologne raid, contributing significantly to the low loss rate, but the Germans soon reorganized their resources and, by a judicious use of radar, concentrated their fighters as an effective counter. The British then introduced a series of deception plans, designed to force the enemy to concentrate in the wrong places. These had reached an elaborate stage of sophistication by 1943, ranging from night-intruder raids by small groups of fast-moving, hard-hitting Mosquitoes, to the use of 'Window' – small metal strips, cut to the correct wave-length, which could be dropped in huge quantities away from the main bomber stream, confusing German radar defenses by appearing on the screens as incoming aircraft.

The stream concept, despite its limited success as a defensive measure, did have unforeseen, additional advantages, however, for so long as the lead aircraft found the target, all the others had to do was follow the bomber in front, thereby helping to solve the navigation problem. It therefore became normal for the lead aircraft to be equipped with radar devices and to be flown by more experienced crews, and did not take long to extend their duties to include marking

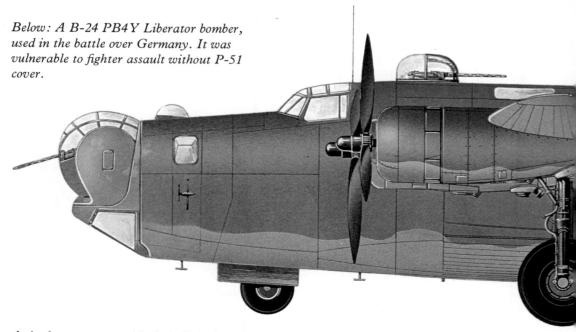

Below: A B-24 PB4Y Liberator bomber, used in the battle over Germany. It was vulnerable to fighter assault without P-51 cover.

A tired crew return with their B-24 from a mission over Germany.

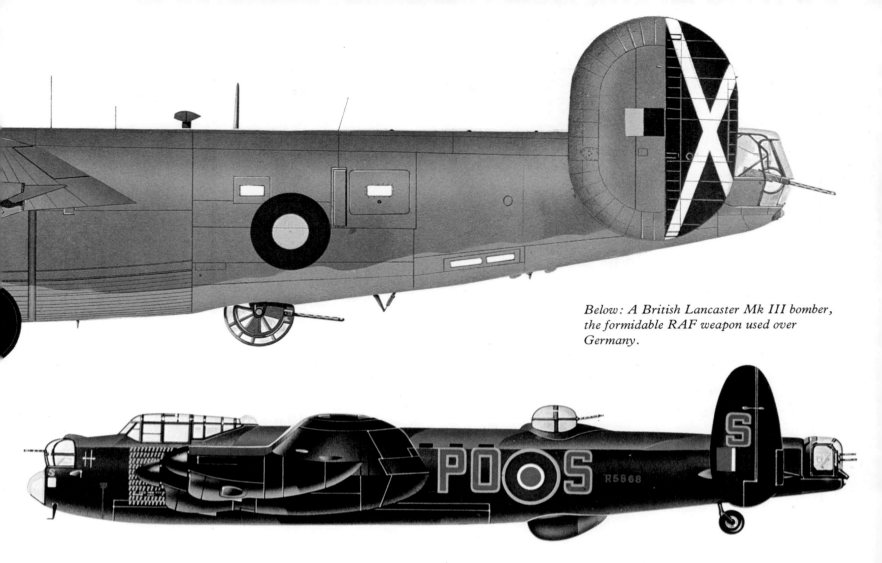

Below: A British Lancaster Mk III bomber, the formidable RAF weapon used over Germany.

the target area, so that the following waves had something definite to aim at. This in turn helped to achieve the concentration of destructive power which was so important to area bombing success. The effectiveness of this 'Pathfinder' technique was in fact shown as early as 28 March 1942 when a selected group of bombers, equipped with *Gee*, was directed to mark the Baltic city of Lübeck with red flares and incendiaries. Even at this early date, results were impressive – nearly half the city was devastated by fire – and, as the other improvements to technique were gradually introduced and perfected, the idea was used on a regular basis. Indeed, by late 1943 the stream leaders were not only marking the target with a variety of colored flares but were also remaining over the area to guide succeeding aircraft in and to correct bombing 'drift' away from the aiming point: tasks which were usually the responsibility of a Master Bomber, flying the ubiquitous Mosquito.

When techniques like this had been fully developed, Bomber Command was potentially at its most effective, but each new tactic or operational procedure had to be tested in action before it could be

adopted on a regular basis. Throughout 1942, as the stream idea and early radar devices were gradually assimilated, the offensive went in fits and starts, with occasional success, but no real aim beyond a general disruption of German industrial life. This was reflected in the rather vague mandate given to Harris at the Casablanca Conference in early 1943, and it was apparent that some of the misgivings about the campaign, drowned in the popular applause for the Thousand Raid, were beginning to reappear, particularly as the numerical build up of Bomber Command, together with the new technology behind it, was absorbing vast amounts of British industrial effort. In such circumstances, Harris decided to concentrate his bombing as far as possible upon particular geographical areas of Germany, with Berlin as the ultimate prize. To begin with, he chose the industrial heartland of the Ruhr, arguing that to devastate cities such as Dortmund, Duisburg or Essen would destroy the enemy's war economy and provide the practice needed to perfect the new techniques, especially those of the Pathfinder Force.

The Battle of the Ruhr, which was to last until July, began on 5 March 1943

when a force of 442 bombers, led by eight Mosquitoes equipped with the recently-introduced *Oboe* radar device, attacked Essen. This had always been a difficult target, being obscured by a permanent industrial haze, but on this occasion good results were obtained. The Mosquitoes, operating entirely on *Oboe* indications, dropped red target-indicator bombs onto the Krupp works and were well supported by Pathfinder Lancasters which deposited 'back-up' green bombs to illuminate the aiming point completely. The main force then went in, depositing their bombs onto the indicators so accurately that reconnaissance photographs later showed severe damage not only to the Krupps complex but also to the center of Essen. Unfortunately such achievements were difficult to sustain. Although four more major raids were mounted against Essen before July, together with a series of attacks upon Duisburg, Düsseldorf, Dortmund and Bochum, the Germans, aware that the Ruhr was now the primary target, organized their defenses accordingly. Other raids on cities outside the Ruhr were put in to prevent such defensive concentration, but to little avail. During the period of the battle, the Ruhr

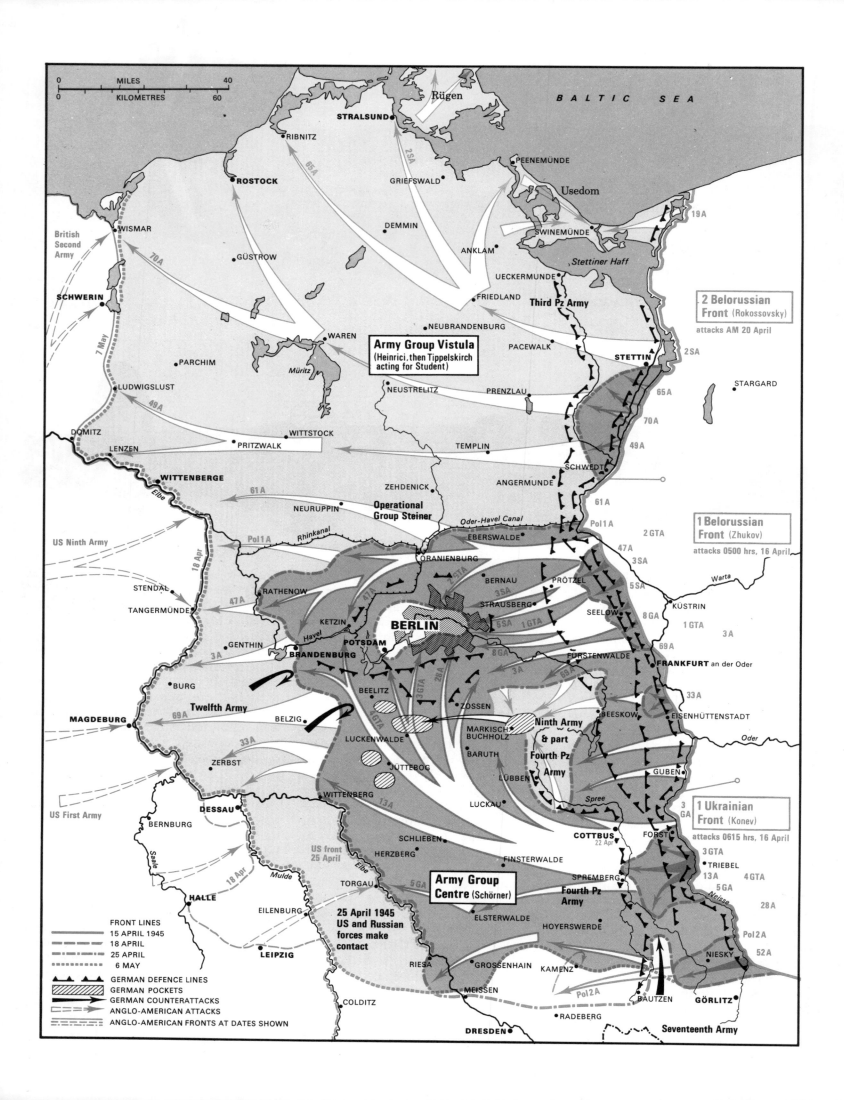

MILES 0 — 40
KILOMETRES 0 — 60

BALTIC SEA

Rügen

STRALSUND

RIBNITZ

PEENEMÜNDE

GRIEFSWALD

Usedom

ROSTOCK

DEMMIN

ANKLAM

SWINEMÜNDE

Stettiner Haff

19A

WISMAR

British Second Army

2SA

UECKERMUNDE

GÜSTROW

FRIEDLAND

Third Pz Army

STETTIN

2 Belorussian Front (Rokossovsky)

attacks AM 20 April

SCHWERIN

NEUBRANDENBURG

PACEWALK

2SA

70A

7 May

Müritz

PARCHIM

WAREN

Army Group Vistula
(Heinrici, then Tippelskirch acting for Student)

STARGARD

65A

LUDWIGSLUST

49A

NEUSTRELITZ

PRENZLAU

70A

DÖMITZ

WITTSTOCK

LENZEN

PRITZWALK

TEMPLIN

49A

SCHWEDT

WITTENBERGE

61 A

ZEHDENICK

ANGERMUNDE

61 A

Elbe

NEURUPPIN

Operational Group Steiner

Oder-Havel Canal

Pol1A

US Ninth Army

Pol1A

Rhinkanal

EBERSWALDE

2 GTA

1 Belorussian Front (Zhukov)

attacks 0500 hrs, 16 April

18 Apr

ORANIENBURG

2STA

47A

3SA

Warta

STENDAL

RATHENOW

BERNAU

PRÖTZEL

5SA

47A

47A

3SA

STRAUSBERG

SEELOW

8 GA

KÜSTRIN

TANGERMÜNDE

KETZIN

BERLIN

5SA

1 GTA

1 GTA

3A

GENTHIN

POTSDAM

8 GA

FÜRSTENWALDE

69 A

FRANKFURT an der Oder

3A

BRANDENBURG

Havel

28 A

3 GTA

3A

69 A

33 A

BURG

Twelfth Army

69 A

BEELITZ

ZOSSEN

BEESKOW

EISENHÜTTENSTADT

MAGDEBURG

BELZIG

4 GTA

MARKISCH BUCHHOLZ

Ninth Army & part Fourth Pz Army

Oder

33 A

LUCKENWALDE

BARUTH

GUBEN

ZERBST

JÜTTEBOG

LÜBBEN

DESSAU

WITTENBERG

13A

LUCKAU

Spree

3 GA

US First Army

1 Ukrainian Front (Konev)

attacks 0615 hrs, 16 April

BERNBURG

Saale

SCHLIEBEN

US front 25 April

HERZBERG

FINSTERWALDE

COTTBUS
22 Apr

FORST

3 GTA

HALLE

18 Apr

Mulde

TORGAU

5 GA

Army Group Centre (Schörner)

SPREMBERG

Fourth Pz Army

TRIEBEL

13A

4GTA

5 GA

EILENBURG

25 April 1945 US and Russian forces make contact

ELSTERWALDE

Neisse

28 A

LEIPZIG

HOYERSWERDE

Pol2A

RIESA

GROSSENHAIN

KAMENZ

NIESKY

52 A

COLDITZ

MEISSEN

Pol2A

BAUTZEN

GÖRLITZ

RADEBERG

DRESDEN

Seventeenth Army

FRONT LINES

———— 15 APRIL 1945
– – – 18 APRIL
— - — 25 APRIL
········· 6 MAY

GERMAN DEFENCE LINES
GERMAN POCKETS
GERMAN COUNTERATTACKS
ANGLO-AMERICAN ATTACKS
ANGLO-AMERICAN FRONTS AT DATES SHOWN

was not destroyed and Bomber Command losses were high. A total of 872 heavy bombers failed to return: a loss rate of 4.7 percent which could not be allowed to continue.

In an effort to escape the German defenses, while at the same time testing the new techniques of bombing at longer range, Harris shifted his area of operations to the city of Hamburg in late July. As with the Ruhr, the initial results were promising – indeed, from the German point of view they were catastrophic, for in four major raids on the nights of 24, 27, 29 July and 2 August 1943 Hamburg was virtually obliterated by fire. Altogether some 50,000 Germans were killed, 40,000 injured and over 1,000,000 forced to flee the city in panic. But once again, the success was only temporary, caused by a combination of factors which were almost impossible to repeat. German defenses were confused by the sudden change of emphasis away from the Ruhr and were plunged into chaos by the first use of 'Window.' In addition, Hamburg, although at extreme range, was ideal for the use of H_2S, and target indication was therefore exceptionally accurate. Finally, the city burned easily, being built to a significant degree of wooden buildings, and once these caught alight they produced the awesome spectacle of a 'fire-storm,' caused by hot air rising and cold air, rushing to take its place, acting as incredibly effective bellows. The center of the city literally melted. Harris immediately saw this as a complete vindication of his belief in area bombing, but could not repeat the success. In this phase of the offensive, which lasted until November, the pattern of the Ruhr was quickly re-established. After their initial surprise, German defenses reorganized themselves with commendable speed, countering the use of 'Window' by a technique known as 'running commentary,' where a ground controller guided concentrations of night fighters onto a bomber stream, and bomber losses started to rise again. Harris tried to get round this by diversionary raids and occasional attacks upon areas away from Hamburg, but his early initiative gradually evaporated. By November a further 695 bombers had been destroyed, representing a loss-rate still in excess of four percent, and German cities, including surprisingly Hamburg, were still operating.

Time was running out, however. The Pointblank offensive was set to end on 1 April 1944, so that heavy bombers could be released to support the Overlord invasion plan, and if Harris was to convince his superiors that area bombing could work, he needed to do so quickly. Heartened by the destruction of Hamburg, which suggested that the potential for victory existed within Bomber Command, he announced his intention to 'wreck Berlin from end to end.' The new campaign began on 18 November 1943 and, as with the Ruhr and Hamburg, initial success was achieved. A total of 444 bombers attacked the German capital, evaded the night fighter defenses, most of which had been committed against a smaller raid on Mannheim-Ludwigshafen, and returned home for the loss of nine of their number. Nor did this appear to be merely 'beginners luck,' for in four further attacks on Berlin in the same month, the loss rate was only just four percent, comparing favorably with the earlier battles. It began to look as if the tables were finally turning to favor the British.

But this did not last. During December the German defenses reorganized themselves yet again, and in most of the major attacks, including four on Berlin, the night fighters were able to infiltrate the bomber stream with comparative ease, destroying on average 4.8 percent of the committed force. Indeed, in one raid against Berlin a total of 40 bombers were destroyed, representing an 8.7 percent loss; something which could not be sustained by Bomber Command for any length of time. But things did not improve in January 1944, when Harris launched nine major raids, six of them against Berlin and the others against Stettin, Brunswick and Magdeburg. In the Berlin raids the loss rate was 6.1 percent, while in the other actions it rose to 7.2 percent. The lowest losses were against Stettin, but this was purely fortuitous as the German night fighter controller misinterpreted his radar reports and committed his aircraft to the defense of Berlin. On other occasions this rarely happened and it was not unknown for the Germans to intercept the bombers over the North Sea, before they had even crossed the coast of Europe. Once again, the British initiative was gradually slipping away.

The situation reached a climax on 19 February 1944, when 120 bombers failed to return from a double attack upon Leipzig and Berlin. The Leipzig raid was by far the more costly, resulting in the destruction of some 78 bombers (9.5 percent of the force), the majority of which fell victim to fighter concentrations on the outward flight: a route

A Martin B-26 Marauder over the Weser.

Another B-26 opens her bomb bay.

B-24s on a daylight raid over Germany.

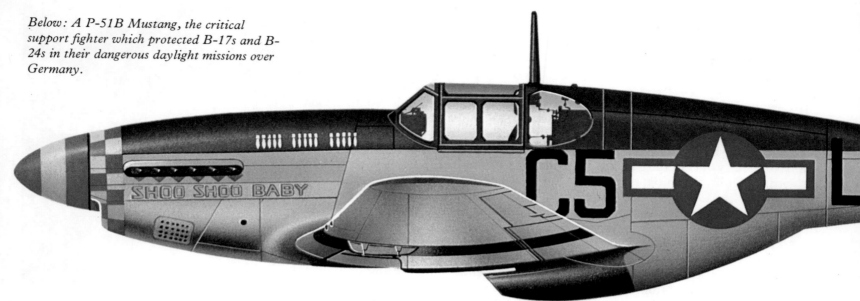

Below: A P-51B Mustang, the critical support fighter which protected B-17s and B-24s in their dangerous daylight missions over Germany.

which took them from their bases in eastern England, across the North Sea, over Holland and into Germany. Bomber Command favored this northern route as the most direct, but it had become dangerously predictable. An alternative southern route, by comparison, appeared to be poorly defended – the Leipzig bombers had returned by this, flying into France and then across the Channel to England, and had suffered few losses – and this placed Harris in a dilemma. If he continued to go straight for Berlin, the Luftwaffe clearly had his route mapped out and losses would be heavy; if he switched to targets in southern Germany, losses would fall, but the main prize of Berlin would have to be forfeit. In the event, he chose the latter option, raiding Berlin only once more, on 24 March, during this phase of the offensive. Casualties diminished – during much of March, as southern targets such as Stuttgart, Frankfurt, Augsburg and even Schweinfurt were hit, the loss rate never exceeded four percent – but the British had been forced to dance to the German tune. Enemy defenses had deflected the intended blow upon Berlin and had forced Harris not only to change his tactics but also his strategic aim.

This was undoubtedly the crucial turning point in the battle, but the fighting was by no means over. On 24 March a final attack, resuming use of the northern route, was made upon Berlin. On this occasion the fighter defenses were caught unawares, with many squadrons concentrated in the south to protect the towns recently attacked, but the losses to Bomber Command were still exceptionally heavy; representing 9.1 percent of the committed force. The majority of these were due to anti-aircraft fire, which took advantage of unpredicted winds

Three P-51 Mustangs in formation over the Reich.

scattering the bomber stream into heavily defended areas. A raid on Essen two nights later seemed to offer some hopes for the resurgence of British success, for only nine bombers were lost out of a force of 705, but the worst was still to come. On 30 March, as a last desperate effort before the Overlord preparations took priority, Harris committed 795 aircraft – the bulk of his force – to an attack upon Nuremberg, hoping to repeat his earlier success against Hamburg. The raid was a disaster. The bombers were sent in on the suspect northern route, crossing the coast at Bruges before proceeding to Charleroi. They then flew due east in a straight line for 250 miles to

Fulda, making the run to the target from northnorthwest. No diversionary raids were mounted and the weather was clear with no protective cloud cover. German fighters were easily fed into the stream by their controllers, destroying the frightening total of 95 heavy bombers, the majority during the straight run from Charleroi to Fulda. Furthermore, later evidence indicated that few of the survivors dropped their bombs on Nuremberg, with the result that damage was slight. It was not an auspicious end to the Battle of Berlin.

The reasons for this overall lack of success were many and varied. Berlin was a difficult target at the best of times,

The P-51 used its six .50 cal machine guns with deadly accuracy against Me-109s.

involving a round trip of some 1150 miles for the bombers, and was, for obvious reasons, one of the best-defended localities in Germany. Because of its distance from England, night-time raids could only be carried out in winter when the hours of darkness were long, and this produced the problem of weather. High winds, clear skies or even dense cloud contributed to difficulties of planning, for predictions in Britain could only be based on information gained through weather reconnaissance aircraft and conditions could change quickly. On more than one occasion the bombers might set out in ideal bombing weather, but find that their advantages of cloud cover disappeared over Europe, leaving them vulnerable to fighter interception. In an aircraft which was loaded down with gasoline and bombs, protected by inadequate .303in machine guns, and incapable of flying much faster than 180 knots fully laden, the prospects of surviving an attack by a Ju 88 or Me 110 were fairly remote. In addition, even if the target was reached, the chances of destroying it were reduced by the lack of radar aids, for Berlin was beyond the effective range of *Oboe* and lacked any distinguishing H_2S features. Unlike the Ruhr and Hamburg, there was also no new technological innovation which could be produced to give the bombers an initial advantage. Harris' dependence upon night-flying aids, new techniques, diversions and sudden shifts of emphasis to gain the initiative had been gradually undermined by a steady rise in the efficiency and effect of German defenses.

It was perhaps fortunate that the heavy bombers were committed to Overlord from 1 April, for after the casualties of late March it was extremely doubtful if concentrated, deep penetration night raids could have continued. Bomber Command had suffered a costly defeat, losing a total of 1047 aircraft between 18 November 1943 and 31 March 1944,

Rounds of ammunition are loaded on a P-51 for the use of their six machine guns.

while failing either to wreck Berlin or to end the war. The Overlord commitment, which lasted until the end of the Normandy breakout in August 1944, was a welcome pause in the bombing offensive, enabling both the British and Americans to reassess their ailing strategies. The result was that in November a Combined Bomber Offensive at last became reality. The Americans, attacking by day with P-51 escort, destroyed what remained of the Luftwaffe and its support services, clearing the skies of fighters altogether and enabling the British to attack at night, free from interception. But by then the war was nearly over and the offensive could be carried out for only

seven months. During that period the damage inflicted upon a rapidly-diminishing Reich was immense, contributing significantly to final victory in May 1945, but the bombers did not win the war on their own. German morale did not crack and her industry, although badly hit, did not collapse entirely. The interwar theorists were wrong. Just as Schweinfurt proved to the Americans that unescorted daylight raids were impractical, so the Battle of Berlin showed the British that night-time area attacks were little more than an unsophisticated bludgeon. So long as the enemy was able to defend his air space, the bombers could be stopped.

D-DAY 1944

6 June 1944

We shall fight on the beaches . . .
WINSTON S CHURCHILL.

When on 4 June 1940 the Prime Minister of Great Britain, speaking for his countrymen, made this famous assertion the beaches he had in mind were very different from the shore where, only four years and two days later, the greatest landing of all time was to take place.

On 6 June 1944 a great Allied Army attacked the Germans' vaunted Atlantic Wall and, in a single day, cracked it. That in a nutshell is the astonishing story of D-Day. And truly it *is* astonishing. Whatever anyone else may have thought, the soldiers of Hitler's Germany considered themselves the foremost warriors of their time. Had not their fathers hurled back Kitchener's Army on the first day of the battle of the Somme and inflicted 56,000 casualties upon them (1 July 1916)? How could the Allies, many of whose military formations had seen no action, cross the channel and break through the fortifications upon which the Todt Organization had labored for four years?

The Allied commanders for the invasion of Europe were appointed at the end of 1943:

Supreme Commander	General Dwight Eisenhower
Deputy Commander	Air Chief Marshal Sir Arthur Tedder
Chief of Staff	Lieutenant General Walter Bedell Smith

For the cross-channel phase, Operation Neptune, all three commanders were British:–

Admiral	Sir Bertram Ramsay, R.N.
General	Sir Bernard Montgomery (21st Army Group)
Air Marshal	Sir Trafford Leigh-Mallory

Initially the 21st Army Group was to comprise two armies,
First American Army: Lieutenant General Omar Bradley,
Second British Army: Lieutenant General Sir Miles Dempsey.

Rommel inspects the Atlantic Wall before the Allied landings.

Eisenhower planned D-Day and gave the go-ahead.

Preparations had begun as long ago as 1941 when Vice-Admiral Lord Louis Mountbatten was made Chief of Combined Operations. Planning had begun under Lieutenant General Frederick Morgan, who, during the Casablanca conference had been appointed CO-SSAC or Chief of Staff to the Supreme Allied Commander (Designate), and who actually received his directive on 26 April 1943.

The layout of the German Armies along the invasion coast of France and the Low Countries was known to the Allied planners in very considerable detail and this was, of course, a factor of immense importance.

The German Commander in Chief of Army Group West was Field Marshal Karl Rudolf Gerd von Rundstedt, a sober, conventional strategist of vast seniority and experience, whose belief in the final victory of Hitler's Germany had been seriously eroded by events in the USSR. He had been dismissed from the command there after the Russians retook Rostov (30 November 1941). He regarded the Atlantic Wall as 'an enormous bluff.' Von Rundstedt had 60 divisions, of which 11 were armored, under his command. With France, Belgium and Holland to hold he felt that his forces, three armies (First, Seventh and Fifteenth) and Armed Forces Netherlands, were seriously over-extended. He was, not unnaturally, worried by the tremendous Allied air superiority, so much so indeed that he proposed a withdrawal to the German frontier. Hitler was not pleased, and sent that ardent tactician, Rommel, his laurels only slightly tarnished by the disastrous end in North Africa, to command in France. Still von Rundstedt was retained as overall commander. Both agreed that the main ports must be held to the last man, but while von Rundstedt thought in terms of a counterattack by 'a centrally located army' before the Allies could consolidate their beach-head, Rommel summed up his creed in this way: 'The war will be won or lost on the beaches. The first 24 hours will be decisive.'

Rommel's experience in the later stages of the North African campaign had shown him that massed armored forces could not operate successfully when the enemy had air superiority. The armored divisions in reserve behind the Fifteenth and Seventh Armies would be canalized on roads and railways, and, given the Allies mastery in the air, would be seriously held up. This was to prove an accurate forecast.

The two field marshals achieved a rather lukewarm compromise, with the infantry well forward, and most of the armor kept well back. Rommel diligently inspected the beach defenses, and galvanized the defenders, who lulled perhaps by the successful defense of Dieppe in 1942, had latterly tended to neglect their wire and their obstacles; their trenches and their minefields.

Study of the northern French coastal defenses reveals that von Rundstedt considered an invasion of the Pas de Calais to be a likely Allied opening gambit. It was in this area that the Atlantic Wall was deepest, here that the best formations were assembled. It was the very pivot of the German defense system.

But if von Rundstedt's gaze was fixed on the Calais coast, Rommel ranged farther afield. In May 1944 Spitfires on air reconnaissance of the Normandy beaches, at nought feet, discovered them to be bristling with fresh obstacles. Hitler himself, who, for all his military faults had a strange tactical flair, had begun to think of Normandy. On 20 March he told a conference: 'At no place along our front is a landing impossible except perhaps where the coast is broken by cliffs. The most suitable, and hence the most threatened, areas are the two west-coast peninsulas, Cherbourg and Brest, which are very tempting and offer the best possibilities for the formation of a bridge-head, which would be systematically enlarged.' General Warlimont, Deputy Chief of Operations (OKW) tells us that: 'Hitler was the first who came to the conclusion that Normandy was the most probable spot. . . . Besides his deductions from troop movements Hitler based his conclusions on the consideration that the Allies from the outset would need a big port which had to be situated in such a way as to be quickly protected by a rather short front line. The conditions would be essentially met by the port of Cherbourg and the Cotentin Peninsula.'

The Führer ordered reinforcement of the Normandy beaches, but by 1944 there was not much to spare for the Western Front. If he could not get the men he wanted Rommel was not short of mines and he produced a plan based on the idea that 'large minefields with isolated strong points dispersed within them are extremely difficult to take.' His plan was to form an impregnable thousand-yard strip along the French shore, with a similar zone to defend the coast defenses from the rear. It called for 20 million mines, and by 20 May over four million were already laid.

Meanwhile von Rundstedt clung to his belief that the Pas de Calais was the likeliest objective. Both Hitler and Rommel were prepared to concede that two attacks were possible: one in Normandy and another near Calais.

Reinforcements were hard to come by. Indeed between April and December 1943, 27 trained German divisions, five of them armored, were transferred from the West and replaced by heterogeneous forces, still in course of formation and training, from the *Ersatzheer* (replacement army). Hitler promised to strengthen the Luftwaffe with 1000 ME 262s, but they did not arrive. Rommel asked for the High Command Reserves

General Eisenhower briefs the parachutists who were to be the first to land in Normandy in the early morning hours of 6 June 1944.

Part of the D-Day armada of hundreds of ships which disembarked for the Norman coast before the D-Day landings.

Corps HQ I SS Panzer Corps, Panzer Lehr Division and 12th SS Panzer, to be brought up within an hour's drive of the coast, so as to strengthen the defenses of Normandy and Brittany. This, on the advice of von Rundstedt, OKW declined to do.

Rommel asked for 24 anti-aircraft bat-teries to be deployed between the Rivers Orne and Vire, and a brigade of *Nebel-werfer* ('Moaning Minnie' mortars) to be placed near Carentan. Neither mate-rialized. Meanwhile the Todt Organi-zation was gradually being withdrawn into Germany to deal with the ever-increasing bomb damage.

The German Third Air Fleet, com-manded by Field Marshal Hugo Sperrle, was stationed in France. It consisted of squadrons of bombers and torpedo bom-bers, day and night fighters, and recon-naissance planes. Of some 890 planes, about 150 were reconnaissance and transport aircraft.

Certainly the measures Rommel pro-posed would have made the Allies task vastly more difficult than it proved. But even without them it was difficult enough. SHAEF (Supreme Head-quarters, Allied Expeditionary Force) had at its command 37 divisions. It was calculated that to transport this force to France must take about seven weeks. And as we have seen, von Rundstedt had at his command no less than 60 divisions. How to redress the balance: that was the question. The factors involved were many and varied.

In the first place the Allies had com-mand of the Sea. This is not to say that there were no longer any German ships or craft, or submarines, capable of in-flicting damage on the invading force: simply that the Germans could not con-test the passage in a fleet action.

The German Naval Force Command Group West was commanded by Ad-miral Krancke, who had his HQ at Paris.

German Ration Strength, France 1 March 1944

Army	806,927
SS and Police	85,230
Volunteers (Foreigners)	61,439
Allies	13,631
Air Force	337,140[1]
Navy	96,084
TOTAL ARMED FORCES	1,400,451
Armed Forces Auxiliaries	145,611

[1] Includes flak formations (100,000 +) and 'paratroops' (30,000 +)

	4 April	28 May
Static coast divisions	26	25
Infantry field-force & parachute divisions	14	16
Armored and mechanized divisions	5	10
Reserve divisions	10	7
	55	58

These U-Boats (Group Landwirt) were for anti-invasion duty, but 14 were not immediately ready for sea. The other 35 sailed before midnight on 6 June.

In the air, too, the Allies were supreme. This meant not only that they could pound the defenses at will, but also that, by bombing other sections of coast, they could help the Deception Plan. They could, in addition, isolate the battlefield by destroying the bridges of the Rivers Seine and Loire, and they could further delay German reinforcement of the beach-head by destroying the French railway system.

In this latter task the Free French Forces of the Interior would also play its part. This Army, representing many shades of French political opinion, is thought to have numbered 100,000 men eager to liberate their country from its odious bondage, capable by ambush and sabotage of inflicting serious delay on German troop movements.

In addition to the Armies that actually existed the Allies produced a phantom one, 'The First Army Group,' which played a rôle which many a real formation might have envied. It was concentrated in Southeast England, and by its wireless traffic persuaded the Germans that it would be imprudent to withdraw troops of Fifteenth Army from the coast between Antwerp and Le Havre.

The Commander in Chief, Northern Command, Lieutenant General Thorne, assembled in Scotland a fictitious 'Fourth Army' of three corps, which, by indiscretions in its wireless traffic, revealed its preparations for landing in Norway.

Turning to the Allied troops we find fresh formations, fully up to their established strength and thoroughly equipped. Some units and formations had seen a good deal of fighting in the Middle East, but the majority were going into action for the first time. But these had been training for years. The official historian, Ellis, states the case simply and fairly:

'Never before had Britain sent into battle large forces which were so well equipped, well balanced and elaborately trained. The war had been in progress for over four years and experience from many seas and many battlefields had been brought to bear on the task that lay ahead.'

The higher commanders were, on the whole, more than adequate. The well-advertised brilliance of Montgomery should not blind us to the solid quality of

The Atlantic Wall was a misnomer, which Rommel reported to Hitler too late.

Flag Officer Channel Coast was Admiral Rieve (HQ Rouen); and Flag Officer Atlantic Coast was Admiral Schirlitz (HQ Angers). Their forces were based at 20 ports from Ijmuiden to St Malo and from Brest to Bayonne:–

	Channel Coast	Atlantic Coast
Destroyers	–	5
Torpedo-boats	5	1
Motor torpedo-boats	34	–
Minesweepers	163	146
Patrol vessels	57	59
Artillery barges	42	–
U-Boats	–	49

Bradley, or the practiced fighting skill of Dempsey.

Where and When to Land? This is the question that the amphibious warfare staff ask themselves when they begin to devise the plan for a combined operation. In World War II the factors that used to be taken into account included the range of fighter cover. It was, of course, unhealthy in the extreme to try to form a beach-head beyond the distance at which your own fighters could take on such enemy aircraft as might appear. At Dieppe (1942) which was within the then range of fighter cover, the Germans had only lost 48 planes to the 106 lost by the British.

The best means of delaying the build up of German reinforcements was to take on their tanks with rocket-firing fighter-bombers, Typhoons and Thunderbolts, and so once again the range of aircraft was a vital planning factor.

Another factor was the availability of landing craft. This was bound to limit the number of divisions that could be landed on D Day.

The COSSAC staff quickly narrowed the choice of areas where a landing could be made to the coast of the Pas de Calais, and the Caen sector of Normandy. The former had obvious disadvantages:–

1 Formidable defenses,
2 High cliffs,
3 Only small parts in the Dover area for the assembly of invasion shipping,
4 Restricted exits.

If this were chosen the lodgment area would have to be extended to include either the Belgian ports or those of the Seine. Altogether this did not seem to offer a very promising operation of war.

The Normandy coast had none of these disadvantages. Its beaches were partially protected from the prevailing westerlies by the Cherbourg Peninsula, and it was less strongly fortified. The time during which a fighter could operate over the assault area was seriously curtailed, and the direct sea crossing was increased to 100 miles. However, on the whole, the naval and air staffs were prepared to accept these drawbacks.

Meanwhile, of course, planning for Overlord was influenced to a great extent by the demands of other theaters for their share of Allied resources; landing craft, divisions and equipment of every kind.

'Put shortly, the British Chiefs of Staff thought (in the fall of 1943) that the success of Overlord, *on the limited scale on which it was being planned*, would be jeopardized unless diversionary oper-

General Patton confers with Eisenhower. Patton had hoped to participate in D-Day.

Minesweepers exploding mines off Utah Beach on the morning of D-Day.

ations in Italy or elsewhere occupied substantial German forces in south Europe and so prevented their transfer to the Western Front. The American Joint Chiefs of Staff feared, on the other hand, that such diversionary operations might absorb too large a share of Allied resources, and, if so, Overlord might fail through starvation.'

The Overlord planners had a good idea what they were up against in France. They had to break the Atlantic Wall, and defeat the two field marshals, von Rundstedt and Rommel, with what help the French Resistance Movement might be able to render them. The enemy still had vast armies, but they were deployed on three fronts with no central reserve.

Distribution of German Divisions at the beginning of 1944

Russian Front	179
France and the Low Countries	53
Balkan States	26
Italy	22
Scandinavia	16
Finland	8
Germany	0
	304

Germany's war production was, incredible though it may seem, despite the Allied bomber offensive, still increasing. She had new weapons, new submarines; jet-propelled aircraft; better tanks than the Allies, and self-propelled long-range missiles. These last, Hitler hoped, would, at the eleventh hour, win him the war. The planners eventually decided to make the assault with five seaborne and three airborne divisions.

The Logistic background to Operation Neptune was described neatly, a month before D-Day by a supply officer who told *Picture Post*:

'We've got a fairly big job on. Something comparable to the city of Birmingham hasn't merely got to be shifted: it's got to be kept moving when it's on the other side.... We must take everything with us – and take it in the teeth of the fiercest opposition. We are, in fact, undertaking the greatest amphibious operations in history, so vast in scale and so complex in detail that the supreme consideration must be the orderly carrying out of a Plan.' (Tute)

There is not space here to describe the myriad devices which ensured the success of the operation. Two, however, demand mention: Mulberry and Pluto.

Forward 14-inch guns of the USS Nevada *blast German positions ashore at Utah Beach.*

An LCM evacuates casualties from the landing area and returns them to a hospital ship.

The Mulberry was a man-made harbor, providing an outer roadstead where ocean-going vessels could anchor, and an inner roadstead, where concrete caissons formed a breakwater, linked with the shore by steel piers. Before the end of June a million men were to pour over the British Mulberry off Arromanches and the open beaches. PLUTO was a novel device for the supply of gasoline through pipe lines under the ocean.

As D-Day approached the great men on either side had problems of every sort, some of which are worth a mention. King George VI had to use his personal authority to prevent his pugnacious Prime Minister from sailing with the invasion fleet in *HMS Belfast*!

Churchill and Eisenhower had to persuade General de Gaulle to broadcast to the French people at a time when President Roosevelt would not allow him to exercise sovereignty in the liberated territories. The General was mortified because Eisenhower omitted from his own address all mention of the French Committee of National Liberation. But the wily Frenchman got round this when the time came by saying that 'The orders given by the French government [his

Barrage balloons protect the D-Day armada against low-flying strafing aircraft of the Luftwaffe.

own committee] and by the leaders which it recognized must be followed precisely.'

Eisenhower's problems were many and varied. Some of the rehearsals were chaotic, especially one at Slapton Sands in May, when German E-Boats got in among the craft and sank two LSTs with 700 men of the US 4th Division. Ten of the missing officers were authorized to have *Bigot Top Secret* papers, and not until all their bodies had been recovered could SHAEF security rest assured that their secrets were still safe. Then again there was a grave disagreement between Eisenhower and Bradley, and Leigh-Mallory who thought that to fly the two American airborne divisions across the Cotentin Peninsula was too hazardous. Eisenhower supported Bradley who 'would risk them to insure against failure of the invasion.'

Finally Eisenhower had to make the big decision, after one postponement, that 6 June must be D-Day. The meteorological report was favorable for that

morning; Montgomery and Ramsay were both for going ahead, and so Ike, with admirable *sang froid*, simply said 'OK Let's go,' and the Admiral, secure in the knowledge that there was wireless silence, went to bed. Before he retired for the night, Winston S Churchill said to his wife: 'Do you realize that by the time you wake up in the morning 20,000 men may have been killed?'

Across the Channel the opposition had for the most part satisfied itself that the long-awaited invasion was not due just yet. The bombers began to drone towards France, and the ten great German coast defense batteries. Lancaster, Halifax and Mosquito aircraft, 1056 of them, went over and dropped 500 tons of bombs on each of them. Eleven aircraft did not return.

On the morning of 5 June von Rundstedt at his headquarters in the Château de Saint-Germain received the Luftwaffe's daily report: 'The enemy command is still trying by all means to prevent us from observing his activities.

The continued air attack on Dunkirk and the coast as far as Dieppe leads us to suppose that the enemy will attack in that sector.' The report concluded with the words: 'However, it is unlikely that the invasion is imminent.' With this the Field Marshal concurred, and after signing his own sitrep for OKW set off for *Le Coq Hardi* and a luncheon which was not spoiled by the fact that 5000 or so Allied ships and craft were moving out into the Channel, simply because he was not aware of it.

The Airborne Assault

The 6th Airborne Division: Major General Richard Gale

This division, with the 1st Special Service Brigade under command, had the task of securing the Eastern flank of the lodgment area. It was to seize and hold the Orne bridges at Benouville and Ranville between Caen and the sea; to silence the Merville Battery which threatened

US troops disembark at Utah Beach as the Allied invasion gathers momentum.

the left flank of the seaborne landings, and to deny the enemy the country between the Rivers Orne and Dives, part of which was flooded, part of which was the jungle known as the Bois de Bavent and part of which was the low ridge running between Sallenelles and Ranville, parallel to the Orne, which overlooked the whole of 3rd British Division's area.

And so in the middle of the night 38 and 46 Groups of the Royal Air Force flew them from their airfields south of Oxford to dropping zones near Ranville (N), Trouville (K) and Varaville (V), where they were to begin landing about 20 minutes after midnight.

The task of the 5th Parachute Brigade was to capture and hold the Benouville and Ranville bridges over the Orne and the Caen Canal, and to protect the dropping zone N, where the 6th Airlanding Brigade was to come in later. Until Caen should fall these bridges carried the only road to the high ground east of the Orne. The Allies could neither afford to leave

them in German hands nor to see them destroyed.

These bridges were the target of a *coup de main* party. Five platoons of the 2nd Oxfordshire and Buckinghamshire Light Infantry, under Major Howard, and 30 officers and men of the 249th Field Company, Royal Engineers, crash landed in six Horsa gliders a few minutes after midnight, rushed the bridges, and took them both within 15 minutes. They proved to be free of explosives.

Some of 5th Brigade were dropped in the right places, and managed to reinforce the *coup de main* party after about two hours. There was confused fighting around the neighboring village of Benouville and Le Port.

Fifteen of the 32 aircraft carrying the 12th Battalion dropped their loads accurately; seven were within a mile of their target; ten were wildly adrift. The task was to hold the eastern approaches of the Ranville Bridge and by 0400 hours they had occupied the Bas de Ranville and taken prisoners belonging to the

736th Grenadier Regiment (716th Infantry Division). The 13th Battalion's task was to protect, clear and improve N, and to complete the bridgehead by taking Ranville itself. This was achieved by 0400 hours and prisoners were taken from 125 Panzer Grenadier Regiment of the 21st Panzer Division, whose station was southeast of Caen. When Major General Gale glided in with the third flight, about 0330 hours, it was to find the Orne bridges securely held by 5th Parachute Brigade.

Meanwhile the main body of the 3rd Parachute Brigade, though many of its troops were landed in the wrong places, carried out a number of their tasks successfully. The Troarn, Bures and Varaville bridges over the River Dives were blown up, the Canadians took an HQ and a signal station. They also had a fierce but inconclusive fight around the Château de Varaville.

Lieutenant Colonel Terence Otway and the 9th Parachute Brigade had one of the worst jobs of all. It was to take the

Merville Battery, and, moreover, to take it before daylight when its four guns could dominate Sword Beach. When at 0255 hours Otway marched on the battery he had with him only 150 men with their personal weapons. The big guns were in steel-doored concrete emplacements six feet thick, two of which were covered by 12 feet of earth.

The reconnaissance party cut the outer wire, marked, with their feet, paths through the minefield and neutralized a number of trip-wire booby-traps. Otway broke his men up into seven parties: two to breach the main wire; one for each gun and one to stage a diversion at the main entrance. In the brief and bloody fight that followed the parachutists overwhelmed the garrison. The four guns, which proved to be 75mm, were put out of action. At 0445 hours a pigeon taken from the signal officer's pocket, took off to carry the glad tidings to England, while Otway led his 80 survivors to the high ground near Le Plein, and formed a defensive position around the Château of Monsieur Leboucher at Amfreville.

Before day dawned the 3rd Parachute Brigade was fairly firmly ensconced on the ridge from Sallenelles to Troarn, which runs down the west side of the Bois de Bavent. They had already performed deeds of desperate valor, as in the

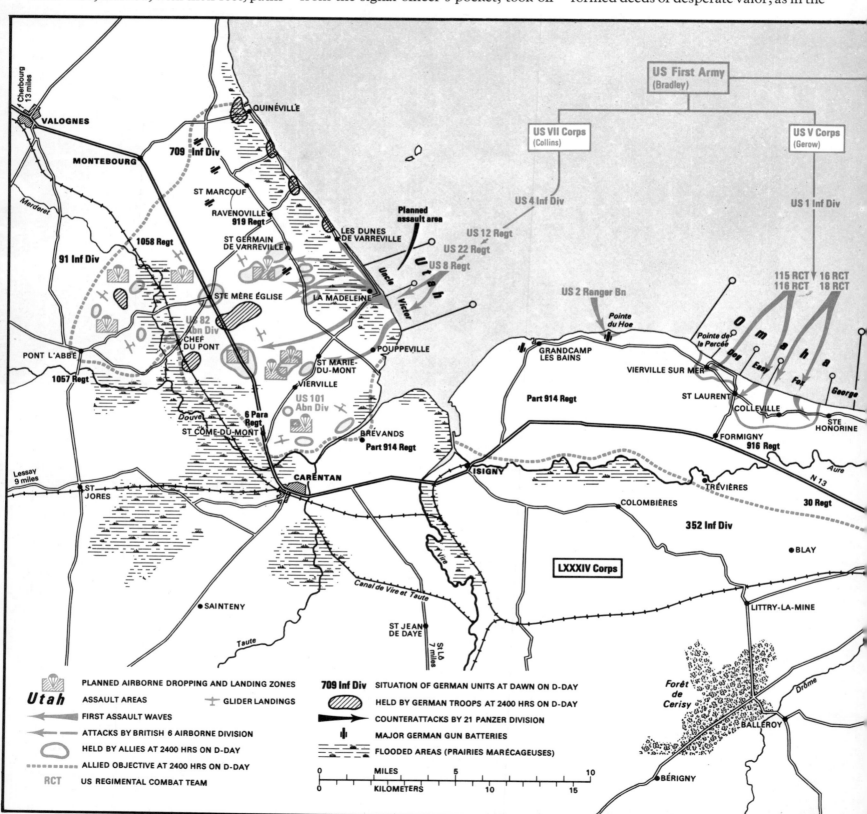

PLANNED AIRBORNE DROPPING AND LANDING ZONES

Utah ASSAULT AREAS — GLIDER LANDINGS

FIRST ASSAULT WAVES

ATTACKS BY BRITISH 6 AIRBORNE DIVISION

HELD BY ALLIES AT 2400 HRS ON D-DAY

ALLIED OBJECTIVE AT 2400 HRS ON D-DAY

RCT US REGIMENTAL COMBAT TEAM

709 Inf Div SITUATION OF GERMAN UNITS AT DAWN ON D-DAY

HELD BY GERMAN TROOPS AT 2400 HRS ON D-DAY

COUNTERATTACKS BY 21 PANZER DIVISION

MAJOR GERMAN GUN BATTERIES

FLOODED AREAS (PRAIRIES MARÉCAGEUSES)

MILES   0   5   10
KILOMETERS   5   10   15

case of Major Roseveare, who rode through Troarn in a jeep, and under fire from every doorway, blew up the bridge.

By dawn, thanks to the operations of the 6th Airborne Division, there was chaos in the ranks of the 711th Division between the Orne and the Dives, and an important tract of territory east of the Orne was firmly in British hands. Here at about midday reinforcements began to arrive in the shape of the 1st Special

Service Brigade under Brigadier Lord Lovat, elements of which soon fought their way on to the vital Le Plein feature and held it against all comers.

The 82nd and 101st US Airborne Divisions

The rôle of the two American airborne divisions was to aid the assault by the United States First Army and to help it to capture the Cotentin Peninsula. The

82nd, dropping astride the River Merderet was to seize Ste Mere Eglise and by holding bridgeheads across the river to facilitate the advance of forces landed on Utah beach. The 101st Airborne Division was to take Carentan and to secure the western exits of the flooded area

D-Day invasion area in Normandy. Omaha and Utah for Americans; Gold, Juno and Sword for the British.

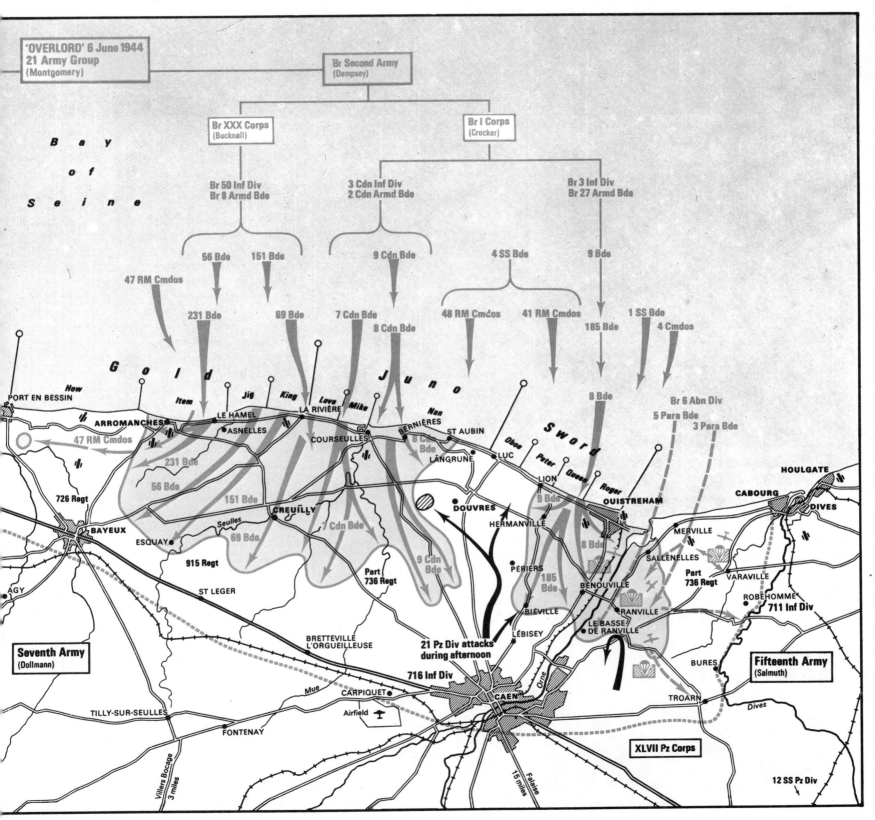

USS Tide *sinking after having been struck by a mine on 7 June.*

The assault wave hits Omaha Beach. The blunders made there almost cost the Allies the battle.

Nervous US troops in an LCVP prepare themselves to hit Omaha Beach on D-Day.

behind Utah. It was to hold the line of the River Douve, north of Carentan, and to join up with the troops on Omaha beach.

The dog-leg approach of the aircraft of the American IX Troop Carrier Command was not easy to execute, though it was protected by Mosquitos of the Air Defense of Great Britain, and masked from German radar by Stirling bombers dropping 'window' northeast of St Malo. Window was metalized strips of paper dropped to confuse enemy radar. Heavy flak and small arms fire, as well as thick cloud, broke up the formations and the drops were very scattered. Everywhere small groups of men, leaping into the dark, struggled manfully to carry out their part in a complicated plan. The 82nd Division lost 60 percent of its equipment.

Unpleasant though it was for so many of the Americans to discover that they had been landed in the wrong places, their dispersion totally confused the Germans. Toward midnight the staff officers of LXXXIV Corps at St Lo toasted their austere general, whose birthday it was, with a glass of Chablis. Erich Marcks, who had left a leg on the Eastern Front, looked surprised, stood up, the joint of his artificial limb creaking, and raised his hand in a friendly but nevertheless cool gesture. It was not exactly an orgy, and just as well for at 0111 hours the field telephone rang and a message came through from the 716th Division: 'Enemy parachute troops dropped east of the Orne estuary. Main area Breville-Ranville and the north edge of the Bavent Forest. Counter measures are in progress.' 'Perhaps,' an officer suggested, 'they are only supply troops for the French Resistance.' By this time, all over Normandy, keen Frenchmen were cutting telephone wires. General Falley (91 Airlanding Division), endeavoring to discover what was going on, was bushwhacked by an American patrol. This was reported to General Matthew Ridgway (82nd Airborne Division), who with a mere eleven officers and men had set up his HQ in an orchard. 'Well, in our present situation,' he said, 'killing Division Commanders does not strike me as being particularly hilarious.'

The Seaborne Landing

Utah Beach

NAVSITREP 1
TO NAVAL COMMANDER WESTERN TASK FORCE
FORCE U ARRIVED TRANSPORT AREA WITHOUT INCIDENT COMPLETE SURPRISE ACHIEVED NO ENEMY ATTACK FIRST WAVE DESPATCHED TO BEACH AS SCHEDULED.

And in went the first of the D-Day seaborne assaults: H-hour: 0630 hours. A 90 minute run in against a strong offshore breeze, and a choppy gray sea, under a bombardment make the shores of France leap into the air. A terrific explosion and LCT 707 turned turtle. She had hit a mine. And then the German shore batteries opened up. The American admirals, by way of showing that they had minds of their own, had rejected Admiral Ramsay's advice to launch the landing craft within eight miles of the shore. Wary of risking their ships within range of the German batteries they launched the troops 11.5 miles out to sea. The men had their sea sick pills and their vomit bags.

At about 0555 hours, 7500 yards off shore and 12 minutes off schedule, PC 1261 hit a mine. Then an LCT hit another and sank almost immediately. The leading wave was now several thousand yards south of the scheduled landing place. The surviving LCTs closed the shore, and 28 DD Shermans swam clumsily in. The 8th Infantry Regiment went ashore in fine style, and, although they were not in the right place, this did not matter. But it could have: they might have attempted to push up the beach, in the teeth of enfilading fire, to get to the place where they should have landed. That this did not come to pass is generally attributed to former President

Two LCIs (Landing Craft, Infantry) land troops in the first assault on Omaha.

'Teddy' Roosevelt's 57 year old son, Brigadier General Theodore Roosevelt Jnr, who had talked his Divisional Commander into letting him go ashore 'to steady the boys.' And he did just that; walking up and down the beach, walking-stick in hand. It was he that made the decision to push straight on inland from where they were. It was he that got the NOIC Utah, Commodore Arnold, to shift the follow-up waves from Red sector to Green. It was not in the book but it was three hours before the German batteries shifted their fire to Green beach. By that time the United States troops had secured a broad stretch of beach and were pushing inland, along the southern (Pouppeville) causeway, to relieve 101st Airborne in Ste Mère Eglise, the first French town to be liberated by the US Army.

There were other heroes on Utah beach besides the legendary and rheumatic Roosevelt. Still, he carved his niche in history that morning, and he took a big risk, for had his men failed to clear the causeway by nightfall, he would have organized the biggest traffic jam of all time on Utah beach. By that evening some 23,250 men with 3500 vehicles were ashore.

Omaha Beach

And at Omaha 34,250 got ashore on D-Day. They did not get very far inland, but the wonder is that they got ashore at all, for the German position was a strong one, defended by better troops than those at Utah, and the American planning was less than brilliant.

Over-impressed by the potential of German artillery fire the invaders were lowered 12 miles out, with the consequence that those of the landing craft that were not swamped, were swept away eastward, landing the seasick survivors of the eight assault battalions late and in the wrong place. Of one battalion of 29 amphibious tanks only two struggled ashore.

The Americans had decided on 40 minutes pre-arranged fire support before H-Hour (0630 hours) – the British bombarded their beaches for two hours before H-hour. Admiral Kirk (Western Task Force) reported afterward that 'the period of bombardment was extremely heavy but was of too short duration to silence or neutralize all the defenses, particularly in the Omaha area.' Much of the supporting fire fell too far inland, but the Germans, who, besides big guns in eight concrete bunkers, had 35 anti-tank guns in pillboxes, and 85 machine guns, were on target. Ten craft of the first flight were sunk, one hit by mortar fire simply disintegrated. In this chaos the American soldiers made their way across 600 yards of flat sand, shingle, wire, mines and assorted obstacles. Wounded men fell into pools and runnels and drowned, dragged down by their heavy loads.

The second wave came ashore 25 minutes later to find the first pinned at the water's edge, seeking cover from the enfilading fire behind the beach obstacles. There was at least one company which, 10 minutes after the ramps went down, had not a single officer or sergeant left unhit.

The Army-Navy Special Engineer Task Force, endeavoring to take on by hand the beach obstacles for which Major General Hobart had designed his 'funnies,' lost 41 percent of their

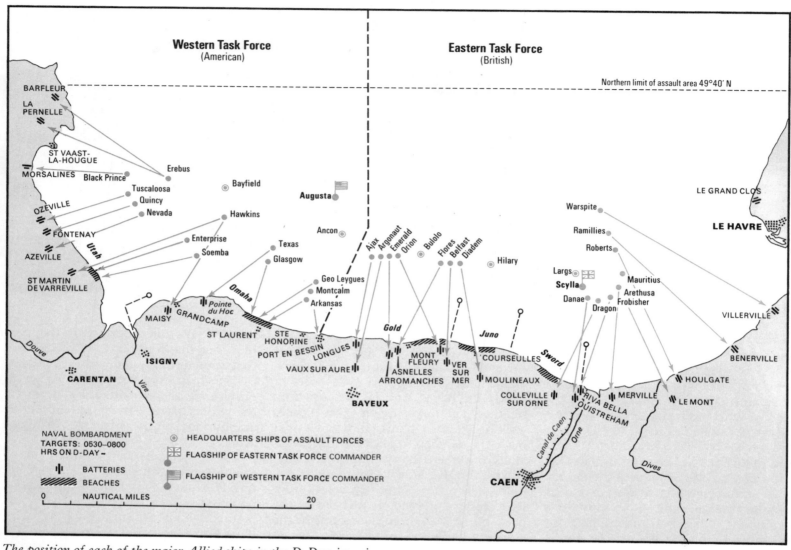

Northern limit of assault area 49°40' N

BARFLEUR
LA PERNELLE
ST VAAST-LA-HOUGUE
MORSALINES
Erebus
Black Prince
Tuscaloosa
Quincy
Nevada
OZEVILLE
Hawkins
Bayfield
Augusta
LE GRAND CLOS
Warspite
LE HAVRE
Ramillies
Roberts
Ancon
Ajax Argonaut
Emerald
Orion Bulolo
Flores Belfast
Diadem
Hilary
Largs
Scylla
Mauritius
Danae Arethusa
Dragon Frobisher
VILLERVILLE
FONTENAY
AZEVILLE
Utah
Enterprise
Soemba
Texas
Glasgow
ST MARTIN DE VARREVILLE
Geo Leygues
Montcalm
Arkansas
Omaha
Gold
Juno
Sword
BENERVILLE
MAISY GRANDCAMP
Pointe du Hoc
ST LAURENT
STE HONORINE
PORT EN BESSIN LONGUES
VAUX SUR AURE
ASNELLES
ARROMANCHES
MONT FLEURY
VER SUR MER
COURSEULLES
MOULINEAUX
COLLEVILLE SUR ORNE
RIVA BELLA
OUISTREHAM
MERVILLE
HOULGATE
LE MONT
ISIGNY
Douve
Vire
CARENTAN
BAYEUX
Canal de Caen
Orne
Dives
CAEN

NAVAL BOMBARDMENT
TARGETS: 0530–0800
HRS ON D-DAY –

⊚ HEADQUARTERS SHIPS OF ASSAULT FORCES

FLAGSHIP OF EASTERN TASK FORCE COMMANDER

FLAGSHIP OF WESTERN TASK FORCE COMMANDER

BATTERIES

BEACHES

0   NAUTICAL MILES   20

The position of each of the major Allied ships in the D-Day invasion.

LCI-412 *hits Omaha Beach. Troops were
pinned down on the shoreline and casualties
were heavy.*

strength mostly in the first half hour. Too often the obstacles they prepared for demolition could not be blown because men were taking cover behind them. 'They're murdering us here,' said Colonel Canham. 'Let's move inland and get murdered,' and there were brave men to follow him.

Still, waves of men and vehicles poured in to add to the confusion. But at 1000 hours – not before time – General Huebner, the assault commander, took a grip on the proceedings. He stopped any more vehicles going in, called for naval gunfire support, and sent in more fighting troops. Destroyers closed to within 1000 yards of the shore. The 1st US Division – the Big Red one – war-hardened in North Africa, in Sicily and at Salerno, shook themselves and clawed their way forward, through the mine-fields, toward Colleville-sur-Mer. For the 29th Division it was a rough baptism of fire, but, though hard hit, small groups infiltrated as far as Vierville and St Laurent.

Still the German Commandant, well-pleased with his morning's work, and dreaming, no doubt, of his *Ritterkreuz*, reported at 1330 hours that the invasion had been stopped on the beaches. Five minutes later the Chief of Staff of 352nd Division was passing to von Rundstedt the good news that they had thrown the invaders back into the sea.

Oddly enough it was almost at the same moment that V Corps (General Gerow) sent a message to USS *Augusta*, Bradley's HQ ship: 'Troops formerly pinned down on beaches Easy Red, Easy Green, Fox Red advancing up heights behind beaches.'

At one time – 0913 hours to be precise – General Omar Bradley had liked the look of things on Omaha so little that he had signaled 'If required can US Forces be accepted through *Jig* and *King*.' But this *most immediate* signal did not reach SHAEF until late in the afternoon. The chaos that such a change of plan would have meant is practically unthinkable – though one can hardly imagine Montgomery agreeing to it in any case. The point is, however, that there was a time – round 0900–1000 hours, when a swift counterattack might just have thrown the Americans off Omaha and into the sea. However, General Marcks found other tasks for his reserves.

By nightfall, despite the loss of approximately 3000 men, 50 tanks, 26 guns, 50 landing craft and ten larger vessels, the Americans at Omaha held a bridgehead two miles deep on a front of four miles.

Pointe-du-Hoe

In between Utah and Omaha, at the summit of a cliff so steep as to be virtually unassailable, was one of the ten powerful German coast defense battery positions. Colonel Rudder and the 2nd Ranger Battalion had the task of silencing this battery. The USS *Texas* bombarded the fortifications from H minus 40 minutes to H minus 05. The Rangers landed at H plus 40 and by that time the Germans had returned to their positions. The Rangers, pinned under the cliffs, were being cut to pieces, when the destroyers *Satterlee* (US) and *Talybont* (British) closed the point and opened a fire so accurate that the Rangers were able to scale the cliff with ropes and ladders and establish a foothold. Rudder led his men into the casemates to find no guns. The Germans had concealed them two and a half miles to the rear.

The British Second Army was to land in an area held by 13 infantry battalions

LSTs continue to pour troops ashore on Omaha once the beachhead was secured.

Omaha after the first landings had been made. A traffic jam of massive proportions developed.

German prisoners are taken at Omaha toward the end of the first day of the assault.

with some 500 mortars and machine guns and not less than 260 guns. Most of these belonged to the German Seventh Army, but on the east flank the Fifteenth Army was to some extent involved.

Weather and Allied aircraft discouraged patrols by the German navy or the Third Air Fleet on 5 June, and it was the Fifteenth Army that gave the first warning. At 2230 hours on 5 June, having intercepted British Broadcasting Company code messages to the French Resistance, the Fifteenth Army told its corps and headquarters to expect an invasion within 48 hours. Von Rundstedt, Sperrle and Krancke all considered that no major landing was imminent, however, the latter ordered a state of 'immediate preparedness' for the Navy, and both the Seventh and the Fifteenth Armies ordered the 'highest alert.' But by that time the 711th and 716th Infantry Divisions were already reporting the British airborne landings east of the Orne to the HQs of LXXI Corps (Rouen) and LXXXIV Corps (St Lo).

Before 0200 hours the Fifteenth Army, hearing that British paratroops had been landed in the 711th Division's area asked that 12th SS Panzer should be moved up. This was refused.

At 0215 hours on 6 June Major General Pemsel, Chief of Staff of Seventh Army, told General Speidel, Rommel's Chief of Staff at Army Group B, that the sound of engines could be heard from the sea on the eastern Cotentin coast, and that ships had been detected in the sea area Cherbourg. In Pemsel's opinion this spelled a major operation. Speidel did not agree nor did von Rundstedt.

At 0235 hours Seventh Army gave the 91st Airlanding Division, its reserve in the Cotentin, to Marcks (LXXXIV

Corps), so that with the 709th it could clear up the situation in the Ste Mère Eglise-Carentan area.

By 0330 hours landing craft had been noted off the mouth of the Vire, and sailing quickly toward the Orne estuary. A few minutes earlier Krancke had ordered light craft to patrol the Baie de la Seine. The three destroyers in the Bay of Biscay were ordered to Brest, and the *Landwirt* group of U-Boats, held especially for anti-invasion duties, was brought to instant readiness. Before 0500 hours, von Rundstedt gave in to the arguments of Fifteenth Army and gave orders for the 12th SS Panzer Division to be moved up in rear of the 711th Division ready for 'immediate intervention,' and for Panzer Lehr to make ready to do the same. This was *before* the Allied naval bombardment began.

At 0700 hours 21st Panzer Division (Major General Feuchtinger) was put under the command of LXXXIV Corps to help deal with 6th Airborne east of the Orne.

Gold

The 50th Div Group made the assault on Gold beach with two Brigade Groups up. The 231st Brigade was to capture Jig beach and the 69th was to take King. The coast there, unlike Omaha, is low-lying and sandy, though there are patches of soft clay on the foreshore and much of the hinterland is soggy grassland.

The 231st Brigade, which had been through the 'siege' of Malta, and the Sicily and Italy landings was a splendid formation, consisting of three fine old regular battalions. It went in on a two battalion front: 1st Hampshire right; 1st Dorset left. The men knew they must take the strong defensive positions in fortified houses at Le Hamel, and take

them quickly. The bombardment, as it happened, did the Germans little damage, but though Le Hamel held out against 1st Hampshires, inflicting heavy casualties, the brigade landed well and 1st Dorsetshire and 2nd Devon pushed on inland, while 47 (Royal Marine) Commando, came in on their heels, sustaining 43 casualties, and made for its objective, Port-en-Bessin, on the inter-Allied boundary.

A thousand yards to the east the 69th Brigade touched down punctually. The 6th Green Howards, landing west of La Rivière, and with the close support of engineer tanks took the strong point at Hable de Heurtot. It was an excellent piece of work during which Sergeant Major Hollis won the Victoria Cross. The battalion went on to capture the battery position at Mont Fleury. Softened up by the bombers and 12 direct hits from HMS *Orion*, the gunners surrendered their four guns without a shot.

At La Rivière 5th East Yorkshire had a hard time, and it took them several hours and 90 casualties to clear the village. Then at 0820 7th Green Howards landed and made for Ver-sur-Mer, where there were no enemy, and took the battery behind it. Bombing and two hours attention from HMS *Belfast* had depressed the 50-man garrison, who packed up. Their 4×10cm. gun howitzers had fired 87 rounds. So the two assault brigade groups of the 50th Division were firmly ashore and fighting their way inland.

Juno

The 3rd Canadian Division Group landed with its 7th and 8th Brigades forward on either side of the little seaport of Courseulles. The landing was delayed by rough weather, and almost everywhere the infantry landed ahead of the DD tanks. Luckily the covering fire of destroyers and support craft was very effective, and there was little enemy firing before the touchdown. The tide was rising fast and the resolute crews of the larger landing craft drove on shore despite the obstructions, while the smaller ones wriggled between them as best they could. Of the 306 landing craft of Force J, 90 were lost or damaged that morning, but they got the troops ashore, and, despite a heavy swell, a tide considerably higher than expected, obstacles covered with water, and a strong current on the starboard quarter, they usually got 'the brown jobs' ashore with very few casualties.

Courseulles was well-defended and did not fall to the 7th Brigade until late

The British landing force and the Mulberries built on Gold Beach, Arromanches.

afternoon. The 8th Brigade took Bernières and St Aubin-sur-Mer both of which were bravely defended. At 1130 hours 9th Canadian Brigade began to come ashore and by 1400 hours the whole division had landed, with its four regiments of field artillery and its armor, and despite the chaos and congestion at Bernières and elsewhere, was sorting itself out. No 48 (Royal Marine) Commando had a difficult landing at about 0900 hours under close-range machine gun fire from St Aubin, and rushed the sea-wall. Some 200 survivors set off to attack Langrune, which it took without difficulty. It was then held up by a strong point, which did not surrender until, next day, a Sherman appeared. This stout resistance had been put up by two officers and 33 other ranks of 736 Grenadier Regiment.

Sword

The British 3rd Division decided to land on a single brigade front, the idea being to put as much weight as possible behind its thrust for Caen.

It landed at the right place and the right time, with very effective covering fire. Of the 40 DD tanks of the 13th/18th Hussars 28 got ashore to support the infantry. Here as elsewhere the crews of the landing craft performed marvels. Astonishing though it may seem the 20 bearing the assault wave got the leading companies of 1st South Lancashire and 2nd East Yorkshire ashore without a casualty. They landed between Lion-sur-Mer and La Brèche at 0730 hours, and got across the beach without much loss. 41 (RM) Commando, much reduced by casualties on the beach, came in to capture Lion-sur-Mer. No 4 Commando and two French troops of No 10 (Inter-Allied) Commando landed and took Ouistreham. While part of the South Lancashires strove to overcome the La Brèche position, the rest made for Hermanville-sur-Mer which they occupied by 0900 hours.

No 3 Commando, [Ed Note commanded by Brigadier Peter Young] went in with the second flight of Lord Lovat's 1st Special Service Brigade. The great battleship *Ramillies* belched forth 15-inch shells as the five LCI sailed past, each with about 90 men aboard. Three were hit on the run in by a gun on the front at Ouistreham. They landed at La Brèche at 0905 hours and passed through the East Yorkshires, setting off inland without undue difficulty, though they came under fire from a 'smack-bang' gun

US troops prepare to land on Utah Beach.

Gold Beach seen from a Marauder aircraft.

Port-en-Bessin was the first port to be taken

One of the boys who did not make it past the beach.

at the back of Ouistreham as they were crossing the long flat meadow inland of La Brèche. Their objective was Cabourg far to the east of the Orne, and they had to cross the Benouville Bridge. The bridges were under rifle fire from the south, and a dozen men got across with one man killed, but instead of going on to Cabourg Lord Lovat sent them to hold Le Bas de Ranville, where the 21st Panzer Division was expected. It was about 1300 hours. By 1530 hours the whole Commando was across the bridge.

Much has been written about the failure of 3rd Division to get into Caen on D-Day. The point is that if they had got a move on in the morning they could have won ground for nothing, which they had to fight for in the afternoon. That is how it goes in a combined operation. After a while the surprise wears off and the defenders rally. In this case the 21st Panzer Division came up through Caen and counterattacked.

The German High Command felt it was essential to mount a counterattack as quickly as possible. The great thing was to pitch the Allies into the sea before they could get set. This meant bringing up fresh divisions, which could relieve and reinforce the infantry divisions, which were holding out with more or less success in the strong points of the Atlantic Wall.

A number of divisions were near enough to reinforce the German troops fighting to seal off the beach-head, but as the following table shows only one went into action on D-Day.

the ring: to eject the Allies *armored* divisions were needed, and they were needed early on. Only one German armored division counterattacked on D-Day and that was 21 Panzer, commanded by General Edgar Feuchtinger. Some of his infantry, battalions of the 125th and 192nd Panzergrenadier Regiments, went into action during the morning and they, like the 736th Grenadier Regiment of the 716th Division, made repeated attacks on the 6th Airborne Division, which, though unsuccessful, were pressed home. Taking into account the 352nd Division's optimistic reports from Omaha, General Marcks decided to send the 21st Panzer into action against the British in the Caen-Ouistreham area, west of the Orne.

General Feuchtinger had a well-equipped division, whose 16,000 men included veterans of Rommel's Afrika Korps. He had 127 Mark IV tanks, 40 assault guns and 24×88mm anti-tank guns, but the division was dispersed over a wide area. The tanks were a few miles northeast of Falaise.

Air reconnaissance kept an eye on the advance of the 21st Panzer and at about 1100 hours General Dempsey asked for air attack on troop movements into Caen from the south and southeast, and the response was magnificent. Even so Feuchtinger managed to get an armored regiment (90 tanks) and two battalions through Caen, and to mount an attack northward toward Lion-sur-Mer. By this time (about 1600 hours) the 8th Brigade had a firm grip on Hermanville,

Colleville sur Orne and Ouistreham, but the German strong points, whose code names were *Daimler* and Hillman were still holding out. The 9th Brigade was still assembling and the 185th Brigade was making for Caen down the west bank of the Canal. 2nd Shropshire Light Infantry had reached Biéville.

The tanks of the Staffordshire Yeomanry were supporting the forward troops of both the leading brigades, and about 1600 hours they spotted German tanks advancing from Caen. A squadron just had time to get into position west of Biéville, when 40 German tanks, moving very fast, came in to the attack. The Yeomanry and the anti-tank guns of the Shropshires each knocked out a couple of them. The Germans turned away taking cover in woods, pursued by the Staffordshire Yeomanry and fired on by field artillery. When they reappeared they had more casualties. Reinforced they made for the Periers Ridge, where a squadron posted on Point 61 lay in wait for them. Three more German tanks were knocked out, and once more they withdrew. So far the British reckoned that they had destroyed 13 tanks for the loss of one self-propelled gun. Typhoons had dive-bombed other tanks in the Western outskirts of Caen knocking out at least six. Feuchtinger recorded that he began the day with 124 tanks of which only 70 were left by nightfall.

Exactly how far the 21st Panzer got is a matter for conjecture. It seems that the leading tanks were not far short of Lion-sur-Mer, when they drew back. The

21st Panzer	6 June
12th SS Panzer	7 June
Panzer Lehr	8 June
353rd Infantry Field Division	9 June
17th SS Panzergrenadier	11 June
2nd Panzer 3rd Parachute	12 June

One can, of course, criticize the details of the German build up. They could have done with more infantry, and 77 and 84 Field Divisions might both have been thrown into the battle early on. Still, that is not the real point. The fact is that infantry divisions could do little but hold

The end of 6 June on Utah; thousands of men ashore and thousands more on their way.

division reported to Rommel that it had 'been halted by renewed landings,' and the telephone log states: 'Attack by 21st Panzer Division rendered useless by heavily concentrated airborne troops, ...' Clearly the Germans were discouraged by the arrival just before 2100 hours of gliders with 6th Airlanding Brigade, making for the drop zone N, near Ranville. It was certainly an impressive spectacle, and the effect of this reinforcement on the morale of each side was incalculable. The arrival of this strong brigade removed any immediate threat to the bridgehead east of the Orne. With the withdrawal of the 21st Panzer Division the Allies were left in comparative peace to sort themselves out ready for whatever the morrow might bring. By the evening of D-Day the Allies had landed 156,115 men from the air and from the sea.

With the Atlantic Wall broken one would suppose perhaps that a great armored battle would have followed, with tanks ranging about the plains of Northern France as Rommel had once ranged about the Western Desert. It was not to be. This was not because the Allied general, having failed to read the works of Captain Basil Liddell Hart and Major General 'Boney' Fuller, did not understand the use of armor, or because the officers of the armored car, British and American, did not know that 'leadership is done from in front.' It is much simpler than that. The reason was that the Germans had far better tanks. Why then did Rommel not hurl Montgomery into the Channel? There is a fairly simple reason for that too: lack of gasoline. The Germans' supply difficulties were so great that they were deprived of their mobility. They dug their tanks into the hedges of the *bocage* and used them as pillboxes. Fighting in a country, where practically every field is surrounded by an anti-tank obstacle, the two armies came to a standstill, which lasted until 26 July when General George Patton, at the head of his US Third Army broke out of the bridgehead and began an advance, which challenges comparison with the *Blitzkrieg* of 1940.

The Battle of Normandy was over. The German Seventh Army was destroyed, and Rommel had fought his last fight. It cannot be pretended that everything had 'gone according to plan' on D-Day, or in the long fight for Caen that followed. But it was an ambitious plan and enough of it went right. The success of the attack on the Atlantic Wall on 6 June 1944 laid the foundations for all that followed: in short, for the liberation of Western Europe, and the destruction of Hitler's evil Empire.

LSTs and barrage balloons crowd the shore as trucks move men and equipment inland.

Casualties wait for evacuation on Juno Beach on the afternoon of D-Day.

Allied Troops Landed on D—Day

SEABORNE

American	Utah	23,250		
	Omaha	34,250		
		57,500		
British and Canadian	Gold	24,970		
	Juno	21,400		
	Sword	28,845		
		75,215	**132,715**	

AIRBORNE

American	15,500	
British	7,900	
	23,400	**23,400**
		156,115

Operation Neptune

Allied Naval Forces

	British	U.S.A.	French	Polish	Norwe-gian	Greek	Nether-lands
Battleships	3	3					
Cruisers	17	3	2	1			
Monitors	2						
HQ Ships	3	2					
Destroyers	65	30	1	2	3		
Frigates	11	2	4				
Corvettes	17		2			2	
Sloops	4						2
Asdic Trawlers	30						
Fleet Minesweepers	88						
Minesweepers		9					
Patrol Craft		17					
	240	66	9	3	3	2	2

Landing Ships & Craft	4126
Ancillary Ships and Craft	736
Merchant Ships	864

Sherman tanks and other vehicles under British com

*A GI inspects trenches along the beach
abandoned by their German defenders.*

...d pass through Reviers as the beachhead widened.

D–Day: Operation Overlord

Chronological Background

1 Sept 1939	German invasion of Poland
10 May 1940	German invasion of the Low Countries
27 May–4 June 1940	Dunkirk
22 June 1940	France accepts Hitler's Armistice terms
10 July 1940	The Battle of Britain begins
22 June 1941	German invasion of Russia
28 March 1942	The raid on St Nazaire
19 Aug 1942	The Dieppe Raid
8 Nov 1942	Operation *Torch*. The Allies invade North Africa
10 July 1943	Allied invasion of Sicily
3 Sept 1943	Allied invasion of Italy
6 June 1944	Operation *Overlord*
8 May 1945	Unconditional surrender of Germany

Gliders (and C-47s that released them) land paratroops behind enemy lines in Normandy.

King George VI visits Eisenhower in France after the beachheads had been secured.

PHILIPPINE SEA 1944

The Great Marianas Turkey Shoot

In 1943 the Japanese tide of conquest in the Far East was stemmed and American forces began to erode Japan's outer defense perimeter. The Gilbert Islands were secured by the US in late November 1943, and in January 1944 an assault upon the Marshall Islands was equally successful. The Japanese found it impossible to react. The Combined Fleet, based at Truk, was merely a shadow of its former self, with the carriers still in Japan training replacement air groups and the cruiser force, attacked by the Americans at Rabaul, virtually a nonentity. It became even less effective in mid-February when Task Force 58 attacked Truk itself, forcing a withdrawal to Palau. As this threatened the flank of MacArthur's advance in New Guinea, however, Palau was also attacked in late March and Combined Fleet headquarters under Admiral Mineichi Koga, who had replaced Yamamoto when the latter was killed in June 1943, was removed to Mindanao. Unfortunately Koga was killed in the process when his seaplane crashed in bad weather, and he was replaced by Admiral Soemu Toyoda who decided to set up his headquarters in Japan, delegating the sea-going command known as the First Mobile Fleet, to Vice-Admiral Jisaburo Ozawa. It was to be a fatal split, denying initiative to the commander on the spot and subjecting the Japanese Navy to the false hopes and political machinations of Tokyo.

The results were apparent in the intricate plan put forward by Toyoda (Operation A-Go), designed to bring about 'a decisive battle with full strength ... at a favorable opportunity.' The idea was to lure the American fleet into one of two battle areas (Palau or the Caroline Islands), chosen because they were within range of the myriad of island air bases from which Japanese air strength could participate to help balance the American carriers. A portion of the Japanese fleet was to be used as bait, sailing openly into the chosen area, and as soon as the Americans reacted the main portion under Ozawa was to leave its anchorage at Tawi Tawi in the Sulu Archipelago, proceed to an area east of the Philippines and take the enemy by surprise. It was an optimistic scenario, but once the Americans threatened the Marianas Islands, the next logical step after the Marshalls, the Japanese had to do something. The Marianas, consisting principally of the islands of Guam, Saipan and Tinian, were part of the inner defense line round Japan itself and represented an ideal base for American strategic bombers. By May 1944 Toyoda had dispatched the carriers to join Ozawa, despite their lack of trained air groups, and had concentrated a total of 1700 aircraft at shore bases in the Dutch East Indies, the Philippines, New Guinea and the Bismarcks. As American intentions became clear, more than 500 of these machines were moved forward into the Marianas.

This was the first Japanese mistake, for while Vice-Admiral Richmond Turner's Amphibious Force prepared for the assault on Saipan, set for 15 June, the carriers of Task Force 58 roamed far and wide, hitting Japanese bases. After neutralizing strikes against Palau, Yap and Woleai in late March, they moved southward to support MacArthur in Hollandia and, on their return to the Central Pacific in May, pounded Truk, Marcus and Wake Islands. At the same time, shore-based bombers hit the by-passed Marshall Islands of Jaluit and Wotje. Japanese aircraft and installations were destroyed in each attack, gradually undermining Toyoda's plan. The process reached a climax on 11, 12 and 13 June as Mitscher's force moved in to soften up the Marianas and interdict Japanese supply routes through the islands of Chichi Jima and Iwo Jima, 650 miles to the north. By the time the Marines invaded Saipan, the 500 aircraft in the Marianas had been largely eliminated, complete American air superiority achieved and one of the main elements of Operation A-Go effectively destroyed.

Neither Toyoda nor Ozawa was aware

Admirals Spruance and Nimitz.

Rear Admiral Raymond Spruance.

Admiral Mineichi Koga.

Admiral Ernest J King visits Admirals Nimitz and Spruance in July 1944.

Gunners fire their .50 cal machine guns from the deck of an LST on its way to Saipan.

of the true state of air losses (the local commander neglected to tell them for fear of repercussions), and when the decision to seek battle was taken on 13 June, both retained a degree of optimism about its outcome. Practical problems continued to emerge, forcing changes to the original plan. In late May the defenders of the island of Biak, an important air base in the efforts to halt MacArthur's advance, had called urgently for aid, and a special naval force under Vice-Admiral Matome Ugaki, composed of the battleships *Yamato* and *Musashi* with cruisers and destroyers, had been detached from Ozawa's command. This had now to be recalled and directed to rendezvous with the rest of the fleet in the Philippine Sea, a maneuver which was to take time and preclude the original scheme whereby it was 'to lure the enemy fleet.' The two forces met on 16 June, but surprise was quickly lost. American submarines saw and reported both portions, allowing Vice-Admiral Raymond Spruance time to assess the danger and make the necessary dispositions. The last great carrier battle was about to begin.

On the American side, Spruance realized that the Japanese could not approach to within range until 19 June, and was not prepared to advance far into the Philippine Sea to meet them. His first duty was the protection of Turner's Amphibious Force, so he ordered his carriers to complete their neutralization of Japanese bases on Guam, Tinian, Chichi Jima and Iwo Jima before rendezvousing 180 miles west of the

USS Manila Bay *and its P-47s on deck under attack by four Japanese planes from Saipan.*

Lt Gen Smith and Vice-Admiral Turner.

Battleship fires in support of the Saipan landings. The middle gun is in the recoil position.

Marianas on the evening of 18 June. Once assembled, Task Force 58 was formidable. Its 15 carriers were divided into four self-contained task groups (TG 58-1 comprising *Hornet*, *Yorktown*, *Belleau Wood* and *Bataan*; TG 58-2 *Bunker Hill*, *Wasp*, *Monterey* and *Cabot*; TG 58-3 *Enterprise*, *Lexington*, *Princeton* and *San Jacinto*; TG 58-4 *Essex*, *Langley* and *Cowpens*), each with its complement of battleships, cruisers and destroyers, and the total air strength exceeded 900, the majority of which were fighters and dive- or torpedo-bombers. In normal circumstances the task groups would have fought as separate entities, but with the prospect of a major fleet action, Spruance altered their organization. The battleships of the carrier group escorts were formed into a 'Battle Line' (known as TG 58-7) under Vice-Admiral Willis Lee with four heavy cruisers and 13 destroyers transferred from Turner's Amphibious Force as an

escort. This was pushed forward 15 miles ahead of the carriers to act as a shield, with TG 58-4 in attendance to give air cover, while the other three carrier groups were stationed in a north-south line some 15 miles apart. It was basically a defensive formation, designed to trap and destroy incoming Japanese air or surface assaults.

Meanwhile Ozawa's force continued to approach the Marianas from the west. It was organized into three parts. A Force, under Ozawa himself, was centered upon the three big fleet carriers *Taiho*, *Zuikaku* and *Shokaku*, with a screen of cruisers and destroyers and provided the main air strength with 207 aircraft. B Force, commanded by Rear Admiral Joshima, contained the slower fleet carriers *Junyo* and *Hiyo* as well as the light carrier *Ryuho*, which between them mustered 135 aircraft. It was protected by one battleship, one cruiser and nine destroyers. These two groups

operated independently about 12 miles apart, while C or Van Force under Vice-Admiral Kurita, comprising the four battleships *Yamato*, *Musashi*, *Haruna* and *Kongo*, four heavy cruisers, a light cruiser and nine destroyers, screening three light carriers *Chitose*, *Chiyoda* and *Zuiho* with a combined complement of 90 aircraft, sailed about a 100 miles in advance to draw the fire of enemy air strikes and extend the range of reconnaissance seaplanes.

In fact it was in the area of reconnaissance that the Japanese enjoyed about their only advantage, for their float-planes, catapulted from battleships and cruisers, had a greater endurance than their American counterparts. Because of this Ozawa was aware of Spruance's dispositions on 18 June and in a position to plan a strike, at a range of approximately 350 miles, for dawn the next day. Spruance, on the other hand, with reconnaissance aircraft that reached

Painting of the US Pacific Fleet on the day of the Great Marianas turkey shoot.

the limit of their fuel about 60 miles short of the Japanese fleet, spent 18 June in ignorance of enemy movements, his latest reports having come in 24 hours earlier from the submarine *Cavalla*, shadowing A Force. It was not until 1000 hours on 19 June, when the radar of Lee's Battle Line detected a swarm of incoming aircraft, that the Americans were able to react. Even so, they managed to inflict the first casualties, for as Ozawa's A Force launched its strike aircraft, the submarine *Albacore* mounted a surprise assault, damaging the carrier *Taiho*. It was but a foretaste of things to come.

As soon as the Japanese air armada, divided into three waves and comprising nearly 250 assorted dive-bombers, torpedo-bombers and fighters, was detected, the American carriers turned together into the wind, launched any bombers or torpedo aircraft on deck, sending them out of the way to the

'Home to Roost,' a painting depicting the return of US naval aircraft to their carrier.

248

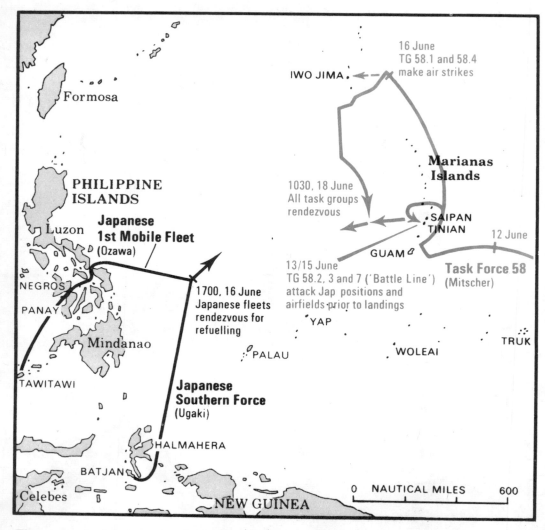

The two navies join in combat in the Philippine Sea.

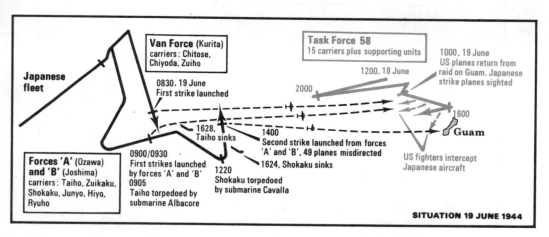

Van Force (Kurita)
carriers: Chitose, Chiyoda, Zuiho

Task Force 58
15 carriers plus supporting units

Japanese fleet

0830, 19 June
First strike launched

1000, 19 June
US planes return from
raid on Guam. Japanese
strike planes sighted

1200, 18 June

2000

1628,
Taiho sinks

1400
Second strike launched from forces
'A' and 'B', 49 planes misdirected

1624, Shokaku sinks

1600

Guam

Forces 'A' (Ozawa)
and 'B' (Joshima)
carriers: Taiho, Zuikaku,
Shokaku, Junyo, Hiyo,
Ryuho

0900/0930
First strikes launched
by forces 'A' and 'B'
0905
Taiho torpedoed by
submarine Albacore

1220
Shokaku torpedoed
by submarine Cavalla

US fighters intercept
Japanese aircraft

SITUATION 19 JUNE 1944

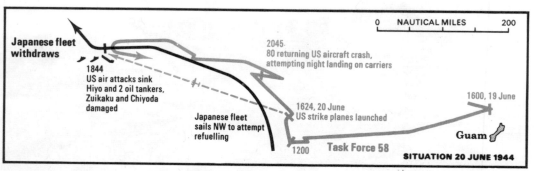

Japanese fleet
withdraws

0   NAUTICAL MILES   200

2045
80 returning US aircraft crash,
attempting night landing on carriers

1844
US air attacks sink
Hiyo and 2 oil tankers,
Zuikaku and Chiyoda
damaged

Japanese fleet
sails NW to attempt
refuelling

1624, 20 June
US strike planes launched

1600, 19 June

1200   Task Force 58

Guam

SITUATION 20 JUNE 1944

Top: The position of both fleets on 19 June 1944.
Above: The position on 20 June as the Japanese withdrew.

eastward, and concentrated solely upon fighters. Nearly 300 Hellcats took to the air, some of them flying over Guam to attack the few shore-based aircraft which the Japanese brought into the battle, but the vast majority advancing to intercept Ozawa's carrier strikes. These interceptions, which continued throughout the morning, usually took place some 45 to 60 miles in front of the American fleet and were so successful that they soon became known as 'The Great Marianas Turkey Shoot.' In the first Japanese wave, from C Force, out of 69 aircraft 42 were destroyed and none penetrated to the American ships. Of the second wave, comprising 128 planes from A Force, more than 100 were intercepted and shot down. The remainder broke through to face the massed gunfire of the Battle Line, and an even smaller remnant managed to reach the aircraft carriers beyond. Minor damage was inflicted upon the *Wasp* and *Bunker Hill* of TG 58-2, but by 1200 hours it was all over. Less than 30 survivors limped back to the Japanese fleet with dangerously exaggerated tales of American carriers on fire and sinking. Meanwhile, the third wave, comprising 47 aircraft from B Force, had flown too far to the north. Just over half of them failed to make any contact with the Americans, returning to their carriers unmolested, but the others succeeded in locating the most northerly task group, where they were pounced on by patrolling Hellcats. Seven of the Japanese aircraft were destroyed: the rest dumped their bombs ineffectively and fled. The Americans, still unaware of the true position of the enemy fleet, let them go.

But if Spruance was unable to hit the source of the Japanese air strikes, the same was not the case with his submarines, and as the morning came to an end a double disaster was inflicted by them upon Ozawa. At 1220 hours the *Cavalla*, after having lost contact with A Force during 18 June, suddenly found herself in an ideal position to attack the *Shokaku*. Three torpedoes tore into her side, starting fires which the crew tried desperately to fight for nearly three hours. But their efforts were in vain: at the end of that time gasoline vapor exploded and the *Shokaku*, one of the last remaining elements of Nagumo's Pearl Harbor force, went to the bottom. At almost the same time the *Taiho*, apparently undamaged by *Albacore*'s earlier attack, also exploded when fumes from a ruptured fuel system ignited. Ozawa's best ships had gone down.

Above: A Japanese twin-engined bomber missed its carrier target in the Battle of the Philippine Sea.

Below: A Grumman F6F Hellcat takes off from the USS Yorktown (CV 10), a replacement for its namesake sunk at Midway.

In the meantime, further Japanese air strikes, launched from the *Zuikaku* of A Force and the three light carriers of B Force, tried to break through to the American ships. Of the planes involved, only about half located the southern carrier task group and were promptly hit by waiting Hellcats. Few of the Japanese machines survived. The remainder, 49 strong, headed for Guam to refuel before restarting their search. But they were unaware of the true state of affairs on the island, dominated by the Americans since dawn. Set upon by 27 Hellcats, 30 Japanese planes were shot down over the sea or as they tried to land on the battered airstrip. By 1600 hours the Americans had cleared the air entirely of enemy machines and, except for action against the occasional shore-based raider, no more air fighting took place on 19 June. The Japanese air arm had been all but destroyed. Of the 373 aircraft sent out from Ozawa's carriers, only 130 had returned; a figure which dropped to 102 as pilot inexperience showed itself in a series of crashes as the survivors re-landed. In addition, about 50 land-based aircraft had been destroyed. Such losses were irreplaceable: Japan would be unable to man or equip an effective carrier force again. American losses, by way of comparison, had been only 29 aircraft. Spruance's defensive stance had been more than justified.

But the Battle of the Philippine Sea was not over, for the Americans, brought up to believe that no naval action could be termed a success without the destruction of the enemy fleet, were determined to go over to the offensive.

Below: Avengers and Helldivers en route.
Right: Vice-Admiral Marc Mitscher.

This was not possible immediately, however, as Spruance was still not aware of Ozawa's position. In fact the American Task Force had drifted eastward during the air battle, increasing the distance between the two fleets to something like 400 miles, outside the range of Mitscher's strike aircraft. Therefore, as a first move, Task Force 58 had to turn westward to try and close the gap while sending out reconnaissance missions in all directions. No sign of the Japanese was reported during the remainder of 19 June, and it began to look as if Ozawa had escaped.

If the Japanese commander had realized the full state of his losses there is little doubt that he would have withdrawn swiftly to Japan, but Ozawa was unaware of the extent of his defeat. Not only did he believe the stories brought back to him about American aircraft and carriers destroyed, but he was also convinced that many of his missing strike planes had landed on Guam or neighboring islands and were ready to take to the air again. As a result, on 20 June, having withdrawn northwestward to rendezvous with replenishment tankers he was prepared to renew the battle at the earliest opportunity. It was only when his communications staff intercepted a signal from an American aircraft at 1615 hours on 20 June, reporting contact with the Japanese fleet, that worries began to arise. Refueling was postponed and Ozawa retired still further northwestward, hoping to outpace the Americans before nightfall and so avoid an air strike which, with only 100 operational aircraft left, he would be unable to counter.

He very nearly succeeded. When the Americans received the long-awaited signal of contact at about 1600 hours, the chances of putting in a successful strike were slim. The enemy fleet was only just within range and, even if aircraft were launched immediately they would have to be relanded after dark, a procedure for which the American pilots were not trained. But Spruance and Mitscher were not going to let the opportunity slip by, and within half an hour of the reported sighting 77 Dauntless dive bombers, 54 Avenger torpedo bombers and 85 Hellcat fighters had taken to the air, heading west into the setting sun. Their mission was a resounding success. After a section broke away to deal with Ozawa's refueling force of six tankers, the remainder swept aside the thin screen of Zero fighter protection and pounded the Japanese fleet, concentrat-

The carrier Zuikaku *and two destroyers under heavy US naval air attack on 20 June 1944.*

ing upon the carriers. After 20 minutes of frenetic action the *Hiyo* had been torpedoed and sunk, the *Zuikaku* crippled, the *Chiyoda* set on fire, the battleship *Haruna* and cruiser *Maya* damaged. In addition, a further 65 planes of the Japanese naval air arm had been destroyed, leaving Ozawa with less than 40 operational machines. Admitting defeat at last, he fled to Okinawa. American losses were slight, for although nearly 80 of the returning aircraft crashed as they tried to reland after nightfall, few crew members were killed. Indeed, after widespread rescue operations only 16 pilots and 33 aircrew were reported missing. The Battle of the Philippine Sea – an American victory of epic proportions – was over. The Japanese naval air arm had been destroyed and her carriers had reduced to impotence, denied the ability either to strike or to defend themselves in future battles. American naval and air superiority was virtually complete – the final naval battle of the Pacific War, at Leyte Gulf in October 1944, was needed to eliminate the Japanese fleet entirely – and the inexorable advances upon the Japanese homeland could continue virtually unopposed. The lesson was clear: in naval as in land warfare in the twentieth century, air power was the essential key to victory.

Gunners and radiomen relax aboard the USS Monterey (CVL.26) *before a strike on Guam.*

Carrier-based planes hit Ushi Point airfield on Tinian in June 1944.

LEYTE GULF 1944

The Battle of Leyte Gulf marks the end of an era in several respects. Not only was it the Japanese Navy's last engagement as an independent fighting force, and the last major naval encounter of World War II, but it was also the last great sea battle fought to date. Appropriately enough, it has the additional distinction of being the largest naval battle in history, one in which every weapon except the mine was employed on both sides. Leyte Gulf saw too the introduction of Japan's new desperate, and deadly, air tactic – the famous kamikaze suicide plane.

As agreed by Churchill and Roosevelt in the early stages of the war, the American Joint Chiefs of Staff directed the war effort in the Pacific theater, the British controlled the Middle East and India, while Europe and the Atlantic were under joint Anglo-American command. After the Battle of Midway, two commanders came to dominate the American war in the Pacific: General Douglas MacArthur and Admiral Chester Nimitz.

Nimitz held the Central Pacific Command. The Navy saw the action in the Pacific as essentially its bailiwick – Europe was the Army's war – and was determined to have the deciding voice in setting policy. Nimitz and the Naval Chief of Staff, Admiral Ernest King, wanted to launch an amphibious campaign west from Hawaii across the central Pacific to Japan, via the Gilbert, Marshall, Caroline, and Mariana Islands, arguing that no one would be safe until the 'spider web' Japan had established throughout Micronesia had been swept up. Their particular concern was to avoid putting Navy forces under the Army's command.

That, of course, was just what MacArthur was asking for. As Commander in the Southwest Pacific area – Australia, New Guinea, the Philippines, and most of the Netherlands East Indies – he planned to launch his own drive to Japan via New Guinea and the Philippines. Further, he proposed that the entire Pacific fleet be placed under his command to cover his advance along the 'New Guinea-Mindanao Axis.' There was no way he would accept the purely defensive role laid out for him by Nimitz and King.

In effect, MacArthur and Nimitz were competing to see who could defeat Japan first. Far from disapproving of this interservice rivalry, President Franklin Roosevelt actually encouraged it. The Commander in Chief believed that the competition would spur each side on to greater efforts and produce faster results. Unfortunately the situation got out of hand, and was to have an important effect on the Battle of Leyte Gulf. The Navy's hatred of MacArthur was so open and virulent that it 'seemed childish,' according to Secretary of War, Henry Stimson. MacArthur later wrote that 'of all the faulty decisions of the war, perhaps the most inexpressible one was the failure to unify the command in the Pacific. . . .' – though what he meant, of course, was the failure to unify command under *his* direction.

It must be noted, however, that if the rift between MacArthur and Nimitz was as wide as some analysts have described, American efforts in the Pacific would have been paralyzed and the war there would never have been won. In fact, the two had much in common: highly-trained minds that could cut through non-essentials to reach the heart of a problem; the ability to instill tremendous loyalty in their men; and above all, the will to win. Although they honestly differed in their views on the best way to win the Pacific war, a great deal of mutual respect and a high degree of cooperation kept the operation running fairly smoothly. When Nimitz needed air support from long-range, land-based bombers, MacArthur provided it. and when the general needed carriers or other naval vessels, he borrowed them from the admiral. In other words, neither ever allowed differences of opinion over strategy to deflect him from his primary objective – to defeat the Japanese.

By the beginning of 1943 the Amer-

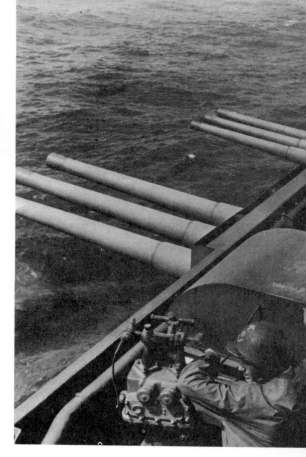

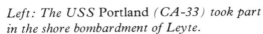

icans had gained control of southeastern New Guinea, Guadalcanal, and Tulagi, and had definitely gained the initiative in the Southwest Pacific.

MacArthur was leading one wing of a two-pronged attack, moving along the north coast of New Guinea toward the Philippines. His strategy was based on achieving local air superiority with land-based planes to cover his advancing troops, and on isolating each successive Japanese base before subjecting it to the final air, ground, and naval assault. His 'island-hopping' program had been successful, but had also proved too slow, so he devised 'leap-frogging' tactics. This involved striking where the Japanese were weakest ('hitting them where they ain't') and by-passing the stronger garrisons, leaving them to wither away, isolated from supplies and reinforcements.

Nimitz, meanwhile, was striking across the Pacific, through the Marshalls, Marianas, and Palaus, toward Iwo Jima and Okinawa. His offensive was based on a combination of fast carrier task forces and hard-hitting amphibious groups. Carrier-based planes would knock out Japanese air defenses over the island target; fleets would move in to blast the shore defenses; and finally Marines and soldiers would land to overcome the last resistance. Once an island was secured, airfields would be established, the Navy would build up harbor and supply facilities, and the whole island would be turned into a forward supply base for the capture of the next objective.

The methods used in both areas involved months of hard, bloody, dangerous fighting – but they worked. By June 1944 Nimitz had worked his way through the Marshalls and Gilberts and was ready to attack Saipan, the key Japanese fortress in the Marianas. Imperial General Headquarters quite rightly decided to meet the attack with the full force of the Japanese fleet. Not only would the loss of Saipan sever their communications with Japanese forces in the south, but the island's position only

1350 miles from Tokyo would make it an ideal base for long-range bomber strikes against the Home Islands. In the greatest air battle of the war, 15 American carriers with 900 planes met nine Japanese carriers with 370 planes. During 'The Great Marianas Turkey Shoot' the Japanese lost 315 of those planes, a carrier, and several battleships and cruisers. The losses in planes, and especially in pilots, were irreplaceable at that stage in the war; the fall of Saipan showed the prospect of defeat so clearly that it led to the fall of General Hideki Tojo's war government.

At the end of July, MacArthur had gained control of New Guinea and was poised to cross the Celebes Sea to Mindanao, but the argument on future strategy was still fiercely contested. King and most other Navy planners in Washington wanted to by-pass the Philippines in favor of an attack on Formosa or even the Home Islands themselves. MacArthur waxed eloquent on the need to recapture the major part of the Philippines – partly for strategic reasons, but primarily because he had given his word to return. Failure to do so, he maintained, would compromise American honor and prestige in the Far East for many years to come. Nimitz was in the middle. He took a dim view of skipping over the Philippines altogether, but was willing to consider by-passing Luzon if major air and naval bases could be established in the central and southern Philippines.

The stalemate seemed unresolvable when President Roosevelt intervened and decided to have a meeting with Nimitz and MacArthur at Pearl Harbor to discuss the next moves. During the meeting on 26 and 27 July, MacArthur and Nimitz talked while the President and the others listened. In the end, all were convinced of the merits of MacArthur's 'Leyte then Luzon' concept. In September the Allied Combined Chiefs of Staff, meeting at the Octagon Conference in Quebec, agreed that MacArthur and Nimitz should converge on Leyte in December. but within a week Admiral William Halsey, who had sent out task forces of his Third Fleet headed by the new Essex class fast carriers to soften up Morotai, Yap, and the Palau Islands, reported meeting few Japanese planes and no warships. His story of the 'amazing and fantastic' lack of Japanese resistance put a different light on the matter. Without opposition, MacArthur's forces could make one long hop from New Guinea to Leyte, by-passing

Mindanao completely. In an unusual example of strategic flexibility the Octagon Conference moved the date of the Leyte Mission up to 20 October.

By this time the Japanese were in grave difficulty, despite their many advantages, largely because Imperial General Headquarters had been operating with an outdated concept of war. For example, although the Japanese could and did design better warships and airplanes than the Americans, they did not give naval air power – the weapon upon which their defense should have relied – top priority. During 1943 America built 22 aircraft carriers; Japan produced only three and never managed to recruit enough pilots to man even a restricted air arm. Japan controlled 80 percent of the world's rubber along with vast quantities of oil, tin, tungsten, manganese, and iron ore – but had no way to exploit those resources. A large merchant fleet was needed, but battleships had been given priority over an expanded merchant navy. By 1943 Japan was already facing a severe oil shortage and curtailed naval operations because it no longer had the tanker capacity to transport the oil from the Netherlands East Indies. As a result of this basic economic weakness in their defense structure, the Japanese had been grimly hanging on since their defeat in Guadalcanal and Papua. Instead of fighting to win, they were now simply trying to hold on as long as possible.

Of all the services the newest, the naval air arm, suffered most. Between 1942 and 1944 Japan lost 8000 navy planes and enormous numbers of pilots. The planes could be replaced, albeit with difficulty, but the men could not. Casualties increased as the quality of new recruits and training procedures fell. With the death of Admiral Isoroku Yamamoto, the major supporter of naval air power was gone and the Navy soon returned to its first love, the battleship.

By March 1944 Japanese strategists could foresee the American invasion of the Philippines, long before Allied planners had managed to agree on it themselves. Japan was most concerned with holding Luzon, thus maintaining communication with Malaya and Indonesia. But she had to be prepared to defend not only all the Philippine Islands, but Formosa and the Ryukyus as well; if the inner defense line that extended from the Kuriles through the Home Islands to the Philippines was breached, Japan would

Right: US naval units off Leyte represented the largest fleet at battle stations in history.

Admiral Chester W Nimitz, who masterminded the entire Leyte operation.

Admiral Jisaburo Ozawa, who commanded the Japanese aircraft carriers.

Admiral William F ('Bull') Halsey, whose performance at Leyte was widely criticized.

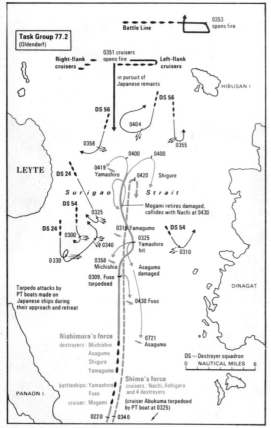

Map labels:
- Task Group 77.2 (Oldendorf)
- 0353 opens fire
- Battle Line
- 0351 cruisers opens fire
- Right-flank cruisers
- Left-flank cruisers
- in pursuit of Japanese remants
- HIBUSAN I
- DS 56
- DS 56
- 0404
- 0358
- 0355
- LEYTE
- 0400 0400
- DS 24
- 0419 Yamashiro
- 0420 Shigure
- Surigao Strait
- Mogami retires damaged, collides with Nachi at 0430
- DS 54
- 0325
- DS 24
- 0315 Yamagumo
- DS 54
- 0300
- 0325 Yamashiro hit
- 0340
- 0310
- 0330
- 0358 Michishio
- Asagumo damaged
- 0309, Fuso torpedoed
- DINAGAT
- 0430 Fuso
- Torpedo attacks by PT boats made on Japanese ships during their approach and retreat
- 0721 Asagumo
- Nishimura's force
  destroyers: Michishio Asagumo Shigure Yamagumo
- DS = Destroyer squadron
- 0 NAUTICAL MILES 6
- battleships: Yamashiro Fuso
  cruiser: Mogami
- Shima's force
  cruisers: Nachi, Ashigara and 4 destroyers
- (cruiser Abukuma torpedoed by PT boat at 0325)
- PANAON I
- 0220 — 0340

The Battle at Surigao Strait.

Japanese cruiser is hit by US carrier-based bombers off Leyte in the battle.

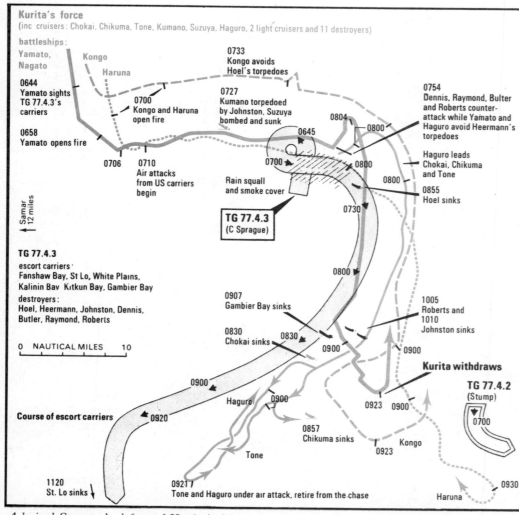

Map labels:
- Kurita's force (inc cruisers: Chokai, Chikuma, Tone, Kumano, Suzuya, Haguro, 2 light cruisers and 11 destroyers)
- battleships: Yamato, Nagato
- Kongo
- Haruna
- 0733 Kongo avoids Hoel's torpedoes
- 0644 Yamato sights TG 77.4.3's carriers
- 0700 Kongo and Haruna open fire
- 0727 Kumano torpedoed by Johnston, Suzuya bombed and sunk
- 0754 Dennis, Raymond, Bulter and Roberts counter-attack while Yamato and Haguro avoid Heermann's torpedoes
- 0804
- 0800
- 0658 Yamato opens fire
- 0645
- 0700
- 0800
- Haguro leads Chokai, Chikuma and Tone
- 0706
- 0710 Air attacks from US carriers begin
- 0700
- 0800
- 0855 Hoel sinks
- Samar 12 miles
- Rain squall and smoke cover
- TG 77.4.3 (C Sprague)
- 0730
- TG 77.4.3
  escort carriers: Fanshaw Bay, St Lo, White Plains, Kalinin Bay Kitkun Bay, Gambier Bay
  destroyers: Hoel, Heermann, Johnston, Dennis, Butler, Raymond, Roberts
- 0800
- 0907 Gambier Bay sinks
- 1005 Roberts and 1010 Johnston sinks
- 0 NAUTICAL MILES 10
- 0830 Chokai sinks
- 0830
- 0900
- 0900
- Kurita withdraws
- TG 77.4.2 (Stump)
- 0900
- Course of escort carriers
- 0920
- Haguro
- 0900
- 0923 0900
- 0700
- 0857 Chikuma sinks
- Kongo
- Tone
- 0923
- Haruna
- 1120 St. Lo sinks
- 0921 Tone and Haguro under air attack, retire from the chase
- 0930

Admiral Sprague's defeat of Kurita's force was the principal naval action at Leyte.

lose her lines of communication through the Formosa Straits and the South China Sea and all the resources of the southern colonies, and would be forced to fall back on the resources of China alone.

In July/August 1944, then, Japanese planners drew up four separate *Sho* (or victory) plans. *Sho-1* covered the Philippines while the others concerned Formosa-Ryukyus, Honshu-Kyushu, and Hokkaido-Kuriles. *Sho-1* was a typically Japanese plan that employed divided forces, diversions, unexpected attacks, and an elaborate time schedule. First the Northern Force under Admiral Ozawa, built around the four carriers *Zuikaku*, *Zuiho*, *Chitose*, and *Chiyoda*, would lure the main American force – Halsey's Third Fleet – to the north, away from the real objective. Then the Center Force commanded by Admiral Kurita, consisting of the giant battleships *Yamato* and *Musashi*, nine cruisers, and a destroyer screen, would come south of Luzon through the San Bernardino Strait into Leyte Gulf. At the same time Admiral Nishimura's Southern Force would move up on the gulf through the Surigao Strait between Leyte and Mindanao. The two forces would converge, destroy shipping in the gulf, smash the Allied bridgehead, and presumably depart before the Third Fleet could return. The carriers were being used as decoys because the naval air force had already been virtually eliminated – there were only 116 planes on Oyawa's four carriers, and less than 200 in land-based air groups in the Ryukyus, Formosa, and Manila. If the plan succeeded the American army at Leyte would be destroyed as completely as the navy had been three years earlier at Pearl Harbor, and Japan would have gained at least a year's breathing space.

Ideally, *Sho-1* would be timed to catch the Leyte landings in their 'naked' stage, as troops and equipment were being launched. But Japan's oil shortage was so great that if *Sho-1* was activated too soon, the ships would be short of fuel for the real engagement. Japanese intelligence had predicted a landing at Leyte during the last ten days of October, but could be certain of neither the time nor the place. Thus the Commander in Chief of the Combined Fleet, Admiral Soemu Toyoda, had to wait until American ships were actually seen entering Leyte Gulf before activating the plan. He was taking a last desperate gamble – that his forces, free from air attack, could make contact with the enemy and destroy them with overwhelming gun power. The Combined Fleet would probably be destroyed. But if the Philippines were lost, and Japan cut off from her only supply of oil, the fleet would be immobilized anyway. In other words, *Sho-1* was a huge kamikaze operation.

Allied preparations for the Leyte landing began in September, immediately after the schedule was advanced by the Octagon Conference. Morotai was taken, to become a staging base for short-range fighters and light and medium bombers. Early in October, MacArthur's forces and those of the US Seventh Fleet under Admiral Thomas Kinkaid began to gather along the shores of New Guinea. The invasion group, when finally assembled, would contain 738 ships including 157 combat vessels, 420 amphibians, 73 service ships, and 84 patrol boats, as well as minesweeping and hydrographic specialist craft. Supporting the convoy was Halsey's Third Fleet – 17 carriers, six battleships, 17 cruisers, and 64 destroyers. Altogether it was the most powerful naval force ever assembled (though not as large as the force that would attack Okinawa the following April). On 10 October the minesweepers began to lead the enormous convoy away from the New Guinea coast, toward the island of Leyte.

Between 12–14 October a major air attack was launched against Formosa;

The big guns of an American battleship soften up defenses on Leyte prior to the landings.

A Japanese destroyer is sunk by a B-25. This direct hit proved fatal to most of the crew.

Admirals Oldendorf (left) and Kinkaid (center) prior to the Leyte battle.

although Japan's weakness in the air had made the giant hop from New Guinea to Leyte possible, it was still necessary to destroy what remained of her land-based air power. Vice-Admiral Marc Mitscher, Commander of Task Force 38 which was part of the Third Fleet, sent a host of planes from his nine carriers against the island. More than 200 Japanese fighters rose to meet them but, as their commander Admiral Fukudome later lamented, they were 'nothing but so many eggs thrown against the wall . . . .' More than a third were lost on 12 October alone. Overall, Task Force 38 destroyed more than 500 Japanese planes and 40 transports and other vessels. A series of raids by China-based B-29s wreaked even more havoc on the island.

During the next week Japanese air bases in Luzon, Mindanao, and the Netherlands East Indies were attacked from the air, and a naval force was sent against the Kurile Islands. There was little resistance from the Japanese, who were hoarding their planes for the 'general decisive battle' ahead.

For once the Allies had no advance knowledge of Japanese plans. MacArthur's staff discounted the idea that Japan might oppose the landings. General George Kenney, Commander of the Far East Army Air Forces considered that Leyte would be 'relatively undefended,' and on 20 October MacArthur's headquarters announced that the Japanese Navy would not use the San Bernardino or Surigao Straits because of navigational hazards and lack of space to maneuver. Admiral Halsey hoped very much that the Japanese fleet would come out and fight, but was not at all certain it would.

Events during the main landings did not dispel this view. The minesweepers had reached the entrances of Leyte Gulf on 17 October. By midday on 18 October the four islands (Dinagat, Calicoan, Suluan, and Homonhon) that mark the entrance to Leyte Gulf from the Philippine Sea had been taken by the 6th Ranger Infantry *Enterprise* under Lieutenant Colonel H A Mucci. Rear Admiral Jesse Oldendorf had moved his fire support ships into the gulf and was bombarding the southern landing beaches to cover the underwater demolition teams. Bombardments continued through the next day, while planes from three groups of escort carriers (usually known as Taffy 1, Taffy 2, and Taffy 3) commanded by Rear Admiral Thomas Sprague attacked Japanese airfields and defenses on Leyte, Mindanao, and in the Visayans.

A-Day, 20 October, dawned with perfect weather and light surf. The fire support ships began their preliminary bombardment at 0700 hours and the troops began landing on schedule at 1000 hours, meeting only light mortar fire. After the first wave had landed, the moment for which MacArthur had been waiting for two and a half years arrived. Accompanied by Sergio Osmeña, who had become President of the Philippines following the death of Manuel Quezon, the general embarked in a landing craft, got out into the water, and strode ashore. Standing on the beach, in a downpour of rain, he broadcast a message to the Philippine people: 'People of the Philippines, I have returned. By the grace of Almighty God, our forces stand again on Philippine soil – soil consecrated by the blood of our two peoples.' He urged the Filipinos to 'rally to me .... In the name of your sacred dead, strike! Let no heart be faint. Let every arm be steeled.' His words had an overwhelming impact in the Philippines and he urged Roosevelt, in a note dramatically scribbled out on the beach, to grant the Philippines independence immediately after the successful liberation campaign.

By midnight on 21 October, 132,000 men and 200,000 tons of equipment had been landed on Leyte; the airfields at Dulag and Tacloban, as well as the docking facilities in Tacloban town, were in American hands. By 22 October the amphibious portion of the operation was over. Of the hundreds of ships that had jammed the Leyte Gulf, only 28 Liberty Ships and 25 Landing Ships Medium (LSMs) and Landing Ship Tanks (LSTs) remained. On land, General Walter Krueger and the Sixth Army remained to root out the 60,000 Japanese who were still fiercely defending the island.

All this time there had been no sign of the Japanese fleet, and it looked as if the

Above: The 14-inch guns of USS Portland *barrage the Leyte shore prior to the landings.*

A Kongo Class battlecruiser, one of four modernized by the Japanese Navy between the wars. Their speed was increased from 23 to 30 knots.

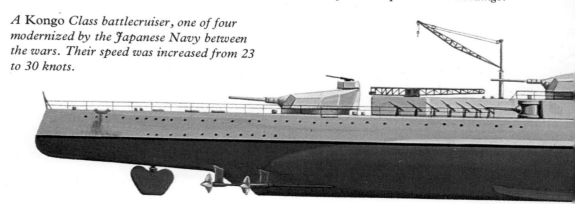

predictions of a virtually uncontested operation had come true. But in fact, Toyoda had only been informed on 17 October that the Allies were approaching Leyte Gulf, and had activated *Sho-1*. The next day Kurita's main battle force left Lingga Roads. On 20 October, after stopping for fuel at Brunei Bay in North Borneo, the force split. Kurita, with five battleships and most of the heavy cruisers, headed for the Sibuyan Sea and the San Bernardino Strait. Nishimura's Southern Force crossed the Sulu Sea heading toward the Surigao Strait, supported by two heavy cruisers, a light cruiser, and seven destroyers – all under the command of Admiral Shima. Meanwhile, Ozawa and the Northern Carrier Force had slipped out of the Inland Sea on their decoy mission.

At 0116 hours on 23 October two American submarines, *Darter* and *Dace*, who were patrolling the Palawan Passage between Palawan Island and the South China Sea, made radar contact with Kurita's Center Force. They sent off a report to Halsey, who received it gladly at 0620 hours; it was the first news he had of Center Force since it left Lingga. Twelve minutes later, *Darter* emptied her bow torpedo tubes at the heavy cruiser *Atago*, Kurita's flagship, which sank almost immediately. The two submarines managed to sink another heavy cruiser and put a third out of commission before the day had ended. Early the next morning, however, *Darter* ran hard aground in the difficult channel and had to be abandoned. Kurita, who had swum over and raised his flag in the giant battleship *Yamato*, took Center Force on into the Sibuyan Sea.

The submarine's timely warning had enabled Halsey to prepare a warm reception for Kurita, and by noon on 24 October he had deployed three of Task Force 38's fast carrier groups on a broad front: Rear Admiral Fred Sherman's group in the north, Rear Admiral Bogan's off the San Bernardino Strait, and Rear Admiral Davison's off Samar. Sherman was in the best position to damage Kurita, but before any of the groups could launch a strike, three waves of 50 to 60 Japanese planes each flew in from Luzon armed with bombs and torpedoes. Although many were shot down, one dive bomber broke through the anti-aircraft fire, escaped the Combat Air Patrol, and hit the light carrier *Princeton* which sank later that day.

Bogan and Davison were able to launch attacks, and since most of the Japanese planes were busy attacking Sherman, the Americans were able to hit Center Force hard. The great battleship *Musashi* sustained hits from 19 torpedoes and 17 bombs, and sank with most of her crew.

At 1400 hours, Kurita, his repeated requests for air cover denied, pulled the Japanese ships west to regroup and assess damages; with four battleships, six heavy cruisers, two light cruisers, and ten destroyers left, Center Force was still a formidable force. Kurita asked permission to wait until nightfall before running the San Bernardino Strait, but Toyoda ordered him straight ahead. The Battle of the Sibuyan Sea had put him seven hours behind schedule and there was already no way he could keep his dawn rendezvous in Leyte Gulf with Nishimura and the Southern Force.

Meanwhile, while Kurita was fighting in the Sibuyan Sea, Southern Force was making its own way toward Leyte Gulf. Nishimura's squadron – the battleships *Fuso* and *Yamashiro*, the heavy cruiser *Mogami*, and four destroyers – was in the

PT boats under heavy Japanese bombardment at Leyte. A Liberty ship stands at the left.

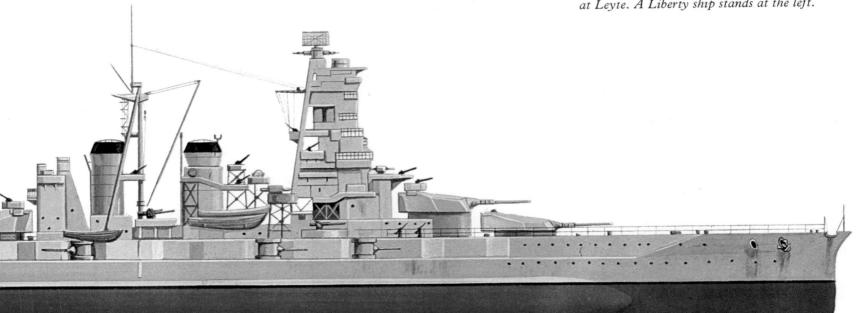

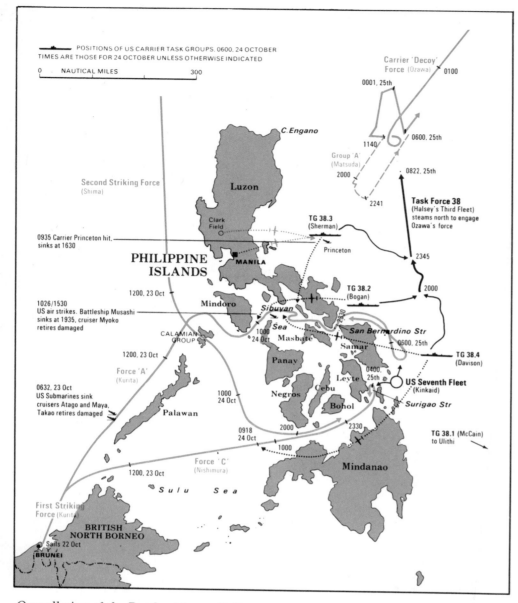

Overall view of the Battle of Leyte Gulf.

LSTs hit the beaches of Leyte once the battle at sea was won.

lead, with Shima's supporting force several hours behind. They were first sighted by planes from the carriers *Enterprise* and *Franklin* at 0905 hours on 24 October. Admiral Kinkaid of the Seventh Fleet correctly estimated that the Japanese force intended to break into the Gulf via the Surigao Strait that night, and shortly after noon had alerted every ship under his command to prepare for the attack. At 1830 hours Nishimura knew that Kurita would not be able to rendezvous as scheduled; nevertheless, when he received a message from Toyoda about an hour later directing that 'all forces will dash to the attack, trusting in divine guidance,' he pushed on toward the strait without even waiting for Shima to catch up. Without air cover, the only chance he believed he had lay in getting into the Gulf under cover of darkness.

But Kinkaid and Rear Admiral Oldendorf, who commanded the Bombardment and Fire Support Group from the heavy cruiser *Louisville*, had laid a neat trap for anyone who tried to enter the gulf that night. Six battleships, four heavy cruisers, and four light cruisers were deployed along a 15-mile battle line between Leyte and Hibusan Island, where the Surigao Strait enters Leyte Gulf. Two destroyer divisions were sent down the strait to launch torpedo attacks, a third was in readiness as a follow-up, and a fourth attended the battle line. Since there were no radar-equipped aircraft available for night reconnaissance, 39 torpedo boats patrolled the strait, with orders to report any contact with the enemy and then attack.

The first contact was reported at 2230 hours, but none of the subsequent PT boat attacks managed to do any damage. At 0300 hours on 25 October the destroyer divisions began their attacks. The Japanese were sailing in a straight line with the destroyers *Michishio*, *Asagumo*, *Shigure*, and *Yamagumo* in front, followed by *Yamashiro*, *Fuso*, and *Mogami*. The *Fuso* was hit first, dropped out of line, and began to burn and explode. The *Yamashiro* was hit twice, and all the destroyers except *Shigure* were sunk or disabled. None of the American destroyers were damaged. Nishimura, now left with only three ships – *Yamashiro*, *Mogami*, and *Shigure*, plowed straight ahead toward his objective, neither ordering evasive action nor taking any notice of his damaged ships.

The formidable American battle line (three heavy and two light cruisers on the left, one heavy and two light cruisers on

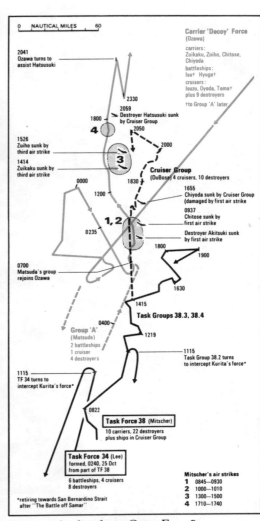

Lt Gen Walter Krueger and Vice-Admiral Thomas Kinkaid on 20 October before the landings. *The carrier battle at Cape Engaño.*

the right, and six battleships with a destroyer screen in the center) stretched across the mouth of the Strait; and as the three Japanese ships approached, Oldendorf found himself in the same position as if he were crossing the Japanese T. In other words, he could turn his ships at right angles to the approaching enemy and rake them with devastating broadsides, to which the Japanese could only reply with the forward guns. The American line opened fire at 0351 hours. *California*, *Tennessee*, and *West Virginia*, who were equipped with the new Mark 8 fire control radar, scored most of the hits. The other battleships, with the old Mark 3 radar, had trouble finding targets. In 18 minutes the American ships fired almost 300 rounds of 14-inch and 16-inch shells. The Japanese ships died slowly, and their commanders bravely carried on while their ships were blasted from beneath them.

At 0355 hours, *Mogami*, burning fiercely but still firing and launching torpedoes, reversed course and began to move south; just after 0400 hours her bridge was shelled, killing the commander and his staff and bringing the

ship to a halt. By this time, *Yamashiro*, who had also turned south, was burning brightly against the night sky. As the American battleships moved in for the kill, two torpedoes from the destroyer *Newcombe* hit and the old battleship quickly sank with Nishimura and most of the crew aboard.

Admiral Shima, following with the Second Striking Force, had intercepted messages from Nishimura as early as midnight that warned him he was in for a fight. At 0300 hours he turned north into the strait, already able to see flashes of gunfire from the battle ahead. An American PT boat patrolling the channel knocked the light cruiser *Abakuma* out of formation with a torpedo. Undaunted, Shima carried on. Half an hour later he passed the burning *Fuso* which had broken in half. He took the two hulks, which were silhouetted by their own flames, to be two ships – the *Fuso* and the *Yamashiro* – and his fears increased. Next he came upon the *Shigure*, heading south, and then *Mogami*, apparently dead in the water. The radar showed a group of American ships some six to eight miles north of *Mogami*. Shimu ordered an

attack and the *Nachi* and *Ashigara* swung over. But *Mogami* was not standing still – she was actually creeping south at about eight knots, being desperately navigated from her engine room. *Ashigara* managed to avoid a collision but the flagship *Nachi*, in the lead, collided with the *Mogami* and tore a hole in her own bow. Meanwhile Shima's four destroyers had failed to make contact with the Americans. Shima decided that to continue north would be folly, and just before 0500 hours the entire force, including the crippled *Mogami*, began to withdraw. As dawn appeared Oldendorf began a general pursuit down the strait with nearly a score of cruisers and destroyers. The *Mogami* and the destroyer *Asagumo* were sunk; the *Abakuma* went down the following day. Protection of the Leyte beach-head was still the Seventh Fleet's primary concern, however, and Oldendorf decided to break off the pursuit. Shima's remaining two heavy cruisers and two destroyers made it to safety as did *Shigure*, the only survivor of Nishima's force.

While the Battle of the Surigao Strait was going on, Admiral Kurita was cau-

General Douglas MacArthur's well-publicized return to the Philippines was only possible once the naval approaches had been secured.

tiously working his way down the 150 mile length of the San Bernardino Strait. His crews were at battle stations, the lookouts tensely straining their eyes for the first sign of the enemy – but no enemy appeared. Halsey, who believed Kurita to be in retreat, had come to the conclusion that Center Force was no longer a serious threat. He had then taken the entire Third Fleet north to chase Ozawa's decoy force, without alerting Kinkaid to Kurita's presence or leaving a single ship to patrol the San Bernardino Strait. Both Kinkaid and Nimitz, however, believed that Halsey had left a force of heavy ships to block the entrance to Leyte Gulf.

They were soon to learn otherwise. At sunrise on 25 October Kurita emerged from the strait and discovered a group of carriers dead ahead. At 0648 hours, thinking he had stumbled across Mitscher's Task Force 38, he opened fire. The crews of what was actually an escort carrier group code named Taffy 3, under

the command of Rear Admiral Sprague, were taken completely by surprise as they ate breakfast on what was to have been another routine day.

Taffy 3 was one of three elements, or units, in Rear Admiral Thomas Sprague's Task Group 77.4. Each unit consisted of four to six escort carriers or CVEs, three destroyers, and four lightly armored destroyer-escorts. Until now they had been flying routine support missions for the Leyte landings. Each carrier normally had a complement of 18 Wildcats and 12 Avengers.

They were vulnerable targets: small, slow, unarmored, and lightly gunned craft. If the handsome big carriers got most of the glory, the little escort carriers handled more of the tedious, day-to-day routine. Often called 'jeep carriers' or 'baby flattops,' they had many other names as well – of which 'bucket of bolts' is the most polite. Many crewmen insisted that CVE really stood for 'Combustible, Vulnerable, Expendable,' and

indeed the little carriers were never designed for a stand-up fight.

As the shells began to splash around his ships Sprague, a former carrier commander in the Battle of the Philippine Sea, launched whatever planes he had on board. Then the group sped off at the maximum CVE speed, sending out urgent, plain-language calls for help. Taffys 1 and 2, more than 130 miles away, launched their own planes in support. Kinkaid, who up until that time had believed the Third Fleet was covering the San Bernardino Strait, could not help – the Seventh Fleet had yet to refill its ammunition lockers after the Battle in the Surigao Strait. Halsey was much too far away to do any good; although he ordered planes from Admiral McCain's task force to assist, it would be hours before they would arrive. Taffy 3 was on its own.

The Japanese made their first mistake when, in the excitement of the moment, they believed they were seeing carriers instead of escort carriers, cruisers instead of destroyers, and destroyers instead of destroyer escorts. The second mistake came when Kurita, instead of forming a battle line with his heavy ships and sending his destroyers in for torpedo attacks, ordered General Attack. This meant every ship for itself, and threw the Japanese force into total confusion.

Sprague, faced with 'the ultimate in desperate circumstances,' formed his carriers in a rough circle surrounded by the destroyers and destroyer escorts. As the Japanese ships closed in 'with disconcerting rapidity,' he ordered a torpedo attack to divert them and turned the carriers southsouthwest to get nearer Leyte.

Although they had twice the speed, the Japanese ships were unable to close in on the escort carriers, for the tenacious defense put up by Taffy 3's planes and destroyers forced them into constant evasive action. Both planes and destroyers attacked over and over again until their ammunition was gone – and then made dry runs to divert Japanese fire from the carriers.

The bombers managed to put one heavy cruiser, *Suzuya*, out of commission early in the battle, and later sank two other cruisers. One of the destroyers, the *Johnston*, forced the heavy cruiser *Kumano* out of the fighting before being hit herself by three 14-inch and three 6-inch shells. Even when her power was gone and her engine room out she continued to fight, firing her guns manually, until three cruisers came up and blasted her until she had to be abandoned. Meanwhile the other two destroyers, *Hoel* and *Heermann*, carried on the battle. *Hoel* finally sank, having been hit 40 times.

Despite the efforts of their defenders, the American carriers were taking a pounding; the *Gambier Bay* was sunk at 0907 hours, and the *Kalinin Bay* took 13 hits from 8-inch guns. Then at 1230 hours Kurita broke off the action and began to retire; not realizing the damage his cruisers were beginning to inflict on the carriers, he had decided to reassemble his force and make another attempt to get into Leyte Gulf. Just then he learned of Southern Force's defeat in the Surigao Strait. As he turned away, 70 Avengers and Wildcats from Taffy 2 and 3 arrived and a signalman on the bridge of Sprague's flagship shouted 'Goddammit, boys, they're getting away.'

Getting away they were, and just in time – Oldendorf's battleships were waiting for them at the mouth of Leyte Gulf, while both Task Force 38 and

General MacArthur and President Sergio Osmeña of the Philippines come ashore. MacArthur walked in, not on, the water.

The biggest battleship in the world, Yamato, is struck by a bomb in Sibuyan Sea.

land-based planes were being prepared for a massive air attack. Had he not turned back Kurita would have shared Nishimura's fate. As it was, the most powerful force Japan had been able to amass since Midway had been turned back by a small, weak, relatively defenseless, but determined squadron – demonstrating the vulnerability of capital ships without air cover.

But the Taffys' troubles were not yet over. On 25 October Taffy 1 became the first American force to endure a kamikaze attack ('Divine Wind'), and later the same day Taffy 3 was attacked eight times and the *St Lo* was sunk. The kamikaze were a special air corps, organized in a last desperate attempt to make up for Japan's rapidly dwindling air power. It had become nearly impossible for a bomber to score a hit on a ship since the invention of the proximity armed fuze for anti-aircraft shells, but the sacrificial crashing of a plane into an enemy ship would have the same effect by

detonating the bombs on board and setting the fuel on fire. In addition, obsolete planes and untrained pilots could be used. Vice-Admiral Onishi of First Air Fleet had already begun training a kamikaze corps when Rear Admiral Arima attempted the first deliberate kamikaze attack against the carrier *Franklin* on 15 October, and thousands of young Japanese volunteered to sacrifice their lives for the Emperor.

Meanwhile, Halsey and the powerful Third Fleet, who had been assigned to 'cover and support' the Army and to 'destroy enemy naval and air forces in or threatening the Philippines' were somewhere off Cape Engaño. Although the first duty of a covering force in an amphibious operation is to protect the landing force, Halsey saw his primary objective as the destruction of the Japanese fleet – and indeed his orders (which he had helped draft) gave him this option.

The Northern Force under Admiral

Ozawa had left the Inland Sea on schedule, taking a course that would allow them to be seen – but not too soon. Ozawa had one heavy carrier and three light carriers with a total of only 116 planes between them, two 'hermaphrodite' carriers (battleships with cutdown superstructures to make room for a short flight deck), and a screen of three light cruisers and nine destroyers. On the morning of 24 October search planes discovered part of Task Force 38, and Ozawa sent out 76 planes to attack it. Only 29 returned. Finally, at 1540 hours, American search planes located the Japanese carrier force; the report, however, did not reach Halsey until 1700 hours.

Hearing of the sighting, the aggressive Halsey was galvanized into action – and into a critical error of judgment. Dismissing Kurita's force from his mind he ordered all 64 ships and 787 planes of the Third Fleet in pursuit of Ozawa's 17 ships and 116 planes.

At 0430 hours on the morning of 25 October Halsey launched his planes against the Japanese, who were reported to be 200 miles off Cape Engaño on Luzon. The first strike came in at 0800 hours – first the Helldivers, then the strafing Wildcats, and finally the Avengers sweeping in to release their torpedoes from 700–1000ft at ranges of 1400–1600yds. Three more major strikes followed in quick succession. Without a Combat Air Patrol, Ozawa was forced to rely on evasive tactics and anti-aircraft fire – perhaps the most deadly barrage produced by either side during the war. Nevertheless, all four carriers and a destroyer went down during these strikes.

Halsey began getting calls for help from Taffy 3 at 0820 hours, but made no real move to send assistance; he wanted to keep his entire battle force with him to clean up the Japanese 'cripples' after the air strikes and to chase the two battleship carriers. He changed his mind, however, around 1000 hours when even Nimitz began asking what he was doing and what provisions had been made to guard the San Bernardino Strait. At 1055 hours he sent one carrier group and most of the battle line south – much too late to be of any real help.

The remaining cruisers and destroyers followed Northern Force, finishing off a light cruiser and a large destroyer; but one light cruiser, the two battleship carriers, and five destroyers managed to escape. Ozawa, who was considered the ablest Japanese admiral after Yamamoto, had managed to save both Center Force

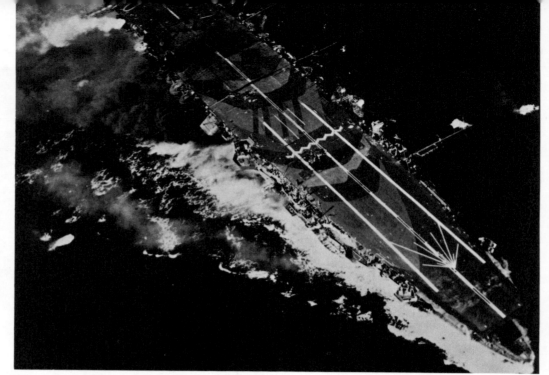

The carrier Zuiho *under attack by planes from USS* Enterprise *off Cape Engaño.*

USS St Lo *(CVE-63) explodes after having been hit by a kamikaze attack.*

'Bull' Halsey made a disastrous run northward which diverted his force from the main battle.

and Northern Force from annihilation, despite the fact that he had 'expected complete destruction' on the mission. Halsey, on the other hand, had piled error upon error. The first, of course, was rising to the bait at all. The second was failing to leave a strong force to block the strait or at least to tell Kinkaid that it was unguarded. The third was his failure to retain a sufficient force to complete the destruction of Ozawa's force at the very end.

By 26 October the battle was over. The Allies had lost a light carrier, two escort carriers, two destroyers, and a destroyer escort. The Japanese were down three battleships, one heavy carrier, three light carriers, six heavy cruisers, four light cruisers, and nine destroyers. The two high points of the battle were Oldendorf's disposition of the Seventh Fleet in the night battle in the Surigao Strait and Ozawa's execution of his decoy mission. The low points were the Allies' failure to destroy either Center Force or Northern Force, and Kurita's failure to sink all of Taffy 3, which he might have done had he been able to retain tactical control of his force and follow up his attack.

The greatest weakness on the American side was the divided command at the top. If one commander, whether MacArthur or Nimitz, had been in overall control, Halsey could not have decamped as he did without asking permission.

There are many reasons for the Japanese defeat: the overwhelming complexity of *Sho-1*; bad co-ordination between commanders; their inability, despite their bravery and competence, to alter their tactics to suit the circumstances; and perhaps most important, the lack of air power. If Leyte Gulf holds one great lesson, it is the helplessness of a modern fleet without air cover.

Leyte Gulf was the last main fleet action in history – and in view of the revolutionary changes in naval warfare, is likely to remain so. It is perhaps fitting then that it was also the last engagement of a battle line, a tactical device for naval combat that dates from the reign of James I and that was first used successfully in the Battle of Lowestoft in 1655. As Oldendorf crossed the T at the mouth of Surigao Strait the battle line went into oblivion along with the Greek phalanx, the galleys of Salamis, the Spanish pikeman, and the English longbow.

Although battleship tactics began to change early in the twentieth century with the development of the mine, torpedo, and submarine, the battleship itself remained the backbone of every navy until well into World War II. Between 1939 and 1945, however, the carrier came into its own; and by the Battle of Midway, as we have seen, it had become the dominant factor in naval warfare. For the rest of the war, battleships – at least in the American navy – were assigned support roles for carriers and amphibious landings. During the postwar period the major navies ceased building battleships altogether.

Today another technological revolution – the development of the atomic submarine and its associated, sophisticated weaponry – might well mean that the carrier is well on the way to assuming an auxiliary role alongside the battleship. Whatever happens, it is clear that a great era in naval history ended with Leyte Gulf: the last, huge, naval engagement to date.

PT-321 rescue survivors in the Surigao Strait during the Battle of Leyte Gulf, the greatest naval battle in history.

JAPAN RAIDS 1944-45

In December 1940 Secretary of the Treasury, Henry Morgenthau, presented a rather strange proposal to President Roosevelt. Despite American neutrality in the Sino-Japanese war, it was suggested that a number of B-17 bombers should be given to the Chinese leader, Chiang Kai-shek, on the understanding that they would be used to attack Tokyo. Roosevelt gave his enthusiastic support, having watched with growing concern the Japanese air raids upon Chinese cities since 1937, and Chiang Kai-shek, understandably, was delighted. Unfortunately on 22 December General George Marshall, Chief of Staff of the US Army, pointed out that there was a shortage of B-17s for his own air service and that none could be spared for the Chinese venture. Reluctantly, the plan was dropped.

Bearing this episode in mind, it might be imagined that the bombing of the Japanese homeland, with the familiar aims of destroying both civilian morale and the industrial base of the country, would have been initiated by the Americans immediately after Pearl Harbor. This was not the case. With the exception of a daring raid upon Tokyo by carrier-launched B-25 twin-engined bombers, led by Colonel James Doolittle on 18 April 1942, no American aircraft assaulted the air space of Japan until June 1944. It was not that the Americans did not want to hit the enemy homeland but that, for a wide variety of reasons, they were incapable. The story of the campaign is a classic example of the practical problems confronting even the most sophisticated nation in the organization and conduct of strategic bombing, reinforcing the lessons of both the British and American offensives against Germany. Yet, ironically, the raids against Japan, culminating in those using atomic weapons in August 1945, probably came closer to vindicating the theories of people like Douhet and Mitchell than any others before or since.

Plans for a bombing campaign against Japan bubbled just beneath the surface of American strategy throughout 1942, but foundered on the first and most persistent problem – that of geography. With the massive expansion of her Empire in the aftermath of Pearl Harbor, Japan had created an extensive buffer zone around the home islands, leaving America in possession of no territory from which existing bombers could operate. A continuation of Doolittle's idea of using carriers was impractical, for even presuming any could be spared, Japanese sea supremacy, particularly in home waters, was so secure that they would be extremely vulnerable. One possibility, suggested by Roosevelt himself, was the stationing of bombers in the eastern provinces of Russia, but Stalin, after lengthy prevarication, refused permission. This left only China – the area originally proposed in 1940 – but the practical problems were immense. To begin with, there was a complete lack of suitable airfields and an apparently insuperable problem of supply, with no Chinese ports open to traffic and the Burma Road cut by advancing Japanese armies. In addition, even if air bases were constructed there was no guarantee that Chiang Kai-shek's troops could protect them for long enough to get a bombing campaign going. Finally – and this was perhaps the overriding problem – there was no aircraft in American service with the range to carry bombs from Central China to Japan – a trip of 1500 miles. Such considerations, coupled with the pressing need to stem the Japanese tide of victory in the Pacific, prevented the planning of a bombing campaign for the first 20 months of the Far Eastern war.

But Roosevelt never gave up the idea entirely. At the Casablanca Conference in January 1943 he discussed the possibility of bombing Japan with the British, and seven months later at Quebec finally decided, in the absence of any other remotely feasible option, to launch the raids from Central China. According to the President's arguments, the problems of supply and ground protection could be solved by basing the bombers in eastern India and merely refueling them

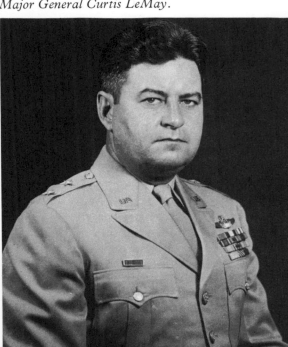

Left: The bomb-damaged drydock containing 59 two-man submarines at Kure which were never used.

at special fields around Changsha on their journeys to and from Japan, while the question of range would be answered as soon as a new bomber, the Boeing B-29 Superfortress, became available. In theory it all sounded very straightforward, but in practice the problems were only just beginning.

The first of these concerned the B-29 itself. It owed its origins to the American air expansion of 1939, when Roosevelt, worried about events in Europe, had successfully pressed for the formation of a viable strategic bombing arm. Major General Henry Arnold, Chief of the Air Corps, immediately instigated an inquiry into long-term needs, and this concluded that a 'Very Long-Range' bomber was essential. A statement of desired characteristics was drafted and sent to leading aircraft manufacturers in America, asking for designs and contract bids. When these were received in May 1940, two were chosen for prototype construction, although it was apparent that the one from Boeing was potentially the winner. It was a radical design, contemplating an enormous machine with a wing span of 141ft and a fuselage 93ft long. It was expected to enjoy a top speed of 382mph at 25,000ft, a range in excess of 7000 miles and a bomb-carrying capacity of 2000lbs, the whole being protected by ten .50in machine guns and a 20mm cannon in the tail. A wooden mock up was ready for inspection by November 1940, and the air chiefs were so impressed that six months later, before the aircraft had even been test flown, an order for 250 was put in.

Major General Curtis LeMay.

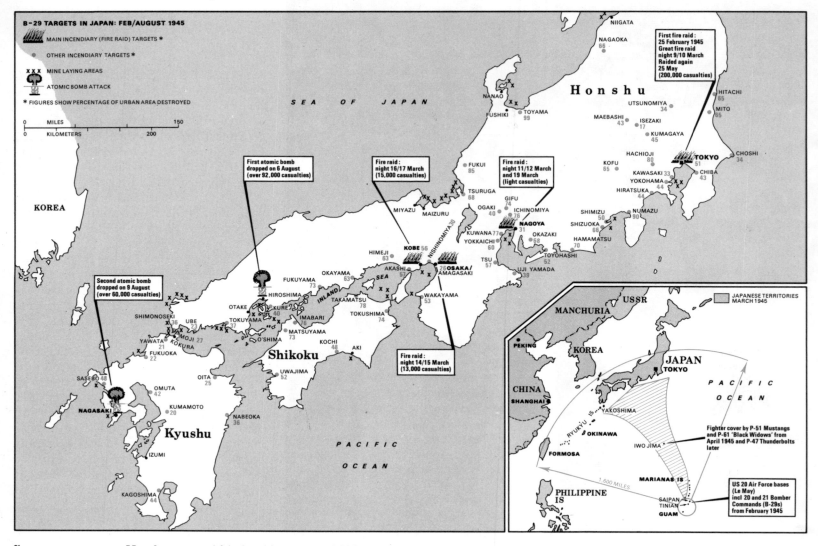

Japanese targets on Honshu came within bombing range of US planes once Saipan, Tinian and Guam were liberated.

Boeing built a completely new factory at Wichita, Kansas, and the first squadrons were confidently expected to be ready for service by late 1943. This dead line was never satisfied as delays in the development of the B-29 followed one upon the other.

The main difficulty arose because throughout the development phase the Boeing engineers were constantly breaking new technological ground. Their most persistent bugbear was weight. An aircraft of this size and potential was necessarily heavy to start with, but as new requirements arose from combat experience over Germany in 1942 and 1943, the addition of self-sealing fuel tanks and armor plating increased the weight considerably. Even after a special 'weight reduction board' had dispensed with such luxuries as soundproofing in the cabin and auxiliary crew bunks, the aircraft was still an incredible 105,000lbs, without the addition of bombs. It clearly required extremely powerful engines just to get off the ground. Four Wright R-3350 18-cylin-

der, air-cooled power packs were chosen, but they presented an entirely new range of problems. When the first prototype was eventually rolled out for testing in early September 1942 it was found that the engines were barely able to last an hour without burning up and, even after extensive modifications, it was engine failure which, on 18 February 1943, caused the second prototype to crash, killing the test pilot Eddie Allen and his entire crew of Boeing experts. This alone set the production program back by four or five months. At the same time other new design features were being constantly introduced, the most impressive of which was a novel type of armament system incorporating a small automatic computer which had the capability of correcting the guns for range, altitude, air speed and temperature, as well as a central control mechanism which enabled any gunner (except the man in the tail) to take over more than one of the five power-driven turrets. Such innovations necessitated more electrical power than the existing generators could provide, so

125 new electric motors had to be fitted to each aircraft. All this took time, until by spring 1943 it began to look as if the B-29 was never going to enter squadron service, let alone deliver bombs to Japan.

In an effort to speed the process up, the Army Air Force decided to take over the entire program itself, and on 18 April 1943 Arnold authorized the establishment of a 'B-29 Special Project' under Brigadier General Kenneth Wolfe. He was given responsibility for production, test-flights and crew training and, as commander of the newly-activated 58th Bombardment Wing, directed to prepare the B-29s for commitment to China by the end of the year. This was an impossible schedule, for by December 1943, although Wolfe was well ahead with a scheme to train 452 crews, each of 11 men, the aircraft were still not available. Only 67 of his pilots had even seen a B-29 and preliminary training was being carried out in B-17s. As a result, just before the Cairo Conference of that month, Arnold was forced to report that the bombing of Japan could not begin until mid-1944 – two and a half years after Pearl Harbor. Roosevelt was bitterly disappointed and did not disguise his anger, insisting that the first raid should be carried out no later than 1 May 1944.

But production problems at Boeing were not that easy to solve. By the beginning of 1944 only 97 B-29s had been built, and of these only 16 were flyable. The rest were at special conversion centers, undergoing yet another series of modifications. On 15 January Wolfe – now in control of 20th Bomber Command, of which the 58th Wing was only a part – had no aircraft at all ready for combat, and the new Presidential deadline looked as unattainable as the old. Once again, Arnold had to intervene, this time to sort out the troubles at the conversion centers. By taking personal charge of the whole process he managed, by force of personality, to get the planes moving at last, and in late March the first battle-worthy B-29 was handed over to Wolfe. By 15 April 150 were ready, being flown to India as soon as crews could be provided. The problems were by no means over – a number of bombers crashed *en route* because of over-heated engines, necessitating further delaying modifications – but by 8 May 148 had arrived in the Far eastern theater. They were stationed originally at Kharagpur, Chakulia, Pairdoba and Dudhkundi in eastern India, but as early as 24 April a number flew 'over the Hump' of the Himalayan foothills to the forward bases around Chengtu in Central China. Almost immediately, new problems emerged to delay the start of the offensive still further.

The first of these was supply, for despite a declared intention to make 20th Bomber Command completely self-sufficient, with its own transport element of C-46s, Wolfe soon found that he could not move sufficient stocks of fuel and bombs from India to Chengtu in time for a first raid on 1 May. Even when he stripped B-29s down and used them as transports, he was only able to deliver 1400 tons of supplies to the Chinese bases by that date, and of the 660,000 gallons of fuel needed, he had less than 400,000 on hand. He was forced to call upon the extremely hard-pressed Air Transport Command in the theater, but this merely brought him into conflict with local commanders, jealous of the official independence of the bombing squadrons. Consequently it was not until early June that a preliminary mission against railway stock at Bangkok could

An assembly line for B-29s, which were first put into action en masse against Japan.

B-24 Liberators unload their bombs over Iwo Jima in February 1945.

take place and not until 14 June that the first raid upon Japan could be launched. Seventy-five bombers were briefed to attack the iron and steel works at Yawata on the island of Kyushu, with depressing results. Seven B-29s aborted before leaving their bases because of mechanical trouble, four returned early for the same reason, three crashed on take off or landing and one came down in China. Of the remainder, 32 were forced to drop their bombs by radar because of cloud cover, 21 failed to locate the target and six jettisoned their loads indiscriminately. Little damage was inflicted.

Nevertheless, Washington was impressed, and on 16 June Wolfe was directed to send his bombers 'the length and breadth of the Japanese Empire.' He was unable to oblige. Fuel stocks in China had been virtually exhausted by just one raid and logistical problems were so bad that it was impossible to build up supplies quickly. The Washington demand was unrealistic, and Wolfe said so. In early July he was recalled to America and replaced by Major General Curtis LeMay, a man of considerable experience, having commanded a B-17 squadron in Europe. He did not arrive until 29 August, and during the intervening period Wolfe's deputy, Brigadier General La Verne Saunders, continued as best he could. Kyushu was revisited by 15 B-29s on 7 July, fuel stocks were carefully restored, and on 9 and 10 August respectively, long-range attacks were made against steel works at Anshan in Manchuria and fuel plants at Palembang in Sumatra, the latter involving a stop-over at RAF bases in Ceylon. The results, however, continued to be poor and the Japanese began to react, destroying their first four B-29s on 20 August when Yawata was revisited. It was a very slow and unsatisfactory start to what should have been a 'decisive' campaign.

When LeMay arrived, he immediately introduced a series of new tactical ideas based upon his experiences in Europe. He insisted upon adherence to the prevailing B-17 doctrine of high-altitude, precision attacks in daylight, organized the B-29 squadrons into self-defending 'box' formations, and even borrowed the British technique of 'pathfinder' crews to lead the attack and mark a suitable aiming point. These innovations certainly improved the character of the bombing as well as crew morale, but did nothing to solve the basic problem of supply. All fuel and bombs had still to be flown from India to the Chinese bases – a

Wrecked Japanese aircraft at Atsugi Field after an American air raid which devastated it.

Japanese women flee from their factory as air raid sirens warn of the approach of US bombers.

Col Paul Tibbetts and his B-29 Enola Gay, *which delivered the atomic bomb to Hiroshima.*

journey of more than 1000 miles by air which actually consumed more gasoline than was being delivered – and this made the raids upon Japan spasmodic, lacking the concentrated force which was needed to make them effective. If long-term damage was to be inflicted, more convenient bases, situated in good supply areas and, ideally, closer to Japan, had to be found. This was realized as early as 1943, before the Chinese operations had even begun, when Admiral Ernest King, US Chief of Naval Operations, recommended the seizure of the Marianas Islands 'at the earliest possible date, with the establishment of heavy bomber bases as the primary mission.' Full approval was granted at the Cairo Conference of December 1943, although time was clearly needed before the process could be fully effected. The Chengtu-based raids, despite their problems, had to be continued at least until the Marianas had been seized and airfields constructed. In the event, they were not phased out until

early 1945 having, in the final analysis, achieved little beyond the gaining of invaluable experience.

The island of Saipan in the Marianas group was invaded on 15 June 1944 and secured by 9 July, with the neighboring islands of Guam and Tinian coming under American control a month later. Work on the airfields began as quickly as possible (in the case of Saipan while fighting for possession of the island was still going on) and the first B-29 landed on 12 October, bringing in the commander of the recently-activated 21st Bomber Command, Brigadier General Hansell Jr. By 22 November more than 100 of the bombers had arrived, enabling a series of 'shake-down' missions to be flown, chiefly against tactical targets on the islands of Truk and Iwo Jima. At first, the results were poor, with inaccurate bombing and unnecessary losses, but gradually things improved. By mid-November Hansell decided that the time was ripe for a raid on Tokyo –

the first since Doolittle's visit two and a half years before. The attack was scheduled for 17 July, but the weather closed in, imposing a delay which lasted a week. The Marianas operations were beginning to bear a worrying resemblance to those from China.

This impression was reinforced as the new campaign eventually got under way. On 24 November 111 B-29s were briefed to attack the Nakajima aircraft plant at Musashi, Tokyo. Seventeen returned early with mechanical trouble, only 24 were able to pinpoint the target, six aborted the mission over Japan, dropping their bombs in the sea, one was shot down by interceptor fighters, one ditched in the Pacific on the return flight. The vast majority unloaded their bombs indiscriminately over the Japanese capital and, needless to say, the specified target was hardly touched. Nor was this an isolated incident, for the pattern was repeated in a number of similar raids and losses mounted steadily. By the end of the year it was apparent that drastic changes were required. The prevailing predilection for high altitude, precision attacks in daylight was clearly not producing the desired results: alternative tactics had to be found. As a first step in this direction, Hansell – a keen advocate of the discredited methods – was relieved on 1 January 1945 and replaced by the more experienced LeMay. He too was a believer in precision bombing, having been influenced by the theories of Billy Mitchell during the interwar period, so any new ideas had to be particularly convincing to make him change his mind. Fortunately, the seeds of doubt had been sown during the last few weeks of his command in China.

The key raid in this process of change had taken place on 18 December 1944 against the Chinese city of Hankow on the Yangtze river, captured by the Japanese in 1938 and rapidly built up into an important military center. It was not a strategic target in the theoretical sense, and LeMay initially refused to contemplate it, but after specific orders from America he agreed to co-operate with the local air commander, Major General Claire Chennault, and commit his B-29s in their normal high-altitude role. Chennault opposed these tactics, however, persuading LeMay to send his bombers in comparatively low (18,000 instead of 25,000ft), carrying incendiaries. The raid was an impressive success. Hankow was hit with over 500 tons of fire-producing bombs which gutted the docks, warehouse areas and surrounding sectors of the city. Some of the fires raged uncontrollably for three days.

The lesson was apparent: as Mitchell had pointed out as early as 1924, Far Eastern cities were highly susceptible to fire, being congested and constructed mainly of 'paper and wood or other flammable substitutes.' Precision bombing with high explosives was unnecessary and a waste of effort in such circumstances: area bombing with incendiaries would have a far greater and more immediate effect. The air leaders in America decided to try the switch as soon as news of the Hankow raid came in, issuing orders for test attacks to Hansell on 19 December. Incendiaries, including a newly-developed type containing napalm, which threw out streams of fiercely burning petroleum jelly, were hurriedly shipped out to the Marianas and reports on their use eagerly awaited. But Hansell remained unconvinced – during the time when LeMay was *en route* from China he sent 57 incendiary-

General view of the main business district of Kobe, taken in March 1946.

Supplies of gas ran dangerously short in Tokyo.

carrying B-29s to Nagoya (3 January 1945), but the results were inconclusive – and LeMay himself took some persuading. Only after heavy losses in precision attacks against Tokyo on 27 January did he agree – reluctantly – to switch to fire raids.

The first of the new-style attacks was carried out by 100 B-29s on 4 February against the city of Kobe. Sixty-nine aircraft located the target and results were good: an estimated 2,500,000 square feet of buildings were destroyed or damaged and local industry was clearly disrupted. LeMay was immediately ordered to elevate incendiary raids to top priority and given an extra wing of B-29s to make sure that maximum pressure could be exerted. Gradually, the new bombing philosophy took hold. On 25 February Tokyo was hit and one square mile of buildings destroyed, while on 4 March, on a return visit to the Nakajima plant at Musashi, the old idea of high altitude, precision attack received another blow as 159 B-29s inflicted minimal damage. In fact this particular plant became something of a test case, for after eight separate missions involving a total of 875 aircraft, little more than four percent damage could be discerned. Fire raids were obviously the answer.

Once convinced, LeMay characteristically devoted his full attention to the new idea, conceiving a major and dramatic change in tactics which involved removing all guns (except the tail) from his B-29s, loading them up with as many incendiaries as they could carry, sending them at night to bomb the target from as low as 5000ft, and guiding them in individually with special pathfinders. Tokyo was chosen as the target and the strike took place on the night of 9/10 March. It was a spectacular success. A total of 279 B-29s, led by pathfinders, arrived over the city between 1200 hours and 0200 hours, high winds fanned the fires that were started and before very long the center of Tokyo was one vast sea of flame. About 16 square miles of buildings were completely leveled and the casualties were enormous. Nearly 84,000 people were killed, 41,000 injured and over a million made homeless, all for the cost of 14 B-29s destroyed.

Thereafter, incendiary attacks were put in on a sustained level and by the end of the Far Eastern war in August 1945 the statistics of destruction made terrifying reading. At first the major industrial and populous centers of Japan – Tokyo, Nagoya, Kobe, Osaka, Yokohama and Kawasaki – were the primary targets, and by June a total of 105.6 square miles out of an aggregate 257 had been completely destroyed. Within these figures, the damage to individual cities was immense. On the night of 13/14 March 300 B-29s leveled eight square miles of Osaka, killing 13,135 people; two nights later 15,000 perished in Kobe; on 16 May 170,000 civilians in Nagoya were made homeless as four square miles of the city went up in flames; in two raids against Tokyo on 23 and 25 May, a further 18 square miles were devastated and the city temporarily paralyzed. B-29 losses were by no means light – between March and June well over 100 were destroyed on the fire-raids above – but the results could not be questioned. Indeed, so impressive were they that by mid-June LeMay was able to report his primary targets destroyed and initiate a secondary campaign against 58 smaller Japanese cities with populations less than 200,000. Beginning on 17 June, when four low altitude night attacks were launched against Kagoshima, Omuta, Hamamatsu and Yokkaichi, the process soon reached such a stage of sophistication that the B-29s were sent out on such raids every third day until the end of hostilities. This released them to carry out other campaigns against more specific targets such as oil refineries, merchant shipping and airfields, and there were even instances where a return to precision daylight attacks was both possible and effective. The main theme of the offensive remained, however, and the fire raids never lost their top priority rating. By mid-1945 21st Bomber Command appeared to be the most devastating aerial weapon yet devised.

But once again, despite the improvements in bombing techniques, the strategy of ending the war through such raids did not succeed. Japanese industry certainly suffered, particularly from a process of dispersion away from city areas, which began as early as 1944, but was still managing to produce essential items right up to the end of the war. The fact that something like 8000 aircraft had been stockpiled in the home islands to be used as a last defensive resort should the Allies invade, shows that not all the factories had been burnt out by mid-1945. Similarly, the Japanese people did not panic and civilian morale remained at an adequate, if rather stoical, level throughout the fire raids. In other words, the lessons of this offensive would appear to be the same as those of the offensive against Germany: that the mounting of a strategic bombing campaign is time consuming, costly and fraught with problems, that the bomber does not always get through to hit precision targets by daylight, necessitating a switch to night-time area bombing to counteract losses and lack of results, and that, even then, civilian panic and the destruction of the enemy's war industry does not ensue.

However, this was not the end of the story so far as the offensive against Japan was concerned, for by August 1945 the Americans were able to use an entirely new and devastating weapon – the Atomic bomb. Arnold had been told of its potential existence as early as July 1943, when he was directed to modify B-29s as delivery platforms, a process which was completed, in the utmost secrecy, by the end of the year. Tests with dummy bombs were carried out at Muroc, California, in February 1944 and five months later a special combat unit was organized under the command of Colonel Paul Tibbetts. Known as the 393rd Bombardment Squadron, it was part of a completely self-sufficient 509th Composite Wing which was to be based, again in secrecy, on the island of Tinian in the Marianas. The first of the modified B-29s left the United States in May 1945 and by July the entire Wing was in place, ready to go. It was just in time. On 16 July the scientists responsible for the Manhattan Project successfully tested the first atomic device in the New Mexican desert, the news was flashed to President Truman at the Potsdam Conference and permission immediately granted to use the weapon against Japan. From what was known of its destructive capability, an atomic explosion in an enemy city seemed sure to end the war, hopefully without the need for a costly seaborne invasion.

A mission directive was forwarded to Tibbetts on 24 July, setting the first – and, it was hoped, the only – strike for 6 August against Hiroshima, with Kokura and Nagasaki as alternative targets in case of bad weather. Problems, for once, were few, however, and at 0245 hours on the specified morning Tibbetts took off from Tinian in a B-29 nicknamed *Enola Gay*. He found the primary target in good visibility, dropping his bomb from high altitude at 0915 hours before banking sharply away to escape the blast. Within minutes a tremendous explosion, equivalent to the conventional bomb loads of 2000 B-29s, had killed 78,000 people in Hiroshima and injured a further 51,000. It completely destroyed

Left: The atomic cloud over Nagasaki.

some 48,000 buildings, damaged another 22,000 and left 176,000 people homeless. The Japanese were stunned, but because of communications problems it took time for the government to react. By 8 August the Imperial Cabinet had still not met and the Americans began to doubt the inevitability of surrender. Truman authorized a second raid, using the only other atomic bomb in existence, and on the morning of 9 August Major Charles Sweeney set out in *Bock's Car*. His primary target was Kokura, but after three abortive bombing runs in poor weather, he switched to his secondary, alternative objective, Nagasaki. At 1100 hours he released his bomb, killing 35,000 and injuring a further 60,000 of the inhabitants. The Japanese decision to surrender was taken by the Cabinet a few days later, although the clinching factor in the decision was Soviet Russia's declaration of war one day earlier.

Ignoring the tremendous moral problems involved in the two atomic attacks, the results were exactly what the inter-war theorists had always argued. An enemy power had been forced to surren-

Above: The remains of Hiroshima some time after the atomic blast which wiped out the city on 6 August 1945.

der by air action, without the need for decisive land or naval operations. Up to this point, conventional high explosives or incendiaries had lacked the degree of instantaneous destruction needed to undermine civilian morale or devastate the industrial base, but this was now provided by atomic weapons. The lessons of earlier campaigns therefore tended to be ignored and the new capability emphasized. Regardless of arguments about the inevitability of Japanese surrender because of naval and land victories in the Pacific, the lesson seemed to be that strategic bombing, using atomic bombs, could work. It was a dangerous lesson, particularly when in 1949 the Russians exploded their first atomic device and threatened America with an equal degree of urban destruction should she try to repeat the Japanese attacks against Soviet targets. Japan may have been forced to surrender in 1945, but the weapon used was soon nullified through the process of deterrence, leaving conventional bombs as the only viable alternative in a situation short of total, self-destructive war.

General MacArthur signs the surrender aboard USS Missouri *in Tokyo Bay 2 September 1945.*

DIEN BIEN PHU 1954

Among the great battles of the twentieth century, Dien Bien Phu has a very unique position. Its effects rest in its psychological achievements as the first instance of a subject Asian people defeating their European colonial masters in battle.

Before examining the battle itself attention must be paid to the background and causes behind this incident. For more than 130 years the area now referred to as Vietnam was under French Colonial rule. This reign was unbroken except for a brief time period when Indo-China, which now consists of the countries of Cambodia, Laos, and Vietnam, was occuped by the Japanese during World War II. Although many Vietnamese, particularly the Communist element within the country, fought against the Japanese, the flag of the Rising Sun brought with it two concepts which kindled the flame of nationalism in the Asian people. First, the cry of 'Asia for the Asiatic people' had been used by the Japanese throughout the 1900s, and even by some Chinese anti-colonial groups. The maxim was given great meaning by the administrations of the colonial governments who exploited their colonies' resources and alienated the population by treating the colonized people little better than slaves. The Asians, particularly the educated class, believed they could rule their own countries just as well as any European, and more importantly, they believed that it was their right. Second, the Japanese proved to all Asian people, many times over, that the white man, the Europeans and Americans, could be defeated in battle. Two prime examples were the defeats of Russia during the Russo-Japanese War at the turn of the century, and the early victories of World War II. Although Japan was ultimately defeated, the small flame of nationalism had been sparked off in many countries. With the end of World War II many Asians felt that the time was right to throw off the yoke of oppression and change their status as colonies.

In 1941 the Central Committee of the Indo-Chinese Communist Party sought the liberation of Vietnam from French domination. The leader of the movement was a young, dedicated, international Communist by the name of Nguyen Ai Quoc, who set up a political/military organization known as the Viet Minh. Although that group continued the fight against the occupying Japanese, their ultimate goal was the elimination of every aspect of foreign domination within the country and the setting up of a Democratic Republic of Vietnam. During the Japanese occupation, when a Vichy-French administration still continued in the area, the Japanese promised the Vietnamese people independence under the protection of Japan. That new country of Vietnam was to be governed by an emperor, a Japanese puppet leader by the name of Bao Dai, who established his government in the ancient capital of Hue. With the defeat of Japan many Vietnamese, especially those in the north, felt certain that the French would consider relinquishing their imperialistic grip and would help establish an independent country which would probably have the same status as the members of the British Commonwealth during that same time. As Allied troops replaced the Japanese, the French reestablished their colonial rule. Many of the Vietnamese, especially those in the south, considered this inevitable and were willing to fall in line again under the French government. For the people of the north, who supported the Viet Minh and their young leader, who had changed his name to Ho Chi Minh, control of the power strings and the right of self-determination were to become the major issues.

On 2 September 1945 the Democratic Republic of Vietnam was proclaimed by Ho Chi Minh, who called for the abdication of the puppet emperor. Within a few weeks of this event formal elections were held. The Viet Minh won most of the 400 seats in their National Assembly and Ho was proclaimed President. With Ho Chi Minh securely in power, the new government demanded the total withdrawal of the French from not only Vietnam but all of Indo-China, and the complete independence of Vietnam. During that time the Viet Minh were not only receiving support from the Chinese Communists but also from American OSS teams, who had been working constantly with Ho and his military adviser Vo Nguyen Giap. The French were having an extremely difficult time in their attempts to reestablish control, due mainly to the intervention of the Americans and Chinese. It was not until late 1945, when all the OSS teams were finally pulled out of Indo-China, that the French managed to gain control.

In 1946 the French agreed to recognize the Vietnamese Republic, but only under the stipulation that they remain in union with France, and that a referendum be held to discover if the people of both the northern and southern regions wished to be united under the Ho regime. Throughout 1946 lengthy discussion meetings took place in both Hanoi and Paris without either faction displaying a willingness to concede anything to the other. By December of that year armed conflict had broken out between the Viet Minh, also known as the 'National Front,' and the French. Most of the conflict was confined to the northern and central regions as the people of the south remained surprisingly loyal to the French. For the vast majority of observers of the Vietnam situation, whether at first or second hand, the complexity of the issues at stake seemed to be understood only by a handful of politicians representing the French or infant Republic government. Ho took his government north and centered it around the city of Hanoi, proclaiming that he was the only true representative of the will of the northern people. The French situated their colonial government in the southern city of Saigon and made preparations to destroy the rebels and secure Indo-China under French rule.

When war broke out between the two the Viet Minh had a military force of approximately 60,000. They were for the most part inexperienced in guerrilla warfare, but had received some training and were well versed in the teachings of method used by Mao Tse-tung and the Chinese Communist movement. It is virtually impossible to discuss the military arm of the Viet Minh without going into some detail about its founding father, General Vo Nguyen Giap. Although much has been written proclaiming Giap to be a military genius, he had no actual military experience prior to 1946. All of his tactics and ideas on guerrilla warfare were based on the Chinese methods. Although he is said to have been brilliant in school, and in fact was selected to study in Paris, Giap was a revolutionary at heart and seldom out of trouble with the authorities. In 1938 he decided to devote himself to the causes of communism and the independence of his country. It was through this man, who was made general of Communist armed forces by Ho Chi Minh, that one of the greatest victories, at Dien Bien Phu, would be won.

From 1946 through 1953 the French, with allied Vietnamese units, fought the Viet Minh to a stalemate. Neither side had managed to gain any substantial victory, and by 1953 the entire southern region and most of the major populated areas in central and northern Vietnam remained under French control. The Viet Minh managed to turn the rural sectors of the north, primarily those along the Song Hong (Red River) Valley and the Chinese and Laotian borders, into their strongholds. Although most of their activity was confined to the north, the Viet Minh also found sanctuary in the Mekong Delta Region and managed to carry out highly efficient guerrilla operations from those areas. Over the years Viet Minh forces received training from the Chinese along the border. With the culmination of the Korean conflict the Chinese diverted large quantities of arms and munitions, heavy vehicles, artillery, anti-aircraft weapons, and all manner of modern weaponry to enable the Viet Minh to fight more effectively against the French. By the late months of 1953 the Viet Minh had doubled their number in troops, and though French propaganda played them down as little more than backward guerrillas the truth was that they were nothing of the sort. The Viet Minh had become a well-armed, well-disciplined army based on traditional military lines, conducting an extremely effective war against their European colonial masters.

Another important event in 1953 was the French government's appointment of a new overall commander for its forces in Indo-China. General Navarre took over command from General de Lattre de Tassigny, who relinquished his command because of failing health and returned to France. General Navarre was the fourth Commander in Chief of the Indo-China situation. His three predecessors had made very little concrete progress against the Viet Minh and had

Ho Chi Minh, leader of the Viet Minh and President of North Vietnam after Dien Bien Phu.

only managed to fight their way to a stand-off which had given the French the cities and the guerrillas the countryside. Navarre decided that a new strategy was called for. One in which the French would bait Giap into a pitched standing battle, then defeat the guerrillas in a set battle. Through this action the French hoped to achieve a much needed psychological advantage which would ultimately lead them to defeat the Viet Minh.

General Navarre chose a small valley in the northwestern area of Vietnam. The valley held a tiny village which soon came to be known as Dien Bien Phu. It lay approximately 25 miles from the Laotian border, more than 150 miles west of Hanoi, and some 75 miles from the border with China. The French thought that this would definitely put them in the heart of guerrilla territory, forcing the Viet Minh to fight the French on French positions and terms.

The valley at Dien Bien Phu lay in an area which had two main seasons. From November to April winter brought cool weather and drizzling rain. From April to November the weather was sweltering and monsoon-like, and typhoons were not uncommon. The surrounding hillsides were densely covered with forest vegetation.

What prompted the French to select such a site? It was known that the Viet Minh had a headquarters in the Dien Bien Phu area, but the site was also a prime link up point for the French base of Sam Neua, in Laos, and the French garrison of Lai Chau in northern Vietnam along the Song Da (Black River). By keeping a constant bond between the three bases the French hoped to send out deep penetration patrols and engage the Viet Minh in their areas of sanctuary and refuge. Also, Dien Bien Phu would supply a much needed airfield from which the French could operate and continue to put pressure on the guerrillas. Also a garrison at Dien Bien Phu would divide the Communist support between the northwestern area and the Red River Valley. The French realized that if they were successful in tying up the main Viet Minh forces they increased the possibility of not only bringing about the defeat of the Viet Minh, but taking areas belonging to the guerrillas and making the French position much stronger after so many years of stalemate.

On 20 November 1953 more than 1800 French and Vietnamese paratroopers stood in readiness for orders to board their 67 C-47 Dakotas at Gia Lam and

French prisoners taken at Cao Bang in 1950 prior to the stabilizing of the war in 1952.

Ho Chi Minh with a group of young recruits for the Viet Minh in 1953.

Bicycles of the Viet Minh brought most of their soldiers forward to the hills of Dien Bien Phu.

Bach Mai airfields just outside Hanoi. The three paratroops battalions consisted of the 6th Colonial Parachute Battalion, under Major Bigeard; the 2nd Battalion of the Parachute Chasseurs Regiment, commanded by Major Brechignac; and the 1st Colonial Parachute Battalion, commanded by Major Jean Souquet. Not only the officers but nearly 90 percent of the force were seasoned veterans of the French/guerrilla war and World War II. As the paratroopers were forming up outside Hanoi, another C-47 flew through the early morning drizzle with three French officers on board: Lieutenant General Pierre Bodet, Brigadier General Jean Decheaux, and Brigadier General Jean Gilles. It was on these three men that the decision rested as to whether or not the parachute battalions would be dropped into the valley of Dien Bien Phu to commence Operation Castor.

By 0700 hours on the morning of 20 November as the skies began to clear, orders had been given to begin the operation. The roar of the transport aircrafts' engines reached the valley, causing thousands of peasants to stop what they were doing and stare upward in amazement as the hundreds of parachutes of men and cargo drifted toward them. Viet Minh soldiers of the 149th Regiment, on exercise in the valley, rushed to fill their defense positions. At the first drop zone, known as DZ Natasha, a Viet Minh company engaged troops of the 6th Colonials as they touched down. The skirmishing became so fierce that the parachutists were engaging the enemy while still suspended in mid-air. By the time Major Bigeard's troops actually got their feet on the ground the skirmish had turned into a fully fledged battle for the drop zone site. The French soldiers were hindered not only by the confusion of the drop and battle, but by the debris of cargo and equipment which had been dropped with them. Matters were made worse by the fact that the paratroopers were unable to locate their heavy weapons, their machine guns and mortars. Communications within the battalion were limited almost entirely to company runners as many of the radios did not survive the jump.

South of this action on DZ Simone, the 2nd Battalion of the Parachute Chasseurs Regiment landed without any serious confrontations. In any event, although those troops were not engaged by the Viet Minh, they had been scattered over such a wide area that it took several

Vietnam and Indo-China in 1954 at the time of the battle.

hours for their officers to concentrate them into a viable fighting force. By that time three companies of the 6th Colonials had pushed the Viet Minh into the village and with little support continued to drive out the guerrillas. The 1st Colonial battalion had jumped into the area by 1500 hours and formed themselves up in time to help the 6th Colonial Battalion mop up the remaining pockets of resistance. It should be noted that in spite of the fact that they were taken completely by surprise, the Viet Minh regiment not only withdrew in good order but managed to aid the villagers and help them to flee into the mountains. By early evening on 20 November the fighting was over and the French, despite early confusion and mismanagement, had suffered minimum losses with only 13 dead and 40 wounded.

On the following day two more paratroop battalions were dropped into the valley. These were the 1st Foreign Legion Parachute Battalion and the 8th Vietnamese Parachute Battalion. With them on that drop came the man who would command the entire operation at Dien Bien Phu, Brigadier General Jean Gilles. With him was a commanding officer of the parachute battalions, Lieutenant Colonel Pierre Charles Langlais, who broke his leg on the jump. During that phase of the operation the heavy equipment and supplies which were to be used in beginning the construction of the defense works were dropped in on DZ Octavie. Once again the air dropping of equipment took its toll, since many of the supplies were either destroyed on impact or scattered over the valley.

By 22 November total French forces numbered nearly 4500, and with the valley secured the task of building the defensive positions was begun. Over the

French POWs, many from French West Africa, listen to a propaganda message. They were liberated by a French convoy soon afterward.

Vietnamese troops advance against the French fortifications as the siege began.

next few months the actual battle for Dien Bien Phu would be fought. It was not a battle of men and maneuvers, but of logistics, which would set the stage for the final outcome of Operation Castor. The French, because of the site which they had been selected, were completely isolated and in enemy territory and would have to fly in all the basic necessities for the fortification and defense of Dien Bien Phu. French engineers calculated that they would need at least 36,000 tons of equipment and materiel to construct a fortification which could hold against the battering of the Viet Minh in the area. In fact, it would need to withstand the entire Viet Minh Army and provide not only a protective shield for the defenders but create an impregnable fortress from which French operations could be launched.

As the operation unfolded the French sent out large reconnaissance missions which were intended to link with Laotian troops in the mountain area of Sop Bau. Those deep penetration missions failed completely and soon the French resigned themselves to exploring no farther afield than the area around their base camp in their search for concentrations of Viet Minh forces. Although the French made every attempt to mount such patrols as often as possible, they managed to find little or no evidence of the Viet Minh in the area. They also seldom encountered the Viet Minh patrols, although they knew they were operating in the vicinity of the valley.

Giap recognized the importance of the approaching confrontation and proceeded to encase the valley with some 5500 troops. He was also aware that the French could not easily be defeated in one quick set battle, so he organized an elaborate jungle supply route to maintain his army and make preparations for a siege. Where possible Giap's plan was implemented by heavy vehicles, but a large part of the Viet Minh convoy transportation was done on pack mules and bicycles, which carried no less than 200lb of equipment and supplies with each load. These, however, were not Giap's main means of supply. He knew that even though rain might wash out the trails, and French bombers might destroy the road, nothing could stop his ultimate source of supplies. He had developed a seemingly endless human chain which dragged not only food and ammunition but artillery pieces which were eventually assembled and buried in the hillsides above the unsuspecting garrison.

Vietnamese peasants man the trenches before Dien Bien Phu as the net closed around the French.

As the siege continued the battle raged more fiercely, especially around airfields.

During the tours of the camp the French bragged that it was impossible for the Viet Minh to get artillery pieces to the tops of the hills. Should any miraculously appear no Viet Minh gun would fire more than three rounds before being destroyed. On that statement Colonel Piroth, commander of the French artillery batteries at Dien Bien Phu, staked his reputation. As the French scoffed at the idea, Giap's artillery strength climbed to the remarkable number of no less than 140 field howitzers, 50 heavy mortars, between 70 and 80 recoilless rifles, and some 36 light anti-aircraft weapons. The most amazing feat was that the Viet Minh had managed to move 12 Katyusha rocket launchers, the same type as were employed by the Russians at Stalingrad, up the mountains and into firing positions. The French on the other hand felt secure in the knowledge that the garrison had 24 150mm howitzers and four 155mm howitzers. To support this they had 30 heavy mortars whose purpose was not so much counter-battery fire as suppressive fire should the enemy attack any part of the base. French aircraft had managed to fly in ten dismantled M-24 tanks which were assembled at the garrison.

Although 36,000 tons of materiel is a large sum, it is not a phenomenal amount by post-World War II standards, until it is realized that every pound had to be carried to Dien Bien Phu via fixed wing aircraft. It was estimated that it would have taken more than 12,000 individual flights to carry the supplies in on the C-47 transports which the French had on hand. Even though the United States later sent C-119 transports to aid the French in their dilemma, logistically it

was an impossible feat to accomplish. When the actual assault occurred in the early months of 1954, and with the ultimate fall of Dien Bien Phu, the engineers would bear the brunt of the blame and be made the scapegoats by higher ranking officers in command positions attempting to clear their own names of any attachment of guilt. There is no doubt that the engineers, who received no more than 4000 tons of materiel; little better than 10 percent of what they had said was required, and of which 3000 tons was barbed wire; had done all that was within their power to make the garrison secure.

During those preparatory months not only was the construction of defenses vital, but of equal importance was France's ability to sell the idea of its intentions at Dien Bien Phu to the rest of the world. Tours to Dien Bien Phu were an almost daily occurrence. Transport aircraft, which could easily have been converted to carry larger quantities of supplies, ferried high-ranking French officers and politicians, and military and political visitors from various countries. Such military men as General John Daniel, US Army Commander in the Pacific; Malcolm McDonald, British High Commissioner; and General Spears, British Military Attaché, toured Dien Bien Phu but did not bother to question the ability of the fortress to withstand an attack. Although some questions were raised concerning the monsoon season, the French tended to ignore their climatic difficulties and moved on to the discussion of other factors. Another name on the list of 'distinguished' political figures to visit the valley was the then US Vice-President Richard Nixon, who

flew in, toured the site, and left seemingly well pleased with the French effort.

While all of this was taking place the Viet Minh were not sitting idly by. Since the first day of the airborne landing, the Viet Minh Council of War had been analyzing the situation and taking steps to augment their forces in the area to neutralize the French threat. In December the Viet Minh command decided to use the 316th Division to eliminate the Lai Chau garrison. That planned attack never really developed, as the French, in a massive four-day airlift operation, evacuated all but 2000 troops from the garrison. Those 2000, including their French officers and advisers, were forced to make the 60 mile trek to join the forces at Dien Bien Phu. What actually befell that 2000 remains unclear, but only 175 soldiers of the province militia ever arrived at the valley garrison. The remainder were said to have died in ambushes and skirmishes along the route, while many of the militia troops deserted on the march. It is curious to note that not one of the French officers survived the journey.

It was clear that in the area of logistics the French had already lost, and if bad weather or heavy anti-aircraft fire prevented the French from moving supplies the garrison forces would simply have to do without. At no time would the Viet Minh supply source be severed. Another of the main components in the overall picture which the French did not possess was a knowledge of position and target identification. It was not until Giap had opened the siege that the troops within the garrison knew exactly what they were up against. Even so, it was virtually impossible for the French to pinpoint the location of probable targets because of the way in which the Viet Minh had camouflaged their assault weapons. Obviously the opposite was true for the Viet Minh. From their positions on the hills they could easily look down into the valley and identify and get the range of any target they wished. To add to their already overwhelming advantage, the Viet Minh had detailed maps of every key position within the French fortress, including the way in which the positions were constructed, thanks to their forward observers, who had watched the engineers building the complex, months before. The last possibility never seems to have occurred to the French General Staff, and was probably the main reason for the accuracy of the suppressive fire with which the Viet Minh engaged the French.

To elude the French spotters while actual preparations were being made, a large number of dummy positions were built to mislead the French. By the time Giap was ready to initiate the attack the Viet Minh had more guns, more ammunition, better fields of fire, and a near total assessment of the defense works of Dien Bien Phu with a good estimate of the French troop strength. Even more importantly, the Viet Minh were fighting on their own territory with an eight to one superiority in manpower. That numerical superiority was further compounded by the fact that more than half of the garrison forces were composed of colonial troops from southern Vietnam, Laos, and Thailand. It had been proved many other times that such troops were easily demoralized and would often de-

Wounded French troops in February 1954 who were defending the approach points to their fortress.

French helicopter evacuates wounded men from Dien Bien Phu as the encirclement closed.

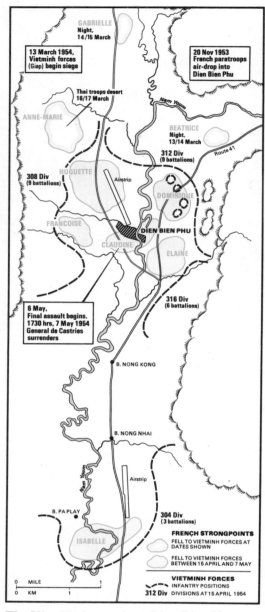

The Viet Minh attack on Dien Bien Phu.

A cache of French arms, some of them of US manufacture, taken by the Viet Minh.

sert at the earliest possible opportunity.

As the preparations of the garrison took shape there developed several key defensive positions. The largest area encompassed the village and the airstrip and contained the command post. The outer defenses were based on interlocking rings which surrounded the main area. Several fortifications were set off by themselves to be used as forward outposts from which the enemy could be engaged on the major avenues of approach into the area. The northernmost outpost was christened Gabrielle. Flanking the main compound and still to the north, Ann Marie and Beatrice formed the next line of defense. To the north, Beatrice was probably the most important as it lay on the only road into the area. The primary defense position was composed of the four interlocking areas of Huguette, Dominique, Claudine, and Eliane. These areas encircled the airstrip

and the headquarters as well as the drop zones used by the paratroopers on their initial assault. Some three miles south of the main defense sector lay one final fortified area, Isabelle. The primary function of Isabelle was not so much as an outpost of defense against the Viet Minh, but as a safety valve should anything go wrong at the main base. It guarded the pass which would allow an escape route out of the valley for the French and had a roughly constructed airstrip built along side it in the event, an air evacuation was necessary but impossible at the main base.

For the defense of Dien Bien Phu the French had finally massed a total of 6500 troops with six batteries of 105mm howitzers, one battery of 155mm howitzers, 32 heavy mortars, ten tanks, and several strike aircraft which operated out of the main airfield. Little did they realize that Giap had assembled no less than five Viet

Minh divisions, of which one was composed entirely of engineers and artillerymen, for the laying of the siege and the ultimate destruction of the French camp.

From November through February the French lost nearly a full battalion of men and officers as casualties in minor engagements and incessant enemy harassment. In spite of all 13 battalions at Dien Bien Phu being considered fully operational the troops knew that their effectiveness was diminished. To make matters worse, because of the encounters with roving bands of guerrillas in the early months of the operation, ammunition stockpiles had decreased so drastically that the main French Headquarters in Hanoi informed the commanders at the compound that because of a logistics problem ammunition was being rationed. Only a set number of rounds could be expended each day in engaging the enemy.

The situation, the restrictions and the lack of support began to harry many of the French soldiers and their colonial allies. The more seasoned troops had begun to believe that the increased enemy activity foretold a major confrontation between the French and Viet Minh in March. In spite of such concern and the feeling of uneasiness and anticipation which prevailed, none would have believed, not in their wildest dreams, what was actually happening.

By the end of the first week in March the time had come for the commands to fix a date for the long-awaited engagement. Colonel de Castries had assumed command of Dien Bien Phu from General Gilles, who had returned to Hanoi to head the entire operation. Through intelligence reports de Castries had decided that the guerrilla attack would commence around mid-March. Little did he realize that as he briefed his officers on the night of 12 March, General Giap was issuing final orders for the launching of the assault at 1700 hours the following day.

The honor of initiating the Viet Minh attack was given to two regiments of the 312th Viet Minh Division and was directed against the outpost Beatrice. Throughout 13 March reports filtered in to French Headquarters about troops movements in front of both Beatrice and Gabrielle. The French, unsure of the target of the attack, decided to adopt a wait and see attitude, which they felt would not endanger or overextend any part of their defenses.

By 1700 hours the tension in the air around the French outposts was stifling. As the minutes ticked by French troops waited for the attack. Waited and wondered when and if it was coming. By 1714 hours many French troops were almost lulled into believing that perhaps they had been mistaken about the impending attack. Little did they realize that they were one minute away from a siege which would last for 56 days.

The first artillery shells hit Beatrice, which was held by the 3rd Battalion, the 13th Demi-brigade of the French Foreign Legion. Almost immediately the 105mm artillery positions located on Beatrice were destroyed. Displaying excellent range the Viet Minh also hit the command post, killing the commander Colonel Gaucher. In the failing light guerrilla soldiers charged the defense perimeters around Beatrice. French troops hesitated for several minutes before returning fire, having been taken completely by surprise as Viet Minh

A French B-26 crashed and Viet Minh celebrate its capture.

French prisoners are marched into captivity after the last redoubts were stormed and taken.

troops sprang up less than 100 yards away from the compound.

At 2100 hours Beatrice was still holding out. Although other French batteries attempted to support the outpost, their efforts were hampered by the fact that much of Beatrice had been overrun and to fire on the enemy was to fire on their own troops as well. Shortly after midnight Beatrice went silent. The hush was broken only by French troops calling out to identify themselves as they tried to make their way into the main complex. Fewer than 200 troops survived Beatrice, having lost more than 75 percent of their battalion in only six hours.

For the French troops and their officers, Beatrice's loss came as a complete shock. No one could believe that in so short a time the guerrillas had not only overrun one of the main defense positions but had decimated a Legionnaire Battalion. As if the tension and shock of

the first major encounter were not enough, the news that the Legionnaires had been so quickly and easily defeated shook the morale of many units. Colonel de Castries notified Hanoi that the situation called for a reinforcement of troops and supplies. He also reported that due to the accuracy of the heavy guerrilla artillery fire the main airfield was closed. Those fighter bombers which were undamaged flew out of Dien Bien Phu for airstrips in Laos early in the morning of 14 March. On that same day the 5th Vietnamese Parachute Battalion was dropped in to reinforce the French position. When they arrived de Castries considered counterattacking the Viet Minh on Beatrice, but as a heavy storm was hanging over the valley and no close air support could be had, the idea was abandoned. In any case de Castries believed that Gabrielle was Giap's next objective and that it was most probably

French POWs were given only Communist literature to read during their imprisonment.

The attempted assault reached within 1000yds of the outpost before guerrilla artillery and the small arms fire from sections of the captured position ripped through the ranks. The force managed to hold on long enough for 150 of the trapped Algerians to escape to the French lines. Apprehending that it would be impossible to reclaim Gabrielle, the counterattack was called off and de Castries reported the developments to the headquarters in Hanoi.

It was almost impossible for the French command to believe that in a period of 48 hours two of the outlying strongholds at Dien Bien Phu had been lost and casualties numbered two and a half battalions killed, wounded, or missing. As if the troops under attack did not have enough problems with Giap, General Navarre in his headquarters in Saigon, and General Cogny in his newly-acquired post as commander of the operation from Hanoi, were attempting to direct the battle from their desks. In a typical French fashion they attempted to find someone on whom to blame the early defeats. The generals managed to find hundreds of scapegoats, ranging from the engineers to the photo-interpreters, from the logistics officers to the air support units, all in an effort to divert attention from their own failure. Indeed, there was an impressive list of charges to be leveled at Navarre and Cogny. They had made the disastrous error of having fallen prey to their own propaganda. For years the French military masters had preached that the guerrillas were nothing more than disorganized bandits, when the fact of the matter was that the Viet Minh were a well-equipped, well-trained fighting force. The knowledge that they, the French commanders, had selected the site for the battle only rubbed the salt into the wound.

By 15 March the morale at Dien Bien Phu had reached a point of near desperation. The feeling of the inevitability of defeat was not confined to the poorly-trained colonial troops but had filtered through the French ranks as well. On the night of 15 March, Colonel Piroth, who had seen the majority of his artillery destroyed in two days by the Viet Minh guns, which he had said would never be able to fire more than three rounds, retired to his bunker and committed suicide with a hand grenade. It was this sort of action which seemed to augur doom for all at Dien Bien Phu. Colonel de Castries was completely overwhelmed by events and his hesitation and

best to keep the troops of the 5th Battalion in reserve for any possible eventuality.

At 1800 hours on the evening of 14 March, as dusk was settling over the valley, the Viet Minh artillery began shelling Gabrielle. That outpost was defended by a battalion of Algerians and eight heavy mortars. The assault troops were of the elite 308th Viet Minh Division. Two of her best regiments, the 88th and the 165th, charged Gabrielle in an attack which could have been a carbon copy of the day before. Because of their elite status the regiments were up to full

combat strength, making the numerical odds against the forces on Gabrielle eight to one. Throughout the night the Algerians, a few Legionnaires from the mortar battery, and the Viet Minh fought hand-to-hand and bunker-to-bunker with everything from rifles to grenades to shovels. Although de Castries had prepared himself for the worst, at dawn the position was still in French hands. Hoping to make the best of the situation, de Castries decided to counterattack with two companies of Legionnaires, a battalion of Vietnamese paratroopers, and six of his ten tanks.

French POWs try their hand at chess during the long months of confinement after the battle. Most of them were repatriated by 1955.

indecision only added to the ineffectiveness of the French troops.

On 16 March more French troops were airdropped to reinforce the camp. Once again Major Bigeard's 6th Colonial Parachute Battalion, who had led the initial assault on the valley in November, were flown in to bolster the morale of the disheartened troops. On that same day, after several days of pounding from the Viet Minh artillery, the 3rd Thai Battalion, which had manned the outpost Ann Marie, deserted *en masse*, leaving the position completely unoccupied. Those troops, sensing the French defeat,

tried to regain their own villages. Those who had nowhere to go dug themselves into the banks of the Nam Noua River to await the battle's final outcome.

On 24 March de Castries realized that his indecision had endangered the lives of every man under him and he relinquished his command to Colonel Langlais, the commander of the airborne troops on the initial drop day. Although officially de Castries was still in charge, he no longer had the will to fight and thought that such a move was for the best. Langlais took the reins and with Bigeard as his adjutant the famous 'para-

chute mafia' was formed. Langlais realized the hopelessness of the situation, but he also felt that if he could formulate a good defensive plan, which would cause the Viet Minh to pay dearly for their efforts, the garrison might be saved. Aware that he could only concern himself with one issue at a time Langlais placed the control of Isabelle in the hands of Colonel Lalande, giving him a free hand in its defense.

Although things were desperate for the French, Giap had his own problems. Casualties suffered in the siege were extremely high and Giap and his Military Front Committee decided that instead of maintaining the direct attack tactics they would attempt to strangle the garrison in a slow, methodical assault which would keep losses down while maintaining the pressure. The Viet Minh went so far as to dig secret tunnels under the French position at Eliane, placing large quantities of explosives in the tunnels. Although losses were cut down, Giap saw that this approach was getting him nowhere. On the night of 30 March, after a prelude of heavy artillery fire, the 312th and 316th Divisions launched their attacks against the positions of Dominique and Eliane, which sat on a cluster of five small hills. The battle lasted for four days and was almost entirely hand-to-hand combat. Both sides lost, gained, captured and recaptured position after position. In a single day the French used more than 13,000 rounds of 105mm artillery ammunition, which took its toll on the Viet Minh and kept them from achieving their objectives. Although the French had held the onslaught, the precious ammunition used was irreplaceable and the Viet Minh were still within the compound.

Two days later Giap decided to hit the French once again and pitted the 308th Division against Huguette. There Bigeard managed to rally a force large enough to counter the guerrillas and when the action drew to a close more than 800 Viet Minh bodies hung on the barbed wire perimeter. He had managed, thanks to the persistence of his paratroopers, to take back one of the Eliane posts, and this small victory gave a boost to the French morale. Although there were several thousand French troops trapped and isolated, the Viet Minh divisions were exhausted and needed to regroup. Thus, throughout the month of

April, while the French position did not improve, Giap was forced to reorganize his forces as he realized that he would have to mount a massive attack on the French garrison, in order to eliminate it at a blow.

At 2200 hours on the night of 1 May, Giap sent orders to his divisional commanders to begin the general offensive. By that date only three days' rations remained in the garrison and the ammunition and artillery rounds were enough for perhaps one last great action. Langlais and Bigeard still hoped that they would be reinforced and resupplied before any major attack came. It was not to be.

From 1 through 6 May the Viet Minh overran position after position. With the passing of each consecutive day the perimeter shrank, but the paratroop mafia refused to surrender and somehow kept the Algerian and Vietnamese units fighting. On 6 May French aircraft attempted to give ground support to their troops but found that they were causing more casualties to their own troops than to the guerrillas. On that same day Giap used his Katyusha rocket launchers to blow up what remained of the French ammunition dump, and with its destruction the few colonial units which had maintained their positions broke ranks and ran.

There was nowhere for the French to make a stand because the Viet Minh had dug tunnels underneath the garrison positions and were exploding them with charges that had been set weeks before. Although the French had made a gallant effort Dien Bien Phu was lost. Giap had brought down the hammer in a crushing blow and at last the valley would be his. On 7 May which is considered the final day of battle, Bigeard took the last tank and attempted a counter charge with the

two remaining companies of paratroopers. By late afternoon, although the garrison never surrendered, it had been completely overrun and the battle for Dien Bien Phu was at an end. In one last effort on 8 May, troops on Isabelle attempted to make a break, but in vain.

After 56 days of siege the French and their allied forces had lost more than 2000 dead, with more than two and a half times that number wounded and missing in action. An eventual 7000 troops were captured as a result of the loss of Dien Bien Phu and of that number less than half survived the prisoner of war camps to return to their countries.

Viet Minh casualties were listed as 8000 killed and 15,000 wounded. The Viet Minh had paid dearly in manpower, but had gained a victory for the revolution. This battle had virtually assured the withdrawal of the French from Indo-China.

How and why did a situation develop whereby the French lost the battle, which they had set up as a trap to destroy the Viet Minh and end the unrest within the colony? The blame must surely rest with the mismanagement, incompetence, lack of military understanding and disregard for proven strategy and tactics on the parts of the supreme commanders of the Dien Bien Phu operation. Not only was the basic operation poorly handled, all the associated operations which were mounted in conjunction with it, were equally badly conducted. The relief effort, Operation Condor, was not only poorly managed but would never have succeeded because the orders issued were so ambiguous they would have been impossible to fulfill. At the very end, when all was lost and Operation Albatross, the planned evacuation effort, was put before the French Command for approval, it was vetoed for no other reason than it was not an honorable manner in which to conduct an army of France.

One could also point at the bad location of the fortifications, the lack of well-engineered defense works, or the absence of fire power and support, but these are all aspects of the second most important failure of the French command: bad logistics. It is one thing to promise and guarantee but it is quite another to deliver. That was the French attitude to logistics during the Dien Bien Phu operation.

Finally, it would appear that an underlying current of racism caused another major miscalculation. The French, through the propaganda of their own

A repatriation committee meets in North Vietnam to plan the evacuation of French prisoners.

military and political releases, or through a refusal to accept that a non-white race had the potential to defeat its imperial masters, displayed a blatant disregard for the capabilities of their enemy.

Dien Bien Phu allowed the victorious Viet Minh to use their supremacy to consolidate their position. They extracted every possible advantage from such a victory, while the French tried desperately to avoid a loss of face by attempting to turn a blundering defeat into an heroic defense by true soldiers of France.

Dien Bien Phu heralded the end of French colonial rule in Indo-China and foreshadowed the end of colonial rule throughout the world. While Dien Bien Phu may have been a military battle and a military defeat, it was in the streets of Paris that the final assault was mounted by a people who had grown tired of war. Dien Bien Phu stands out as a classic example of the ever-changing military and political relationship between First and Third World powers in the 20th century.

French prisoners are forced to sign a document proclaiming their loss of the battle and the war.

People of Haiphong line the streets to cheer their victorious troops who occupied the port in 1955 after the French evacuation.

TET OFFENSIVE 1968

January 1968

In a book that concerns itself with great battles, the Tet Offensive of January 1968 may seem out of place. On the whole great battles are considered to be confrontations and turning points in conflicts after which the victors go on to greater achievements and gains. On military grounds the final victors of the Tet Offensive have always been considered the American and South Vietnamese forces. General William Westmoreland, commander of United States forces, reported to President Johnson claiming 'overwhelming victory' over the North Vietnamese and Viet Cong troops after the end of the initial Communist offense. In his words it was the 'enemy's last gasp' effort, and a sign that Hanoi had decided that a continued prolonging of the war was not in its best long range interest. He made further claims that the hard-core committed Viet Cong were totally destroyed, and that from that point on the United Stated would begin to see the fruits of its labors in Southeast Asia.

Another famous US military man, General Matthew Taylor, in his memoirs *Swords and Plowshares*, published approximately four years after the Tet Offense, said that it was beyond his comprehension why the enemy committed itself to such an undertaking which he described as a suicidal venture, likening it to Hitler's last effort on the Western Front during the desperate days of the Battle of the Bulge.

A more likely appreciation is Bernard Brodie's interpretation of the Tet Offensive: although many years of struggle lay ahead, ultimate North Vietnamese victory would be achieved.

What were the objectives, both military and political, and what did North Vietnam actually stand to gain? Militarily, it seemed to be a 'much to lose-little to gain' endeavor against the forces in South Vietnam. However, politically much more was at stake. Hanoi hoped to prove once and for all that the South Vietnamese government could not pro-

tect itself without American aid and troops. A victory would also be useful as bargaining leverage at the Paris Peace Talks, which were already the target of much debate. And, of unquestionable American political significance, 1968 was a Presidential election year.

On the surface the facts of the offensive speak for themselves, but there was far more to Tet than 'order of battle.' It is highly likely that the Tet Offensive was not merely a confrontation between opposing nations on a given battlefield; more probably it was part of a loosely knit, concerted effort among several Communist Nations in the Far East, whose intentions were to force the United States to reevaluate and reconsider its ideas on US influence and involvement in the Far East. This is a controversial statement, but one which is supported by other incidents which coincided with the Tet Offensive.

The launching of the Tet Offensive itself did not come as a surprise to American and South Vietnamese Headquarters, but the magnitude of the effort did. As early as October 1967 General Vo Nguyen Giap, head of the North Vietnamese military forces, and mastermind of Dien Bien Phu, issued a statement which was construed as one of his occasional troop 'pep talks.' After eliminating the usual display of boasts predicting glorious victory from the rambling report issued from Hanoi, the following points became clear. First, there was to be a specific avoidance of any major main-force encounters with US troops in South Vietnam, except in the northernmost province of Quang Tri, I Corps, which bordered the De-Militarized Zone (DMZ). Stepped-up regional offensive actions by small units throughout the country were also intended. The key point came in a two-part segment of the statement. Giap was convinced that his campaign in the northern province would pin down US

Right: US Air Force security police repel an attack on Tan Son Nhut air base on 31 January 1968 during the Tet Offensive.

Above left: President Nixon visits Vietnam after winning the 1968 election thanks to Tet.

Below left: US Marines hit the beach near Da Nang.

Bottom left: Viet Cong insurgents are captured and herded into a helicopter.

Above: Girl guerrilla is captured by ARVN troops and is bound with the Viet Cong flag.

Above right: US troops clear a village.

forces to such an extent that he went so far as to hint that US troops would find it impossible to go to the aid of any other region of South Vietnam. This meant that for a change the North Vietnamese Army and Viet Cong could decide exactly when, where, and whom they chose to fight. The second part of that statement, when taken at face value, appeared somewhat vague. It made reference to the fact that unless North Vietnam itself were invaded, Hanoi would not require the aid of foreign troops in its military efforts. At the time this statement was taken to hint at possible Chinese involvement which was extremely unlikely.

Throughout the end of 1967 Communist losses in Viet Nam were extremely high, even though the credibility of the 'body counts' – instituted by Defense Secretary MacNamara – was not to be relied on. The body count display of enemy losses was considered an indicator for showing that American military might was accomplishing its mission. The pacification program throughout South Vietnam seemed to be working well in several provinces. Prisoners taken and Communist desertion were on the increase, and the bombing of North Vietnam appeared to be bringing Hanoi nearer to accepting the idea of the conference table. In all it projected a feeling that the end of the Communist struggle was nearing. This false sense of security was on the increase. 'False security' not because of the offensive which was to come, but owing to the lies and deceptions fostered through not only the military experts, but through the Department of Defense and parts of the Intelligence Community as well. Army Intelligence was ordered, late in 1967, to doctor its figures on the total strength of Viet Cong forces in South Vietnam, even though CIA reports indicated twice that number of troops operating in that country. This juggling of figures made the American war effort appear to be on a winning keel. Secretary MacNamara, who through some obsession believed that the war in Viet Nam could be run as a 'big business' with graphs, perpetrated the use of the 'body count.' In so doing he could claim a definite number of kills, and publicly displayed his charts in a show of real 'company productivity.' Piles upon piles of documents of deception, whose principal aim was to make the state of events look better to the American people, soon became indistinguishable, even to the military itself, from the facts. Such was the cause of American assurance of superiority, and the primary source of the shock wave which the Tet Offensive produced.

Throughout January 1968, a crucial month, both factions knew that a squaring off was in process. Within Laos the infiltration of Communist supplies and soldiers was at an all time high. Although a Christmas and Tet holiday truce was agreed upon and instituted in the South – in all but the five Northern Provinces of I Corps – everyone concerned knew that the ceasing of hostilities was only a means to gain time. Each side agreed to the truce, and respected it as long as it suited their actual needs.

On 21 January 1968 the Tet Offensive opened. Communist forces began the siege of a Marine fire-support base at Khe Sanh, six miles from the Laotian border in Quang Tri Province. This attack seemed to herald another Dien Bien Phu.

It is possible that the key to the understanding of the Tet Offensive lies here. A military victory of any proportion in South Vietnam could lead to

the toppling of the already precarious position of those in America who supported the war effort. It must be remembered that France did not lose Indo-China with the fall of Dien Bien Phu, but lost it in the streets of Paris when the tide of public opinion turned against those who would prolong the struggle. Tet was not designed primarily for the purpose of defeating the United States at Saigon, Hue, or Khe Sanh – although an all-out effort was made to secure those defeats – but in Washington and in the hearts of the American people. Disenchantment and rebellion were already beginning to burn in the US. General Giap, through Tet, merely fanned the flames.

Attention was focused around the Marine-held airstrip and fire-support base of Khe Sanh, located 14 miles south of the DMZ and approximately six miles east of the Laotian border. Khe Sanh was dug from a red clay plateau, and surrounded by hills thickly overgrown with trees and bamboo. The base itself was garrisoned by 3500 Marines with artillery support, and ringed by three Marine-held hills to the north and west of the base. To the southwest the Special Forces camp of Lang Vei sat on Route 9, the main east/west road between Laos and the coast. The importance of Khe Sanh lay in the fact that the base could and did provide both a military and artillery strike force against the infiltration and supply routes running out of North Vietnam into Laos and along the border into South Vietnam.

Khe Sanh showed all the signs of

being another Dien Bien Phu situation. It sat in a valley surrounded by hills protecting an air base; the North Vietnamese Army (NVA) had already dug in heavy artillery implacements in both the DMZ and Laos which could strike the base at will; and approximately one week prior to any actual attack the Royal Laotian border outpost of Ban Houei Sane was overrun and its 2000 defenders were killed. Those who escaped abandoned their positions, and many sought refuge at the Lang Vei Special Forces camp.

On 21 January Communist forces began a pre-dawn attack with the shelling of Khe Sanh. Casualties were light, but an ammunition supply dump and several helicopters were destroyed. During that same day, not only was Khe Sanh the scene of minor skirmishing, but probing NVA reconnaissance type engagements were centered on Lang Vei and the three Marine held hills. Because of the heavy artillery barrage, and due to the ever increasing number of Communist troops in the area, the Marine Commander at Khe Sanh decided that his forces were unable to provide the nearby village of Khe Sanh with the security needed, and ordered the evacuation of the village on the following day. Several Marine platoons fought in day long skirmishing in an attempt to keep Route 9 open between the village and the firebase in order for the villagers to reach Khe Sanh and be flown to the safety of Da Nang. As the villagers were being flown out, nearly 1500 more Marines were flown in to reinforce the garrison. Hundreds of tons

of ammunition and supplies were also
ferried into the base by Air Force cargo
planes and Army helicopters from the
bases at Quang Tri and Da Nang.

The 23 January was a long day for
those at Khe Sanh. The NVA began to
ring Khe Sanh with some 18,000 regular
combat troops, the largest single concentration of enemy forces ever massed
in that area. These troops consisted of
the 325th C and 304th NVA Divisions.
To the northeast within 15 miles of Khe
Sanh, the 320th NVA Regular Division
positioned itself around Camp Carroll
cutting the main route of overland support for which the Marines may have
hoped.

On 25 January a blanket of fog rolled
in, completely covering the western half
of Quang Tri Province and parts of Laos.
On that date Khe Sanh received its
heaviest shelling. The 152mm Soviet
heavy artillery pieces, which were deployed in the DMZ, rained down on the
garrison and airstrip in an all day bombardment. Under cover of the attack and
in the poor visibility NVA troops inched
their way forward to within 1000 yds of
the airstrip. Here they increased the
bombardment with mortar fire or dug
themselves in in the hope of gaining a
jump off point in their assault of the
firebase.

When the weather cleared the following morning, there was no doubt among
American military chiefs as to the prime
objective of the day. All Air Force combat missions, regardless of their previous
assignments, were reallocated to give
support to the growing battle area. More
than 450 missions were flown against the
enemy in that first day. Flown without
any real idea of the degree of success they
had attained. Once again enemy gunners
proved their effectiveness as many of the
aircraft had to abort their sortie due to
damage inflicted by heavy anti-aircraft
fire around their targets. In conjunction
with the air attacks, ARVN (Army of the
Republic of Viet Nam) Rangers were
flown in to reinforce the Marines in areas
that were considered weak links in the
garrison. Most of these troops were
given the order to fight to the last man if
the enemy should break through the
barbed wire perimeter. American troops
were locked in battle in their attempts to
reopen Route 9 for their own supply
purposes.

*Above right: Firemen spray foam on a fuel
storage tank after a Viet Cong mortar attack
on Tan Son Nhut base.*
Right: Aerial view of the tank after Tet.

By this time the extensive build up of North Vietnamese forces had grown to alarming proportions. Near the fire support bases of Con Thien and Gio Ilnh, which were within a 35 mile radius of Khe Sanh, the NVA 324th B Division was taking up position. By all Intelligence estimates the enemy troop strength in the area had risen to approximately 50,000, four-fifths of whom were front line regular troops.

General Westmoreland felt sure that the battle for Khe Sanh was only just beginning. Since the Lunar New Year truce was nearly upon them, he believed that that would no doubt be the time for either a continued and extensive build up, or the launching of the main attack. While the truce was still scheduled to begin on 29 February, both sides had previously stated that the truce would not be observed in the five Northern Provinces. It only remained for the US to wait for General Giap to show his hand. General Westmoreland also believed that the coming offensive would be the largest, and most likely the last, major battle of the war. He was at least partially correct.

On 30 January 1968 the Tet Offensive began in earnest. But it was not at Khe Sanh nor any of the other nearby fire bases that the main action was initiated. It was a massive attack of well organized

Top: ARVN and US troops search for guerrillas near Tan Son Nhut air base.
Right: Fire breaks out after a VC strike on Da Nang air base on 30 January 1968.

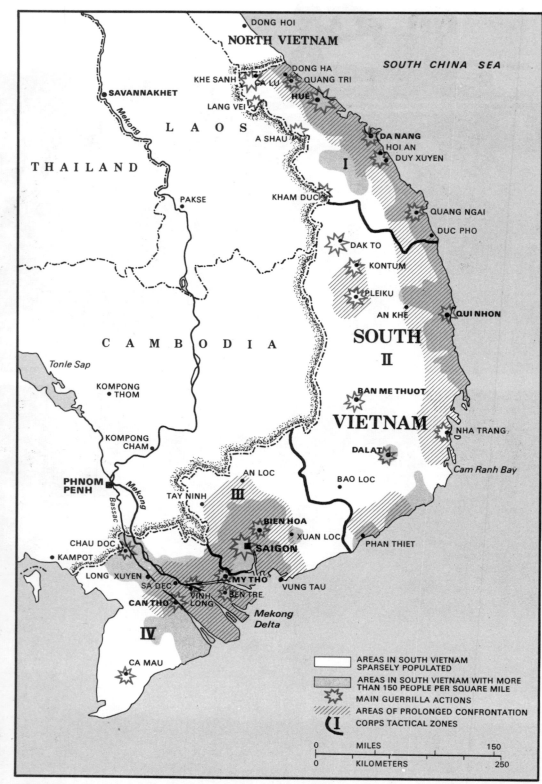

Vietnam at the time of the Tet Offensive, which took months to finally stem and destroy.

Vietnamese government, was at hand. Throughout the day the radio station urged the people of South Vietnam to rise up and throw off the yoke of oppression. Workers and students were called upon to form coalitions within the cities in support of the liberating forces, and to take charge until the battle was won and the Communist saviors were able to set up a permanent government. The VC Radio broadcasts said that an organization was to be formed which would be known as the 'Alliance of National and Peace Forces.' This organization would be a coalition of the intellectual and working classes. Only in a very small number of places were the radio broadcasts taken seriously by the South Vietnamese people. The exception was in the city of Hue, where bands of students and professors marched in support of the Communist forces. It was the failure of the South Vietnamese people to rally in support of the NVA/VC forces which surprised and in many senses defeated the Communist effort.

Numerous attacks and counterattacks could be described. However, in dealing primarily with Saigon and Hue, an overall picture and conclusion can be drawn.

At 0300 hours on 31 January, NVA/VC forces opened their attacks on Saigon, and throughout the rest of South Vietnam. Nearly 5000 troops had infiltrated Saigon during the week prior to the attack. South Vietnamese and US forces were taken totally by surprise, not so much by the actual attack itself but in the strength of the co-ordinated efforts of the attacking units. Later it was discovered that NVA/VC troops had infiltrated Saigon posing as mere visitors to the city, on their way to visit friends and relatives for the celebrations of Tet. None of the infiltrators carried weapons nor any objects which could identify them with their objective. All weapons, ammunition and rations had been smuggled into the city beforehand by the use of laundry trucks, food vendors, and even in fake funerals. Once the troops reached Saigon they were broken into units and briefed on their objectives. One soldier of the Viet Cong, captured during the offensive, told how the troops went so far as to make the necessary prefiring of their weapons during the nightly displays of fireworks which accompanied the festival.

When the actual attack began in Saigon the Vietnamese National Police seemed oblivious to the gatherings of 20 to 30 armed men in hundreds of locations

units of both the NVA and Viet Cong regular troops, which struck out against many towns in the northern and central provinces and in the region known as the Central Highlands of South Vietnam. These attacks, though in many cases beaten off, were only the preemptive assaults, foreshadowing what was to come. The true battlefronts of the Tet Offensive were in two primary areas: the capital city of Saigon and the ancient capital, Hue. Although many engage-

ments took place throughout South Vietnam, from as far north as Dong Ha in the northernmost province of Quang Tri to the small villages and towns of the Mekong Delta region, these two capitals were the keys to the Tet Offensive.

The VC chief radio station, 'Radio Liberation,' announced during this time that the long awaited 'great offensive,' which would rid the people of Viet Nam from the imperialistic forces of the United States and its puppet South

throughout the city. In some instances these troops had boldly donned their NVA uniforms. The battle went into motion with a unit of one of the NVA/VC 'suicide squads' marching to the gates of Independence Palace and there screaming for the guards to 'open the gates, for we are the liberating army.' From that moment on fighting broke out throughout the city. No one and no place was safe from the Communist attack. Jeep loads of American MPs cruising through the streets on their nightly rounds were gunned down, almost to a man. Over 700 men attacked Tan Son Nhut airstrip and poured over into the MACV compound which lay adjacent to it, hoping to destroy not only the 7th Air Force Command Center, but General Westmoreland and his Headquarters. All along the perimeter of the air base, which consisted of 150 outposts and bunkers, the Communist troops slipped past without a shot being fired, and were able to range within 1000 feet of their objective before being challenged. More than 18 different areas of the base were under heavy attack and it took nearly eight hours of bloody hand-to-hand combat between VC and US forces before the advance was finally halted. American casualties at Tan Son Nhut were extremely high, chiefly due to the fact that the only troops stationed there to counter the attack were rear-echelon support people and MPs. At one point the battle around MACV compound became so desperate that General Westmoreland moved to a windowless command room, ordering all of his Staff Officers to don their weapons and sending many to help with the sand-bagging of defense positions.

In other areas of the city Communist forces raced through the streets engaging the National Police attacking US officer and enlisted men's billets. Radio and television stations and any other targets considered essential to their cause were also strongly attacked. One suicide unit, wearing fake ARVN uniforms, grabbed a section of the Headquarters of the Vietnamese Joint General Staff. This embarrassment was later compounded by the fact that the weapons and machine guns of the guards were turned against the South Vietnamese relief forces attempting to rescue the officers trapped inside the headquarters.

One of the most bizarre events of the day was an early morning parade of VC troops, held in a section of the city and complete with songs and the waving of flags. In a pseudo-appearance of victory,

Men of the 35th Artillery, 9th Infantry Division load their 155mm howitzer in the Mekong Delta.

Hué residents search for their belongings after US Marines freed the town from Viet Cong hands.

other VC troops followed the parade running up and down the streets asking the people to give the names and whereabouts of government officials living in the area. During this same time summary courts were held by the Communists. Unarmed ARVN and American soldiers were taken from vehicles and small compounds and shot by firing squads after being 'tried and convicted' by these courts. These executions were staged for the benefit of the Vietnamese

civilians, who watched how their liberators dealt with 'the enemies of Viet Nam.'

Another major attack, was the attack on the American Embassy by 19 VC commandos. So fortress-like was the embassy that it had earned the nickname of 'Bunker's Bunker,' reflecting both the Ambassador's name and its appearance. At 0300 hours, coinciding with the initial assault, the commandos, wearing civilian clothing and red armbands, attacked the

complex with mortars and blew a hole in
the wall of the Embassy. Although Intelligence had warned of the possibility
of such an attack, only five MPs were on
duty – one more than usual. Without
going into great detail on a move by move
account, this battle can be summarized
as a bloody, hard-fought engagement
which raged for more than five and a half
hours. It was finally ended through the
personal bravery of the Marine guards
who had been virtually alone in their
struggle until at 0800 hours they were
relived by two platoons from the 101st
Airborne Division. They succeeded in
recapturing the compound, but fighting
continued as Embassy officials were
afraid of leaks in security due to areas
through which the commandos might
have passed. American soldiers were
ordered to take no prisoners and to
eliminate everyone within the compound
who was not an American. This resulted
in the deaths of two Vietnamese chauf-
feurs, 'accidentally' killed in the cross-
fire. The total number of American dead
was five.

Later that same day of 31 January,
President Nguyen Van Thieu declared
martial law. Saigon became a closed city,
and atrocities, for which this battle became infamous, were common. Aside
from those crimes perpetrated by the
NVA/VC in the streets and at their court
martials, one of the most widely remembered acts of that first day's fighting
was the street execution of a captured VC
soldier by the Chief of the Saigon Police.
This execution brought heated outcries
from the US Command, not for humani-
tarian reasons, but in fear of more re-
prisals against American troops by the
NVA/VC. As the years have passed it is
this 'atrocity' which has been remembered, and only because Police Chief
Nguyen Ngoc Loan carried out the execution in front of a press photographer
who recorded the entire event on film.

By 1 February Saigon was in total
upheaval. Entire blocks of buildings
burned, while in other parts of the city
the sounds of machine gun and rifle fire
were drowned out by the noise of fighter
aircraft attempting to dislodge Communist troops who held fast to their
recently gained positions. After the dust
of the initial assault had settled, American and South Vietnamese forces had a
fairly good idea where the majority of
Communist forces were located; the Saigon suburb of Cholon. The area had a
history of being anti-government, due
principally to its large Chinese population and the instigations of its Buddhist

Smoke rises from a devastated fuel dump after a mortar attack on Khe Sanh in March 1968.

priests, who were in constant disagreement with the government. The VC
established a headquarters at the Buddhist Pagoda of An Quang, and it was in
Cholon that the American and South
Vietnamese forces met with their stiffest
resistance.

American Headquarters assumed
command of the Saigon defense at this
time, and for the first time US combat
forces were brought into the city itself to
bolster the ARVN ranks. From 2–5
February a see-saw state prevailed as
ARVN and US support troops eliminated pockets of Communist resistance,
only to have them spring up in another
area then return to the 'cleared' sectors
while US and ARVN troops were busy
elsewhere. Tan Son Nhut airbase was
again hit in a running battle which lasted
nearly 36 hours. American troops, who
had helped the ARVN forces eliminate
the Communists within the city proper,
then turned to concentrate their efforts
on the suburbs. This was the primary
area where NVA/VC resistance had to be
quelled before any stabilization could
take place. Over 1600 regular NVA
troops controlled entire blocks of Cholon, and it was actually from 7 February,
through the Communist counteroffensive of 18 February, until 23 of the
month that fighting continued in that
area.

One significant event occurred on 13

February. American B-52 bombers flew
against targets within ten miles of Saigon, the closest they had ever approached the capital city in the entire
war. It demonstrated the enemy's elusive
nature as Intelligence reports claimed 42
deaths as a result of the raids, none of
whom they could positively identify as
Communist troops.

On 18 February with the counteroffensive getting under way, Communist
forces struck out from the Cholon suburb, killing seven National Policemen
and leaving countless others wounded.
Tan Son Nhut air base was once again
attacked and bombed, but ground fighting never moved within the perimeter of
the base.

The overall offensive had begun to
lose impetus. Even though on 20 February US Intelligence sources reported
that no less than three NVA Divisions
were located around Saigon, the battle
for the city itself was rapidly drawing to a
close. There were still a few desperate
attempts to move against the city from
Cholon, but on 23 February American
and South Vietnamese commanders
stated that the NVA/VC forces who had
entered Saigon were effectively overcome. While skirmishing continued on
the outskirts of the city, the battle itself
was over.

There was another prime target
against which the Communist forces

Fire support defends an American outpost near the Cambodian border in December 1968.

moved in their Tet Offensive, and one to which they attached special significance: the battle for the city of Hue. This was the ancient capital of Viet Nam, and as such held special meaning for the people. It was here in the old imperial city that many believed the seat of power should have remained. Hue had a predominantly Buddhist population whose agitation in 1963 had led to the overthrow of Diem, and it had continued to be the seat of student dissidence, religious separatism, and anti-American sentiments in South Vietnam. This city, as can be seen by the intensity of the battle which took place, was probably the most crucial confrontation between the ideologies of the North and South within Viet Nam.

The battle for Hue began on the same timetable as had the Saigon attack. At 0300 hours, 31 January, NVA/VC troops entered the city and within a matter of hours had completely overrun all their military and political objectives except for the Headquarters of the Third ARVN Division. In their preliminary action the VC released more than 2000 political prisoners and 400 of their own troops from the jails of Hue, seized the Citadel surrounding the ancient city which sat on the bank of the Perfume (Huong) River, and raised their flag above its battlements. Hue was the most successful of the Tet attacks, and within hours militants, mainly students and

C-7A transport delivers supplies to Tra Bong.

professors, were rallying to the support of the 'Liberators' and moving throughout the city calling for support against the corrupt government of Saigon. Although it seemed that the tide was moving in favor of the Communist effort, the massive public support and collaboration which they believed would greet their advance never materialized. Those who could not flee attempted to barricade themselves in to await the counterattacks which they knew the US and South Vietnamese armies would soon launch.

Later that same day South Vietnamese forces and several US Marine companies with tank support closed in on the city from all sides. Their main objective was the rescuing of a US Military Advisor unit trapped within the city. Once that mission was accomplished the combined forces turned to the problem at hand; the immediate recapture of Hue. After several days of fighting, ARVN I Corps Commander Lieutenant General Lam and Marine Commander, Lieutenant General Robert Cushman made the decision for an all out attack campaign, realizing at the same time that this action could mean the destruction of many of the ancient historical and religious landmarks within the city. General Westmoreland, in Saigon, believed that Hue was crucial to the enemy's plans of cutting supply lines and tying up American troops before the main attack against Khe Sanh, and it was as a result of his orders for the immediate recapture of Hue that the decision for an unrestrained attack was made.

By 3 February much of Hue had been destroyed, as both US and South Vietnamese fighter aircraft dropped tons of bombs in their attempts to dislodge the VC from their stranglehold on the city. On the ground US and ARVN troops found it no easy task to bring the enemy to grips. They found themselves battling desperately in house-to-house melee, the conclusion of which was the recapture of only a few blocks of city at extremely high cost. The 5 February saw US forces making an attempt to create a breach in the walls of the Citadel, which was in most places 20 feet high and more than 14 feet thick, but with no success. On 7 February the main bridge across the Perfume River, which American and ARVN troops had struggled to keep open, was blown by the VC in a desperate attempt to keep it from falling into the hands of the Americans. It was not until four days later that the US forces managed to cross the river by means of

ARVN soldiers man their machine gun 25 miles northwest of Saigon.

ARVN trooper gets a lift after an injury.

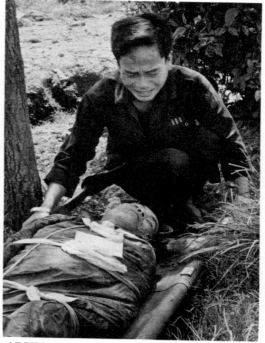

ARVN trooper cries over a friend's body.

assault craft and with the aid of helicopter 'gun ships.' At the same time other American forces took up positions at the northwest corner of the Citadel hoping to trap the enemy forces.

From 11–15 February South Vietnamese forces struggled forward and managed to recapture a few more blocks of the city as American jets pounded Hue into almost total ruin. The fighting within the city was described by one

Marine commander as the worst fighting that Marines had encountered since the battle for Seoul, Korea in the 1950s. The ability and the means to move troops forward during this time was such a problem that it was not uncommon for South Vietnamese officers to commandeer small buses and motorcycles to get themselves and their troops up to the front lines. The most agonizing aspect of the battle was seen not just in the fighting, but in the wholesale destruction of city and population. By 15 February it was not uncommon to see or smell the rotting bodies of not only soldiers, but civilians strewn throughout the streets. As one correspondent summed it up, 'in this once beautiful city a nightmare now exists.' As indeed it did. The bodies of soldiers, men, women and children lay in tangled heaps under the rubble while the rats gnawed at the rotten and blackened flesh. In the destruction of Hue it must have seemed that only the rats would survive.

The troops tried desperately for several days to outflank the enemy, but it was a futile attempt. By 20 February American forces engaged at the Citadel were at one-half combat strength. Combat aircraft were dropping a torrent of rockets and napalm as ground troops began the extended use of sprays containing noxious gasses in the hopes of dislodging the VC. During that same time American and ARVN troops were not alone in their need for reinforcement. All around the Citadel, pockets of enemy reinforcements were being frustrated in their attempts to relieve their comrades. Several were found attempting to dig their way under the wall of the Citadel in their efforts.

On 21 February the battle finally broke in favor of the US and ARVN forces. The bad weather, which had hampered combat aircraft for more than a week in their bombing attempts, lifted and they were able to give more accurate and effective support for the ground troops. With bombs, napalm, rockets, and gas they began to press the VC defenders back. By 22 February the Viet Cong held only the southwest corner of the Citadel, and in the days that followed those pockets of resistance were methodically eliminated. With the coming of night on 24 February there were only a few places within the city where the sounds of gunfire could still be heard. Under the cover of darkness those Communist troops who were still able attempted to melt away and slip out of the city.

The battle for Hue was officially considered to have ended on 25 February. As both sides lay back to lick their wounds, and the South Vietnamese struggled to establish some kind of order, both American and Communist sources gave reports on the battle situation and their losses. The United States claimed 119 Americans, 363 ARVN troops and 4000 enemy troops killed. The Communists reported that

Three VC dead displayed on a road near Saigon.

their own losses were 3000 while there were nearly 1000 Americans and 1200 South Vietnamese troops killed. Hanoi Radio, which could not miss such an opportunity for propaganda, broadcast to the world that over 12,000 Americans and ARVNs were either killed or wounded. Only by gathering together all the families who were notified, or whose sons and husbands were never again heard from, could an accurate death toll be known. Whatever the true number of casualties, one fact of the battle for Hue remains. Not only was that beautiful ancient city destroyed, but the battle made homeless refugees of more than 100,000 Vietnamese civilians. Atrocities were not confined to the battlefield. After the battle ended mass graves were found containing the bodies of nearly 1000 civilians, shot or beheaded and chained together. These were the victims of the VC, people said to have been political enemies to the cause of liberation.

Throughout all of South Vietnam during Tet countless other towns were attacked. These included the major towns of Da Nang, where fighting only lasted for several days, Quang Tri, Qui Nhon, Nha Trang, Pleiku, and Kontum. In all of these towns and hundreds like them the situation was much the same. Either the town was overrun or the military and political headquarters within the towns were the object of the attack.

In almost every case the towns were recaptured within the first week of the offensive. When the Communists' initial offensive and their counteroffense of 18 February were finally over, hundreds of thousands of South Vietnamese people were homeless; thousands were dead. Although soldiers and civilians alike realized that the massive Communist offensive had run its course, the end of the war seemed to have moved farther from their grasp.

To the astonishment of many the Tet Offensive was indeed over. The major offense which had been foretold by Giap in his October 1967 speech reached its conclusion. General Westmoreland and his staff still believed that a strong drive was yet to be made against Khe Sanh. The Special Forces base at Lang Vei was the only section of the Khe Sanh defenses to be overrun during the course of the Tet Offensive in the rest of South Vietnam. The actual battle for Khe Sanh did not take place until the following months of March and April. It was not the battle which many feared it would be, nor was it a Dien Bien Phu for the United States.

What then had Tet truly accomplished? First and foremost it showed that the so-called progress of the South Vietnamese government in their efforts of pacification (that is the gaining of confidence, support and allegiance) and control in the interior of South Vietnam had in fact been unsuccessful. In the first days of Tet Communist forces seized these areas without the slightest show of resistance. The loss of the interior forced both the US and South Vietnamese governments to review the methods of their programs in these areas. Another major problem stemmed from the enemy's ability to mass troops and strike almost at will within South Vietnam. The enormous numbers of Communist troops which were set against targets during the offensive astonished commanders because of the number reported dead in the previous year. Such was the false sense of security which the body count program brought. Many had honestly believed that it was beyond the North's capability to mass such forces.

During the 27 days that the Tet Offensive lasted the South Vietnamese lost more than 100 soldiers per day this in addition to 8000 wounded and 500 missing in action. The US and other troops suffered similar losses with 1500 killed and 7000 wounded. The worst fact was that the war had truly been brought to the people. More than 7000 civilians were killed in less than four weeks and nearly three-quarters of a million were homeless. For their own protection these civilians were resettled near the large populated areas, but it was in those resettlement camps that the civilian death toll rose through disease and epidemics. Thirteen of the 44 provinces of South Vietnam were so badly disrupted and affected by Tet that the pacification program was set back to its very beginnings. In addition it would take nearly six months to get the program working again in another 16 provinces. It was the necessity of beginning the re-pacification and relocation programs which caused the South Vietnamese government to adopt a new policy of rebuilding the ruins of Tet, rather than, as they had hoped, the building of a nation for the future.

This is not to say that the Communists walked away unscathed. Their losses were staggering at nearly 40,000 dead or wounded. In the vast majority of areas held by ARVN troops the Communists made no headway whatsoever due to the ARVN's determination to fight rather than desert their positions, as had once been their tendency. There was also poor communication and lack of co-operation in many areas between the NVA and VC forces. A crucial complication for the Communist cause was the disillusionment of many within the ranks of the

Above: Defoliation exposed this Vietcong control site which was destroyed by the US.

Below: USS Bennington *was a safe haven for naval aircraft off the Vietnamese coast.*

Above right: Flares dropped from an AC-47 expose a VC position outside Saigon.

Right: ARVN troops move their tank up to Quang Tri after the Tet Offensive.

Viet Cong due to the failure of the people to rise up in support of the 'liberation.' The Communist forces had truly expected, and had based much of their thinking and tactics on the belief that the South Vietnamese would promote their cause. Finally, and of major importance to the future, was the Communists' loss of experienced personnel, sacrificed in suicidal missions throughout the country.

Varying viewpoints and conclusions have been drawn when the final results of Tet were examined. Some have said that the weeks of battle resulted in stalemate, for although the Americans and South Vietnamese held the populated areas much of the interior was in the hands of the NVA/VC. Others claim that Tet was an overwhelming victory for the US and its allies, in that the most powerful Communist offense since Dien Bien Phu had been repelled and ARVN forces had

proven that they could and would fight to hold their own. The Communists had played their trump card, sacrificed all, and still they had completely failed to crush the South Vietnamese and their supporters.

Although these points can be argued and substantiated, when looking at Tet as an overall picture and in reference to the war years that followed, the accomplishments of the NVA/VC would affect the foreign policy of its adversaries in the years to come. Because of Tet and the *Pueblo* incident in Korea American military and political leaders began to re-evaluate the position of the United States in the Far East. The American people were suddenly made agonizingly aware of the war in Viet Nam, and though demonstrations and riots against the war had taken place prior to Tet, the sea of unrest grew stronger after that point in time. It was in those days after the Tet

Offensive that Americans began to question whether the lives lost, or world opinion, justified the presence of the United States in Viet Nam. It should be remembered that in the 1968 Presidential elections, the theme which put Richard Nixon into the White House was one of finding a means to wind down the war in Viet Nam and withdrawing from Southeast Asia as gracefully as possible.

Tet and its strategic importance as a decisive battle rests not on the battlefields of South Vietnam, but on the effect it had on a nation as mighty as the United States dividing its people, and laying the groundwork for the eventual withdrawal, in haste and disillusion, of the American Armed Forces.

Below: A Vietcong guerrilla is interrogated following a raid by an US corpsman and his interpreter.

Above: Men of the 25th Infantry Regiment return to fire support base Jamie.

Left: ARVN troops return with the body of a comrade killed near the Cambodian frontier.

Below: ARVN general executes a Viet Cong officer in civilian clothes during Tet.

NORTH VIETNAM RAIDS 1965-73

The apparent success of the atomic strikes in August 1945 had dramatic and far-reaching ramifications so far as American air power was concerned. To begin with, it produced the result that Billy Mitchell had been campaigning for in the 1920s and 1930s – an independent air force. In 1946 an autonomous US Air Force was established, owing its *raison d'être* almost entirely to a special Strategic Air Command (SAC) under General LeMay, charged with the task of mounting atomic attacks in the event of a future war. This was all very well so long as the Americans possessed a monopoly of atomic weapons, but as soon as any potential enemy acquired a similar capability of guaranteed mass destruction, SAC became a little superfluous except as a deterrent or as a last resort. This was seen to good effect during the Korean War (1950–53) when the Americans, although undoubtedly capable of destroying North Korea and the bases in southern China merely by committing LeMay's B-29s, were restrained by a fear that such actions might cause the Russians and/or the Communist Chinese to enter the conflict, escalating it into a war of cataclysmic proportions. The new air force was therefore kept closely in check, with limitations upon targets, areas of attack and types of attack being strictly imposed by American political leaders. It was a new kind of conflict – soon to be called Limited War – into which the strategic use of air power in the World War II sense did not, and could not enter. The Americans were to experience a similar need for restraint during their long and bitter involvement in Vietnam.

American interest in the political stability of Indo-China (Vietnam) dated back to early 1950 when the French, embroiled in a guerrilla war which they were finding increasingly difficult to fight, requested military and economic assistance. President Truman's administration evaluated the situation and, through National Security Council Memorandum 64 on 27 February, laid down the bases of what later became known as

the 'Domino Theory.' It was decided that 'all practicable measures (should) be taken to prevent further Communist expansion in Southeast Asia,' for since Mao Tse-tung's success in China the previous year it was felt that other states in the area would progressively follow suit. As Ho Chi Minh's Viet Minh guerrillas in Vietnam seemed the most active Communist fighters, they had to be stopped first, otherwise Vietnam would be merely a prelude to the fall of Laos, Cambodia, Thailand and Burma. This line of argument was gradually to involve the Americans in Southeast Asia, beginning in the early 1950s as aid was given first to the French and then, after their defeat in 1954 and the division of Vietnam along the 17th parallel, to the South Vietnamese under President Ngo Dinh Diem. Much of this aid took the form of air power, and as American aircraft were provided to the French or South Vietnamese air forces, USAF personnel went with them.

At first, in the absence of North Vietnamese aggression the American advisers kept a fairly low profile, but after the Central Committee of the North Vietnamese Workers' party declare its intention to unify Vietnam by force in May 1959, the situation gradually began to change. Guerrilla forces, using the Ho Chi Minh trail through Laos and Cambodia, infiltrated the South and began operations, ambushing Diem's forces and cutting strategic highways around Saigon. The South Vietnamese armed forces were weak and badly organized, forcing the Americans to provide overall plans and command techniques for the defeat of what seemed to be a full-scale insurgency, directed from Hanoi. The newly-inaugurated President Kennedy authorized increased military assistance in 1961, including the commitment of part of the 4400 Combat Crew Training Squadron USAF (code named Farm Gate), ostensibly to familiarize South Vietnamese pilots in the use of the T-28 trainer aircraft. By February 1962 American Farm Gate crews were flying combat missions, including the first de-

Left: Side view of a Lockheed T-33 at Eglin AFB Florida prior to its use over Vietnam.

Below left: B-52 releases its bombs over North Vietnam.

foliant strikes designed to destroy jungle cover for the Viet Cong guerrillas.

American planning aid culminated in the National Campaign Plan of fall 1962, whereby the guerrillas were to be driven back and defeated in three combat phases by South Vietnamese forces. The process began in January 1963, but ran into immediate problems, caused chiefly by a lack of adequate air cover which, in certain desperate situations could only be rectified by USAF commitment. Things got worse as 1963 progressed, for political troubles in Saigon – troubles that were to lead to Diem's overthrow and death in a military-inspired coup in November – affected South Vietnamese moral and allowed the Viet Cong to score a series of victories, the full effects of which could be kept in check only by further American air strikes. By early 1964, when General William Westmoreland arrived in Saigon as new head of the American Military Assistance Command Vietnam (MACV), things had deteriorated to such an extent that his first reaction was to ask for increased USAF commitment, including the provision of B-57 Canberra light bombers. Secretary of Defense, Robert McNamara, intent upon a policy of early withdrawal from Southeast Asia, refused permission, but within eight months was forced to change his mind. On 2 August 1964 North Vietnamese gunboats attacked the US destroyer *Maddox* in the Gulf of Tonkin. President Johnson reacted by ordering retaliatory air strikes upon coastal bases and oil storage facilities in North Vietnam on 5 August, and two days later Congress, in the 'Gulf of Tonkin resolution,' authorized him to use ... all measures – including the commitment of armed forces – to assist the South Vietnamese. The movement of two B-57 squadrons to Bien Hoa and F-100 and F-102 squadrons to Da Nang indicated that air power was to play a major role.

The retaliatory air strikes of August 1964 were followed by a number of small raids on 2 December, when USAF and Navy planes hit North Vietnamese lines of communication being used to support the Viet Cong in the South, but sustained attacks north of the Demilitarized Zone (DMZ) on the 17th parallel did not begin until early 1965. The Americans

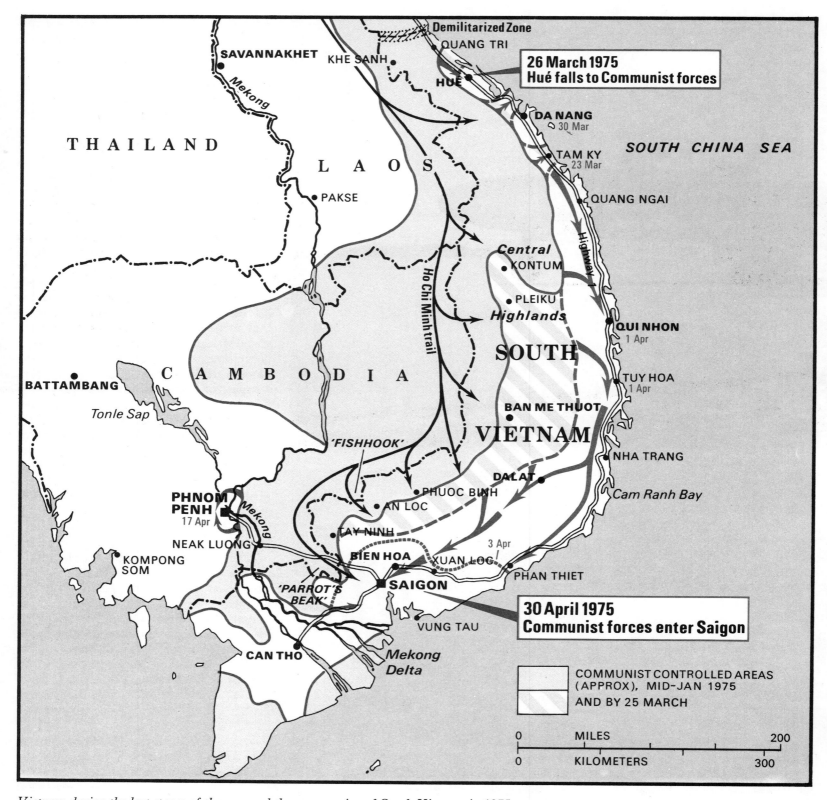

**26 March 1975
Hué falls to Communist forces**

**30 April 1975
Communist forces enter Saigon**

COMMUNIST CONTROLLED AREAS
(APPROX), MID-JAN 1975

AND BY 25 MARCH

Vietnam during the last stages of the war and the overrunning of South Vietnam in 1975.

were understandably wary about beginning an air offensive against another sovereign state, particularly when that state had powerful allies in the Communist world, and this led to stringent controls being strictly imposed. At first, in the Flaming Dart operations of February 1965 – mounted in response to Viet Cong attacks upon Pleiku and Qui Nhon – American pilots were briefed to hit military installations only and to make

sure that no civilians were killed, even if this meant aborting the mission. A 19-day bombing pause then ensued, partly to see what reaction the North Vietnamese would make (they made none) and partly to lay down definite guidelines for the future. When the raids began again on 2 March, with F-105s and B-57s hitting ammunition dumps at Xom Bong about 35 miles north of the DMZ, they went under the code name

Rolling Thunder – a name which was to persist until the end of the first bombing phase in 1968.

Rolling Thunder operations had three basic aims. First, it was hoped they would impede North Vietnamese infiltration into the South by hitting supply lines, bridges and rear areas north of the DMZ: a campaign of pure interdiction. Second, it was hoped that raids upon the enemy would help raise morale of the South Vietnamese, suffering under a succession of ineffective governments which did not end until June 1965, when the Armed Forces Council installed Major General Nguyen Van Thieu as Chief of State. Finally, and perhaps most importantly, it was intended to impose a penalty upon Hanoi for its continued support of aggression in the South, it being argued that if lines of communication, supply dumps and war-supporting facilities were hit hard enough, the North Vietnamese would be forced either to withdraw or to agree to some kind of peace settlement. This final aim was the closest the Americans came to strategic bombing in the traditional sense and in fact, in practical terms, their offensive bore little resemblance to any of World War II. Political restraints effectively prevented a concentrated use of air power over the North. Certain areas, chiefly around the populous centers of Hanoi and Haiphong, as well as a buffer zone near the Chinese border, were officially termed 'sanctuaries' into which no raids could be mounted; targets were carefully controlled, often by the White House itself; and selected portions of the North Vietnamese war effort, including port facilities and, initially, air defense systems, were not allowed to be touched. This made the planning and execution of raids extremely difficult and frustrating, particularly when Soviet or east European ships could be seen quite openly offloading war material in Haiphong harbor, but was a manifestation of the news and difficult art of limited war.

The initial Rolling Thunder operations in 1965 were carried out by the 2nd Air Division under Lieutenant General Joseph Moore, stationed at bases in South Vietnam and Thailand, as well as naval aircraft from carriers of the 7th Fleet in the Gulf of Tonkin. The principal aircraft in use was the F-105 Thunderchief, a machine which had been mass produced in the 1950s for tactical strike but was not much good as a fighter. This necessitated the provision of fighter cover, and from May 1965 the F-4 Phantom took this role, gradually extending it to include strike missions. Later, in 1968, the new swing-wing F-111 fighter was based for a time in Thailand, but was never a central feature of the Rolling Thunder operations. The same was true of a number of more obsolete designs, including the F-100 Super Sabre, and B-57 Canberra: both were used at some time over the North, but neither was of central importance.

President Nixon meets with Admiral John McCain, US C in C Pacific Fleet, and Henry Kissinger.

Super Sabres (F-100s) drop their bombs on Vietcong targets in the demilitarized zone in 1965.

This, more than anything else, emphasizes the primarily tactical nature of the campaign, and this is reinforced when it is realized that the B-52 Stratofortress – the main weapon of SAC – was actively restrained from mounting attacks upon strategic targets, being kept well away from the Hanoi-Haiphong area throughout the period of Rolling Thunder. In fact whenever the B-52s from Guam or Thailand were committed north of the DMZ, as in April 1966 when they hit the Mu Gia pass on the Ho Chi Minh trail, they operated under a different command structure and the code name Arc Light. Their main contribution to the bombing of North Vietnam was to come later.

It was probably because of all these limitations and restraints, that American efforts north of the DMZ were initially unsatisfactory. Despite a progressive rise in sortie rates, culminating in September 1965 when over 4000 were flown, a number of problems arose, leading Westmoreland to conclude that 'there was no indication of North Vietnamese willingness to negotiate or terminate support of the Viet Cong.' Some of the difficulties were geographical – the heavy forests and jungle terrain made target location almost impossible in many instances, while the annual northeast monsoon virtually put a stop to all missions between October and March – but other difficulties were operational. Pre-strike reconnaissance tended to warn the defenders so was rarely used; post-strike reconnaissance was difficult because of the terrain. The types of target chosen for attack were easily camouflaged or moved, while North Vietnamese defensive measures steadily increased in size and effectiveness. During 1965 the number of anti-aircraft guns north of the DMZ rose from 1000 to well over 2000 and, in April, the first surface-to-air missiles (SAMs) were located. By the end of the year 56 SAM sites had been reported, although in August, after the first American planes had been destroyed by Soviet-built SA-2 heat-seeking missiles, a special Iron Hand mission directive had permitted retaliatory strikes. In addition the North Vietnamese Air Force, safely stationed in sanctuary areas around Hanoi and equipped with Soviet-supplied MIG 15s, 17s and, after December 1965, the more modern 21s, posed a constant threat. By the end of the year some 50 USAF and Navy planes had gone down over the North, chiefly to anti-aircraft fire as they flew low to avoid the SAMs, and the results were disappointing. None of the objectives of Rolling Thunder had been achieved, and what little concentration of force that might have been exerted had been dissipated by a political policy of imposing bombing pauses – the longest was over Christmas and New Year 1965 – to test Hanoi's reaction. This usually took the form of a rapid build up of strength and increased infiltration into the South.

An USAF RF-101 Voodoo flies low over the Vietnamese jungle as it nears its target.

Presented with such poor results, President Johnson had no choice but to approve a series of heavier air strikes in late-spring 1966. In addition to the targets already allowed, gasoline, oil and lubricant (POL) storage facilities at Haiphong, Hanoi, Nguyen Ke, Bac Gian, Do Son and Duong Nham were listed in the mission directives, together with power plants in the Hanoi area, road and rail communications with China and a ground control intercept radar station at Kep. The first strike, against POL facilities near Hanoi, took place on 29 June, and thereafter all the new targets were hit, the sortie-rate culminating again in September, just before the monsoon, when a total of 12,000 strikes took place. By that time the Americans were beginning to announce a degree of success, citing the destruction of thousands of enemy trucks and watercraft, hundreds of railway cars, bridges, supply areas and up to two-thirds of North Vietnam's POL storage tanks. It was estimated that Hanoi had been forced to divert about 300,000 workers to repair the damage inflicted by the bombing, while US commanders in the South reported a significant reduction in 'battalion-sized attacks,' implying a fall in the rate of infiltration. The only cause for concern appeared to be a strike in December 1966 against the Van Vien vehicle depot actually in Hanoi which had led to civilian deaths and a diplomatic outcry.

But the picture was not quite as rosy as American leaders made out. The North Vietnamese, although undoubtedly hurt by the strikes, fought back with increasing ferocity as the year progressed. POL supply bases were disposed or concealed underground, the rail links with China were kept open by a heavy commitment

Below: A Northrop F-5 fighter interceptor used for photographing North Vietnamese positions north of the DMZ.

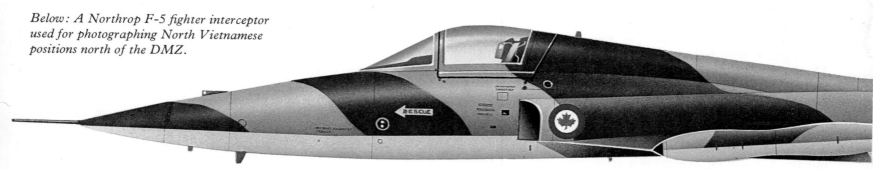

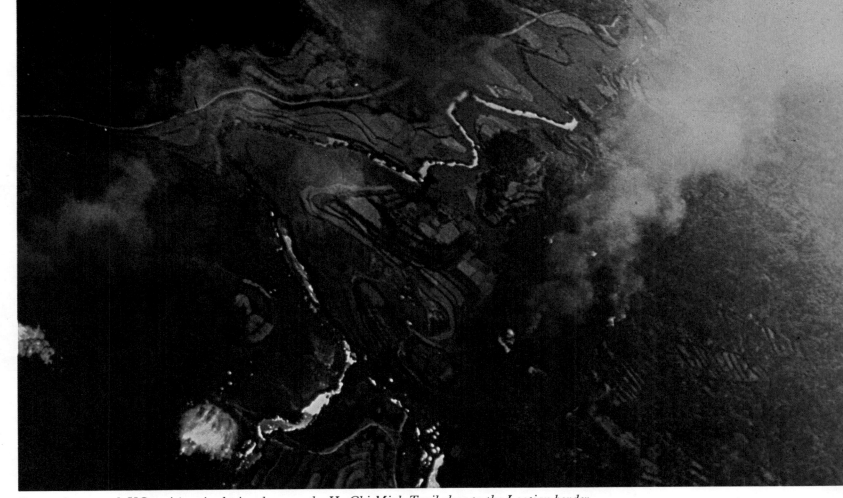

Supersabres attack VC positions in the jungles near the Ho Chi Minh Trail close to the Laotian border.

of manpower which repaired the damage as fast as the Americans could inflict it, and as the port of Haiphong was still off-limits to the air-raiders, extra war supplies could easily be brought in. Furthermore, the North Vietnamese air defenses had begun to take a mounting toll of American aircraft. The number of reported SAM sites rose to about 150 and although their effectiveness was negated to some extent by Electronic Counter-Measures (ECM), a policy of rapid site movement and dummy construction by the North Vietnamese posed worrying problems as American pilots never knew exactly when to expect a SAM attack. At the same time the North Vietnamese Air

Force, operating MIG 21s from bases at Phuc Yen, Kep, Gia Lam, Kien An and Hoa Loc in the Hanoi sanctuary area, went onto the offensive. The first sustained air-to-air combats took place on 3 September 1966, and thereafter the Americans were forced to divert F-4 Phantoms from their primary strike missions to Combat Air Patrol duties. As the MIG 21 enjoyed greater maneuverability, the usual American tactic was to fly low and, when the enemy was sighted, use the higher acceleration and speed of the F-4 to fire Sidewinder air-to-air missiles in hit-and-run attacks. During 1966 23 MIGs were shot down in this way, but by the end of the year the Americans had lost 455 aircraft to the various defense systems north of the DMZ. Needless to say, Hanoi was still supporting aggression in the South and was not initiating peace negotiations.

This led to more changes in the Rolling Thunder mission directives, as Washington approved new targets even closer to Hanoi in January 1967. Vital industrial and lines of communication targets were hit, forcing the North Vietnamese to commit nearly 100 MIGs to the air defense battle. Little damage was inflicted by the Americans, but in Operation Bolo on 2 January the 8th Tactical Fighter Wing USAF under Colonel Ro-

bin Olds managed to set an extremely successful fighter trap. Baited by what appeared to be a normal F-105 strike, the MIGs suddenly found themselves engaged in the largest aerial combat of the war. Olds' F-4s shot down seven MIGs in 12 minutes without loss to themselves and, after two more were destroyed in a similar operation two weeks later, the North Vietnamese Air Force was obliged temporarily to stand down and regroup. This enabled the F-105s and F-4s together to hit a variety of vital targets, including the Thai Nguyen iron and steel plant and the *Canal Des Rapides* road and rail bridge, both close to Hanoi. The MIGs did not return to the battle until spring 1967, reaching the height of their commitment in May, when a total of 72 engagements were reported by American pilots. As 20 MIGs were destroyed in the process, the Americans seemed to be winning at least an element of air supremacy, and this was reinforced between April and August when strikes against the air bases at Kep, Hoa Lac, Kien An and Phuc Yen were permitted. The only airfield spared was Gia Lam, Hanoi's International Airport, and 18 MIGs remained there unmolested, but the rest of the North Vietnamese Air Force withdrew across the border to bases in China. It was a notable American victory, costing only twenty-five aircraft destroyed.

But this did little to obtain the objectives of Rolling Thunder, and on 20 July 1967 the target list was revised yet again, this time permitting attacks upon 16 additional fixed targets and 23 road, rail and waterway segments inside the Hanoi-Haiphong area. Bridges, bypasses, rail yards and military storage areas were hit in an effort to slow down or halt all movement between the two cities or to points north and south. Some of the targets had to be visited time after time because of North Vietnamese rebuilding efforts – for example, on 2 August Hanoi's Paul Doumer bridge was hit, destroying the center span, but had to be struck again on 25 October and 19 December – and by the end of this, the third full year of bombing, Hanoi's leaders seemed to be no nearer discussing a peace settlement than they had been in 1964. The Soviets and Communist Chinese continued to pour aid into the area through Haiphong, leaving American air leaders with a distinct impression that they were being ordered to fight with one hand securely tied behind their backs. Even political leaders in Washington, aware of mounting domestic and international opposition to the war, were looking for an honorable way out of the bombing campaign.

This was provided, surprisingly, in early 1968 when the North Vietnamese and Viet Cong apparently tried to force an end to the war through overt military action. On 21 January the Marine base at Khe Sanh was attacked and besieged, and nine days later, during the Vietnamese New Year (Tet), co-ordinated assaults of unprecedented strength were made against 36 provincial capitals throughout South Vietnam. Both operations were eventually countered, chiefly through a massive use of air strikes, but the casualties sustained in the process by American forces led to renewed domestic pressures upon the Johnson administration and a change in war policies. On 31 March the President terminated all bombing north of the 20th parallel and, as a *quid pro quo*, the North Vietnamese agreed to meet US delegates at Paris to discuss the possibility of a peace settlement. After months of deadlock, the two sides came to an essential understanding which enabled Johnson to order an end to all air, naval and artillery bombardment of North Vietnam from 0800 hours (Washington time) on 1 November. After three years and nine months, during which over 300,000 sorties had been

A gasoline dump near Hanoi bursts into flames after an air raid in June 1966.

Above: The destroyer USS Everett F Larson. *Below: Guided missile from USS* Oklahoma City.

flown and nearly 650,000 tons of bombs dropped, the Rolling Thunder operations were over. In retrospect they achieved little, for although the flow of manpower and supplies from the North into the South was probably reduced whenever important targets were destroyed, the resilience of the North Vietnamese people and the constant support that they received from other Communist states successfully negated American air efforts. If the full strength of the USAF and Navy could have been committed, the picture would obviously have been different, but in an age when nuclear weapons restraint upon the use of force is essential, in the final analysis it is difficult to fault the Rolling Thunder strategy. It was at least useful as a bargaining chip in establishing peace negotiations.

But the Paris understanding of 1968 did not mean that the war in Vietnam was over, and the next three and a half years saw a gradual return to American strikes north of the DMZ, chiefly in retaliation for North Vietnamese attacks upon American reconnaissance aircraft. These had been permitted to fly selected missions by the Paris delegates, but when they were fired upon in early 1970 President Nixon did not hesitate to order 'protective reaction strikes' against SAM sites, anti-aircraft systems and airfields in the North. When these had no effect, 'reinforced protective reaction strikes' were authorized, the first being flown in early May 1970 when nearly 500 USAF and Navy planes hit air defense localities near the Barthelemy and Ben Karai passes. Thereafter they became a regular feature of American policy – in February 1971 Operation Louisville Slugger was mounted against newly-reported SAM sites, while a month later, in Operation Fracture Cross Alpha, 234 strike missions were devoted to anti-aircraft defenses north of the DMZ – and by late 1971 had been extended to curb enemy road construction near the 17th parallel. By September POL storage areas south of Dong Hoi appeared on the mission directives, in November strikes were permitted against new MIG bases at Vinh and Quan Lang and, in late December, the heaviest air attacks since 1968 took place when over a 1000 sorties were flown in four days south of the 20th parallel.

The main reason for this process of escalation in late 1971 was a feeling among American leaders that the North Vietnamese were using the absence of sustained air attacks upon their country

A B-52 bomber pilot, captured after being shot down over North Vietnam, meets the Hanoi press.

Three US prisoners arrive in Vientiane, Laos after their release by the North Vietnamese.

to build up forces in preparation for an all-out offensive upon the South. They were not wrong, for by spring 1972 invasion forces numbering some 200,000 men, with armor and artillery support, were massed near the DMZ as well as in Laos and Cambodia. They moved into South Vietnam on 29/30 March, taking Quang Tri City in the north, advancing from Laos into the Central Highlands and from Cambodia into the Binh Long and Tay Ninh provinces, northwest of Saigon. American air power was immediately thrown in to stem the tide, with F-105s, F-4s and B-52s, together with Navy and Marine aircraft, pounding enemy supply dumps between the 20th parallel and the new battle lines in the South. Nixon suspended the Paris

peace talks on 8 May and authorized a renewed air offensive, known as Operation Linebacker, against the North. It was a policy change of great importance, representing a far more concentrated commitment of air power than had been the case with Rolling Thunder. For the first time USAF and Navy aircraft were permitted to mine Haiphong and other North Vietnamese ports, while hitting hitherto restricted targets anywhere within range. Bridges in Hanoi itself and along the rail links with China were successfully attacked, and fuel dumps, warehouses, marshaling yards, power plants, POL pipe-lines and SAM sites were all destroyed in a campaign of unprecedented effectiveness. Many targets which had defied destruction before were taken out by newly-developed laser or TV-guided smart bombs – for example, the Than Hoa bridge, scene of many unsuccessful Rolling Thunder strikes, was destroyed by just one F-4 equipped with such weapons – and by late June, as the North Vietnamese invasion faltered, the Americans congratulated themselves upon a successful campaign.

This feeling of success was reinforced on 13 July when the North Vietnamese agreed to resume peace negotiations, and for a time it seemed that a settlement was only just round the corner. Indeed, by 23 October Nixon was so optimistic that he ordered a halt to all air operations north of the 20th parallel as a final incentive to Hanoi. But it was a false dawn, for once again the North Vietnamese appeared to be using peace discussions as a cover for more aggressive preparations, and when they walked out of the Paris talks on 13 December a continuation of the war was inevitable. Nixon had grown tired of prevarication, however, and was determined to negotiate terms which would allow an honorable withdrawal of American forces from Vietnam. In an effort to force the North Vietnamese back to the conference table, he therefore initiated a further series of concentrated air attacks, nicknamed Linebacker II, using everything short of nuclear weapons against the North.

The Linebacker II operations spanned an 11-day period, 18–29 December 1972, with a 24 hour pause on Christmas Day, and involved the mounting of attacks upon anything to do with North Vietnam's war effort. F-105s, F-4s and F-111s flew over 1000 sorties against targets hitherto on the restricted list: rail yards, power plants, communications centers, dockyards and all MIG bases; while, for the first time, B-52s were permitted to strike the Hanoi–Haiphong area. This was a dramatic departure from previous policy, for the B-52 was an awesome machine. Originally built in the 1950s as SAC's long-range, deep penetration nuclear bomber and extensively modified since 1965 to carry conventional ordnance, it had been responsible for some impressive tactical strikes in the jungle areas of South Vietnam and Laos, when carpet bombing had destroyed huge tracts of forest through which the Viet Cong had been operating. But with the exception of occasional raids just north of the DMZ, principally against choke points on the Ho Chi Minh trail, the big bombers had been kept well south of the North Vietnamese capital for fear of diplomatic repercussions.

Bombs destined from North Vietnam are unloaded from a ship at Guam.

An F5-A Freedom Fighter armed with two napalm bombs en route to a Vietnamese target.

F-105 Thunderchief heads for its target in October 1968.

Their commitment to Linebacker II was therefore an indication of Nixon's determination and promised a degree of force which up to now had been missing from American air efforts.

In the event, the B-52s were decisive. Bombing round-the-clock in poor weather conditions, they inflicted more damage in 11 days than had been suffered by the North Vietnamese over the previous eight years. In the Hanoi area the Gia Lam railroad yard was devastated, 31 barrack buildings at Bac Mai were leveled, warehouse and railway facilities at Yen Vien and Van Dien were destroyed. An estimated 80 percent of North Vietnam's electrical power production was wiped out, together with 25 percent of her POL supplies. The Haiphong gasoline storage area was hit repeatedly, destroying 20 50,000 gallon tanks, at Than Am and Bac Giang POL facilities were razed, and at Thai Nguyen a power plant was put out of action. In addition the North Vietnamese Air Force was virtually wiped out and air defense systems destroyed. The process was costly – during Linebacker II 26 American aircraft were lost, including a sobering total of 15 B-52s – but by 28 December complete air supremacy had been achieved. The Americans roamed the skies of North Vietnam for two more days before Hanoi agreed to resume negotiations. Nixon's policy of punitive air action had worked. On 15 January 1973 the bombing of North Vietnam was stopped and eight days later a nine-point cease-fire agreement, effective from 28 January, was signed in Paris. American involvement in a war which was to terminate in a North Vietnamese victory in 1975, was finally over.

The USAF came out of the war with a certain degree of satisfaction, particularly over the success of the Linebacker operations, and considerable experience in modern air warfare. The lessons of Vietnam were essential to the use of force in the nuclear age, ranging from the need for constant political control of air actions, even if this meant accepting less success than the potential of the air force was capable of achieving, to the importance of technological change, indicated by the dramatic effects of smart bombs in early 1972. In addition, the experiences of 1965–73 added further proof to the argument that the old theories of strategic air power, although still relevant in the nuclear contest, bore little relation to anything beneath the level of total war. The use of air power in a purely conventional sense can no longer involve the destruction of enemy cities even if the capability to do so exists: it must be carefully controlled at all times to prevent unnecessary escalation. American air leaders and politicians learned this lesson in Vietnam too late.

An F-4, armed with a Sparrow missile, comes in for a landing at Phu Cat AB in May 1971.

INDEX

Numerals in italics indicate an illustration of the subject mentioned.

ACKNOWLEDGEMENTS

The editor would like to thank Richard Natkiel of *The Economist* who provided all the maps. Helen Downton, Jinbo Terushi and Graham Bingham provided the line illustrations and artwork. A special thanks goes to Stuart Perry who designed the book.

The editor would like to thank the following libraries and agencies for the photographs on the following pages:

Bison Picture Library: 62–63 (both), 64, 66, 72 (top), 82–83, 87 (bottom), 89, 90, 93 (bottom), 95 (top 3), 96, 97, 99 (top), 100 (both), 101, 102–103 (all 4), 104–105 (all 3), 106–107, 115 (bottom), 116 (right), 136 (top), 166 (both), 170 (top), 174 (top), 175 (top right), 176 (bottom), 178–179, 183, 190–191 (top), 202 (top), 203 (both), 227, 246–247 (all 3), 275 (bottom).
Navy Department, National Archives: 1, 128 (center left), 134–135 (both), 137 (bottom), 138–139 (bottom), 146 (center), 148–149 (all 6), 151 (top), 152 (bottom), 153 (bottom), 157 (all 4), 159 (both), 160, 161 (bottom), 162, 163 (all 3), 228 (bottom), 229

(both), 234 (top and bottom), 236, 237 (top 2), 244 (top), 249 (bottom), 251 (all 3), 252 (bottom), 255 (top right), 258, 259, 263 (center), 264 (top and center), 265, 267 (bottom right).
Naval Historical Foundation, Washington DC: 6, 15 (top), 19 (both), 20, 123 (both), 124, 127 (both), 128 (top, center right and bottom), 129 (top), 132 (top 2), 137 (center), 139 (top), 141, 142 (both), 151 (center), 153 (top), 154–155 (both), 158, 244 (bottom), 245 (top), 249 (top), 252 (top), 253 (bottom), 254–255 (bottom), 255 (top left and center).
US Air Force: 2–3, 118 (bottom), 119 (all 3), 129 (bottom), 190–191 (bottom 2), 192 (bottom 2), 194

(top 2), 195, 198, 214, 215, 217 (both), 218, 221 (all 3), 222, 223 (both), 245 (center and bottom left), 266–267, 269 (both), 270 (top), 274, 275 (top), 294–295 (all 4), 298, 299 (both), 302–303 (all 4), 306–307 (both), 314 (all 3), 315.
Novosti Press Agency: 8–9, 13 (bottom), 21, 23 (top), 24 (all 3), 25, 26 (top 2), 27 (left), 29 (center), 30 (bottom), 31, 75 (bottom), 181 (center), 185 (all 3), 187, 188 (top, center left and bottom), 189 (both), 201, 204, 205, 206 (both), 207 (all 3), 208, 211 (all 3).
Popperfoto: 85 (top), 116 (left), 144 (bottom).
Bundesarchiv: 168 (bottom), 170 (center), 175 (top left).
Mainichi: 270 (bottom), 272 (bottom).
Orbis: 88, 231.
Heinrich Hoffman: 168 (center).
Robert Hunt Library: 4–5, 10–11, 13 (top), 14 (both), 15 (bottom), 16 (both), 17 (both), 18 (all 3), 22, 23 (bottom), 26 (top left and bottom), 27 (right), 29 (top and bottom), 30 (top 2), 32, 33 (all 3), 34 (both), 35 (all 3), 36–37 (all 6), 38–39 (all 3), 40–41 (all 5), 42–43 (all 3), 45 (all 3), 46–47 (all 4), 49 (all 3), 50 (all 5), 54, 55 (both), 56 (both), 57 (both), 58–59 (all 4), 60,

61, 65 (both), 67, 68–69 (all 4), 70, 71, 72 (bottom), 73, 74, 75 (top 3), 76, 77 (all 3), 78 (both), 79 (all 3), 80 (all 3), 81 (all 3), 84, 85 (bottom), 86, 89 (bottom), 91 (both), 93 (top), 95 (bottom), 98–99 (bottom), 109, 110–111 (top), 112 (all 3), 113, 115 (top), 117 (all 3), 118 (top), 120–121 (all 3), 122, 125, 126, 129 (center), 130, 131, 132 (bottom), 133 (top), 136–137 (bottom), 137 (top), 138 (top), 140 (both), 145, 146 (top and bottom), 151 (bottom), 152 (top), 161 (top 2), 165, 167 (all 3), 168 (top), 170 (bottom), 171 (both), 172, 173 (both), 175 (bottom 2), 176 (top 2), 177, 180, 181 (top), 184, 186, 188 (center right), 192 (top), 193 (bottom), 196, 197 (both), 200, 202 (bottom 2), 213, 216, 224–225 (all 3), 226, 228 (top), 230, 234 (center), 235, 237 (bottom), 238, 239 (all 4), 240, 241 (both), 242–243 (all 4), 244 (center), 245 (bottom right), 253 (top), 256, 257 (all 3), 260, 261, 262, 263 (top), 264 (bottom), 271, 272 (top), 277, 278–279 (all 3), 280–281 (all 3), 282–283 (all 3), 284–285 (all 3), 286, 287, 288, 289 (both), 291, 292–293 (all 5), 297 (both), 300 (all 3), 301 (all 3), 304–305 (all 4), 309 (both), 312 (all 3), 313 (both).